LAWS AND LEGISLATION

SELECTED ISSUES IN MARITIME LAW AND POLICY

LIBER AMICORUM PROSHANTO K. MUKHERJEE

LAWS AND LEGISLATION

Additional books in this series can be found on Nova's website under the Series tab.

Additional e-books in this series can be found on Nova's website under the e-book tab.

LAWS AND LEGISLATION

SELECTED ISSUES IN MARITIME LAW AND POLICY

LIBER AMICORUM PROSHANTO K. MUKHERJEE

MAXIMO Q. MEJIA, JR.
EDITOR

nova publishers
New York

For permission to use material from this book please contact us:
Telephone 631-231-7269; Fax 631-231-8175
Web Site: http://www.novapublishers.com

Library of Congress Cataloging-in-Publication Data

Selected issues in maritime law and policy : liber amicorum Proshanto K. Mukherjee / Editor: Maximo Q. Mejia, Jr., Maritime Law and Policy, World Maritime University, Sweden.
p. cm.
Includes index.
ISBN: 978-1-62618-508-1 (hardcover)
1. Maritime law. I. Mukherjee, Proshanto K. honouree. II. Mejia, Maximo Q. (Maximo Quibranza), 1965- editor of compilation.
K1150.S45 2013
341.4'5--dc23

2013019730

Published by Nova Science Publishers, Inc. † New York

CONTENTS

Proshanto Kumar Mukherjee, FNI, MRIN, LLB (Dalhousie), PhD (Wales), Barrister-at- Law (Law Society of Upper Canada), Solicitor (Ontario Supreme Court), Master Mariner.

FOREWORD

Trade is the life blood of a nation and shipping is the global means by which trade is conducted. At the heart of shipping is maritime law which, in virtually all its facets, represents the legal order and framework of governance for trade and shipping. Maritime law is of ancient vintage steeped in tradition. Its origins are said to be lost in antiquity dating as far back as the Babylonian Code of Hammurabi of 1500-3000 B.C. and the Hindu Code, the Manu Samhita of 900 B.C. As a practitioner's creed and an academic discipline it enjoys a measure of uniqueness that is at once exotic and utilitarian. The challenge of maritime law as a profession whether in practice or in academia is perhaps only surpassed by the lure of the seafaring profession. Professor (Dr.) Proshanto K. Mukherjee to whom this book is dedicated by his esteemed peers and colleagues epitomizes both these professions.

Professor Mukherjee started life in shipping as a cadet on the Training Ship *Dufferin* in India where he was born. He spent some 16 years at sea eventually acquiring command by reaching the rank of Master. He then proceeded to read law at Dalhousie University in Canada, qualified as a barrister and solicitor in Ontario and entered the legal profession specializing in maritime law. Later he obtained his Ph.D. in law from the University of Wales. Among his other accomplishments, he served as a practicing lawyer, a senior policy adviser in the Canadian Hydrographic Service and a maritime legislation consultant for the International Maritime Organization (IMO) from the times when I served as its Secretary General. In 1989 I appointed him as the founding Senior Deputy Director and Professor of Maritime Law at the IMO International Maritime Law Institute. He served in that capacity for seven years and performed as a brilliant academic and an accomplished administrator. He subsequently served as IMO Legal Adviser for the Caribbean Region and eventually as ITF Professor of Maritime Safety and Environmental Protection at World Maritime University where he rose to become Director of Doctoral Studies and Vice President of Research before retiring in March 2011. He continues to serve as Professor of Maritime Law and Policy at WMU on a part-time basis and is also presently Director of the Maritime Law Programme and Professor of Maritime Law at the Faculty of Law, Lund University. Over his 14 years at WMU, Professor Mukherjee made a distinguished and significant contribution to the development of that esteemed institution of which I was the founding Chancellor and where I continue to be Chancellor Emeritus. WMU enjoys immense global respect and recognition today and Professor Mukherjee has been one who has unflinchingly contributed to the University's attainment of that stature.

I have been closely associated in my long official career at national and international levels with maritime academic personalities of the highest international eminence and I respect and admire Professor Mukherjee as being among the very best of them in the world. In the field of maritime law, especially the IMO convention regimes, he is undoubtedly a contemporary leader and luminary of distinction. His long list of publications touching on virtually every aspect of maritime law bears evidence of his intellectual prowess and natural affinity for research and scholarship in maritime law. Professor Mukherjee is a teacher and mentor of outstanding calibre and unfailing dedication. His students past and present, scattered across the globe many of whom are accomplished lawyers, judges and academics will unhesitatingly bear testimony to that fact.

I feel privileged to have known Professor Mukherjee intimately over a substantial period of time in the maritime world and I continue to hold him in the highest respect and esteem. This book is a fitting tribute to a personality of such eminence and distinction and, along with the editor and authors who have laboured hard to produce it, I am honored to be able to contribute to it through this Foreword.

Chadrika P. Srivastava
Secretary-General Emeritus, International Maritime Organization

Genova, 9 August 2012

PREFACE

This book is dedicated to a respected colleague and distinguished academic: Professor Proshanto Kumar "PK" Mukherjee. As an expression of our deepest esteem and admiration, I have had the privilege of receiving chapter contributions from some of PK's closest friends in academia to publish a book on selected issues in an area of study that lays closest to PK's heart – maritime law and policy. This volume is our way of articulating through publication what we have not been able to collectively and fully communicate in extemporaneous speech. The occasion is the conclusion of PK's engagement at the World Maritime University (WMU) in Malmö, Sweden, an institution to which he has devoted more than 25 years of service, first as a visiting professor and later as a resident member of the faculty.

PROFESSOR PROSHANTO K. MUKHERJEE

Professor Mukherjee's involvement in maritime law and policy began early in his life. In 1963, he entered as an officer cadet on board the training ship *Dufferin* in Bombay, India on a scholarship from the Government of West Bengal. He went on to serve a total of sixteen years at sea from cadet to master, on ships of various types (freighters, container ships, tankers, bulk carriers, passenger ships, hydrographic ships and scientific research ships) under various flags (Indian, German, British and Canadian). As a mariner, he even gained particular expertise and experience in navigation in ice-covered waters in the polar regions of the Canadian Arctic.

After his seagoing career, during which time he also migrated from India to Canada, he read law at Dalhousie University Law School in Halifax, Nova Scotia, where he specialized in Marine and Environmental Law, graduating with a Bachelor of Laws (LLB) in 1977. He served articles with Robert J. Green Q.C., Director of Legal Services, Department of Justice, Government of Canada, Ottawa; was called to the Law Society of Upper Canada (Ontario Bar) as Barrister-at-Law; entered in the Rolls of the Supreme Court of Ontario as a Solicitor; and appointed Notary Public in and for the Province of Ontario. PK then served as Senior Adviser on Maritime Policy and International Affairs in the Canadian Hydrographic Service (CHS), Department of Fisheries and Oceans, Ottawa; Canadian delegate to the Marine Environment Protection Committee (MEPC) of the International Maritime Organization (IMO); Environment Committee of the Organization for Economic Co-operation and Development (OECD); Canadian representative on the International Hydrographic

Organization (IHO) Group of Experts on Technical Aspects of the Law of the Sea (TALOS); and Chairman of the Liability and Compensation Working Group of the Inter-departmental Task Force on Tanker Safety and Pollution Prevention, Government of Canada. He also practiced as a Barrister and Solicitor in Ottawa, Ontario, as an Associate in the firm of Barnes, Sammon, Naftel, and subsequently as a sole practitioner. The areas of PK's legal work in the government included criminal prosecution, civil litigation, tax litigation, and fisheries law. His areas of legal work as a private practitioner included intellectual property law, estate law, matrimonial law, commercial and corporate law, and municipal law.

In 1989, PK was appointed Founding Senior Deputy Director and Professor of Maritime Law of the IMO International Maritime Law Institute (IMLI) in Malta. As Professor of Maritime Law, his academic responsibilities included planning and organizing the Shipping Law and Maritime Legislation programs; preparing curricula; scheduling visiting professors; teaching the foundation courses in Shipping Law and Maritime Legislation; engaging, scheduling and supervising lecturers; supervising tutorials, maritime legislation drafting projects, and dissertations; setting and marking examinations; serving on the Board of Examiners of the Institute; and organizing graduations. Aside from his academic duties, he was responsible for administration and supervision of the Institute's day to day operations; budgetary and financial management; supervision of staff and liaison with governments and international organizations, agencies, and institutions involved in maritime law. While at IMLI, Professor Mukherjee also received appointments as Visiting Professor at the World Maritime University as well as Lecturer on Maritime Law at the International Oceans Institute (IOI) in both Halifax, Canada and Valletta, Malta. It was also during his time in Malta that Professor Mukherjee enrolled in doctoral studies at the University of Wales. In 1996, he was awarded the degree of Doctor of Philosophy (PhD) after successfully defending his thesis, "The Development of Maritime Legislation: An Enquiry into its History, Principles, Uniformity and Preparation."

In 1998, Dr. Mukherjee joined WMU as the International Transport Workers' Federation (ITF) Professor of Maritime Safety and Environmental Protection. At WMU, he was Programme Co-ordinator of the specializations currently named Maritime Safety and Environmental Administration, Maritime Law and Policy, Marine Environment and Ocean Management, and Maritime Education and Training. His duties embraced all academic and administrative functions, to include planning, preparation, and organization of academic programmes; teaching at the postgraduate level; research and publication; supervision and internal assessment of postgraduate dissertations and doctoral theses; setting and assessment of examinations; engagement and scheduling of visiting faculty; supervision of resident faculty and support staff; and delivering the maritime law and administration courses in the WMU outreach programs at Dalian and Shanghai Maritime Universities in China.

In addition to the above duties, Professor Mukherjee was appointed WMU's Director of Doctoral Studies and assigned the task of implementing the joint WMU-Swansea University doctoral program in Maritime and International Commercial Law as well as WMU's own PhD program in Maritime Administration. He served as supervisor as well as examiner of several doctoral candidates, not only at WMU but also at Swansea University, Cardiff University, University of Greenwich, Greenwich Maritime Institute, and Lund University. Professor Mukherjee was eventually designated Vice President (Research), responsible for coordinating the University's various research efforts.

PK's teaching, research, and consulting expertise has been, and continues to be, highly sought after in many countries around the world. He is, or has served as, Director and Lecturer to the National Judicial Training Institute for Judges of the Superior Courts of Ghana at seminars sponsored by the Ghana Shippers Authority and Ghana Ports and Harbours Authority, as well as in similar judges' seminars sponsored by Nigerian Shippers Council. In the late 1990s, he served as IMO's Legal Adviser for the Caribbean Region and acted as Head of the Legal Component of the Wider Caribbean Initiative on Ship Generated Waste (WCISW), an IMO/World Bank project headquartered in Port of Spain, Trinidad and Tobago and involving 22 participating countries in the Caribbean and Central American Region. His responsibilities included serving as legal adviser, drafting regional model marine pollution legislation both principal and subordinate, for the implementation of various international conventions on maritime safety and marine environmental matters; organizing and/or chairing workshops and training seminars; advising various Government Ministries and agencies of the Caribbean Region; supervising regional and sub-regional legal consultants; and acting as legal adviser to the Caribbean Port State Control Secretariat in Bridgetown, Barbados and the Regional Marine Pollution Emergency Information and Training Center for the Wider Caribbean (REMPEITC-Caribe) Office in Curacao.

As IMO Maritime Legislation Consultant, Professor Mukherjee has undertaken numerous missions for several jurisdictions to draft maritime, marine environmental, ports and inland waters navigation legislation and to provide advice on the establishment and operation of numerous Maritime Administrations including the Bahamas, Bangladesh, Cambodia, Democratic Peoples' Republic of Korea, Ghana, Grenada, Guyana, Hungary, Indonesia, Jamaica, Latvia, Oman, the Philippines, Mauritius, Mozambique, Sri Lanka, Trinidad and Tobago, and Vietnam.

Independent of his role as IMO consultant, he has also provided legal and policy advice and drafted maritime legislation on shipping law, marine environmental law, commercial maritime law and maritime labour law in the British Virgin Islands, Canada, Cayman Islands, Latvia, Malaysia, and Romania. He served as Legal Consultant for the International Centre for Ocean Development (ICOD), United Nations Economic and Social Council (UNESCO), and Food and Agricultural Organization (FAO). Professor Mukherjee was appointed to the Economic and Social Council for Asia and the Pacific (ESCAP) Group of Legal Experts in Maritime Legislation to revise and update the Manual entitled *Guidelines for Maritime Legislation* for publication of its Third Edition. He has acted as Legal Counsel to law firms in Malta, London, Amsterdam, and Oslo on international maritime law matters. He has been in-house Counsel to the Latvian Shipping Company as well as Legal Consultant to Cayman Islands Shipping Registry, Ministry responsible for shipping in Mauritius, Langkawi International Yacht Registry, Malaysia, Government of Latvia, and the Government of Oman.

As Legal Consultant to the Cayman Islands Shipping Registry, Professor Mukherjee was responsible for reviewing, updating and the preparation of shipping and marine environmental legislation of the Cayman Islands, both principal as well as subordinate; advising on shipping policy matters; and generally providing legal advice on all matters of maritime law to the Cayman Islands Maritime Administration. He performed the functions of Legal Advisor for the Shipping Sector Consultative Committee and the Shipowners' Advisory Council; Legal Consultant for the Swedish Maritime Administration on behalf of WMU for provision of consultancy services to the Government of Romania under EU Twinning project to assist Romania as a candidate country for accession to implement European maritime legislation and administrative requirements; Member of the Comité Maritime International (CMI) Working Group on Unfair Treatment of Seafarers; WMU Advisor to the Government of India on the establishment of the Indian Maritime University; and Legal Consultant to the Baltic Master Projects I and II on behalf of WMU.

Professor Mukherjee has been appointed to numerous honorary positions, most recently as Chancellor of the Colombo International Nautical and Engineering College (CINEC), Maritime Campus, Colombo, Sri Lanka. He is also Adjunct Professor of Maritime Law at Chung-Ang University in Seoul, South Korea; Visiting Professor at Korean Maritime University in Pusan, South Korea; Visiting Professor in the Faculty of Law at Dalian Maritime University in Dalian, China; Visiting Professor in the Faculty of Law at University of Antwerp (*Hoogleraar Universiteit Antwerpen*) in Belgium; Visiting Professor at the National University of Juridical Sciences in Kolkata, India; Faculty Member of the Hague Academy of International Law, Seminar for Advanced Studies in Public and Private International Law, The Hague, Netherlands; and Honorary Research Fellow at Swansea University.

Professor Mukherjee retired from his full-time administrative and faculty positions at WMU in March 2011, but remains Professor of Maritime Law and Policy and continues to teach in the course specialization that he conceived and led since joining in 1998. In 2011, he assumed the duties of Director of the LLM and PhD Program in Maritime Law at Lund University in Lund, Sweden, a joint WMU-Lund program that he helped develop in 2007.

Professor Mukherjee is the author of *Maritime Legislation*, published by WMU Publications in 2002; the book is set for revision in 2013 and publication under the Springer Verlag label. The book has received excellent reviews and is widely acclaimed as the only comprehensive text on the subject. He has numerous publications to his credit embracing virtually every aspect of public and private maritime law that include articles in peer-reviewed journals and conference and symposia proceedings. He is co-editor of *Maritime Violence and Other Security Issues at Sea*, published by WMU Publications, 2002. He co-authored the Fourth Edition of the renowned shipping reference *Farthing on International Shipping*, to be released in 2013 also by Springer. He was previously a member of the Advisory Board of Editors of the Journal of Maritime Law and Commerce and is presently a member of the Editorial Advisory Board of the WMU Journal of Maritime Affairs, and of the Editorial Board of the Journal of International Maritime Law.

THIS BOOK

The international nature of the maritime industry means that ships are subject to the varying legal jurisdictions of the ports in which they call. Law and policy provide a framework necessary for establishing order and harmonization in a highly regulated global industry; they are vital instruments for promoting the safety, security, and commercial efficiency of shipping as well as the protection of the marine environment, in an atmosphere of competing national-*contra*-global as well as private-*contra*-public interests. Furthermore, it is of great importance that the legal and policy aspects of maritime activities closely follow the rapid pace of technological and commercial developments. Students and practitioners in maritime law and policy need to be constantly familiar with trends in the shipping industry and possess a solid comprehension of the international legal regimes that not only encourage the sustainable development of global maritime commerce, but also regulate its conduct.

I would like to take this opportunity to express my most heartfelt gratitude to eminent colleagues who have given freely of their time to produce superlative chapters that both speak to select topics of general interest to the maritime public and that are truly worthy of a publication bearing the name of our honoree. What we have attempted with this work is a book that presents a mix of background information and insightful analysis by leading experts on a wide range of some of the most pressing and contemporary maritime law and policy topics – ranging from the development of maritime standards (Mbiah) to the challenges of operating flags of convenience (Mensah), from the latest convention on the international carriage of goods by sea (Basu Bal) to liability and compensation issues related to ship-source marine pollution (Jacobsson, Xu, Kojima), from the intricacies of marine insurance law (Thomas, Gauci) to the vagaries of the conflict of laws (Manolis), and from the legal framework for maritime piracy (Menefee) to the linkages between political stability, economic development, and piracy (Mejia). This book hopes to serve students, faculty, and researchers in the fields of law, policy, and general maritime studies, as well as other maritime professionals in the public or the private sector – including advisers on maritime law and policy and marine environmental protection issues – who wish to acquire advanced knowledge in a selection of international maritime law and policy issues.

I would also like to take this opportunity to acknowledge my debt of gratitude to Dr. C. P. Srivastava, Secretary-General Emeritus of the International Maritime Organization, for graciously honoring this volume with a Foreword.

I wish to conclude this Preface in the same way that it began – with a few more words about our honoree. Professor Mukherjee, or "PK" as he is fondly known to friends, is many things to many people. He is, *inter alia*, an engaging lecturer, versatile teacher, prolific writer and researcher, dynamic public speaker, masterly wordsmith, maritime consultant, legal counsel, supervisor and examiner, maritime legislation expert, WMU Vice President, CINEC Chancellor, IMLI Senior Deputy Director, master mariner, Arctic navigator, barrister, solicitor, globetrotter, Bollywood fanatic, vindaloo master, philanthropist, devoted father, proud grandfather, and last but not least: loyal friend to both colleagues and students. As a mentor and direct supervisor, he encouraged me to grow as an academic and afforded me countless opportunities to exercise responsibility. As a friend and colleague, he was always ready to listen to and discuss my ideas and schemes no matter how frivolous they may have been. With PK's departure from WMU, the big question is, "How do we fill those size 12 shoes he is leaving?" I don't think anyone really has a ready answer. We will simply have to keep trying. For the time being, we are reassured by PK's pledge to continue to help deliver parts of the Maritime Law and Policy specialisation at WMU for at least the next few years. It is truly a great comfort knowing that for the moment, it is still not really "farewell" but more like, "see you around!"

Maximo Q. Mejia Jr.
Professor, Maritime Law and Policy, World Maritime University

Malmö, Sweden, 4 February 2013

In: Selected Issues in Maritime Law and Policy
Editor: Maximo Q. Mejia, Jr.
ISBN: 978-1-62618-508-1

Chapter 1

THE ROLE OF THE INTERNATIONAL MARITIME ORGANIZATION IN THE DEVELOPMENT OF MARITIME LAW AND POLICY

Kofi Mbiah*[*#]*
Chairman of the Legal Committee of IMO
Chief Executive Officer of the Ghana Shippers Authority

> "the bed out of which all the social sciences spring is history, there they find to greater or lesser degree, subject matter and material, verification or contradiction" [1]

The history of the formation of the International Maritime Organization (IMO) is as rich as it is colourful and would therefore be an appropriate place to begin the consideration of any matter involving the IMO and, *a-fortiori,* its role in the development of maritime law and policy. The establishment of an international organization to deal with issues of safety of navigation was first attempted in 1889 when an International Maritime Conference [2] was held in Washington D.C. dubbed "the Washington Conference". This conference did not however see any merit in establishing a permanent international body to deal with the issue of safety of navigation, most probably for fear that a permanent body would establish rules and regulations that would be a fetter on "freedom of navigation".

In 1948, an international conference in Geneva adopted a convention formally establishing the IMO as one of the Specialized Agencies of the United Nations [3] (the original name was the Inter-governmental Maritime Consultative Organization (IMCO) [4]. The name was changed in 1982 to IMO [5]. For the purposes of this chapter I will use IMO regardless of the time period under discussion. The IMO convention entered into force in 1958 and the first meeting of the organization was held in 1959. The objectives of the organization are summarized in Article 1(a) of the convention and it states:

[*] Email: kmbiahami@gmail.com.

[#] Any viewpoints and opinions expressed in this paper are solely that of the writer, and do not necessarily represent the views of the Legal Committee, the International Maritime Organization, or the Ghana Shippers Authority.

a) To provide a machinery for co-operation among Governments in the field of governmental regulation and practices relating to technical matters of all kinds affecting shipping engaged in international trade; to encourage and facilitate the general adoption of the highest practicable standards in matters concerning maritime safety, efficiency of navigation and prevention and control of marine pollution from ships; and to deal with administrative and legal matters related to the purposes set out in this Article;
b) To encourage the removal of discriminatory action and unnecessary restrictions by Governments affecting shipping engaged in international trade so as to promote the availability of shipping services to the commerce of the world without discrimination; assistance and encouragement given by a Government for the development of its national shipping and for purposes of security does not in itself constitute discrimination, provided that such assistance and encouragement is not based on measures designed to restrict the freedom of shipping of all flags to take part in international trade;
c) To provide for the consideration by the Organization of matters concerning unfair restrictive practices by shipping concerns in accordance with part II;
d) To provide for the consideration by the Organization of any matters concerning shipping and the effect of shipping on the marine environment that may be referred to it by any organ or specialized agency of the United Nations;
e) To provide for the exchange of information among Governments on matters under consideration by the Organization.

The present Convention of the IMO has, however, better organized the various articles of the Convention to reflect modern trends and to give vent to the broader aspirations of member states. The Convention now sets out in Article 1, the "PURPOSES OF THE ORGANISATON". It is from the purpose of the organization that we can appropriately evaluate the role of the IMO in terms of its contribution to Maritime Law and Policy. Article 1(a) which underpins the purpose of the organization clearly spells out what encompasses the mandate of the organization.

Through the overall objectives, it is clear that governmental regulation in matters affecting shipping engaged in international trade is the gravamen of the purpose article. Such regulation is expected to involve the highest practicable standards involving maritime safety, efficiency of navigation and prevention of marine pollution from ships. Also encapsulated within this purpose clause is the formulation of administrative and legal matters that give vent to the key areas outlined within this article. Out of this broad framework is developed the functions of the International Maritime Organization [6].

FUNCTIONS

The role of the IMO with respect to the development of Maritime Law and Policy is appropriately captured through the provision of Article 2 dealing with Functions, and which provides for the drafting of Conventions, Agreements, or other suitable instruments for the benefit of governments and other intergovernmental organizations.

It is through this medium that IMO has substantially carried out is mission over the last sixty (60) years. The drafting of Conventions, Agreements or other suitable instruments are carried out through the Committees of the IMO. Article 2 spells out the functions as follows:

a) Subject to the provisions of Article 3, consider and make recommendations upon matters arising under Article 1 (a), (b) and (c) that may be remitted to it by Members, by any organ or specialized agency of the United Nations or by any other intergovernmental organization or upon matters referred to it under Article 1 (d);
b) Provide for the drafting of conventions, agreements, or other suitable instruments, and recommend these to Governments and to intergovernmental organizations, and convene such conferences as may be necessary;
c) Provide machinery for consultation among Members and the exchange of information among Governments;
d) Perform functions arising in connexion with paragraphs (a), (b) and (c) of this Article, in particular those assigned to it by or under international instruments relating to maritime matters and the effect of shipping on the marine environment;
e) Facilitate as necessary, and in accordance with part X, technical co-operation within the scope of the Organization.

Article 3(b) of the convention provides:

In order to achieve the purpose of the organization set out in Article 1, the IMO should provide for the drafting of Conventions, Agreements or other suitable instruments and recommend these to governments and to intergovernmental organizations, and convene such conferences as may be necessary. Today, this Specialised Agency of the United Nations has 169 Member States and 3 associate Members [7].

Mission Statement

The Mission Statement of the International Maritime Organization is as stated in Resolution A 1011(26) and is incorporated in the strategic plan for 2010-2015:

> "The mission of the International Maritime Organization (IMO) as a United Nations Specialized Agency is to promote safe, secure, environmentally sound, efficient and sustainable shipping through cooperation. This will be achieved by adopting the highest practicable standards of maritime safety and security, efficiency of navigation and prevention and control of pollution from ships, as well as through consideration of the related legal matters and effective implementation of the IMO's instruments with a view to their universal and uniform application".

The key words in the Mission Statement which reverberate the essence and work of the IMO are not merely in the adoption of the relevant instruments, important though this may be, but more in the effective implementation of the instruments and their universal and uniform application. Following Resolution A 900(21) [8] on "Objectives of the Organization in the 2000's", the work of the IMO is now defined through its Mission and Strategic Plan, developed to cover a period of six years. The latest plan is to span the period 2010 to 2015 and sets out the trends, developments and challenges presently facing the organization and the strategic directions as well as objectives that this specialized UN body whishes to pursue in relation to identified challenges; challenges that are very often introduced by Member States through the submission of appropriate papers on particular subjects.

The strategic plan also provides for specific outputs and deliverables expected during the biennium, and all Committees are expected to provide their inputs into the global Strategic Plan of the Organization. The Assembly, meeting every two years, then receives the reports on the various Committees' progress of work and provides further directions as appropriate. These are then included in the Work Programme for another biennium.

STRUCTURE OF IMO

The Assembly

The governing body of IMO is the Assembly, made up of all members of the IMO. The Assembly meets once every 2 years but may also meet in extraordinary sessions where necessary.

It is responsible for a number of Resolutions that guide the conduct of work at the IMO. The Assembly is the highest decision making body of the organization. It is seized with the following functions:

a) To elect at each regular session from among its Members, other than Associate Members, its President and two Vice-Presidents who shall hold office until the next regular session;
b) To determine its own Rules of Procedure except as otherwise provided in the Convention;
c) To establish any temporary or, upon recommendation of the Council, permanent subsidiary bodies it may consider to be necessary;
d) To elect the Members to be represented on the Council as provided in Article 17;
e) To receive and consider the reports of the Council, and to decide upon any question referred to it by the Council;
f) To approve the work programme of the Organization;
g) To vote the budget and determine the financial arrangements of the Organization, in accordance with part XII;
h) To review the expenditures and approve the accounts of the Organization;
i) To perform the functions of the Organization, provided that in matters relating to Article 2 (a) and (b), the Assembly shall refer such matters to the Council for formulation by it of any recommendations or instruments thereon; provided further that any recommendations or instruments submitted to the Assembly by the Council and not accepted by the Assembly shall be referred back to the Council for further consideration with such observations as the Assembly may make;
j) To recommend to Members for adoption regulations and guidelines concerning maritime safety, the prevention and control of marine pollution from ships and other matters concerning the effect of shipping on the marine environment assigned to the

Organization by or under international instruments, or amendments to such regulations and guidelines which have been referred to it;

k) To take such action as it may deem appropriate to promote technical co-operation in accordance with Article 2 (e), taking into account the special needs of developing countries;

l) To take decisions in regard to convening any international conference or following any other appropriate procedure for the adoption of international conventions or of amendments to any international conventions which have been developed by the Maritime Safety Committee, the Legal Committee, the Marine Environment Protection Committee, the Technical Co-operation Committee, or other organs of the Organization.

m) To refer to the Council for consideration or decision any matters within the scope of the Organization, except that the function of making recommendations under paragraph (j) of this Article shall not be delegated.

The Council

It is worth mentioning that at the time of its formation, the IMO was made up of thirty-six (36) member states which as indicated earlier, had, by 2012, risen to 169 member states with three (3) associate members.

The increasing size of the membership at various times necessitated the amendment of the IMO convention for greater involvement of more member states in the decision making process. The subtle agitations of developing nations in the 1960's and 1970's came to the fore in the 1980's and were placed on the front burner leading eventually to an amendment of Article 17 of the Convention in 1993 increasing the membership of Council to 40 Members States [9].

Indeed, it is pertinent to point out that at its inception, the IMO was made up, in terms of structure, of the Assembly, and the Maritime Safety Committee. Article 28(1) of the 1948 Convention provided that:

> The Maritime Safety Committee shall consist of fourteen members elected by the Assembly from the members, Governments of those nations having "an important interest in maritime safety", of which not less than eight shall be "the largest ship-owning nations" and the remainder shall be elected so as to "ensure adequate representation" of members, Governments of nations with an important interest in maritime safety such as nations interested in the supply of large numbers of crews or in the carriage of large numbers of berthed and unberthed passengers, and of major geographic areas [10].

The Convention of the IMO, emanating from the 1948 Conference set out a three-tier structure for the IMO. These were the Assembly, the Maritime Safety Committee and the Council. The Maritime Safety Committee was made up of 14 member states while the Council was made up of 16 member states which in accordance with Article 17 of the Convention was set up as follows:

a) Six shall be governments of the nations with the largest interest in providing international shipping services
b) Six shall be governments of other nations with the largest interest in international seaborne trade
c) Two shall be elected by the Assembly from among the Governments of nations having a substantial interest in providing international shipping services
d) Two shall be elected by the Assembly from among the Governments of nations having substantial interest in international seaborne trade

The Council, as presently reconstituted, performs the executive and policy making role of the organization. All instruments, formal recommendations and resolutions must be approved by Council before submission to Assembly. The Council is now made up of 40 members elected every 2 years. The membership is now divided into Categories A, B, and C of 10 members each for groups A and B and 20 members for Category C.

Group A - countries with the largest international shipping services
Group B - countries with the largest international seaborne trade
Group C - states not elected under A or B that have special interests in maritime transport or navigation and whose presence in the Council will ensure representation of the world's major geographic areas. It is important to note that the world's major geographic areas is not defined and has sometimes posed some difficulties [11]. The Council meets twice a year.

The Committees

The Maritime Safety Committee

Any discussion of the role of the IMO and its maritime law and policy formulation cannot appropriately be undertaken without starting from the Maritime Safety Committee (MSC), as that is where it all began [12].

The original mandate of the IMO is reflected in its historical antecedents. In view of the importance placed on Maritime Safety as encapsulated in the formation of the Maritime Safety Committee, the mandate of the IMO was captured rather succinctly in the functions of the Maritime Safety Committee as constituted in 1948.

It stated amongst its functions that:

> "The Maritime Safety Committee shall have the duty to consider any matter within the scope of the organization and concerned with aids to navigation, construction and equipment of vessels, manning from a safety standpoint, rules for the prevention of collisions, handling of dangerous cargoes, maritime safety procedures and requirements, hydrographic information, log-books and navigational records, marine casualty investigation, salvage and rescue and any other matters directly affecting maritime safety" [13].

At its formation, the Maritime Safety Committee was the IMO and the IMO was the Maritime Safety Committee. The functions of the Maritime Safety Committee thus reflected the entire aspirations of the drafters of the IMCO Convention.

The main function of the Maritime Safety Committee has not changed in any significant way from that ascribed to it in 1948. It outlines the core issues relating to safety and the formulation of rules relating to safety at sea.

In this regard, the Maritime Safety Committee has over the years churned out a number of instruments that could rightly be defined within the purview of the development of maritime law and policy. It has formed the basis of the development of national and regional instruments by governments and intergovernmental organizations [14]. The development of instruments and the formulation of policies by the MSC is undertaken through its Resolutions, Guidelines and the issuance of circulars to member governments, intergovernmental, non-governmental bodies and industry [15].

The Maritime Safety Committee is now made up of all IMO member states. Its work is carried through various sub committees. These include the following:

- Bulk liquids and gases;
- Carriage of Dangerous Goods,
- Solid Cargoes and Containers,
- Fire Protection,
- Radio Communication and Search and Rescue,
- Safety of Navigation,
- Ship Design and Equipment,
- Stability, loadlines and Fishing Vessels Safety,
- Standards of Training and Watch keeping,
- Flag State Implementation.

The main functions as reflected in Article 29 of the IMO Convention were to consider aids to navigation, construction and equipment of vessels, manning from a safety standpoint, rules for the prevention of collisions, handling of dangerous cargoes, maritime safety procedures and requirements, hydrographic information, logbooks and navigational records, marine casualty investigation, salvage and rescue, and any other matters directly affecting maritime safety.

Marine Environmental Protection Committee (MEPC)

Responsible for all matters relating to the prevention and control of marine pollution from ships. The MEPC has developed a number of international instruments codes and guidelines dealing with the protection of the marine environment. Indeed to this day the MEPC has been instrumental in the development of a number of international instruments and policies dealing with the protection of the marine environment. The MEPC has developed Conventions, Codes and Guidelines dealing with the following environmental issues:

a) Harmful Aquatic Organisms in Ballast Water
b) Recycling of Ships
c) Prevention of Air Pollution from Ships
d) Marine Pollutions Conventions and Protocol (MARPOL 73/78)
e) The Oil Pollution Preparedness and Response Convention (OPRC)
f) Identification of and Protection of Special Areas and Particularly Sensitive Sea Areas
g) Reception Facilities
h) Harmful Anti-Fouling Systems for Ships
i) Noise from Commercial Shipping and it Adverse Impact on Marine Life,
j) Guidelines for Port State Control etc.

The Legal Committee (LC)

The Legal Committee was established in the aftermath of the Torrey Canyon Disaster in 1967. It deals with the legal problems arising from an incident and any legal matter within the scope of the IMO.

The Technical Cooperation Committee (TCC)

The Technical Cooperation Committee coordinates the work of the IMO in providing technical assistance in the maritime field, especially to developing countries.

The Facilitation Committee (FC)

The Facilitation Committee was established in 1972, to amongst others deal with issues relating to the elimination of unnecessary formalities in international shipping.

The IMO chose for the celebration of the 2011 Maritime Day, the theme "Piracy: Orchestrating the Response". Together with other Committees of the IMO, the Legal Committee took note of the need to mount a worldwide decisive and effective response to deal with this menace which had assumed alarming dimensions. The Legal Committee has been seeking ways to ensure that states have appropriate legislation to bring perpetrators of these heinous crimes to book.

These are the main bodies through which the IMO executes its mandate. In view of the fact that a number of IMO instruments are channeled through the Legal Committee, it will be appropriate to place emphasis on the work of the Legal Committee, highlighting some of its achievements in the formulation of International Maritime Law and Policy The Legal Committee is indeed the factory which produces a good number of the IMO's international instruments that Member States adopt and implement.

The Formation of the Legal Committee

The Torrey Canyon Incident

The *Torrey Canyon* orginally built with a 60,000 ton capacity was later enlarged in Japan to 120,000 tons. At the time of the accident, the tanker was owned by the Barracuda Tanker Corporation, a subsidiary of Union Oil Company of California, but chartered to British Petroleum.

The vessel sailed from Mina al-Ahamadi in Kuwait on 19th February 1967 with a full load of 120,000 tons of cargo. On March 18th 1967, owing to a navigational error, the *Torrey Canyon* struck Pollard's Rock between the Cornish Mainland and the Scilly Isle. This resulted in a significant amount of pollution damage to the marine environment. Various attempts were made to deal with the spill but to no avail. When the disaster struck, a decision was taken to bomb the vessel and blow up its oil tanks and that was done. The cleanup involved 78 separate fire brigades, 38 military units, with a crisis summit being called by Prime Minister Harold Wilson of the United Kingdom. The coasts of the UK and France were affected by the spill. The contamination blighted Cornwall's beaches and tourist industry for many years.

Claims were made by the British and French Governments against the owners of the vessel. The settlement was the largest ever in marine history for an oil claim at that time.

The *Torrey Canyon* disaster brought to the fore, issues that had technical, legal and commercial dimensions. How to keep ships more safe and improve navigation regulations, who should be liable, how and who to pay for loss, or damage in such incidents, became issues of grave concern to the international maritime community.

The *Torrey Canyon* disaster was unprecedented in the annals of oil pollution incidents. It was thus generally felt that the existing regime of international law was incapable of dealing with all the issues that arise as a result of the magnitude of such an incident. These concerns were expressed in a paper submitted by the United Kingdom to the International Maritime Organization. It stated amongst others that:

> "as the causes of such damage are inherent in the type and quantity of this cargo, it is for consideration whether tanker owners or operators should accept liability, independent of negligence, to cover damages arising out of pollution caused by accidents to tankers. In either case it would be for consideration; a) Whether some form of insurance might be made compulsory and b) Whether special principles should be agreed to enable Governments and other injured persons to recover costs of fighting pollution in the sea, cleaning polluted beaches and so on".

This indeed was to form the bedrock for later deliberations for the development of international instruments for liability and compensation, with direct action, insurance and prompt compensation to victims. It is to be noted that the Torrey Canyon affected both British and French Interests. The French Government supported the position that the legal, technical and commercial issues that arose in the wake of the *Torrey Canyon* disaster were to be best dealt with within the IMO. The IMO rose to the occasion.

Before the formation of the IMO, the responsibility for drafting and developing international treaties and other maritime legal instruments rested with the CMI, established in

1896 through Belgian Commercial and political interests. Their introduction into the medium of international legislative drafting came through a proposal to the International Law Association to codify the entire body of international maritime law [16].

The CMI's effort led to the development of the Salvage and Collisions Conventions of 1910, the Limitation of Liability Conventions of 1924 and 1957, the Liens and Mortgages Convention of 1925, the Arrest of Seagoing Ships Convention 1952, the Convention on Carriage of Passengers by Sea 1961 and the convention on Liability of Operators of Nuclear Ships 1962 amongst others.

The proposal that the issues regarding the *Torrey Canyon* incident be dealt within the framework of the IMO, was accepted by the IMO executive body, the Council, which then decided to form an Adhoc Legal Committee. The Committee was thus formed and it held its maiden meeting on 21st and 22nd June 1967. There was common agreement amongst members of the Adhoc Committee which was later endorsed by the Council, for collaboration between the CMI and the Committee for the progression of its work. This collaboration has been most beneficial to the Legal Committee till this day. The Adhoc Committee thus metamorphosed into the Legal Committee of the International Maritime Organization.

The Legal Committee is mandated by the IMO convention to deal with any legal matters within the scope of the organization. Its membership is open to all members of the IMO.

It is also empowered to perform any duties within its scope which may be assigned by or under any other international instrument and accepted by the organization [17].

The Work of the Legal Committee

The deliberations of the newly formed Committee which was to become one of the instrumental Committees of the IMO, led to the development of the International Convention on Civil Liability for Oil Pollution Damage (1969) [18] and the International Convention Relating to Intervention on the High Seas in cases of Oil Pollution Causalities 1969 [19].

The Legal Committee has since then developed a number of international instruments, Resolutions, and Guidelines which have served the international maritime community very well. These have been so successful that there have been concerns within industry that there would be over-regulation which will stifle the practice of shipping.

Born out of the fear of over-regulation, especially by states with large fleets, the General Assembly in 1993 passed resolution A.778(18) [20] indicating that proposals for new conventions or amendments to existing conventions be entertained only on the basis of clear and well documented compelling need. This is what has commonly been referred to as "the compelling need".

What amounts to a clear and well-documented compelling need has always been a matter of intense debate, especially when juxtaposed against claims that the IMO is only called into action after a catastrophe of dramatic proportions [21]. Be that as it may, the Legal Committee has often reached consensus on whether there is the compelling need for the development or otherwise of a new convention or the revision of an existing one. Undoubtedly, however, the intense debates are likely to continue for a long time to come..

The work of the Legal Committee in the development of international legal instruments have often been informed by these questions:

a) Is the subject covered by an existing International Legal Regime?
b) Is it appropriate to leave the matter to be self-regulated by the industry?
c) Will it promote uniformity?
d) If it has to deal with liability, what type of damage ought to be covered ?
e) Should the liability regime be based on fault or should there be strict liability?
f) Should there be a cap on the compensation available?
g) Should there be compulsory insurance with direct action?
h) Should an international Fund be set up and who should contribute?
i) Which courts should have jurisdiction?
j) What should be the geographical scope of the convention
k) Should acceptance be based on tonnage or number of countries or both, etc.

In view of the concept of the "freedom of the seas" (*mare liberum*), Member States of the International Maritime Organization have always been loath to extend international regulations to cover areas beyond the territorial seas [22]. This view was strongly held by a number of countries and it is thus not surprising that some of the conventions developed by the IMO" [23] limited the scope of pollution damage to damage caused on the territory, including the territorial sea of a contracting state and to preventive measures taken to prevent or minimize such damage [24]. By 1992 however, the need to extend the geographical scope of coverage had been realized, and protocols adopted to amend the conventions extended the geographical scope to include pollution damage caused in the Exclusive Economic Zone [25].

Contribution to the Development of Maritime Law and Policy

One area where the work of the Legal Committee has greatly manifested itself is the area of liability and compensation. The efforts of the Legal Committee in this area can only be described as laudable and commendable. The development of the Civil Liability Convention (CLC) following the *Torrey Canyon* incident, set the stage for the development of other liability and compensation regimes that will serve the international maritime community for several years to come.

After the 1969 conference which established the Civil Liability Convention, the alarm bells for dealing with a catastrophic disaster did not cease. There were many within the International Community who felt that the limits of liability established by the CLC were rather on the low side and feared that in the event of a catastrophic spill, the limits would be inadequate to compensate the victims. Following from these concerns, the IMO convened another conference in 1971, which resulted in the adoption of a convention establishing the International Fund for Compensation for Oil Pollution Damage.

The Fund is made up of contributions from cargo owners, who are receivers of oil imports rather than shipowners. This was generally meant to spread the risk between the shipowner who carries the cargo and the oil importer who is the beneficiary. The Fund, which entered into force in 1978, is meant to deal with situations where in the event of an accident, the limits of liability under the CLC are exhausted, and there is the need to pay additional compensation.

Time was not a good friend to the twin conventions, the CLC and the FUND, as technology improved and the capacity of tankers grew with the improvement in technology. Therefore the limits were increased in 1992 and again in 2000 to take account of the likelihood of more catastrophic incidents than that which was witnessed during the *Torrey Canyon* and *Amoco Cadiz* [26] incidents.

Despite these increases there were a number of countries which still had apprehensions that the existing limits may not be enough to deal with cataclysmic and catastrophic incidents. This was fuelled by the *Exxon Valdez* incident off Prince William Sound (USA) in 1989; an ecological tragedy of monumental proportions involving about 270,000 barrels of crude oil spilling in very pristine surroundings. The clamour for increased limits was accentuated by this incident, leading the United States to pass its own legislation on Marine Pollution, the Oil Pollution Act of 1990. (OPA 1990).

In 2003, therefore, a Diplomatic Conference was called at the instance of the Legal Committee of the IMO for the establishment of a Supplementary Fund for a third tier compensation regime for oil pollution damage. This was made optional as some countries were apprehensive that the limits were going to overburden oil importing countries.

In the area of Liability and Compensation, another concern raised by member states, was the inadequacy of the international regime dealing with the carriage of passengers, especially as the cruise business grew in Europe and America. In 1974, the Legal Committee adopted the Athens Convention on the Carriage of Passengers and their Luggage by Sea with the limits of liability being increased in 1990 and in 2002. The 2002 protocol in addition to increasing the limits, also revised the basis of liability and introduced the concept of compulsory insurance for the shipowner.

The Legal Committee is also credited with the comprehensive review of the 1957 Convention on Global Limitation of Liability for Maritime Claims, leading to the adoption of the 1976 Limitation of Liability for Maritime Claims Convention which also saw its limits increased by virtue of the 1996 protocol. A further increase in the limits was adopted by means of the tacit amendment procedure in 2012.

One subject that continued for several years to engage the minds of the international maritime community was the need for a liability and compensation regime for the carriage of hazardous and noxious substances by sea. After long years of work, the IMO through the Legal Committee adopted in 1996, the Convention on Civil Liability and Compensation for the Carriage of Hazardous and Noxious Substances by Sea [27]. It is worth noting that after over a dozen years of its adoption the convention did not meet the ratification criteria to enter into force; so in April 2010, the Legal Committee revisited the HNS Convention made some modifications to the text, and adopted the 2010 HNS Protocol. It is hoped that with the amendments made to the convention, states should now be more willing to ratify the HNS Convention and Protocol.

As pointed out earlier, the Legal Committee has indeed made a great deal of contribution in the area of liability and compensation for pollution damage. There was however one area that in common parlance [28] was referred to as the "orphan". There is no doubt that the IMO has put in place a comprehensive regime for dealing with incidents of oil pollution from ships through the work of the Legal Committee. It is however worth noting that by the 1990's the size of vessels had increased phenomenally, to the extent that some containerships were carrying more oil as bunkers than some tankers that had generally been brought under the international oil pollution regimes.

It was thus felt that a "compelling need" had been established to provide a regime that would deal with pollution from ships' bunkers in the event of an accident. This led to the adoption of the International Convention on Civil Liability for Bunker Oil Pollution Damage, 2001; as previous regimes did not cover spills arising out of bunkers from vessels which were not tankers.

The Legal Committee has also only recently adopted the Nairobi Wreck Removal Convention in 2007. The work of the Legal Committee has spanned a number of areas within the realm of the rule of international maritime law.

The efforts of the Legal Committee has not only been focused on liability and compensation issues. The Legal Committee has also addressed issues of the suppression of unlawful Acts Against the Safety of Maritime Navigation as well as fixed platforms on the Continental Shelf, leading to the adoption of the SUA Treaties. This Convention was developed in the wake of the *Achille Lauro* [29] incident and it formed the basis for addressing the legal issues relating to the suppression of unlawful acts at sea. These Rules were updated after the tragic events of "nine- eleven" in the United States of America. The SUA Protocols of 2005 were designed to deal with issues of maritime violence including acts of terrorism not envisaged by the 1988 Rome Convention on the Suppression of Unlawful Acts at Sea.

Current and Future Work

The Work Programme of the legal committee for the next biennium thus includes the following:

a) Keep under review the adequacy of the legal framework to suppress unlawful acts against ships and fixed platforms through the SUA convention and its Protocol
b) Promulgate information on prevention and suppression of acts of piracy and armed robbery against ships
c) Assist developing regions in their introduction and implementation of effective security measures and measures against piracy and armed robbery against ships.
d) Actively participate in the work of the Joint IMO/ILO Adhoc expert Working Group on issues relating to safeguarding the human rights of seafarers
e) Strategies to facilitate entry into force of 2002 Athens Protocol, 2005 SUA Protocols and 2007 Nairobi wreck removal Convention
f) Adoption of HNS Protocol 2010 as soon as practicable

It is to be noted that these are not exhaustive and may be modified and added on from time to time as the exigencies permit.

The massive pollution occasioned by the blowout on the *Deep Water Horizon* in the waters off the United States of America and the *Montara* incident which occurred in Australian waters but ended up polluting Indonesian waters, have sounded a wake-up call to the IMO to consider putting on the Work Programme of the Legal Committee, the consideration of an international regime for liability and compensation for damage caused to the marine environment by trans-boundary oil pollution arising out of offshore exploration and exploitation activities. This issue has been brought to the fore by Indonesia and has been the subject of intense debate in the Legal Committee. The Committee however did not have the appetite for the development of a new convention in this regard and has recommended the development of guidelines to assist states which may need such assistance in the development of their national legislation on the subject.

CHALLENGES

The challenges for the Legal Committee in the coming years are enormous. Enormous not because a lot of work has not been done already but enormous because the work that has been done should be seen to bear fruits. One of the major challenges of the Legal Committee is how it gets wide acceptance and application or implementation of the instruments it has developed [30]. Thus, the Legal committee has turned its attention to providing the appropriate guidelines, working through the Technical Cooperation Committee's Integrated Technical Cooperation Programme (ITCP) to support countries which are in need of support for the implementation of instruments developed by the IMO.

It is worth recalling that the Legal Committee was engendered as a result of a catastrophe. It has, since its establishment, dealt with a good number of issues relating especially to liability and compensation confronting the international maritime community. It may seem that the Committee is at the end of its work unless a new incident arises that calls for the development of a new convention. At present there is no new convention being developed by the Legal Committee. Within the framework of a "compelling need" for new legislation and the fear of over-regulation by industry, there is a quandary as to what next the Legal Committee would embark upon by way of an international instrument.

This is indeed a challenge that the Legal Committee must confront boldly or else it risks becoming moribund. There is no doubt that there are still gaps in the international regime for maritime transport and unless uniform approaches are adopted in dealing with them, there would be regional and national solutions which will not inure to the benefit of the global character of shipping. At its 99th Session, the Legal Committee decided not to pursue the development of a new international treaty dealing with transboundary pollution, but to develop guidelines that would assist states which are in need of guidance as to how to approach such situations. The legal issues regarding piracy need to be addressed boldly within the framework of an international convention. There is however no appetite for the development of such a convention within the Legal Committee. The Committee has decided that the existing legal framework is enough to deal with the scourge of piracy. The Committee working through the Integrated Technical Cooperation Programme (ITCP), would however assist states to develop appropriate legislation to enable states which require a strengthening of their national legislation deal with acts of piracy.

The Legal Committee should consider the development of model laws capable of being adopted by states for ready implementation with minimal amendments as may be required within particular domestic jurisdictions and legal systems. The Legal Committee should set itself the task of reviewing all the instruments it has developed with a view to revising them where need be and coming out with ways of ensuring their successful implementation. There is no doubt that the Legal Committee, since its establishment, has made a very significant contribution in serving the rule of international maritime law.

EXECUTING IMO'S MANDATE

Since 1959, this United Nations Specialized Agency has provided a forum for co-operation among Governments in the field of governmental regulations and practices relating to all kinds of shipping engaged in international trade. The IMO has also, over the years, facilitated the adoption of comprehensive multilateral treaties for a wide range of technical measures and in particular, the adoption of the highest practicable standards designed to enhance safety, security and efficiency of shipping. Among the numerous achievements include the adoption of over 50 major multilateral conventions and Protocols as well as over 800 codes, recommendations and guidelines which have served the international maritime community in the business of international transportation by sea.

The IMO indeed has a wide scope of operation and has, over the years, assumed a number of responsibilities dealing especially with the development of technical rules and regulations with respect to the safety, and security of ships as well as the protection of the marine environment.

Through various committees the IMO executes it mandate, which has also involved design and equipment of ships, fire protection, safety of navigation, radio communication, search and rescue, training and certification of seafarers, flag state implementation, port state control and ways for enhancing security on ships, including dealing with the scourge of piracy.

In view of the broad membership of the IMO – 169 sovereign states, the international instruments adopted by it enjoy wide international acceptance and implementation. Indeed for a good number of the IMO conventions, the parties that have adopted the instruments represent over 90% of the worlds merchant fleet and for a business such as shipping which is international in character, it is indeed remarkable. In its quest to ensure that the dynamic business of shipping keeps abreast with technological and other changes, the IMO keeps under constant review its multilateral treaties and causes amendments to its provisions where the dictates of a new order so require.

The IMO's success in the discharge of its mandate will not have true meaning unless there is appropriate implementation of the numerous treaties it has churned out. To ensure that member states are adequately equipped with the know-how to implement these instruments, the IMO has an elaborate Technical Cooperation programme that provides capacity to member states, especially developing countries and least developed countries and small Island Developing states. Because the work of IMO transcends a good number of operators in the industry, the IMO's efforts at building capacity covers port states, shipowners, ship managers, ship operators, ship builders, equipment manufacturers, training institutions, insurance companies and many others in the field whose operations impact on the business of international shipping. Thus the IMO's policy formulation has extended to cover all these areas and have formed the basis for the development of industry standards. Since 2003, the roll-out of IMO's plans and programmes for the benefit of member states and the world at large has been based on the development of High Level Action Plans with the requisite Strategic Directions towards the execution of its mandate. In reflecting on its performance the former IMO Secretary General, Admiral Mitropolous recalled the need for an international agency regulating maritime transport in view of the international nature of shipping. The IMO's role in this respect continues to underpin its activities, especially the development of technical regulation in the areas of safety, security and the pollution of the marine environment. In underscoring the international character of shipping he noted: "The ownership and management chain surrounding any particular vessel can embrace many different countries; it is not unusual to find that its owners, operators, shippers, charterers, insurers and the classification society, not to mention the officers and crew, are all of different nationalities and that none of these is from the country whose flag the ship flies" [31]. Oftentimes shipping is referred to as a dangerous occupation. Anytime disaster strikes and there are high profile cases, the international community is quick to chastise, admonish, and call for more standards to prevent future occurrences. In most of these situations the IMO has responded appropriately. Cases in point include, The *Titanic, The Torrey Canyon, The Amoco Cadiz, The Exxon Valdez, Estonia, Erika, Prestige and the Costa Concordia* etc. In the words of Mitropoulos: the "IMO's work has demonstrated beyond doubt, that international standards – developed, agreed, implemented and enforced universally – are the only effective way to regulate such a diverse and truly international shipping industry" [32]. As indicated earlier, by the year 2008, the IMO's Conventions [33], its codes, guidelines and recommendation had been noted as the reference point for any action involving the safety, security and prevention of marine pollution from ships. Today, IMO's rules and regulations formulated in the interest of industry are best described as from "cradle to grave" – i.e. the development and application of standards from the embryonic stages of ship construction to the time it is finally broken up (not laid to rest) in the scrapyard and eventually recycled. A unique manifestation of the acceptance and application of the international rules developed by the IMO is expressed through the wide acceptance of conventions such as the Safety of Life at Sea Convention, SOLAS, the Tonnage Convention, the Loadlines Convention, The Standards of Training Certification and Watchkeeping (STCW) and the Marine Pollution Convention (MARPOL 73/78) which reflect over 98% of the World's total fleets. As indicated earlier, the work of the IMO is now [34] executed through its Strategic Plan and the High-Level Action Plan [35]. Amongst the good number of actions taken by the IMO in respect of its mandate of safety, security and the protection of the marine environment are the following;

a) *Safety of Passenger Ships*: In its quest to improve upon safety of Passenger Ships, the MSC in December 2006 adopted new amendments to the SOLAS Convention. These amendments emphasize the need for measures to prevent a casualty from occurring in the first place and provides for the design of ships that would ensure safety of passengers in the event of a casualty at sea.
b) *Goal-Based New Ship Construction Standards (GBS):* These standards are meant to ensure that hull standards developed by classification societies meet the safety goals and functional requirements established by IMO.
c) *Seafarers Training and Certification*: Experience has shown that a number of disasters have occurred due to the human element. Efforts to address shortcomings in relation to the Human Element have thus been increased by the IMO. In this regard

the IMO has continuously revised its standards of training and certification of seafarers incorporated in the STCW Convention.

d) *The International Safety Management (ISM) Code:* Through SOLAS 1974, the IMO developed a code for safety management which was made mandatory for oil tankers, bulk carriers and passenger ship in 1998 and for all other ships in 2002. The Safety Management Code or the ISM Code as it is commonly referred to, provides elaborate provisions on standards of operation and the requisite training to be adopted by shipowning companies. There is no doubt that the code has proved a useful addition to the development of standards of safety for the shipping industry.
e) *Search and Rescue* Since the adoption of the International Convention on Maritime Search and Rescue (SAR Convention) in 1979, IMO has strengthened its efforts at ensuring that in the event of a casualty at sea an appropriate framework exists for search and rescue of victims. The SAR was revised in May 1998 and entered into force in January 2000. The revised annex to the SAR Convention clarifies the responsibilities of governments and puts greater emphasis on the regional approach and coordination between maritime and aeronautical SAR operations. In this regard IMO has through its Technical Cooperation programme aided with the setting up of regional maritime rescue coordination centers (MRCC's) for improving upon search and rescue operations for casualties at sea. Between 2006 and 2008 the IMO has commissioned three MRCC's in Mombassa Kenya, Cape Town, South Africa and Lagos Nigeria.
f) *Carriage of Dangerous Goods in Packaged Form*: Through an amendment of SOLAS the IMDG code [36] has been developed by IMO which has set an international standard for the safe carriage of packaged dangerous goods [37].
g) *Safety of Fishing Vessels*: The IMO has also developed standards for the Safety of Fishing Vessels with collaboration from the FAO [38] and the ILO [39].

In October 2012 a Diplomatic Conference was held in Cape Town South Africa to adopt An Agreement to the Protocol to the Torremolinos Convention of 1993 relating to the 1977 Torremolinos International Convention for the Safety of Fishing Vessels. It is to be noted that the safety of fishermen and the vessels with which they ply their trade has always been a major and integral part of the concerns of IMO. Even though the interest of the IMO in this regard was manifested in the development of a convention way back in 1977, legal and technical obstacles worked against the entry into force of the convention. Thus the 2012 Agreement on the Implementation of the 1993 Protocol is expected to deal with the technical and legal obstacles that have so far impeded the implementation of the protocol. When the Agreement enters into force, countries which are parties to it could consider implementation of the technical requirements of the 1993 Torremolinos Protocol under the terms and conditions contained in the Agreement. This is yet another demonstration of IMO's role in the development of Maritime law and policy in the wider sphere of international maritime transport.

Flag State Implementation

The role of the flag state in Maritime Transportation has long remained one of the cherished principles of maritime navigation. Through its Flag State Implementation policies, the IMO has set global standards for flag, port and coastal states with respect to the ship, its navigation, in relation to safety, security and the protection of the marine environment.

Port State Control

One area where IMO has been effective in dealing with the substandard ships has been through the development of port state [40] control mechanisms. With the support of the IMO, nine regions have established regional port state control regimes through Memoranda of Understanding (MOU's) and this has thus left very little or no room for sub-standard ships to operate. The role of the Port State Control Authorities is enhanced through the exchange of information and maritime data on the IMO Global Integrated Shipping Information System (GISIS).

The IMO Voluntary Member States Audit Scheme

This is also one of the unique developments of the IMO established in furtherance of its objectives of ensuring that the mandatory instruments adopted by member states are effectively implemented. Indeed, at its 88th Session, in June 2002, the IMO Council considered and approved in principle a proposal by 19 member states for the development of an IMO Model Audit Scheme taking inspiration from the ICAO Universal Safety Oversight Audit Programme. After a number of reviews of the main tenets of the scheme, it has now been adopted as a standard peer review mechanism by which the work of maritime administrations are measured with respect to implementation of IMO instruments [41].

Amongst others, the scheme is purposed to transform the monitoring and implementation of IMO instruments. Some of the expected benefits include:

a) improved and full reporting to IMO on the implementation treaty obligations;
b) better investigations of casualties and port state control detention;
c) more rigorous delegation of authority to recognized organizations;
d) better trained and properly certificated seafarers;
e) better communication between flag and port States;
f) acceptance of the need to improve performance;
g) closer monitoring and accountability by companies (shipowners); and
h) greater awareness of the need to establish measures to protect coastal and marine resources.

There is no gainsaying the fact that the Voluntary IMO Member States Audit has proven very successful and now there are incessant calls to make this mandatory.

Maritime Casualty Investigation

Maritime Casualty Investigation requires global standards and adherence to uniform practices in view of the very different legal regimes within which an investigation may be undertaken [42]. The IMO has put in place appropriate guidelines for Maritime Casualty Investigations.

Integrated Technical Co-Operation

The global adoption of International Instruments and their universal applicability is paramount to the success of the business of international shipping. In this regard, states should not be left behind due to lack of capacity. The IMO's ITCP thus ensures that countries that require the strengthening of their capacities with respect to implementation of IMO instruments are duly provided with the wherewithal to do so.

Piracy and Armed Robbery against Ships

Despite all the contributions of the IMO towards safe navigation and maritime security, in recent times, the issue that has left an indelible and unsavory mark on the work of the IMO is the scourge of piracy. Reports of attacks on ships, traversing the Gulf of Aden and the Somali Coast are as disturbing as they are alarming. There is no doubt the effort and energy pumped into dealing with this scourge of the oceans. The IMO has undertaken various initiatives to deal with the issue of piracy.

Indeed, for the year 2010, the IMO adopted for its slogan for the celebration of the World Maritime Day the catch phrase: "Piracy: Orchestrating a Response". IMO's collaboration with various UN agencies in this regard is remarkable. Mention can also be made of the Djibouti Accord and the U.N. Working Group on Piracy.

There is no gainsaying the fact that intractable as the menace of piracy may seem, the IMO is working assiduously towards curbing it. In this regard, the Legal Committee is expected to provide guidelines through the IMO's ITCP Programme to member states who require expertise in bringing their criminal law regimes up to date, to enable them fortify the said legislation and to expeditiously bring the perpetrators of these heinous crimes to justice.

Fair Treatment of Seafarers

The Legal Committee of IMO has adopted guidelines for the fair treatment of seafarers in the event of a maritime accident. The guidelines are to ensure that seafarers are treated fairly and humanely and that detention, if necessary at all, should be for no longer than is necessary for the purpose of gathering information.

THE ISPS CODE

After the gruesome events of September 11 2011, the International Maritime Community was prodded to a rude awakening that maritime transport and its paraphernalia could be used as instruments of terrorist activities. The IMO, as it had done in times past, rose to the occasion, and in December 2002 adopted an amendment to the SOLAS Convention which enshrined the new International Ship and Port Facility Security Code (ISPS Code). A number of countries have already put in place measures to implement the code, and this has proven useful to the international maritime community. Indeed its purpose of providing a standardized consistent framework for evaluating risk and enabling Governments to offset changes in threat with changes in vulnerability for ships and port facilities of appropriate security levels and corresponding security measures seems to have been largely achieved [43].

CONCLUSION

It is clear that from very humble beginnings in 1948, the IMO has matured into a fully fledged international organization within the United Nations system with the capacity to provide the requisite technical rules and regulations for the conduct of international shipping.

It is also evident that the contribution of the IMO to international shipping is remarkable and cannot be gainsaid. The IMO's sterling contribution to the service of international shipping and, in particular, the development of maritime law and policy can be summed up in the words of its former Secretary General, Efthimios Mitropoulos when he said:

> "the celebration of the 60th anniversary of the IMO would provide an opportunity to pay tribute to the sterling work the organization has been delivering since its inception in 1948 as a specialized agency of the United Nations; as an institution serving the common public good; and as the regulator and partner of an industry, which while credited with carrying the overwhelming volume of world trade safely and efficiently, also displays a caring attitude vis-à-vis the environment both marine and atmospheric". Undoubtedly this sums up the enduring work and mandate of the IMO as captured in the phrase: "safe, secure and efficient shipping on clean oceans".

It is worth noting that in working to achieve its mission of promoting safe, secure, environmentally sound, efficient and sustainable shipping through cooperation [44], the IMO has worked with various bodies, Governmental as well as Non-Governmental to develop the comprehensive body of IMO Conventions, Codes, Guidelines, Agreements, Recommendations and Resolutions that have governed every facet of the technical regulation of international shipping [45].

It is also worth mentioning that the high levels of adoption and implementation of IMO Conventions is traceable to the consensus building mechanisms adopted by the various Committees of IMO in arriving at most if not all of its decisions relating to the development of international maritime law instruments.

Over the years, the work of the IMO has expanded and covered various facets of shipping beyond its original maritime safety intentions. Now the work of the IMO broadly covers such areas as; Maritime Security and Piracy, Protection of the Marine Environment as well as the atmosphere, the development of legal regimes for liability and compensation and other issues dealing with Maritime Labour and the Human Element.

The work of IMO has now encompassed issues of Technical Cooperation and advisory support to Developing Countries, Facilitation of Shipping through a reduction in Administrative Burdens and the provision of data and information to relevant bodies on matters relating to shipping.

Today, apart from the development of Conventions that represent the main body of law through which technical enforcement is undertaken, the IMO has also provided "subsidiary international legislation, (soft law) in the form of Codes, Guidelines, Agreements, Resolutions, and Circulars, some of which even though not binding on member states are compelling in their application to matters affecting international shipping.

The IMO has indeed proven through its work over these last 64 years (1948-2012) that it has accomplished its mandate of the development of international maritime law and policy for the highest practicable standards of maritime safety and security, efficiency of navigation and the prevention and control of marine pollution from ships. While acknowledging that it has enjoyed the collaboration of other international bodies in the discharge of its mandate, it undoubtedly stands out as the international body within the United Nations System that has developed a comprehensive set of technical rules for universal and uniform application in the business of international shipping.

REFERENCES

[1] A.L Rowse, *Public International Law*.

[2] See McDonald Eula," "Towards a World Maritime Organisation – A half Century of Developments in Ocean Shipping published by the Division of Publications/Office of Public Affairs (International Organisations and Conference Series IV International Maritime Consultative Organisation 1 (publication 3196). Also see E/conf.4/13.

[3] Other Specialized Agencies of the United Nations include; The World Health Organisation (WHO), International Labour Organisation (ILO), the International Civil Aviation Organisation (ICAO), The Food and Agriculture Organisation (FAO) etc. These belong to the class of organisations within the UN system which are autonomous but work through the coordinating machinery of the United Nations Economic and Social Council.

[4] For a detailed report of the 1948 conference see Cates John M. "UN Maritime Conference – Geneva 1948" published by the Division of Publication/Office of Public Affairs in their International Organisation and Conference Series IV: International Maritime Consultative Organisation 1 (publication 3196).

[5] For further information on the choice of name and acronym see Lampe H Wilhelm, "The" "New" International Maritime Organization and its Place in the Development of International Maritime Law", *JMLC* vol.14, No. 3, July 1983.

[6] Article 2.

[7] www.imo.org.

[8] Also see Resolution A 909(22) on Policy Making in IMO – Setting the Organizations Policies and Objectives.

[9] See an article on the membership of the IMO Council written by Ademun-Odeke titled: "From the 'Constitution of the Maritime Safety Committee' to the Constitution of the Council": Will the IMCO Experience Repeat Itself at the IMO Nearly 50 Years On? The Juridical Politics of an International Organization; Texas International Law Journal Vol. 43:55. For a thorough discussion on the formative years of the Maritime Safety Committee see, Constitution of the Maritime Safety Committee of the Inter Governmental Maritime Consultative Organisation, Advisory Opinion, 1960 I.C.J. 150.

[10] K.R. Simmonds, The Constitution of the Maritime Safety Committee of IMCO, 12 INT'L and COMP. LQ. 56, (1963).

[11] See an extensive consideration of the issues that attend to representation of the interests of Member States in Ademun-Odeke, supra.

[12] See Ademun-Odeke, op cit.

[13] Article 29 (a).

[14] See also Constitution of the Maritime Safety Committee of the Inter Governmental Maritime Consultative Organization, 54 AM. J. INT'L L 884 (1960).

[15] See www.imo.org., Maritime Safety Division, List of MSC Resolutions.

[16] See Rosalie Balkin, presentation published in Current Maritime Issues and the International Maritime Organization by Myron H. Norquist, John Norton Moore, University of Virginia, Centre for Ocean Law and Policy.

[17] N. Gaskell (2003) Decision Making and the Legal Committee of t he IMO, *International Journal of Marine and Coastal Law*; 18(2) 155-214.

[18] Commonly referred to as the CLC or the Civil Liability Convention 1969.

[19] Commonly referred to as the Intervention Convention 1969.

[20] On Work Methods and Organization of work indicating the Committees and their subsidiary bodies.

[21] Indeed some people have said that" maritime laws are written in the blood of past disasters". It is however important to note that for some of the actions taken by the IMO, it needs to be proactive in filling the lacunae in international maritime law.

[22] This was the case during the development of the limits of the territorial seas during the Law of the Sea negotiations. The limits of the territorial sea, over which states exercise sovereignty were eventually extended from three nautical miles to twelve nautical miles under UNCLOS.

[23] The Civil Liability Convention and the International Convention on the Establishments of an International Fund for Oil Pollution Damage 1971 (The Fund Convention).

[24] See The Civil Liability Convention (CLC 1969).

[25] See also the Nairobi Wreck removal Convention 2007.

[26] In 1978,The Liberian registered VLCC the *Amoco Cadiz* caused the world's worst oil tanker spill at the time and is estimated to have cost over $250million in damages to fisheries and tourist facilities.

[27] Commonly referred to as the HNS Convention.

[28] Within the Legal Committee.

[29] In 1985, members of the Palestinian Liberation front hijacked the Italian cruise liner the *Achille Lauro* with 400 passengers on board.

[30] For a detailed discussion of the challenge, see, Dr. Alan TAN Khee Jin, (Faculty of Law, National University of Singapore), The Sea Transport Industry and the Challenges of State Regulation, *UNITAR Conference on Seas and Security*, 6-8 March 2002, Hiroshima Japan.

[31] See IMO News Issue 3 (2008) opinions expressed by the former secretary General of the IMO, Efthimios S.E. Mitropoulos.

[32] ibid.

[33] About 50 in number.

[34] See IMO Assembly 25th Session, November 2007. The Assembly adopted a new six year Strategic Plan spanning the period 2008-2012. (A 989 (25).

[35] A 990 (25).

[36] International Maritime Dangerous Goods Code.

[37] Also developed by IMO through the Maritime Safety Committee is the International Maritime Solid Bulk Cargo Code (IMSBC).

[38] Food and Agriculture Organisation of the United Nations.

[39] nternational Labour Organisation also of the United Nations.

[40] See U.N. General Assembly Resolution 58/40 on the role of the port state.

[41] See Paper by L.D. Barchue, Sr, Head, Member State Audit Internal Oversight Section, Office of the Secretary General of the International Maritime Organization, titled: Making a Case for the Voluntary IMO Member State Audit Scheme.

[42] See the code of the International Standards and Recommended Practices for a safety Investigation into a marine casualty or marine incident; referred to as the Casualty Investigation Code.

[43] For a detailed discussion on the ISPS Code see: Implementation of the ISPS Code at the IMO Website at www.imo.org.

[44] See Boisson Philippe; Safety at Sea: Policies, Regulations and International Law. Preface by William O'Neil, Paris edition, Bureau Veritas, 1999, ISBN 2 – 86413 – 020 -3 pp44-45.

[45] Some of these bodies include; the United Nations Division on Oceans and the Law of the Sea, (UNDOALOS) The Comite Maritime Internationale, (CMI) The International Transport Federation (ITF), The International Civil Aviation Organisation (ICAO) The International Labour Organisation (ILO) etc. For a more detailed list of Non-governmental organizations in Consultative status, visit the IMO website at http://www.imo.org/About/Membership/Pages/Default.aspx.

In: Selected Issues in Maritime Law and Policy
Editor: Maximo Q. Mejia, Jr.
ISBN: 978-1-62618-508-1

Chapter 2

FLAGS OF CONVENIENCE: PROBLEMS AND PROMISES

Thomas A. Mensah[*]
Inaugural President, International Tribunal for the Law of the Sea,
Manila, Philippines

INTRODUCTION

One of the perennial and intractable problems in international shipping is that posed by ships that are registered in States which operate what are described as "open registries". Open registry states are States which permit merchant ships to be registered under their laws (and fly their flags) even if the owners of the ships are not nationals of the States. Such ships are often also described as "flags of convenience" ships.[1]

Registration is the term normally used to refer to the attribution of national status to a ship. Generally speaking registration is a precondition for the right of a ship to fly a national flag, and registration is evidenced by the issue to the ship of a number of documents which together provide evidence of its nationality and hence the right to operate at sea. The flying of a national flag is the visible symbol of the ships nationality and evidence of its registration. As the Convention on the Law of the Sea puts it, "ships have the nationality of the State whose flag they are entitled to fly"[2].

---

[*] E-mail: tamensah@yahoo.co.uk.

[1] The term "flag of convenience" was originally used to refer to a different type of ship. The 1958 Convention on the High Seas and the 1982 Unite Nations Convention on the Law of the Sea (UNCLOS) both speak of a ship that "sails under the flags of two or more States, using them according to convenience". (Article 6, paragraph 2.of the 1958 Convention and Article 92, paragraph 2 of the 1982 UNCLOS) The use of flags in this way is prohibited by both conventions, with identical provisions stating that such a ship "may not claim any of the nationalities in question in relation to any other State, and may be assimilated to a ship without nationality". The use of the term "flag of convenience" to refer to ships that have no "genuine link" with the State of registry is a relatively modern term, beginning from the period after the end of the Second World War.

[2] Article 91 of the 1982 Convention on the Law of the Sea.

Under traditional maritime law and the law of the sea, every State has the right to fix the conditions for the registration of a ship under its flag.[3] Normally a ship flying the flag of a State is under the jurisdiction of that state, and the laws of that state are applicable to the ship in all matters arising in the course of its operation[4]. The legislation of many States provided that there should be not just a legal link but also an economic and operational connection between the State and ships that are granted the right to fly its flag. To ensure that this would be so, States set out in their domestic law basic requirements that ships had to satisfy in order to be registered under their jurisdiction. For the most part the requirements related, *inter alia,* to the nationality of the owners of the ships, the technical and other conditions of the ships, the nationality of the crew and the composition of the crews serving on the ships[5]

In many cases, the laws and regulations on registration of ships were quite elaborate and sometimes extremely demanding. This was especially so in the United States. The laws in the United States were further strengthened with the passing of the Seamen's Act in 1915. The main purpose of the Act was to provide safeguards for mariners. Among other things, the Act regulated the working hours of mariners, their emoluments and other allowances and even established baselines requirements for the food provided to seafarers on board ships. The Act also provided for more effective enforcement of safety standards on board ships, with specific requirements on the number and quality of lifeboats on board and the minimum number of qualified seamen required on each ship.

ORIGINS OF THE FLAGS OF CONVENIENCE

The stringent requirements in the legislation of the United States placed the operators of United States ships at a competitive disadvantage, as compared to owners and operators in other countries. In response owners and operators of US ships looked for possible avenues to protect their business interests. One of the avenues identified by them was to move their ships to States whose requirements were not so high. Panama was seen as a suitable country for this purpose, and a number of owners moved their ships from the United States register to the Panamanian register. Because of the close association of Panama with the United States at the time, this move did not attract much attention at first, and there was hardly any hostile reaction to the movement of ships to the Panamanian register. The attractiveness of this new arrangement soon became widely appreciated, and some entrepreneurs in the United States decided to establish a similar registry of ships in Liberia. The Liberian registry soon began to flourish, thanks in part to the growing unpopularity of the Panamanian flag. The unpopularity was due to a number of factors, including concerns from labour unions in the United States,

[3] "Generally speaking it belongs to every sovereign to decide to whom he will accord the right to fly his flag and to prescribe the rules governing such grants" The Muscat Dhows Case, Reports of International Arbitral Awards RIAA 1905 XI, p. 83.

[4] It is generally agreed that the flag State of a ship has the right to regulate matters on board the ship, regardless of where the ship may be. For example, Article 4(1) of the 1973/1978 MARPOL Convention provides that the flag State has the right and duty to prohibit violations of the Convention "wherever the violation occurs". On the high seas the jurisdiction of the flag State is exclusive, with only a few special exceptions.

[5] "The purpose of the requirement that a ship should fly the national flag, and be owned, built and crewed by national (or a combination of these) was to ensure a close economic and operational connection between a ship and the country of registration" Bruce Farthing and Mack Brownrigg, Farthing on International Shipping, LLP Business Series (1977), p.186.

dissatisfaction among some European shipping concerns, increases in the fees charged by the Panamanian authorities and escalating political problems in Panama.[6]

In due course, ship registers that are open to non-national owners, and apply less restrictive requirements, have become more numerous and more attractive to shipowners. This is due to a number of factors. On the whole the open registers give to owners the possibility of operating much more cheaply than under the flags of traditional maritime States. This means that ships are able to compete more effectively by reducing operating costs. For example, these ships can avoid additional crew costs by employing seafarers from outside the States that impose strict conditions and terms of employment for their seafarers. Other owners move to open registry countries for less commendable reasons: they flag out from traditional maritime States mainly in order to avoid the obligation to observe national and international laws and regulations that impose strict safety standards or mandate high standards for environmental protection, as well as fair terms of employment and decent working conditions for seafarers working on the ships. On the whole, however, owners move to open registries mainly with a view to reducing their costs.[7]

Thus, from the early 1950s there developed an alternative to the traditional system of ship registration that required that a ship should normally be registered in the country of which the owner or owners (and specified members of the crew) are nationals. The new system permits ships to be registered in states that are not necessarily the states of nationality of either the owners or any members of crews. Under this new system, ships can transfer easily between flags. As a result, it is possible, and indeed usual, for a ship to be owned by a company registered in one country, managed by a company based in another country, with crew members from different or other countries. Ships that are registered and operated under such a system are described as ships that fly "flags of convenience" and countries which permit the registration of ships in this way are said to operate "open registries".

But it is not easy to determine in every case the ships that may correctly be considered as operating under the traditional registration system, as opposed to those that are covered by the open registry system or which fly "flags of convenience". This distinction was not easy even under the traditional system of ship registration since there was no agreement on the specific and necessary links that needed to exist between a ship and the country of its registration.[8] Nevertheless, there was sufficient agreement on the basic criteria that most States used to determine the nationality of ships. Ships deemed to be flying flags of convenience are those which do not satisfy any of these criteria. In 1958, the OECD Maritime Transport Committee produced a rough and ready definition of what should be considered as "flag of convenience"

---

[6] See Rodney P. Carlisle, Sovereignty for Sale: the Origins and Evolution of the Panamanian and Liberian Flags of Convenience, Annapolis, MD: the United States Naval Institute, 1981. Also Richard Coles and Edward Watt, Ship Registration Law and Practice (2nd Edition) Informa, London (2009), paragraphs 3.12 to 3.17.

[7] "It is today not a question of trying to escape from proper safety standards. It is all to do with competing more effectively by reducing operating costs through, for example, avoiding the necessity to have "double crews" because of leave requirements and other crew costs arising from the employment of seafarers from western nations" Farthing, note 5.above, p.188; "Ship owners seek to reduce operating costs by reducing the number of crews employed and/or reducing the wages and associated benefits paid for the crew" Malcolm Willingale, Ship Management, (1998) London LLP Business Series, p.47.

[8] "A number of connecting factors have been put forward as the appropriate test of a vessels nationality. One of the common links required by many States was that the ship be owned by and crewed by nationals of the flag State. A Report by the UNCTAD Secretariat in 1982 listed 28 countries that required their vessels to be manned entirely by nationals, and a further 24 which stipulated that key personnel and/or a given percentage of the crew had to be nationals" Farthing, op. cit. note 5.above, p.184.

ships. The Committee noted that "the laws of certain countries... allow, and indeed make it easy, for ships owned by foreign nationals or companies to fly their flags. This is in contrast to practice in maritime countries (and in many others) where the right to fly the national flag is subject to stringent conditions and involves far-reaching obligations" [9]

Building on this statement a British Committee of Inquiry, chaired by Lord Rochdale, produced in 1970 what was considered as the defining set of characteristics for identifying the countries that operate the "flag of convenience" system. The common features, as identified under the Rochdale formula, were the following:

1. The country of registry allows ownership and/or control of its merchant vessels by non-citizens
2. Access to the registry (of the country) is easy. A ship may usually be registered as a consul's office abroad. Equally important, transfer from the registry at the owner's discretion is not restricted.
3. Taxes on the income from the ships are not levied or are low. A registry fee and an annual fee, based on tonnage, are normally the only charges made. A guarantee or acceptable undertaking of future freedom from taxation may also be given.
4. The country of registry is a small power with no national requirement under any foreseeable circumstances for the shipping registered, but the receipts from very small charges on a large tonnage may produce a substantial effect on its national income and balance of payments.
5. Manning of ships by non-nationals is freely permitted.
6. The country of registry has neither the power nor the administrative machinery to impose any government or international regulation, nor has the country the wish or the power to control the companies themselves.[10]

But even this formulation is not sufficiently comprehensive or clear to be accepted generally as a "definition" of "flag of convenience" or to provide an adequate and useful yardstick for distinguishing a "flag of convenience ship" from a ship registered under the traditional system of ship registration. The difficulty is compounded by the emergence of what have come to be known as "second" or "international" registers. The arrival on the scene of these new types of registry has made the difference between "open registries" and the traditional ship registries less clear-cut in many respects.[11]

DEVELOPMENT OF INTERNATIONAL OR PARALLEL REGISTRIES

The emergence of "international" or "parallel" registers was one of the results of the success of the flag of convenience system of ship registration. As noted above, flag of

[9] OECD Maritime Transport Committee 1958.

[10] Report of the Committee of Inquiry into Shipping (The Rochdale Report) HMSO London, May 1970, Cmnd. 4337, p.16, paragraph 62.

[11] Perhaps the most comprehensive definition of a flag of convenience ship is the one offered by Boczek: "Functionally a flag of convenience can be defined as the flag of any country allowing the registration of foreign owned or foreign-controlled vessels under conditions which, for whatever reason, are convenient and opportune for the persons who are registering the vessel", Boczek, Flags of Convenience – An International Legal Study, (1962), Harvard University Press, p. 2.

convenience registration offers a number of competitive advantages over the traditional system of ship registration. In the main, the flag of convenience registries impose fewer and less stringent requirements either in terms of the costs of registration or the consequential running costs of the ship. These advantages, coupled with the harsh economic climate created by the recession of the 1980s, forced many owners in the traditional maritime nations to move to open registry flags in foreign countries where they could expect to operate more cheaply. For many of these owners, the main reason for their move was not because they wished to escape from the higher technical safety and environmental standards demanded by the traditional maritime countries. Rather they moved because registration under foreign flags enabled them to compete more effectively by reducing their operating costs.[12] For it had become clear to many of them that they could not hope to compete effectively unless they had greater flexibility, especially as regards requirements on ownership and the choice of personnel to crew their vessels. It was to achieve this flexibility that many owners found it necessary to move some of their ships to flag of convenience registries. This led to the phenomenon of "flagging out" of ships from their traditional flag States to other States. Much of the movement was to countries that offered flags of convenience registration. The consequence was that a large proportion of fleets of the traditional maritime nations were registered abroad, leading to a steady contraction in many of the high-cost European fleets. The fate that had befallen the merchant marine fleet of the United States had also affected the fleets of many European maritime countries.

To stem the flow of ships away from their registers, many traditional maritime countries in Europe resorted to new approaches to attract back the owners who had left their registers to register ships abroad. But these countries did not wish to compromise their traditions in their efforts to attract ships back to their registries. Nor were they willing to depart from their long-standing commitment to standards of safety, environmental protection and fair conditions of employment for seafarers or decent social conditions on board ships. The strategy chosen by them to attract their shipowners back was to establish "second "or "parallel" shipping registers that would offer many of the advantages of "flags of convenience" registration, but which would not also permit or condone the lax practices and procedures associated with normal "flags of convenience" ships. Beginning with Norway in 1987, many European maritime countries established new registers in addition to their traditional national registers.[13] These new and parallel registers came to be known as "international shipping registers". The new registers offer to owners "quality registers" which insist on respect for all existing international commitments but also offer significant cost and tax advantages to owners. As previously noted the main aim of the new registers was to attract back the national owners who had left their national registers to take advantage of the more liberal regimes offered by the flag of convenience States. However, it was also hoped that the new registers

[12] "The reasons for the acquisition of a flag of convenience vary and are often misunderstood. First and foremost, there is an economic motivation which might take several forms. Many shipowners register their ships in another country where there was minimal taxation or none at all. This has always been the primary motivation for flag of convenience registration. There may be in the flag of convenience State also greater freedom of operation resulting from less demanding labour legislation requirements". Edgar Gold, New Law of the Sea and Nationality of Ships, p. 268.

[13] The Norwegian International Ship Register (NIS) was established in 1987 by an Act of 12 June 1987. The Register offers many concessions. In particular, there is no nationality restriction concerning the employment of non-Norwegian seafarers, with the exception of the Master who should hold Norwegian citizenship. However, it is possible to apply for dispensation from this requirement. See Richard Coles and Edward Watt, Ship Registration: Law and Practice, op.cit. Note 6 above, paragraph 21.11.

would be sufficiently attractive to owners from other countries who wished to enjoy the benefits of the new regimes without having to cope with the generally unfavourable reputation of the normal "flag of convenience" ships. So the law for the new register provided that registration would be possible even for ships whose owners are not necessarily national of the State of registry. In time the success of the Norwegian initiative persuaded many other countries to adopt the same strategy; and international (second) registers were established in many other States. States providing international or parallel registries include Denmark, Germany, Spain (the Canary Islands), Italy, France (the Kerguelen Islands register), Luxemburg, and Portugal (the Madeira register).[14]

The emergence of "open registers" or "flag of convenience" registers, including the international and second registers of European maritime States, has resulted in a veritable sea change in the global system of ship registration. The consequence is that a large number of ships are now registered in countries of which the owners are not nationals. Further, because of the less stringent requirements regarding the use of non-national seafarers on open registry ships, a large numbers of seafarers from other States can be recruited on these ships. The result is that a very high proportion of the world's ships are now owned by persons, or crewed by officers and ratings, who are neither citizens nor even residents of the States of registry of the ships. Indeed, the situation now is that the countries with the largest ship tonnages in the world are those that operate "open registers", and very few of the traditional maritime states are numbered among the large world registries of shipping.[15] And while it is true that the new international (or second) registries in European countries continue to insist on very high standards of operation and do not tolerate the shady management and operational practices that are popularly associated with the normal "flags of convenience", it is also the case that these registries share many of the characteristics of the original flags of convenience registries, especially with regard to the advantages they offer in the form of reduced costs, tax exemptions and freedom from the bureaucratic restrictions that still exist in the traditional maritime States. For example, the processes of registration and de-registration of ships are likely to be simpler and easier and owners have the ability to employ seafarers who are not nationals or residents of the State of registration. As a result, there is some ambivalence in the attitudes adopted towards the second registries by some of the organizations and institutions that are normally opposed in principle to flag of convenience ships.[16]

OBJECTIONS TO FLAGS OF CONVENIENCE

Flag of convenience registration has been the subject of unfavourable comment and hostile criticism over the years. The objections have been based on legal, politico-economic as well as on safety and environmental grounds. On legal grounds it has been argued that flag of convenience registration is contrary to international law requirements, with particular

[14] See Kappel, The Norwegian International Ship Register: A New Approach of a Traditional Shpping Nation, Bremen (1988).

[15] As of 2009 Panama, Liberia and the Marshall Islands are the three largest registers in terms of DWT and they account for more than 39 per cent of the worlds shipping capacity.

[16] For example, the ITF does not consider that ships registered under the new international registers are "flags of convenience" in all cases. With the exception of those on the German and French second registers, the ITF's attitude depends on whether the ships are owned by nationals of the flag States or the crew wage arrangements are acceptable. See Coles and Watt, note 6.above, paragraph 3.10.

reference to the long-standing rule that there should be a "genuine link" between a ship and the country whose flag it flies. On the economic and political fronts, developing countries have objected to flag of convenience registration because they claim that the practice denies them the opportunity to expand their shipping fleets and thus prevents them from participating equitably in the maritime carriage of cargoes in their import and export trade.[17] But perhaps the most serious objection against "flags of convenience" is represented by the charge that flag of convenience registration allows shipowners to remain anonymous and thus permits and facilitates the operation of sub-standard ships that do not meet basic safety and environmental standards. A related complaint is that flag of convenience registration permits and assists unscrupulous owners to apply sub-standard working conditions for seafarers working on their ships. In addition, flag of convenience registration has in recent times been accused of involvement in criminal activity and terrorism.[18] Finally, flag of convenience ships have been seriously implicated in the widely condemned practice of illegal, unreported and unregulated fishing (IUU Fishing).[19]

Legal Objections to Flags of Convenience

A major and persistent objection against flag of convenience registration has been that it permits shipowners to be legally anonymous and this makes it difficult to prosecute them for civil or criminal offences. It is alleged that, by making it possible to conceal the true owner of ships, the flag of convenience system helps to blur the crucial distinction between, on the one hand, the persons who enjoy the benefit of the property in the vessels and, on the other, the legal owners of the ships. As the 2004 Report of the Consultative Group on Flag State Implementation appointed by the Secretary General of the United Nations put it, "it is very easy, and comparatively inexpensive, to establish a complex web of corporate entities to provide very effective cover to the identities of beneficial owners who do not wish to be known" In similar vein a report by the Organization of Economic Co-operation and Development (OECD) entitled "Ownership and Control of Ships" noted that the corporate structures of companies registering and operating flags of convenience ships are often multi-layered and spread across numerous jurisdictions, thus making the beneficial owners almost impenetrable to law enforcement officials and taxation. The Report concluded that "regardless of the reasons why the cloak of anonymity is made available... it will also assist those who may wish to remain hidden because they engage in illegal or criminal activities,

[17] See Ademuni-Odeke, Protectionism and the Future of International Shipping – Nature, Development and Role of Flag Distrimination, Preferences, Cargo Reservation and Cabotage Restrictions, State Intervention and Mritime Subsidies, Martinus Nijhoff Publishers,(1984), especially Part Four - Problems Caused by and/or arising from the use of the traditional methods of establishing and developing national fleets.

[18] According to David Cockroft, General Secretary of the ITF, " arms smuggling, the ability to conceal large sums of money, trafficking in goods and people and other illegal activities can also thrive in the unregulated havens which the flag of convenience system provides".

[19] "According to the Environmental Justice Foundation (EJF), "flags of Convenience - described by Franz Fishler, former EU Commissioner for Fisheries, as "the scourge of today's maritime world" - represent one of the key ways by which fishermen can circumvent management and conservation measures and avoid penalties for IUU fishing". The EJF believes that "a very large proportion of IUU fishing could be eliminated if the loophole in international law that allows States to issue flags of convenience to fisheries vessels was closed" http//www.ejffoundation.org/page 164.html.

including terrorists"[20]In this connection the Report observed that flag of convenience registration provides anonymity for a ship's beneficial owners through the technique of using "nominee shareholders. In jurisdictions that require shareholder identity to be recorded, a loophole is created if the beneficial owner is enabled to appoint a nominee to act as the shareholder, especially if the nominee cannot be legally compelled to reveal the identity of the beneficial owner. Further, although there is a universal requirement that companies or corporations should have at least one director, some jurisdictions allow the director to be a nominee director. Where this is the case, the nominee director's name will appear on all corporate paperwork in place of the beneficial owner. Hence, like the nominee shareholders, the nominee director cannot be compelled to divulge the identity of the beneficial owners. The Report concludes that the use of bearer shares is "perhaps the single most important (and perhaps the most widely used) mechanism" to protect the anonymity of a ship's beneficial owners. It also noted that physically possessing a bearer share accords ownership of the corporation, and there is no requirement for reporting the transfer of bearer shares, and not every jurisdiction requires that their serial numbers even be recorded.

But perhaps the most commonly invoked legal objection to the flag of convenience registration is the one based on the international law requirement that there should be a "genuine link "between a ship and the state whose flag it flies. The principle of the "genuine link" was first adopted in the High Seas Convention of 1958 and repeated in identical language in the 1982 United Nations Convention on the Law of the Sea.[21] The gist of the principle is that although it is the sovereign right of every State to set the conditions for the registration of ships and to grant to registered ships the right to fly under its flag, this right is not unlimited: it is subject to the paramount requirement that there should be a "genuine link" between every ship and the country whose flag it flies. Indeed, it has been claimed that article 5 of the High Seas Convention (and the even more elaborate corresponding provision (Article 94) of the United Nations Convention on the Law of the Sea, 1982 were intended to provide an indication of what the required genuine link should be. Specifically, it has been asserted that the "genuine link" requirement means that the flag state is required to exercise effective jurisdiction and control over a ship flying its flag in technical, administrative and social matters relating to the ship, and failure or inability to do so results in the loss of the entitlement of the ship to fly the flag of the flag State. Thus in its comments on what was to become Article 5 of the 1958 Convention on the High Seas, the International Law Commission which had prepared the draft articles of the convention stated:

> "Each State lays down the conditions on which ships may fly its flag. Obviously the State enjoys complete liberty in the case of ships owned by it or ships which are the property of a nationalised company. With regard to other ships, the State must accept certain restrictions. As in the case of the grant of nationality to persons, national legislation must not depart too far from the principles adopted by the majority of States, which may be regarded as forming part of international law. Only on that condition will the freedom granted to States not give rise to abuse and to friction with other States. With

[20] OECD Report," Ownership and Control of Ships" 2003.

[21] Article 5(1) of the 1958 High Seas Convention and Article 91(1) of the 1982 UNCLOS.

regard to the national element required for permission to fly the flag, a great many systems are possible, but there must be a minimum national element."[22]

From this, some scholars and state representatives have concluded that, although the drafters of Article 5 of the 1958 Convention wished to leave it to each State to impose its own conditions for granting the right to fly its flag (i.e. to set its own criteria for registering ships), every flag State is, nevertheless, required, as a precondition for the grant of its flag to a ship, to ensure that there is a genuine link between the ship and its registry. Based on this interpretation of the provision, some States and commentators have argued that, since most flag of convenience registry countries are not in a position to exercise such jurisdiction and control over vessels under their flags, no genuine link can exist between such countries and ships flying their flags and, accordingly, that the practice of flag of convenience registration is incompatible with international law.[23]

On the other hand, others have contended that the exact meaning of this provision is far from clear. In particular, they have pointed out that there is no basis for the claim that the requirement of a genuine link should be considered as a "precondition" for the right of a State to register a ship. In the view of some scholars the genuine link requirement is to be regarded as a "consequential" obligation that is placed on the flag State after registration. In other words, there is no support for the view that the existence of a genuine link is to be considered as a necessary requirement that empowers a State validly to register a ship. According to this view the genuine link requirement merely imposes certain obligations on the flag State in respect of ships that it registers, but does not affect the validity of the registration itself.[24]

The objection based on the "genuine link" has been raised in a variety of contexts but with little success. In the United States case of *Lauritzen v Larsen* the Supreme Court rejected the contention that the ability of a State to grant to a ship the right to fly its flag could be challenged by another State, for instance on the ground that there is an absence of a genuine link between the ship and the flag State. The Court stated:

"Each State under international law may determine for itself the conditions on which it will grant its nationality to a merchant ship, thereby accepting responsibility for it and acquiring authority over it. Nationality is evidenced to the world by the ship's papers and

[22] Report of the International Law Commission on the work of its eighth session, (A/3159), article 5 Commentary, II Yearbook of the ILC 1956, p.253 at p.278.

[23] Before the International Court of Justice, the spokesperson for The Netherlands argued that the term "shipowning nation"... ' obviously does not refer to States which are owners of vessels in the legal sense of the word. Neither does it refer to States in whose territories a large tonnage of vessels is registered, since mere registration does not necessarily guarantee the effective exercise of jurisdiction of the State concerned in technical and other matters over ships so registered" The spokesperson continued: States are not completely free in fixing the conditions for the right to fly their flag. In this respect it is significant that Article 5 of the of the Convention on the High Seas, signed at Geneva 29th April, 1955, expressly States: "There must exist a genuine link between the State and the ship; in particular, the State must effectively exercise its jurisdiction and control in administrative, technical and social matters over ships flying its flag." This provision, which forms part of a Convention adopted as a codification of the rules of international law (cf. first paragraph of the preamble), clearly imposes limitations to the freedom of a State to determine which ships "belong" to that State. Written submission of the Netherlands, paragraphs 10 and 11. The spokesperson for Norway stated: "as in the case of the grant of nationality to a person, national legislation on the subject of nationality of ships must not depart too far from the principles adopted by the majority of States which may be regarded as forming part of international law" Oral Statement of Mr F. Seyersted.

[24] See Churchill, note 35.below.

flag. The United States has firmly and successfully maintained that the regularity and validity of a registration can be questioned only by the registering State".[25]

The same approach was adopted by the International Court of Justice in its Advisory Opinion on the *Composition of the Maritime Safety Committee of the Inter- Governmental Maritime Consultative Organization.*[26] The Court ruled that the term "shipowning nation" as used in the in the relevant Article of the constitution of IMCO, referred to a State in which ships are legally registered and not the States of the persons who are the "beneficial owners" of the ship.[27] The ICJ did not accept the argument that the Article had anything to do with "beneficial owned" tonnage. Hence, the Court concluded that the largest ship-owning States are the States with the largest registered tonnage. With regard to the "genuine link" criterion, it was submitted that the Court should apply the reasoning that had been applied in the *Nottebohm* Case and place limitations on the right of a State unilaterally to grant its nationality to ships.[28] However, the International Court of Justice held that this concept was irrelevant in the circumstances of the case and it, therefore, refused to consider or apply it in giving its Opinion.[29]

Admittedly, the Court addressed the issue as one of "treaty interpretation" and it did not enter into the question of nationality or open registers. Nevertheless, the Advisory Opinion had clearly rejected the "genuine link" requirement, at least as a criterion for determining whether a State can legitimately be considered to be the ship-owning State of a particular ship.

The Court's decision amounted to a clarification that, after registration, a ship has the nationality of the State in which it is registered and whose flag it flies, and third States and other parties are obliged to recognize this and are not entitled to determine whether a genuine link in fact exists between such a vessel and the flag State.[30]

This view was further reinforced by the International Tribunal for the Law of the Sea (ITLOS) in its judgment in the M/VSAIGA No. *2* case between St Vincent and the Grenadines and the Republic of Guinea.[31] One of the arguments advanced by the Respondent (Guinea) in the case was that Saint Vincent and the Grenadines did not have standing to bring a claim in respect to the vessel because, although the ship was registered in Saint Vincent and the Grenadines and was flying the flag of that State, there was no genuine link between the

[25] 345 US 571 (1953) (Emphasis supplied).

[26] ICJ Advisory Opinion on the Constitution of the Maritime Safety Committee of the Inter-Governmental Maritime Consultative Organization, ICJ Reports, 1960, p.150.

[27] Ibid. P 24.

[28] In the Nottebohm case, the Court held that although a sovereign State has the right to settle its own rules on the acquisition of its nationality, the State cannot claim that such rules are entitled to recognition by another State unless it has acted in conformity with the general rule that "the legal bond of nationality is in accord with the individual's genuine connection with the State" !955 ICJ Reports, p.23.

[29] Ibid. P.25. The argument that the principle in the Nottebohm case is applicable to ships has been rejected."To derive from the application of criteria of this type to the competence of States to confer nationality upon individuals, principles assumed to be relevant to limiting the competence of States to attribute nationality to ships is, if not an exercise in irrelevancy, certainly a disguised mode of stating that because certain limits have been imposed on States with respect to individuals for some problems, other limits ought to be imposed with respect to ships for other problems". McDougal, Burke and Vlasic, Public Order of the Seas, p.39.

[30] G.P. Pamborides, International Shipping Law – Legislation and Enforcement, Kluwer Law International (Ant. Sakkoulas Publishers, Athens) 1999 p.6).

[31] M/V "SAIGA" (No2) (Saint Vincent and the Grenadines v. Guinea) Judgment, ITLOS Reports 1999, p.10.

ship and the State.[32] The Tribunal did not accept this contention. Rather, it declared that the "genuine link" provision in the United Nations Convention on the Law of the Sea (1982 UNCLOS) was to be viewed as an obligation on the flag State to exercise effective jurisdiction and control over the ship but not as a criterion for determining whether a State has the right to grant to a ship the right to fly its flag. After examining the wording of Article 5 of the 1958 Convention on the High Seas, the report of the International Law Commission on the draft articles presented to the 1958 Conference on the Law of the Sea, the deliberations of the 1958 conference that adopted the 1958 Convention, as well as the discussions leading to the adoption of Article 94 of the 1982 UNCLOS, the Tribunal concluded that:

> "The purpose of the provisions of the Convention on the need for a genuine link between a ship and its flag State is to secure more effective implementation of the duties of the flag State, and not to establish criteria by reference to which the validity of the registration of ships in a flag State may be challenged by other States".[33]

These decisions reflect the general trend to disconnect the "genuine link" concept from the "nationality" issue. This trend has been followed by other courts. For instance, in the case of *Anklagemyndigheden* v. *Poulsen and Diva Navigation,* the European Court concluded that administrative formalities alone are sufficient and that there are no other criteria required for the grant of nationality and *a fortiori,* that nothing further is required to establish a genuine link.[34]

It may, therefore, be concluded that the attempt to challenge the flag of convenience registration on legal grounds has not been successful. Consequently, it is now generally accepted, sometimes reluctantly, that a flag State has the exclusive right determine the conditions on which it will grant its nationality to a ship and that the grant of nationality cannot properly be questioned by another State or group of States or any organization on the basis of an alleged absence of a genuine link between the ship and the State granting nationality.

In effect, the legal position tends to be that, although there is an unquestioned requirement for a "genuine link" between a State and a ship registered in the State or flying its flag, the "genuine link" requirement is not a prerequisite for registration but rather an obligation consequential upon registration.[35]

[32] "Guinea contends that, in the absence of (the exercise by Saint Vincent and the Grenadines of prescriptive and enforcement jurisdiction over the owner or, as the case may be, of the ship) there is no genuine link between the Ship and Saint Vincent and the Grenadines and that, accordingly, it is not obliged to recognize the claims of Saint Vincent and the Grenadines in relation to the ship" Judgment, ITLOS Reports 1999, 10 at paragraph 76.

[33] Judgment ITLOS Reports 1999, p.10, at paragraph 83.

[34] Case C.286/90, Judgment of the Court of 24 November 1992. European Court Reports 1992, p.I06019.

[35] Churchill: "There is no single obligatory criterion by which genuineness of a link is to be established. A State has discretion as to how it ensures that the link between a ship having its nationality and itself is genuine". Robin Churchill, The Meaning of the Genuine Link Requirement in Relation to the Nationality of Ships (70(2000) http://www.oceanlaw.net/hedley/pubs/ITF-Oct 2000. It has also been claimed that the requirement for a genuine link is not part of "customary international law". Churchill and Lowe, Law of the Sea (3rd edition) Manchester, Juris Publishing, Manchester University Press (1999) p.258.

Political and Economic Objections to Flags of Convenience

In addition to the challenge of the legitimacy of flags of convenience on purely legal grounds, there have been objections based mainly on political and economic grounds. Challenges of this type have been raised in a number of contexts, including in the Organization for Economic Coordination and Development (OECD), in the United Nations Conference on Trade and Development (UNCTAD), and in the International Labour Organization (ILO). The objection in the OECD was raised by the traditional maritime countries while the challenge in UNCTAD was mainly at the initiative of the developing countries. In the ILO complaints against flags of convenience have come from States and organizations on the grounds that many owners and operators of flag of convenience ships do not comply with generally accepted international standards relating to terms and conditions of work for seafarers, including the right to fair treatment and decent conditions of work.

The concerns of the traditional maritime states were succinctly expressed by the Statement of the Consultative Ship Group governments. The Statement pointed out that the "growth of open register shipping was leading to a general reduction in standards to lower social and wage benefits for crews, as well as affecting the competitive position of their own merchant marines. They also pointed out that there was no genuine link between the ship and the flag State as required by the 1958 High Seas Convention. For those reasons the countries members of the OECD have supported many of the initiatives aimed at making the operation of flags of convenience difficult, if not impossible.

In UNCTAD, there was serious objection to flag of convenience ships, especially from the developing countries. These countries maintained that the operation of flag of convenience registries (or open registries) denied them the full opportunities to develop their fleets and to participate fairly in the transportation of goods and cargoes in their trade with other countries. In this they were supported by a study produced by the UNCTAD Secretariat for the Manila conference of 1979 entitled "Repercussions of Phasing out of Open Registry Fleets."[36] The conclusions of the study set in train a political campaign whose main purpose was to establish by international agreement the requirement for a genuine link between the flag of a ship and the nationality or residence of its owners, managers and seafarers. It was hoped and believed that effective application of such a requirement would lead eventually the entire elimination of the flag of convenience system.[37]

After extensive discussions, it was agreed in UNCTAD that appropriate measures should be put in place to do away with the practice of flag of convenience registration. The method proposed to achieve this was to adopt an international treaty instrument that would "solidify" the genuine link concept and make it the basic criterion for ship registration by States, and work commenced to prepare an international convention with this aim in mind. A draft convention was presented to United Nations convened Plenipotentiary (diplomatic)

[36] UNCTAD Report: Action on the Question of Open Registries, TD/B/C.4/220 (1981).

[37] To the parties who considered that open registries posed a threat to their interests, the introduction of the genuine link requirement was seen as "a golden gift which would enable them to fight open registries more easily" G.P. Pamborides, International Shipping Law – Legislation and Enforcement, note 30.above, p.5.

Conference in 1986. The conference adopted the United Nations Convention on Conditions for the Registration of Ships.[38]

As noted earlier, one of the principal objectives behind the proposal for the adoption of the 1986 Convention was the "phasing out of flags of convenience"[39]. However, faced with concerted opposition from many countries, including some of the traditional maritime countries, UNCTAD was forced to abandon this radical objective. In the end the original objective of phasing out of the FOC was abandoned in favour of the development of a formal agreement that would set out the conditions under which ships should be accepted for registration by States. In other words, the idea was that the 1986 Convention would seek to re-define the concept of the "genuine link" that has been stipulated in the 1958 Convention on the High Seas and in the 1982 UNCLOS. The original intention was that the 1986 Convention would clarify the "jurisdiction and control" that a flag State needs to exercise over ships registered under its flag in order to satisfy the requirement for a genuine link as prescribed by international law. But even this more modest aim could not be achieved; and the conference could only agree on a list of criteria that, it was hoped, would ensure the identification and accountability of shipowners. The new Convention was also expected to establish mechanisms for the exercise by flag States of their jurisdiction with respect to administrative, technical and economic regulation of ships.[40]

But, in spite of the efforts of the developing countries, the conference could not agree on the criteria to be used to determine whether the registration of a ship by a particular State is legitimate and, hence, that the ship is entitled to fly the flag of that flag State. With regard to specific requirement that there should be a "genuine link" between the ship and the State of its flag, the conference was unable to agree whether this link was to be based on an "economic stake" of citizens of the flag State in the ownership of the ship or, conversely, whether there should be a "nationality requirement" regarding the persons who serve on board the ships. In the end it was agreed to retain both alternatives and to leave it to each flag State to determine which of them it would use as the basis for its registration and the grant of its flag to ships. However, the Convention required that each flag State should make a choice between the two alternative criteria, namely, an "economic link" based on the stake of its citizens or residents in the ownership of the ship (ownership criterion) or a connection based on mariners from the State to crew ships flying its flag (crew nationality criterion).

The ownership criterion requires legislation on appropriate participation by the State or its nationals as owners of ships flying its flag or in the ownership of such ships and on the level of such participation [41]Under the crew nationality criterion, the flag State is required to ensure that "a satisfactory part" of the ship's complement are nationals or residents of the State. It is left to the sole discretion of each State to decide which of the two criteria it wishes to apply in granting the right to ships to fly its flag.[42] A flag State could, of course, decide to apply both criteria.

---

[38] 26 ILM 1236 (1987).

[39] One of the studies prepared in 1979 for the Manila Conference of UNCTAD was on "Repercussions of phasing out of open registry fleets".

[40] See S. G. Sturmey, The United Nations Convention on Conditions for the Registration of Ships, 1987 Lloyds MCLQ 97 and George C. Kasoulides, The 1986 UN Convention on Conditions for the Registration of Ships and the Question of Open Registry, 20 ODIL 543 (1989).

[41] Article 8.

[42] Article 9.

The effect is that, subject to the minimal conditions stipulated in the 1986 Convention, the principle of open registration has been accepted and is now firmly established under the Convention.[43] What is worse, even the minimal conditions in the 1986 Convention are unlikely to be operational in the near future because the 1986 Convention has not entered into force and the prospects of it entering into force are far from bright.[44]

Another objection against flag of convenience registration is based on its impact that it has on working and living conditions of seafarers who work on board ships that fly flags of convenience. This is particularly the case with ships whose owners and operators move them to foreign registers in order to avoid stringent requirements on safety, labour and environmental standards. The campaign to counter and eliminate this aspect of flag of convenience registration has largely been undertaken within the ILO, as part of its general mandate to improve working conditions and eliminate practices that deny to workers the right to decent living and working conditions. In its work in relation to seafarers, ILO has considered it necessary to concentrate special attention and efforts on the problem arising from the operation of flag of convenience ships.[45] In one of the documents prepared during the preparation of ILO's Convention No. 147, it was noted that many seafarers work aboard ships that are registered in States that do not exercise effective jurisdiction and control over their ships. The paper then observed that workers on ships registered in these States "often have to work under unacceptable conditions, to the detriment of their well-being, health and safety and the safety of the ship on which they work".

The first major step in ILO's campaign was taken in 1976 with the adoption of the ILO Convention No. 147. The aim of Convention No. 147 was to improve employment conditions in merchant ships, and to expand the ability of port States which are parties to the Convention to take steps to protect the health and safety of seamen on merchant vessels that call in their ports. The Convention prescribes a set of standards relating to safety, social security, and shipboard conditions of employment as well as living arrangements that must be observed in merchant shipping registered in States Parties to the Convention. These are the standards set out in a number of earlier ILO Conventions that are listed as an Appendix to the 1976 Convention. The earlier conventions cover, among others, minimum age, medical examination, articles of agreement, officer's competency certificates, food and catering on board ships, crew accommodation, occupational accidents, sickness or injury benefits, and repatriation. Convention No. 147 also seeks to implement by reference some other previous ILO conventions, such as those dealing with freedom of association, protection of the right of seafarers to organize and bargain collectively, and standards of hours of work and manning necessary to ensure safety of human life aboard ships.[46] The Convention gave to States

[43] See Moira McConnel, "Business as Usual: An Evaluation of the 1986 UN Convention on Conditions for the Registration of Ships" in Journal of Maritime Law and Commerce 435 (1987); also Wefers Bettink, "Open Registry, the Genuine Link and the 1986 Convention on Registration Conditions for Ships" in Netherlands Yearbook of International Law, 1987, pp. 70 – 119.

[44] Note 74.below.

[45] The Preamble to the 1976 Convention (No.147) stated that the General Conference of ILO had decided "to adopt certain proposals with regard to sub-standard vessels, particularly those registered under flags of convenience".(emphasis supplied).

[46] The Merchant Shipping Convention, 1976 (No. 147) was accepted as the basic point of reference in the industry for minimal acceptable standards of safety and health, social security and living and working conditions of seafarers. Parties to the 1976 Convention were also required to implement and enforce a number of the basic safety and environmental conventions of IMO.

Parties the option to discharge their obligations under the Convention by adopting implementing laws that are "substantially equivalent" to those stipulated in the Convention.[47]

Following the adoption in 1982 of the United Nations Convention on the Law of the Sea, ILO embarked on a comprehensive review of Convention No.147 in order to ascertain how it had helped to improve the standards of operation for ships, including those registered in flag of convenience registries. ILO evaluated the international standards applicable to ships, particularly those concerned with safety of ships and persons and cargoes on board, human security, and quality ship management. It then examined how flag States could be encouraged and assisted to discharge their duties and obligations with regard to, *inter alia*, labour conditions, crewing, and social matters on ships that fly their flags.

ILO's work on these issues resulted in the adoption in 2006 of the ILO Maritime Labour Convention. The decision of the ILO to develop a major new maritime labour Convention was taken in 2001 in a joint resolution of the international seafarers' and shipowners' organizations, supported by governments. The resolution noted that the shipping industry is "the world's first genuinely global industry" which "requires an international regulatory response of an appropriate kind – global standards applicable to the entire industry".

It was agreed that the new Maritime Labour Convention would have two primary purposes, namely:

(a) to bring the system of protection contained in existing labour standards closer to the workers concerned, in a form consistent with the rapidly developing, globalised sector and (b) to improve the applicability of the system so that shipowners and governments interested in providing decent conditions of work do not have to bear an unequal burden in ensuring protection.

THE NEW MARITIME LABOUR CONVENTION (MLC 2006) WAS ADOPTED IN 2006

The MLC 2006 provides for comprehensive rights and protection at work for the world's seafarers, numbering more than 1.2 million. It aims to achieve both decent working conditions for seafarers and secure economic interests in fair competition for quality shipowners. With an estimated 90% of world trade carried on ships, ILO and its participating members consider that it is "incontestable" that seafarers are essential to international trade and the international economic and trade system.

The 2006 Maritime Labour Convention consolidates and updates more than 68 previous international labour standards related to the maritime sector that have been adopted by the ILO over the past 80 years.48 The Convention sets out seafarers' rights to decent conditions

[47] Article 2(a) of the Convention. Other Articles of the convention specify applicability, and establish the duties and obligations of the Contacting Parties.Article 1 states that the Convention is applicable to every seagoing ship, whether publicly or privately owned, if it engages in the transport of cargo or passengers for the purpose of trade or is employed for any other commercial purpose. National laws and regulations shall determine what ships are to be regarded as sea-going ships for the purposes of the Convention.

[48] See Moira McConnel, "Making Labour History" in Aldo Chircop, Ted L. McDorman, Susan J. Rolston (eds.) The Future of Ocean Regime Building, Essays in Tribute to Douglas M Johnston, Martinus Nijhoff Publishers (2009) pp.349-384; and Peter B. Payoyo "The Contribution of the 2006 ILO Maritime Labour Convention to Global Governance" in Chircop, McDorman & Rolston, op.cit. pp.385-408.

of work on a wide range of subjects. It aims to be "globally applicable, easily understandable, readily updatable and uniformly enforced".[49]

It is interesting to note that, in spite of the declared wish and intention of the States and other participants in the work of ILO to seek to abolish flags convenience ships altogether, neither the 1976 Convention (No 147) nor the 2006 Maritime Labour Convention addressed the issue of flag of convenience, as such. Further, no attempt was made in either convention to pursue the objective to "abolish" flag of convenience ships and open registries, or even to interfere with the operation of these registries. True, the ILO and the organizations involved in preparations for the 2006 Convention emphasised that the ability of the flag State to effectively exercise its jurisdiction over ships flying its flag "is a matter of concern". However, they admitted that "the precise criteria or conditions adopted by a State with respect to the grant of its nationality to a ship were a matter beyond (their) purview".[50]

Indeed, the 2006 MLC accepted and incorporated a definition of shipowner that reflects the current received international law position which reserves exclusively for the flag State the right to determine matters relating to the status of ships. For example, The Convention does not seek to define the owner of a ship but merely provides for situations in which some other person (such as the manager, agent or bareboat charterer) has assumed the responsibility for the operation of the ship from the owner if, on assuming such responsibility, such person has agreed to take over the duties and responsibilities imposed on shipowners in accordance with this Convention regardless of whether any other organization or persons fulfil certain of the duties and responsibilities on behalf of the shipowner.[51] Rather interestingly, the Convention leaves it to the competent authorities of the flag State (after consultation with organizations of shipowners and seafarers concerned) to determine whether the Convention should be applied to any ship or particular category of ships.[52]

Objections of Workers and Trade Unions to Flags of Convenience

A third line of attack against flags of convenience has come from the seafarers, organized through their principal trade union organization, the International Transport Workers Federation (ITF).[53] While seafarers representatives have voiced serious concerns with many

[49] The Convention sets out seafarers' rights to decent conditions of work on a wide range of subjects, and has been designed to become a global instrument known as the "fourth pillar" of the international regulatory regime for quality shipping, complementing the key Conventions of the International Maritime Organization.

[50] "The participants took the view that the exclusivity attached by the UNCLOS to the right of States to fix the conditions for the grant of nationality, as affirmed by the authoritative interpretations of ITLOS in the MV Saiga case (No.2) and subsequent cases, as well as other agreements, indicated that the question relating to the precise criteria or conditions adopted by a State with respect to the grant of its nationality to a ship were a matter beyond the purview of the organizations. However, participants in the meeting also considered that issues relating to securing the objective and purpose of the "genuine link" requirement, that is, assuring the ability of the flag State to effectively exercise its jurisdiction over ships flying its flag, were maters of central concern to all organizations and formed a substantial part of their programmes of regulatory initiatives and technical cooperation activities in the shipping and fishing sectors".

[51] Article II(1)(j) of the2006 MLC.

[52] Article II(5).of the 2006 MLC.

[53] ITF Official Booklet: "Flags of Convenience – The ITF Campaign; Also Herbert R. Northrup & Peter B. Scrasse, "The International Transport Workers Federation FOC Shipping Campaign 1983-1995", University of Denver Transportation Law Journal, Spring1996 – 23 Transp. L.J. 369.

aspects of the operation of flag of convenience ships, their main objection has been the failure of many flag of convenience ships to comply with international and national standards, particularly those relating to the terms of employment and working and living conditions of the men and women who serve on board their ships. According to the ITF, flag of convenience registration provides ships with the means to avoid labour regulations in the countries of ownership of the ships (which may not be the countries of registration) as well as "licence to pay low wages" to seafarers working on the ships. Some flag of convenience ships also subject seafarers to long hours of work in unsafe and uncongenial conditions. Moreover, since ships registered in flag of convenience registries have no true nationality, they are in effect beyond the reach of the national trade unions of seafarers in any single State.

In the view of the ITF, the most important criterion to be used to determine that a ship is a "flag of convenience ship" is whether the nationality of the shipowner is the same as the flag that the ship is flying. In 1974 the ITF adopted the following definition of a flag of convenience ship: "Where beneficial ownership and control of a vessel is found to lie elsewhere than in the country of the flag the vessel is flying, the vessel is considered as sailing under a flag of convenience".[54]

ITF also considers that ships that are not bound by the labour contracts and collective agreements represent a threat to the interests of its member seafarers. The ITF campaign which was formally launched in 1948 had two elements. The first was a "political" campaign designed to establish by international governmental agreement a requirement for a "genuine link" between the flag that a ship flies and the nationality or residence of its owners, managers and seafarers. ITF also believes that enforcement of such a requirement would "eliminate the flag of convenience system entirely". Allied to the political campaign is an industrial campaign whose purpose is to ensure that seafarers serving on flag of convenience ships, regardless of nationality, will be protected from exploitation by shipowners.

As part of the political campaign, the ITF has played an active role in the work within both ILO and UNCTAD to get flags of convenience registries abolished altogether. For this purpose the ITF has consistently insisted on the requirement of the genuine link between ships and their flag States. For the reasons indicated above, this aspect of the campaign has not been wholly successful, and there is little prospect of any such success in view.

A possible reason why the ITF has so far not achieved complete success in its campaign to abolish flag of convenience ships may be that there is some inconsistency between the two objectives that it seeks to achieve by the campaign. It appears that the ITF seeks to achieve two mutually inconsistent objectives. The first is to promote the concept of "genuine link" between ships and their flag States with a view to achieving the complete abolition of all flag of convenience ships; but the second is to ensure that seafarers who happen to work on flag of convenience ships are protected from exploitation and are guaranteed satisfactory working and living conditions. This means that, whilst the ITF seeks to make operations difficult or even impossible for flag of convenience ships, it also finds it necessary and useful to deal with flag of convenience ships, because to do otherwise would deny ITF assistance to the seafarers who work on these ships and thus leave them to the mercy of the very parties from whom they need to be protected. Consequently, the ITF has felt obliged to adopt a more

[54] "The ITF believes here should be a "genuine link" between the real owner of a vessel and the flag the vessel flies, in accordance with the Unite Nations Convention on the Law of the Sea (UNCLOS). There is no "genuine link" in the case of FOC registries" ITF Booklet: What are Flags of Convenience?

pragmatic approach by which it has been willing to treat with some flag of convenience ships so long as they are willing to accept and apply what the ITF considered to be "minimum acceptable standards" These are the standards incorporated into the ITF Standard Collective Agreement which sets the wages and working conditions for all crew serving on flag of convenience ships. Flag of convenience ships that are covered by acceptable ITF agreements are issued with the ITF Blue Certificate by the ITF Secretariat; and a ship with such a certificate is exempted from industrial action by ITF and its affiliated member unions in ports. The ITF calculates that, to date, no less than a quarter of all FOC ships worldwide are covered by ITF agreements, thus giving direct protection to more than 120,000 seafarers. Compliance with ITF agreements is monitored through a network of inspectors who operate all over the world. These inspectors monitor the payment of wages and the existence of employment and working conditions on board ships that conform to those stipulated in the ITF agreements. Where necessary, the inspectors are able and authorised to take appropriate action to ensure that the applicable standards are enforced.[55]

Of course, the other side of the coin is that, by entering into these agreements, the ITF is forced to permit ships that are covered by the ITF agreements to operate without interference. This means that a flag of convenience ship that signs the appropriate agreement can expect to operate unhindered, not because it has somehow acquired the "genuine link" with the country of registry but rather because it in agreed to meet the standards required by ITF. The ship does not cease to be a "flag of convenience ship"; but its operation is tolerated because it no longer presents a danger to the interests that the ITF considers to be paramount. The dictates of principle have, commendably, been trumped by more pragmatic considerations.

A More Realistic Approach to Flag of Convenience

Although the political and industrial campaigns to abolish flags of convenience ships have not been universally supported by all countries and organizations, there has always been general agreement that certain features of the flag of convenience system are undesirable and should to be rectified or abolished. In particular, it is agreed that appropriate measures should be taken to sanction flag of convenience ships that do not comply with international standards for the safety of ships (and persons and goods on board ships), for the protection and preservation of the marine environment, and for fair treatment of seafarers, including prevention of abuse and denial of rights to seafarers.

The approach adopted for this purpose has shifted from the original approach that sought to deny or question the right of sovereign states to grant their flags to foreign ships. Instead the new approach is based on the adoption and implementation of measures that require and encourage flag States to exercise effectively the jurisdiction and control over ships that fly their flags. The purpose is to make it impossible or difficult for ships to disregard the basic standards for safety and environmental protection with impunity or to ignore the rights of seafarers to decent working conditions on board ships without sanction.

Further, the new approach has been adopted because the international shipping community has realised that it is not realistic to expect to achieve the changes needed in the attitudes, or in methods of operation of those who own or operate flag of convenience ships,

[55] ITF Home page: Flags of Convenience Campaign.

solely or primarily through reliance on the flag States. It is now accepted that reliance on flag State jurisdiction and control alone will not be sufficient to rid the oceans of the most undesirable effects of flag of convenience registration. At the same time, it is also recognized that successfully tackling the undesirable practices of flag of convenience ships does not necessarily require the total abolition of flags of convenience ships. Experience over the years, including the failure of so many previous attempts to "outlaw" flags of convenience ships, has convinced many states and organizations in the shipping world that seeking to prevent the very existence of flag of convenience ships is not a realistic or worthwhile effort. In particular, they acknowledge that conceding a significant role for the flag State is not incompatible with the goal to achieve a form of global governance over ships that delivers effective enforcement of standards for ship safety, environmental protection and respect for the rights and welfare of seafarers.

PORT STATE CONTROL IN THE FIGHT AGAINST SUB-STANDARD SHIPS

This main basis of the new approach has been the mechanism of port state control. In recent times, this mechanism has been accepted for use (and used quite effectively in many areas) by the organizations and institutions that have participated in the campaign to eliminate and reduce the undesirable practices of flag of convenience ships and other sub-standard ships. The principal organizations involved in this campaign include IMO and the ILO.[56]

The widest and clearest declaration of the principle of port state control is in the United Nations Convention on the Law of the Sea,(1982 UNCLOS), mainly in the provisions relating to the prevention an d control of marine pollution from vessel-sources.[57] These provisions assert the powers and rights of coastal and port States to enforce applicable and generally accepted international standards against ships that are operating in their territorial seas or exclusive economic zones or which voluntarily enter into their ports.

Port State control was in fact used in a number of important treaty instruments prior to the adoption of the 1982 UNCLOS. As far back as 1954, the International Convention for the Prevention of Pollution by Oil (1954 OILPOL Convention) included provisions that permitted the authorities of a State Party to the Convention to demand and inspect documents on board a ship within its ports in order to ascertain that the ship complied with the provisions of the Convention[58] An even more direct application of the principle of port state control and enforcement was in the 1969 Civil Liability Convention. Article VII of the Convention gives the right to (and imposes the obligation on) each State Party to ensure, under its national law, that a certificate of insurance, as required by the Convention, is in force in respect of any ship, *wherever registered*, entering or leaving a port in its territory, or arriving at or leaving a an off-shore terminal in its territorial sea.[59] The principle was applied even more stringently under the 1973 MARPOL Convention for the Prevention of Marine Pollution from Ships, as

[56] ILO used port State control extensively in both the 1976 (No.147) Convention as well as the 2006 MLC. IMO uses port State control in all its major safety and marine pollution conventions. Port State control is also relied upon indirectly by the ITF.

[57] Articles 218 to 221 and Articles 223 to 234.

[58] 1nternational Convention for the Prevention of Pollution of the Sea by Oil 1954 (327 UNTS 3) Article IX, paragraph 5.

[59] Article VII, paragraph 11 (emphasis added), International Convention on Civil Liability for Oil Pollution Damage, 1969 973 UNTS 3.

modified by the Protocol of 1978.[60] Under MARPOL States Parties are entitled to inspect ships in their ports to ensure that the ships carry certificates required under the Convention or that they meet the requirements of the Convention. Where a ship does not meet the requirements, the State of the port is empowered (and required) to take such steps as will ensure that the ships shall not sail until it can proceed to sea without presenting an unreasonable threat of harm to the marine environment.[61] Although such a provision would normally apply to ships of States that are parties to MARPOL, the Convention stipulates that it can (and should) be applied also to ships of States that are not parties to the Convention. This is the effect of the provision of the Convention which states that "with respect to the ships of non-parties to the Convention, Parties shall apply the requirements of the present Convention as may be necessary *to ensure that no more favourable treatment is given to such ships"* [62]

The emergence and acceptance of the port State control mechanism has provided an important tool for those whose objection to flags of convenience is not primarily based on "legal principle" or economic self interest, but rather because they wish to do away with certain undesirable practices that have come to be associated with a large number of ships flying flags of convenience, such as the failure of the owners to observe basic standards and requirements and the unwillingness or inability of flag states to exercise their jurisdiction and control to enforce these standards and requirements. Effective use of port state control ensures that ships cannot disregard applicable standards with impunity. It means that, if a ship fails to implement the standards expected of it (including those that qualify as "generally accepted" under the 1982 UNCLOS), the ship can be sanctioned if and when it enters a port or off-shore installation of a State that has agreed to apply those standards. This will be so even if the flag State of the ship has not agreed to accept or apply the standards in question.[63]

The port state control mechanism has significantly transformed the debate on the issue of flags of convenience ships. In the past opponents of flag of convenience ships (and the undesirable practices attributed to such ships) appeared to be engaged in losing battle in their efforts to abolish the system as a whole. This was partly because they were for the most part using increasingly ineffective legal, political or industrial methods. It now appears that the international shipping community has found a new weapon which, if used effectively and consistently enough, can put the necessary pressure on States that operate flag of convenience ships (and also on the ships themselves) to desist from the practices which make flag of convenience registration so objectionable. Although there are many who object to flags of convenience registration as a matter of principle and would be happy to see the end of the system completely, there are others who are only concerned about the undesirable practices that are associated with flag of convenience ships. In other words, many of the persons and institutions that attack flags of convenience do so not just because the ships are registered in foreign flag States, but usually because flag of convenience States are considered to be more prone to encourage and condone the operation of sub-standard ships. Hence, it is reasonable to assume that, if owners of flag of convenient ships do not deliberately disregard international standards of safety, environmental protection and fair conditions of work for

[60] 1973/78 MARPOL Convention 1340 UNTS 61.

[61] Article 5, paragraph 2,.of the 1973/78 MARPOL Convention.

[62] Article 5, paragraph 4 of the MARPOL Convention (emphasis added). Similar provisions are in all IMO conventions that provide for inspection of ships in ports by the authorities of the port States.

[63] On port state control generally see Dr. Z Oya Özçayir, Port State Control (2nd Edition) London LLP (2004).

seafarers, some of these persons and institutions may be willing, perhaps reluctantly, to tolerate the existence and operation of these ships. Accordingly, it is reasonable to believe that effective and more widespread use of port state control could, by helping to eliminate or significantly reduce the undesirable practices of some flag of convenience ships, also make such ships less undesirable.

Because of its immense potential to influence the behaviour of flag of convenience ships and their flag States, port state control has been accepted and used in all the organizations and contexts as a bedrock mechanism for the effective implementation and enforcement of international standards on all ships. In the 1982 UNCLOS, port state jurisdiction and control is declared to be one of the overarching principles of public international law of the sea for the regulation of international shipping. Similarly, within the International Maritime Organization (IMO), the campaign against sub-standard ships has at all times been buttressed by the mechanism of port state jurisdiction and control. And in the ILO, port State jurisdiction and control has been elevated to a prominent position in the programme to establish and implement international standards to protect the rights of seafarers and their entitlement to fair terms of employment and decent conditions of work. As previously noted, the 2006 ILO Maritime Labour Convention identifies port state control as one of the principal mechanisms to be used by States and labour unions to enforce the international standards for fair treatment of seafarers that are mandated in that Convention.

For the ITF, the possibility that ships will be inspected in foreign ports (by officials of the port states or by ITF inspectors) gives considerable satisfaction because it means that fewer ships will be able to continue to flout international regulations or blatantly disregard international standards without detection and sanction. The same is true of the FAO where the crusade against of IUU fishing is widely agreed to be directly linked with effective control of flag of convenience registration of fishing vessels.[64]

Finally port state control has been the mainstay of the highly effective regional enforcement mechanism first introduced by the 1982 Paris Memorandum on Port State Control.[65] The MOU mechanism has now been extended to more than eight regions of the world. By pooling their resources, the regional partners participating in the various MOUs have helped to establish a fairly effective regime that takes advantage of the now universally accepted device to persuade flag States and ship operators that it is in their own interests for their ships to observe basic international standards for safety, environmental protection and respect for seafarers' rights and welfare. In this way the various MOUs have demonstrated how concerted and focused action can help to concentrate the minds of those who would otherwise seek to disregard the legitimate need and wish of the global community for responsible shipping. In the current atmosphere, responsible shipping can only mean shipping that genuinely strives to serve world trade and commerce, while giving due regard to safety, environmental protection and the interests and welfare of those who serve on board ships.

In all these areas, port state control has provided a telling example of how national and international law can be made more effective through co-ordinated action. In particular, it has

---

[64] FAO considers IUU Fishing to be linked with FOC. See David J. Doulman, Illegal, Unreported and Unregulated Fishing: Mandate for an International Plan of Action, Document AUS:IUU/2000/4.2000 http://www.fao.org/DOCrep/005/Y3274E/y3274e06.htm The Environmental Justice Foundation(EJF) states that "a large proportion of IUU fishing could be eliminated if the loophole in international law that allows States to issue flags of convenience to fisheries vessels was closed".

[65] Text in 21 ILM 982.

shown that it is possible to design an effective regime that is able to affect the behaviour of States and non-state actors directly while, at the same time, recognizing and respecting importance of state responsibility.[66] In port state control, it appears that the international maritime community has found a mechanism that enables other States to intervene in matters relating to ships that are registered in other States, without having to question or undermine the sovereign right of States to grant their flags to ships or to determine the conditions under which such grant will be made. By accepting that other States can, in appropriate cases, intervene in the interests of maritime safety, the marine environment, and seafarers' rights, the shipping community has clarified that it is no longer necessary to maintain that ships should be considered as an extension of the territory of the State of their registry in all situations and for all purposes.[67]

Evaluation of Flags of Convenience

It has to be acknowledged that the many and determined attempts to abolish the practice of flag of convenience registration (or to make the operation of flag of convenience ships difficult if not impossible) have on the whole been unsuccessful. Consequently, flag of convenience ships are still with us and it looks like they are here to stay. That being the case, the more advisable and helpful exercise appears to be to examine the phenomenon of flag of convenience registration and operation dispassionately in order to identify the negative and undesirable aspects that need to be eliminated or reduced and, perhaps more importantly, to determine whether there are any positive aspects and advantages that could be put to maximum use in the service of shipping and world trade.

In the first place, it must be noted that the blanket claim that flag of convenience ships are all sub-standard and should, therefore, be prohibited is not borne out by available evidence. While there are features and practices of flag of convenience ships that are clearly undesirable, it does not necessarily follow that everything about flags of convenience ships is undesirable or necessarily against the interest of international shipping.[68]

One of the more common charges against flag of convenience registration is that it permits the operation of sub-standard ships. This is because the flag States are unwilling or unable to exercise effective jurisdiction and control over the ships and this, consequently, permits ships registered with them to disregard or flout safety and environmental standards.

---

[66] The use of port state control by IMO has been seen as establishing a "regime that expressly responds to the transnational character of the shipping sector by focussing on effectiveness whilst remaining firmly focussed on the traditional international law principles of State responsibility". Moira McConnel, "Making Labour History etc." note 48.above, p.362.

[67] "In terms of freedom of the seas, the acceptance by the flag States of a mechanism for the direct intervention of other sovereign States in matters affecting its registered ships has been a significant departure from the principle that those ships are an extension of its own territory" Farthing, note.5.above, p.193.

[68] "The most widespread belief was that the FOC States allowed owners to by-pass the more stringent safety requirements of their own states. It is this image of sub-standard FOC that has received the widest publicity and is the least founded on fact. There have been (and still are) sub-standard vessels on all registries, and the safety record of FOC states has only been marginally worse than that of the rest" Edgar Gold, The New Law of the Sea and Nationality of Ships, note 12 p.268. Although the ITF presumes that FOC ships are sub-standard, it does not apply this presumption to FOC ships which sign ITF agreements. On these the ITF states: "In our experience, their ships are relatively safe, and on-board conditions are generally good" ITF Official Booklet: Flags of Convenience, p.39.

Flag of convenience registration are also accused of allowing unscrupulous owners to disregard international standards on fair labour terms and decent working conditions for seafarers. There is no doubt that some flag of convenience registry countries, either deliberately or by omission, allow or permit ships registered with them to evade international and national requirements. It is also the case that there are features of flag of convenience registries that make it easier for ships registered with them to disregard international standards with relative impunity. But this is not always the case. For one thing, the flouting of international standards is not confined to flag of convenience ships. In any case, there are effective measures such as port State control which, properly implemented and enforced, can persuade or oblige flag States to take their responsibilities more seriously or, failing that, would enable other States to apply effective sanctions against delinquent ships. The widespread use of port state control in many international shipping conventions and, particularly, the more co-ordinated implementation that has been made possible through the regional Memoranda of Understanding have shown that it is possible to have open registry or flag of convenience ships that satisfy international and national standards for safety, environmental protection and respect for seafarers' rights and welfare. In similar vein, the success of the ITF in persuading or forcing owners and operators of flag of convenience ships to accept ITF Standard Collective Agreements means that it is possible to make flag of convenience ships agree to apply decent wages and conditions of work to crew, regardless of nationality of the ships or of the members of the crews. Ships that apply these standards do not constitute any more threat to the interests of seafarers than do ships registered in traditional maritime States.

The same approach is adopted by IMO in its programme against sub-standard ships at sea. Flag of convenience ships that satisfy the standards set in IMO instruments are not described as "sub-standard", and they are not deemed to pose any greater hazards to safety of shipping or to the marine environment merely because they fly flags of convenience. In sum, a flag of convenience ship need not be a sub-standard ship, and the flag of the ship does not necessarily determine whether such a ship meets relevant national and international standards.

In its programme for the elimination of sub-standard ships, IMO has found port state control to be a useful sanctioning mechanism which has the virtue of impartial application to all ships. This has been made even more effective with the application of the "no more favourable treatment" principle for the inspection of ships in ports.[69] It has further been assisted by the regional arrangements based on the various Memoranda of Understanding. There is now in place a virtually worldwide system for policing and targeting sub-standard ships of all types and flying under all flags.

IMO has also recognized that relying solely on port state control is not likely fully to achieve the objectives of safety, environmental protection and respect for the rights and welfare of seafarers. Accordingly, attention has also been given to measures that highlight the duties of flag States. For example, ships are still required to be certified and inspected by the flag State or by an organization designated to act on behalf of the flag State.[70] In this way the system demands on-going compliance with international standards, and also assists weaker

[69] Note 62 above.

[70] In most cases the institutions chosen for this purpose are Classification Societies. On the role and possible uses of classification societies, See Jonathan Lux, Classification Societies, LLP (1993); and Jurgen Basedow and Wolfgang Wurmnest, Third Party Liability of Classification Societies – A Comparative Perspective (Hamburg Studies in Maritime Affairs) Springer 2005.

flag State Administrations who are obliged to ensure that their ships operate in accordance with international standards. Where flag States lack the capacity to meet their obligations, they are assisted, through the Technical Co-operation Programmes of IMO and other bodies in the United Nations system, to improve the human and institutional infrastructures that will enable them to exercise the full measure of jurisdiction and control required by general international law and under specific conventions and instruments.

In another sense, the system also operates indirectly to check on a state's implementation of its international obligations. Further, it provides a powerful economic incentive to shipowners to register their ships in flag States that have a record of reliable flag State certification. In some cases port States, alone or in concert with others, find it necessary and useful to" target" the ships of particular flag States based on the regularity that ships of those flags are found to contravene applicable standards. Ships targeted in this way could suffer considerable losses resulting from longer times they need to stay in port for inspection and, where necessary, corrective action. For that reason responsible operators may find it more convenient to move their ships away from such flag States in order to avoid being "tarred with the same brush".

The approach of IMO in this sector has been found useful and acceptable because it manages to deal effectively with the international law concerns about state sovereignty without compromising the ability of states to enforce the necessary standards on ships. By promoting international cooperation and the use of voluntary regional arrangements such as Memoranda of Understanding on port state control and other agreements on the inspections of foreign ships, IMO has found a way to tackle the problem caused by failures of flag state to discharge their responsibilities that generally is the basis of the concern with the genuine link requirement. In many contexts, the concern with the existence of the genuine link between a ship and its flag State arises largely from the failure of some flag States to discharge their responsibilities, and not merely because some ships are registered outside the states of nationality of their beneficial owners.

As noted above, it has been claimed by many developing countries that the existence and operation of FOC ships somehow prevents them from participating adequately in the provision of shipping services and having an equitable share in the maritime transportation of their own import and export trade. However, not much evidence has been given to support this claim. On the contrary, it is perhaps more true to say that the inability of developing countries to play an effective role in world shipping is due more to the lack of capital and expertise than to the existence or operation of flag of convenience ships.[71]Indeed, it can reasonably be argued that the long and largely unsuccessful campaign by the developing countries (organized in the Group of 77 in UNCTAD) to "phase out" flags of convenience

[71] The list of LDC which are able to self-supply themselves with shipping services, economically and technically is very short. Among the major grievances of LDCs is lack of capital and shortage of foreign currency. Building a whole new fleet or even buying second hand vessels is a very big operation which requires huge capital investments. Even if LDCs receive loans from the World Bank and other funds, and even if the shipyards grant them special credit arrangements, still their debit in balance of payments will increase. The creation of a merchant marine is essential for the economic strength and independence which all LDCs strongly desire. Yet because LDCs do not have the resources for establishing national fleets, they switch dependencies from foreign shipping services to dependence on foreign financing and get caught in a vicious circle. LDCs have no experience in operating and maintaining shipping services. People will have to be trained and external expertise will have to be used since the shipping industry is a very specialized field which requires a high degree of skill not only in operating the boasts but also in managing the business" Amos Herman, Shipping Conferences, Lloyds of London Press, Ltd. (Kluwer Law and Taxation Publishers, 1993 pp. 161-162.

shipping was not just a waste of valuable time and energies, but actually represented a shooting in the foot by the developing countries. In the first place there was no reasonable basis for the suggestion that the mere abolition of flag of convenience ships would enable the developing countries to increase their tonnages. The assumption that, upon the abolition of the flag of convenience registration system, owners of flag of convenience ships would choose to reflag their ships in other developing countries, instead of in the registries of the traditional maritime States, has no basis in fact or logic.[72] There is no reason why a shipowner in the United States or Greece would wish to de-register a ship from Liberia or Panama and re-flag it in the Philippines or Nigeria. And in any case, it is not clear why an American owned ship that is moved from the Liberian flag to the Nigerian or the Philippines flag would cease to be a flag of convenience ship, merely because it is able to draw some of its crew from the country of registry, even though the real owners of the ship are still in a different country.

It would appear, therefore, that the long campaign by UNCTAD to phase out flag of convenience ships did not in the end bring much benefit to the developing countries. Indeed, by giving the impression that the 1986 Convention was part of a programme against the very principle of "open registries" (instead of the effort to eliminate the undesirable features and practices of the flag of convenience system) the members of the Group of 77 might have helped to underplay the other and less controversial aims of the 1986 Convention. What is more the impression that the true aim of the 1986 Convention was to do away with flags of convenience registration has perhaps ensured that the Convention itself will not enter into force at all. This is to be regretted since some of the very progressive elements of the 1986 Convention, such as the requirement that the owner of a ship should have a credible and easily identifiable presence in the state of registry[73] and other provisions that aim to remove or reduce the anonymity of owners and shareholders of ships, will probably not be implemented because many countries whose ratifications are needed to bring the Convention into force refuse to ratify because they object to parts of the Convention that they consider to be incompatible with the continued existence of flag of convenience ships.[74]

In addition, because of the assumption that the main concern of the proponents of the 1986 Convention was to make the concept of the "genuine link" the main criterion for the validity of a ship's registration, the Convention (and the discussions leading to its adoption) provided the opportunity and justification for many traditional maritime countries to establish second or parallel ship registers. In effect, the establishment of these new registries enabled the countries concerned to get the best of both worlds. For with the second or international registers the maritime countries are able to get round the legal objection to open registries based on the absence of the "genuine link" while still enjoying most of the advantages of the open registry system. The result is that the flag of convenience system has not been abolished

[72] "Most of the LDCs feel that if the FOC system is abolished, many shipowners from the traditional maritime nations will reflag their ships in LDC registries because of a ready supply of labour at wages below the ITF mandated levels" Rex S. Toh & Sock Yong Phang, "Quasi-Flag of Convenience shipping: the wave of the future" Transportation Journal, Winter 1993 edition.

[73] Article 10 of the 1986 Convention requires the flag State to provide in its laws that the company or person owning the ship should either (a) be established or has its principal place of business in the territory of the flag State; or (b) at least have a representative person or company in the territory of the flag State who can be held to account legally for the owner's responsibilities, including any financial obligations.

[74] Pursuant to Article 19 the Convention is to enter into force 12 months after it has been ratified, accepted etc. by "not less than 40 States, the combined tonnage of which amounts to at least 25per cent of world tonnage".

but rather appears to have been recognized and accepted. At the same time, the share of the developing countries in world shipping remains as low as it was at the beginning of the UNCTAD campaign, and perhaps lower. Thus, it may be true to say that the campaign in UNCTAD against flags of convenience has not achieved much, and may in fact have been counter-productive.

POSSIBLE ADVANTAGES OF FLAGS OF CONVENIENCE

The outright objection to the flag of convenience system may perhaps also have denied to the developing countries some of the potential benefits of flag of convenience ships. Among them the following may briefly be mentioned.

First, as was indirectly recognized in the discussions leading to the adoption of the1986 UNCTAD Convention, flag of convenience registration can help countries to increase the tonnage of ships flying their flags, and thus enhance their share of merchant shipping. For the developing countries this appears to be one way in which they can increase their share in the maritime transport of goods, especially those featuring in their export and import trades. Such increase may help to redress the imbalance in trade that was at the heart of the complaints against the current system of world maritime trade. Many of the developing countries had hoped and expected that the 1974 UNCTAD Convention on the Code of Conduct for Liner Conferences would contribute to redress this imbalance, especially as a result of the Convention's endorsement of the 40/40/20 principle for sharing of liner trade between ships registered in importing and exporting countries, respectively. But the Code of Conduct Agreement has not worked as expected; and to many it has virtually become a dead letter.[75] This is due, at least in part, to the fact that few developing countries have the registered shipping tonnages that enable them to take advantage of the cargo sharing formula mandated by the1974 Code of Conduct Convention.[76] And because of their antipathy to the very principle of flags of convenience, developing countries in general are unwilling to contemplate the possibility of registering foreign owned ships under their flags. And in the absence of the capital and expertise required to develop national fleets of their own, there is very little scope for these countries to equip themselves sufficiently to be able to play the equitable role in world shipping that is their right and desire.

Another possible benefit of flag of convenience registration for a developing country is that it could enable the country to secure much-needed employment opportunities for citizens who wish to go to sea. As has already been seen in many States, a strict adherence to the traditional requirement that ships should not only be owned by nationals of the flag States but also that a certain component of the crews should be nationals of these states would have denied much needed job opportunities to the large numbers of developing country seafarers who currently serve on board ships in many countries, including some ships registered in traditional maritime countries. It is also a well-known fact that, for a variety of reasons, more and more young men and women in the traditional maritime countries have lost the urge to go

[75] See Rex S Toh & Sock-Yong Phang, note 72 above.

[76] "The UNCTAD Code of Conduct is an excellent tool for controlling conferences, but it is not the right tool for the economic development of national fleets". Amos Herman, Liner Conferences, op.cit. note 71 above p.214.

to sea.[77] Hence a return to the traditional insistence that crew complements should be drawn entirely or even mainly y from nationals of the flag States would not only cause unemployment for many potential seafarers from the developing countries, but would also lead to a serious shortage of qualified and willing seafarers. This would only be to the detriment of the developing countries and also to international shipping industry.[78]

Furthermore, flag of convenience registration in some developing countries could enable these countries to benefit from globalisation and extend their influence in shipping, just as some of them have been able to take advantage of foreign capital and know-how to promote r development in other areas, through co-operation and partnership with industrial and commercial interests from the developed world. For example, a developing country that chooses to register ships beneficially owned by nationals of another country could so organize its system as to enable it to derive more from ships than just the registration charges paid by the owners. Under the laws of United States and some other countries, the authorities of the State of registry of a ship reserve the right, in certain situations, to requisition ships that are beneficially owned by their nationals even if the ships are registered in other states.[79] Based on this model, a developing country that permits non-nationals to register ships in its registry could also provide in its law that ships on its register will be required to participate in the carriage of a specified proportion of the seaborne trade of the State. Such a law would help the State to increase its share of shipping to a level commensurate with its share of the trade with other countries. It would also do away with one of the most common and generally undesirable features of the current flag of convenience system, that is to say, the situation in which a ship registered in a flag of convenience State hardly ever enters the ports of that State and is, therefore, not easily subject to inspection and control by the authorities of that State. A requirement that a ship registered in a State should carry goods to and from the flag state will help both to increase the economic link between the State and the ship and also give the authorities the State the opportunity and facility to exercise the jurisdiction and control over the ship that is the true rationale of the "genuine link" requirement prescribed by international law.

Finally, greater use of flag of convenience by developing countries, if accompanied by safeguards and reforms that eliminate or reduce the negative aspects of the system, can help to spread ship registration among many more countries and provide opportunities for persons and companies in developing countries to play an increasing role in world shipping. This will increase competition among providers of shipping services for the trade of the world. In a world of increasing globalisation and escalating costs of goods and services, greater competition can only be to the benefit of world shipping, and of the global trade which depends increasingly on shipping and shipping services.

[77] This is recognized by IMO and constitutes the basis for it "Go To Sea" campaign whose objectiveis to attract entrants to the shipping industry.

[78] Ibid.

[79] The US has an Effective US-Controlled Ships (EUSCS) system. Effective United States-Controlled Ships are ships owned by US citizens or companies that are registered in countries that have no prohibition to requisitioning of these vessels by the United States under authority of Section 902, Merchant Marine Act of 1936. Such ships can reasonably be expected to be made available to the United States in time of national emergency.

CONCLUSION

Flag of convenience registration of ships appears to be here to stay. The many campaigns that have been waged in many organizations and on numerous fronts have so far not succeeded to make a dent on the system or its long term prospects. But recent developments, including especially the use of port state control in the enforcement regimes of IMO and ILO, have demonstrated that it is possible to get rid of some of the worst features of the system without necessarily abolishing it altogether.

The history of the campaigns mounted at various times by ILO, IMO and the ITF shows that a consistent and widespread use of port State control is one of the best and most effective ways to persuade flag States to exercise the jurisdiction and control over ships registered with them that is required under general international law and in numerous international instruments on shipping. The mechanism of port state control has been found to work well because while it enables all concerned - flag states, port states, ship owners and operators and seafarers and their unions – to implement and apply agreed standards, it does not infringe on any fundamental norms of international law.

Finally, it is helpful to consider whether a reformed and more sanitized form of the flag of convenience registration can be operated in place of the current system and, if so, whether such a system would have any benefits for the shipping community. A dispassionate examination of the current operation of flag of convenience system suggests that it is possible to regulate and clean up the system in a way that can make it contribute positively to the development of shipping services. In the process it may also be made to serve the interests of developing countries, especially by increasing their share of international shipping and thus enabling them to make their share of shipping more equitable than it can otherwise be.

In: Selected Issues in Maritime Law and Policy
Editor: Maximo Q. Mejia, Jr.
ISBN: 978-1-62618-508-1

Chapter 3

CAUSATION IN THE ENGLISH LAW OF MARINE INSURANCE: THE CASE FOR CHANGE

Gotthard Gauci*
Maritime Regulation and Policy, Plymouth Business School,
Plymouth University, Plymouth, UK

1. INTRODUCTION

The requirement of a causative link has been used over the years to rein in claims for damages in tort or claims for damages as a result of a breach of contract. Causation is a concept which has rightly been described as the most 'pervasive and yet elusive' [1]

In contract, reference is usually made to the rule enunciated in *Hadley v Baxendale* [2]: numerous difficulties in connection with this rule have arisen over the years, with a recent authoritative statement from the House of Lords in this respect being the one in *Transfield Shipping Inc. v. Mercator Shipping (The Achilleas)* [3]. In the case of the English law of torts, there are several restrictions implemented on liability through causation, and a defendant can claim that even if the damage would not have occurred but for his negligence, nevertheless the damage was too remote for there to be a valid claim. Nevertheless as will be seen in more detail below, English courts have in recent years confirmed the view that in certain instances, a material contribution to the risk of the damage which occurred will suffice, on policy grounds, to allocate liability to the defendant. The law of marine insurance requires a link of proximate cause and effect between the peril insured against and the loss. This may appear to be a simple rule, but many problems have arisen over the years in this respect, both before and since the enactment of the Marine Insurance Act 1906 [4].

* gotthard.gauci@plymouth.ac.uk.

2. Proximate Causation in the Law of Marine Insurance

This requisite is provided for expressly in Section 55 of the Marine Insurance Act 1906 which provides:

"(1) Subject to the provisions of this Act, and unless the policy otherwise provides, the insurer is liable for any loss proximately caused by a peril insured against, but, subject as aforesaid, he is not liable for any loss which is not proximately caused by a peril insured against..."

The *causa proxima* has been said to be 'the cause proximate in efficiency, and not necessarily the cause nearest in time [6].' The latter option, although opted for in some early marine insurance cases [7], would be a mechanistic and probably unintended approach to causation. In *Leyland Shipping v. Norwich Union, The Ikaria*, Lord Shaw stated:

"To speak of *proxima causa* as the cause which is nearest in time is out of the question. Causes are spoken of as if they were as distinct from one another as beads in a row or links in a chain, but - if this metaphysical topic has to be referred to - it is not wholly so. The chain of causation is a handy expression, but the figure is inadequate. Causation is not a chain, but a net. At each point influences, forces, events, precedent and simultaneous, meet; and the radiation from each point extends infinitely. At the point where these various influences meet it is for the judgment as a matter of fact to declare which of the causes thus joined at the point of effect was the proximate and which was the remote cause.

What does 'proximate' here mean? To treat proximate cause as if it was the cause which is proximate in time is...out of the question. The cause which is truly proximate is that which is proximate in efficiency." [8]

In the case here being discussed, the vessel, after being hit by a torpedo, entered a port which it later had to leave due to a gale which had sprung up and an order by the authorities to move to the outer port. She grounded and eventually was lost. It was held by Lord Shaw that the cause of the loss was the damage caused by the torpedo:

"In my opinion, the real efficient cause of the sinking of this vessel was that she was torpedoed. Where an injury is received by a vessel, it may be fatal or it may be cured: it has to be dealt with. In so dealing with it there may, it is true, be attendant circumstances which may aggravate or possibly precipitate the result, but which are incidents flowing from the injury, or receive from it an operative and disastrous power. The vessel, in short, is all the time, in the grip of the casualty. The true efficient cause never loses its hold. The result is produced, a result attributable in common language to the casualty as a cause, and this result, proximate as well as continuous in its efficiency, properly meets, whether under contract or under the statute, the language of the expression 'proximately caused" [9].

On the basis of this principle, English courts, in the very great majority of cases, approach the problem of multiple causation by picking up one proximate cause out of a number of operating causes relating to one incident. It has been said that '[T]he pragmatic Englishman prefers to avoid the philosophical maze, to cut through to a practical solution' [10]. In *State of Netherlands v Youell* [11], in the context of a dispute relating to a suing and labouring clause, Mr Justice Rix, echoing the provisions of section 55 of the Marine Insurance Act 1906 stated that '...a loss proximately caused by perils of the sea, but remotely caused ... or merely contributed to... by the negligence of master or crew, is recoverable.' In such instances the remote causes, normally excluded on the basis of common sense, are ignored and the one proximate cause is deemed to be the sole cause of the loss; therefore the entire loss would be allocated to the peril designated as the proximate cause. In other words, this will result in an all-or-nothing lottery, reflecting an aversion of English marine insurance law to multiple proximate causes. One can here refer to the 1981 edition of *Arnould's Law of Marine Insurance* which states that 'in the cases which have so far come before the courts the judges, or a majority of them, have always found it possible to isolate a single peril as the proximate cause of the loss which gave rise to the action [12].' The process of elimination of the non-proximate cause has to be carried out on criteria of common sense. As Lord Atkinson said in the aforementioned case of *The Ikaria* [13] 'there is such a tendency in argument ... to split up complex causes into their components and establish a sequence between them, that it is well always to bear in mind the warning given by Lindley L.J. ... that this rule [of proximate causation] must be applied with good sense to give effect to, and not defeat the intention of the contracting parties.'

A similar problem to that in *The Ikaria* arose in the later case of *The Coxwold* [14], where the vessel with that name grounded and a claim was made in respect of a partial loss. At the time of the incident the vessel had been requisitioned by the Ministry of War Transport and was sailing in a convoy, when she lost contact with the vessel ahead due to poor visibility; a lighthouse in the vicinity was not visible due to its operation on reduced power. An issue arose as to the identity of the cause of the loss. The House of Lords decided that the cause of the loss was the warlike operation [15]; Lord Wright stated:

"Once it is clear, as this House finally held in Leyland Shipping Company v. Norwich Union Fire Insurance Society [1918] AC 350, that 'proximate' here means, not latest in time, but predominant in efficiency, there is necessarily involved a process of selection from among the co-operating causes in order to find what is the proximate cause in the particular case. In the words of Phillips on Insurance...:

In the case of concurrence of different causes to one of which it is necessary ... to attribute a loss, it is to be attributed to the efficient predominating peril whether it is or is not in activity at the consummation of the disaster'.

This choice of the real or efficient cause from out of the whole complex of the facts must be made by applying common sense standards. Causation is to be understood, as the man in the street, and not as either the scientist or the metaphysician, would understand it. Cause, here, means what a business or seafaring man would take to be the cause without too microscopic analysis, but on a broad view." [16]

However, the reference to common sense creates the problem as to what constitutes common sense, and reference may here be made to a decision by the High Court of Australia where the court divided 3-2 in relation to the application of common sense in that case [17].

3. Specific Problematic Issues

A. Causation and Delay

Section 55(2)(b) of the Marine Insurance Act 1906 provides that:

'Unless the policy otherwise provides, the insurer on ship or cargo is not liable for any loss proximately caused by delay, although the delay be caused by a peril insured against;'

The Institute Cargo Clauses A, B and C of 1982 provide an exclusion in relation to 'loss damage or expense proximately caused by delay, even though the delay be caused by a risk insured against (except ...)' [18].

The term 'proximate' here causes substantial problems in that it is very difficult to decide whether delay is a cause proximate in efficiency or not, and by definition delay is always caused by another eventuality. Reference was earlier [19] made in this chapter to the celebrated case of *Pink v. Fleming* [20] which however must be treated with caution as it preceded the enactment of the Marine Insurance Act 1906 and was decided on different rules relating to proximate causation.

B. Loss caused by the Expectation of the Operation of a Peril

Problems relating to causation have also arisen when a loss is caused not by the actual peril itself but because of the expectation of the same peril. The case of *Kacianoff v. China Traders Insurance Co* [21] related to a cargo of salt beef insured on a cargo policy covering the risk of capture on a voyage from San Francisco via Vladivostok via Nagasaki. The cargo was discharged at San Francisco and there sold. Notice of abandonment was given to underwriters who refused to accept it. According to Reading, CJ:

> "Was this loss occasioned by a risk within the policy, that is, was it a loss occasioned by capture? The answer is: Certainly not. The vessel never was in risk of capture, because she determined not to undergo the risk, the cargo never underwent the risk, because it was determined to discharge the cargo so as to avoid the risk. Therefore, never having come under the risk and the risk never having begun to operate, no claim can be made on the policy." [22]

A similar issue arose in *Becker, Gray and Co v. London Assurance Corporation* [23]: The case related to a cargo of jute which was to be shipped from Calcutta to Hamburg on board a German vessel. The cargo was *inter alia* insured against loss by 'men-of-war, enemies, and restraints of princes'. While the cargo was in transit, war broke out between Britain and Germany, and the vessel entered a neutral port in order to avoid capture by the enemy; as a result the voyage was abandoned and the insured gave a notice of abandonment and claimed a constructive total loss. The House of Lords decided that the loss was not caused by a peril insured against; according to Lord Sumner:

"My Lords, if there is any real distinction to be drawn between a loss by perils insured against and a loss by successfully avoiding them, between a loss by capture and a loss by the fear of it, one might think that it arises in this case. It was self-restraint, not restraint of princes, that hindered the captain from putting to sea [24].

C. Specific Problematic Wording

The wording used in relation to causation in the Institute Cargo Clauses B & C of 1982 [25] could be a cause of interpretative concern. The following terms are used:

'reasonably attributable to' [26]; 'caused by' [27]; 'attributable to' [28]; 'arising from' [29]; 'caused by' [30]; 'resulting from' [31].

A similar problem arises with the wording of section 39(5) of the Marine Insurance Act 1906 where the phrase 'attributable to' is used instead of 'caused by' [32].

There may be a strong argument that the difference in wording supports a different onus of proof in relation to causation, and this is buttressed by the view that the wording in standard form marine insurance policies is unlikely to have been drafted without strict legal scrutiny. However, in *The Salem* [33], Lord Justice Kerr stated that the phrase 'might have been attributable to', used in clause 8 of the insurance contract in that case, did not alter the well-established principles of causation'. Whilst this interpretation may be an easy way for finding a resolution to the problem, it does not necessarily reflect the presumed intention of the parties, and it seems idle to consider the difference in wording as simply capricious. 'Arising from' [34], resulting from (and other similar wording) may arguably also include a remote cause as being covered by the policy. This view is supported by Clark J in *Beazley Underwriting v The Travellers Companies Incorporated* [35]:

"128. I am prepared to accept that 'arising out of '…does not dictate a proximate cause test and that a somewhat weaker causal connection is allowed….

129. That does not, however, determine what degree of causal connection is required…

130. In my judgment a relatively strong degree of causal connection is required."

This extract is cited by Burton J in *British Waterways v Royal and Sun Alliance plc* [36], who interprets it as perhaps suggesting "'a half-way house' but with a 'relatively strong degree of causal connection'". [37] Moreover, according to the said judge, the term or phrase specifying causation may possibly necessitate a different approach depending on whether one is referring to insurance cover or exclusion of such cover [38].

Clause 27 of ITCH [1995] [39] uses very wide terminology in Clause 27; this provides as follows:

"In no case shall this insurance cover loss damage liability or expense *directly or indirectly caused by or contributed to by or arising from*" [40].

It may be noted that this provision adopts a very wide approach to the causation issue. An operative cause can be direct or indirect. Similar wording is utilised in the Institute Extended Radioactive Contamination Exclusion Clause [41], which has more pre-eminence in that it is elevated to a paramount clause. There is case-law to the effect that the term 'directly' should be interpreted on the same basis as 'proximately'; 'indirectly' should mean 'less proximately' and indicates at least a degree of remoteness [42].

D. Causation and the 'All Risk' Type of Policy

The requisite of causation obviously creates concern for the individual seeking coverage, for he must ascertain that he has obtained coverage in respect of the eventualities that may possibly affect the insured matter. The position is rendered more favourable towards the insured if the policy insures under the all-risks basis available for cargo because there is no specific risk specified in the policy which must be proved as being the cause of the loss. It must be pointed out, however, that no insurer would cover all risks without any limitation; neither should all risks be thought to include certainties. The all-risk cargo cover available under the Institute Cargo Clauses A is subject to a number of exceptions [43]. The matter has been discussed in the case *British and Foreign Marine Insurance Co Ltd v. Gaunt* [44]. In that case, Lord Birkenhead elaborated on the requirement of causation in an all risks policy:

"These words ('all risks') cannot be held to cover all damage however caused, for such damage as is inevitable from ordinary wear and tear and inevitable depreciation is not within the policies...Damage, in other words, if it is to be covered by policies such as these, must be due to some fortuitous circumstance or casualty. ...The damage proved was such as did not occur, and could not be expected to occur, in the course of a normal transit. The inference remains that it was due to some abnormal circumstances, some accident or casualty. We are, of course, to give effect to the rule that the plaintiff must establish his case, that he must show that the loss comes within the terms of the policy; but where all risks are covered by the policy, and not merely risks of a specified class or classes, the plaintiff discharges his special onus when he has proved that the loss was caused by some event covered by the general expression, and he is not bound to go further and prove the exact nature of the accident or casualty which in fact occasioned the loss. In this case the respondent established that the loss must have been due to some casualty, and consequently the judgment of the Court of Appeal on this point is right." [45]

A similar problem can arise in the context of the Institute Theft, Pilferage and Non-Delivery Clause. This provides that:

"In consideration of an additional premium, it is hereby agreed that this insurance covers loss of or damage to the subject-matter insured caused *by theft or pilferage, or by non-delivery of an entire package*, subject always to the exclusions contained in this insurance." [46]

In the case of *Middows Ltd v. Robertson (and other cases)* [47], Mr Justice Hilbery dealt with a contention of the plaintiffs that the loss was caused by non-delivery and decided that 'non-delivery' was a term which 'affected the burden of proof' and that 'it is enough if [the claimant] proves non-delivery and gives prima facie proof that the goods were not lost in any other way than by theft or pilferage.' [48]

4. More Than One Proximate Cause

Although in the very great majority of cases, English courts, applying English law of marine insurance, single out one cause as a proximate cause out of a number of causes, there is the odd case where more than one proximate cause are held to be operative, and even in these unusual cases, English courts resolve this problem by what can veritably be termed an all or nothing lottery. A case where two proximate causes were held to be operative was that of *The Miss Jay Jay* [49]. In that case extensive reference was made to the non-marine case *Wayne Tank & Pump Co Ltd v Employer's Liability Insurance Corp Ltd* [50] and Lawton LJ emphatically stated:

'It is now settled law, at least as far as this court is concerned, that, if there are two concurrent and effective causes of a marine loss, and one comes within the terms of the policy and the other does not, the insurers must pay." [51]

Lawton L.J. then went on to deal with the situation of one cause being included and the other being excluded, and referring again to the same authority referred to above, stated that:

"All three members of the Court, however, considered what should happen when there were two causes which were equal or nearly equal in their efficiency in bringing about the damage, one being under the general words so as to make the insurers liable and the other within the exception so as to exempt them from liability. They all agreed that the exception applied." [52]

A difficulty which arises in the context of for instance the Institute Hull Clauses (1/11/95) is whether the *Wayne Tank & Pump v Employers Liability Insurance* test applies where both a covered peril and an excluded are operative causes but the causation tests are different. The case could arise where a loss is caused to an insured vessel by a pirate maliciously detonating an explosive. Clause 4 of the IVCH states that a loss by piracy is covered, whereas Clause 23 of the same set of clauses excludes loss *arising from* the detonation of an explosive caused by a person acting maliciously. The term 'arising from' can arguably be interpreted as casting a wider net than the term 'caused by'. The question, as yet unresolved, is whether the loss would be indemnifiable at all. It is submitted that the answer would probably be that the insurer would be justified in rejecting the claim on the basis of principles at least analogous to those set forth in *Wayne Tank and Pump v. Employers' Liability*. However, the said scenario is not really one where a loss is caused by two separate causes, but rather by one causative element which constitutes two different perils [53].

In *The Cendor Mopu* [54], the Supreme Court was dealing with a difficult case where a loss to insured cargo affected by inherent vice [55]was held to have been proximately caused by a peril of the sea. It is interesting to note that Lord Mance added 'some words' about a submission, rejected by Lord Saville in the same case [56], that the loss was caused by two proximate causes, and concluded his speech by the following statement:

> "The present hypothesis is of two concurrent risks arising independently but combining to cause a loss. While it may be that the same principle applies (as the Court of Appeal's dicta in the *Miss Jay Jay* suggest), I would at least wish to hear argument on that. I need not go further into this aspect, upon which I have formed no concluded views." [57]

5. Apportionment and the Norwegian Marine Insurance Plan

Causation is dealt with specifically in the Norwegian Marine Insurance Plan 1996, Version 2010, and some relevant parts of which are reproduced below:

"§2-12. Main rule relating to burden of proof. The assured has the burden of proving that he has suffered a loss of the kind covered by the insurance and of proving the extent of the loss.

The insurer has the burden of proving that the loss has been caused by a peril that is not covered by the insurance, unless other provisions of the Plan provide to the contrary.

…."

A very interesting approach to causation is adopted in §2-13 of the said Plan. This provides for apportionment between different insurers in relation to one loss on the basis of the contribution of the risks to the one incident:

"If the loss has been caused by a combination of different perils, and one or more of these perils are not covered by the insurance, the loss shall be apportioned over the individual perils according to the influence each of them must be assumed to have had on the occurrence and extent of the loss, and the insurer shall only be liable for that part of the loss which is attributable to the perils covered by the insurance..."

This provision is however subject to §2-14 dealing with two exceptions to apportionment where a loss is caused by a combination of marine and war perils:

"If the loss is caused by a combination of marine perils, cf. §2.8, and war perils, cf.§2-9, the whole loss shall be deemed to have been caused by the class of perils which was the dominant cause. If neither of the perils are considered dominant, both shall be deemed to have had equal influence on the occurrence and extent of the loss." [58]

The departure from apportionment in §2-14 in relation to war and marine perils has a historical justification. The dominant-cause rule as a departure from the 1930 apportionment rule was introduced into the Norwegian Marine Insurance Plan 1964 and has been retained since. The §2-13 free apportionment rule was found to be a cause of excessive incidences of litigation as a result of cases emanating during the Second World War [59]. The second part of §2-14, where the result is a fifty: fifty split, is reminiscent of section 187(2) of the Merchant Shipping Act 1995 [60], relating to maritime fault, where it is provided that 'if...having regard to all the circumstances, it is not possible to establish different degrees of fault, the liability shall be apportioned equally.'

However, the apportionment rule remains the general rule in the Norwegian Marine Insurance Plan and this is very significant. In the law of tort, English law introduced apportionment in 1945 through The Law Reform (Contributory Negligence) Act 1945, in terms of which causative negligence on the part of the defendant would translate into a reduction of the claimant's demand [61]. Before that law came into force the rule at common law was to the effect that contributory negligence on the part of the plaintiff would block the claimant's claim for damages from the defendant [62], thereby adopting an all-or-nothing approach [63] reminiscent to the one existing in the English law of marine insurance; the courts, in an attempt to avoid the harshness of the common law full defence of contributory negligence, created the use of the rule of last opportunity [64] which was also extended to cases of 'constructive last opportunity' [65]. In English Admiralty law, in the case of collision between two or more ships at fault, an equal division of loss was applied on the basis of section 25(9) of the Judicature Act 1873. This rule was changed by section 1 of the Maritime Conventions Act 1911to the one applied now, i.e. the rule of proportionate fault; this rule can now be found in section 187 of the Merchant Shipping Act 1995 [66]. The contributory negligence defence does not apply to the tort of deceit [67].

Apportionment, whether in tort or in marine insurance, is undoubtedly compatible with expectations of fairness and justice. If damage has been caused by two separate actions, a person should only be responsible for what he has caused and nothing beyond that; the task for an adjudicator would be probably more of a case of ascertainment of quantification than liability. If courts have managed to apply the rules of contributory negligence, there should be no reason why an apportionment rule in marine insurance law should cause difficulty, despite the doubts evident in the implementation of §2.14 of the Norwegian Marine Insurance Plan.

6. The Cendor MOPU [68]

The difficulties created by the general English marine insurance approach to causation on an all or nothing basis can best be highlighted by the recent decision by the Supreme Court in *Global Process Systems Inc v Syarikat Takaful Malaysia BHD, The Cendor MOPU.* In that case an oil rig was the subject matter of an all risks cargo policy [69]. The oil rig was being carried on a barge from Texas USA to Malaysia. It was common ground that the damage was caused by 'fatigue cracking as a result of the repeated bending of the legs under the motions of the barge in the sea' [70]. The policy excluded loss caused by 'inherent vice or nature of the subject matter covered'. Mr. Justice Blair in the court of first instance [71], decided that the 'proximate cause of the loss was the fact that the legs were not capable of withstanding the normal incidents of the insured voyage from Galveston to Lumut, including the weather reasonably to be expected.' [72] The Court of Appeal reversed this decision and overruled the decision in *Mayban General Insurance BHD v Alstom Power Plants Ltd* [73], reliance on which had been placed by the court of first instance. At the end of his leading judgment, Lord Justice Waller stated that it seemed to him that:

'in this case the cargo was properly stowed and was in good condition in the sense that care was taken to consult surveyors as to how the rig should be carried and they certified that it was fit for the voyage. It is not that the legs then simply suffered severe metal fatigue and cracking, i.e. normal wear and tear. Metal fatigue was not the sole cause of the legs. A leg breaking wave, not bound to occur in the way it did on any normal voyage round the Cape of Good Hope, caused the starboard leg to break off. That led to the others being at greater risk and then breaking off. It was not certain that that would happen and although with the benefit of hindsight we know that it was highly probable, that probability was unknown to the insured and that was a risk against which the appellants insured." [74]

The Supreme Court dismissed an appeal [75], and applied the rule that 'perils of the seas are not confined to cases of exceptional weather that was unforeseen and unforeseeable' [76] and also that 'inherent vice or nature of the subject-matter insured has never (before the decision in *Mayban* [2004] 2 Lloyd's Rep. 609) previously been defined as encompassing any fortuitous external accident or casualty that was unexceptional or foreseen or foreseeable.' [77]. This approach is probably at odds with commercial expectations, particularly because the inherent vice probably constituted at least fifty percent of the combined causative element. If the Norwegian Marine Insurance Plan approach had been applicable, a fairer result would probably have been achieved [78]; such a result could also be achieved in English law by appropriate wording in a policy [79].

The application of the inherent vice defence in an all risks policy was also addressed in earlier cases, notably *Noten v. Harding* [80], a case relied on by the insurers in the aforementioned case of *The Cendor MOPU* [81]. The case related to an all risks policy on a shipment of leather gloves. The shipment was made in the monsoon season. On delivery the goods were found to be wet, stained, mouldy or discoloured. According to Bingham L.J.:

> "If the factual cause of the damage to these gloves has been correctly identified, then I think it plain that there was an excepted peril under these policies. The goods deteriorated as a result of their natural behaviour in the ordinary course of the contemplated voyage, without the intervention of any fortuitous external accident or casualty. The damage was caused because the goods were shipped wet. … I regard it as

immaterial that the moisture travelled round the containers before doing the damage complained of." [82]

Towards the end of his judgment, Bingham L.J. further stated:

> "Perhaps most importantly, there is nothing in the facts of this case to suggest any untoward or unusual event of any kind. It was not unusually humid or hot in Calcutta at the time of shipment nor particularly cold in Rotterdam. There is nothing to suggest an unusual period between manufacture and packing of the gloves, nor between packing and stuffing of the containers, nor between stuffing and shipment, nor between shipment and discharge, nor between discharge and unstuffing. There is nothing to suggest that the position of these containers in the stow was unusual. They were, on the evidence, an entirely normal series of shipments for the time of the year. There was on the evidence, no combination of fortuitous events, and the defendant never undertook to insure the plaintiffs against the occurrence of hot and humid weather in Calcutta during the Monsoon." [83]

Similarly, *Wunsche Handelsgellschaft International v. Tai Ping* [84] was a case where damage included damage caused by condensation from cartons containing the goods. This was held to be a case where the exception of inherent vice was applicable. Towards the end of the judgment Moore-Bick J.stated:

'[t]he subject of the insurance was cans packed in cardboard cartons and the loss by sweating in the present case was caused by the natural behaviour of the goods in the course of the voyage no less than in *Noten v. Harding. …'* [85].

7. Policy Changes in the English Law of Torts

Recent ameliorations relate to the rule that it is sufficient for the purpose of the English law of torts that a 'cause' has materially contributed to the damage. For instance in the case of *McGhee v. National Coal Board* [86], a case dealing technically with Scottish Law, Lord Wilberforce, after reviewing a number of cases, stated:

> "But I find in the cases quoted an analogy which suggests the conclusion that, in the absence of proof that the culpable condition had, in the result, no effect, the employers should be liable for an injury, squarely within the risk which they created and that they, not the pursuer, should suffer the consequence of the impossibility, foreseeably inherent in the nature of his injury, of segregating the precise consequence of their default." [87]

The same approach was taken by the House of Lords in the different circumstances of *Fairchild v. Glenhaven* [88] that a victim of an industrial disease which could have been acquired from one of or both of that person's employers, both employers had 'caused' the injury; Lord Rodger stated:

> "Following the approach in *McGhee*, I accordingly hold that, by proving that the defendants materially increased the risk that the men would develop mesothelioma due to

> inhaling asbestos fibres, the claimants are taken in law to have proved that the defendants materially contributed to their illness." [89]

Indeed in that case it was quite possible that one of the defendants had not contributed at all to the damage, but a pragmatic approach based on policy considerations was applied. Lord Nicholls stated:

> "In some circumstances a lesser degree of causal connection may suffice. This sometimes occurs where the damage flowed from one or other of two alternative causes. Take the well-known example where two hunters, acting independently of each other, fire their guns carelessly in a wood, and a pellet from one of the guns injures an innocent passer-by. No one knows, and the plaintiff is unable to prove, from which gun the pellet came. Should the law of negligence leave the plaintiff remediless, and allow both hunters to go away scot-free, even though one of them must have fired the injurious pellet?
>
> ...To impose liability on a defendant in such circumstances normally runs counter to ordinary perceptions of responsibility. Normally this is unacceptable. But there are circumstances, of which the two hunters' case is an example, where this unattractiveness is outweighed by leaving the plaintiff without a remedy." [90]

The *Fairchild* case relieves the claimant from an impossible evidentiary scenario, and it can be justified because all the defendants acted wrongfully and undoubtedly at least one of them was causative of the claimant's damage. Moreover, it is more likely than not that all of the defendants have or should have liability insurance. The issue of apportionment was not addressed in *Fairchild*, and until the case of *Barker v Corus* [91], English courts had been steadfast in refusing to apportion indivisible damage [92]. In *Barker v. Corus*, a defendant had been exposed to asbestos fibres also during a period where he was self-employed, and the question arose as to whether liability of the defendants should be joint and several on the basis that the mesothelioma is indivisible. Lord Hoffman stated in his judgment that the result in such a case could be unfair [93], and that '[a] defendant is liable for the risk of disease which he himself has created and not for the risks created by others, whether they are defendants, persons not before the court or the claimant himself.' [94] Although the issue of actual apportionment was not up for decision, Lord Hoffman hinted at a practical approach to apportionment, when he stated that that '[I]t may be that the most practical method of apportionment will be according to the time of exposure for which each defendant is responsible, but allowance may have to be made for the intensity of exposure and the type of asbestos.' [95] Joint and several liability, however, was later imposed in mesothelioma cases via section 3 of the Compensation Act 2006 [96].

8. Causation in Relation to the Interpretation of the Water Resources Act 1991 [97] – A Pragmatic Approach ?

The celebrated decision of the House of Lords in *Empress Car Co (Abertillery) Ltd v National Rivers Authority* [98] is another example which could lead to a victory of a policy of pragmatism by an environmentally conscious judiciary over strict justice, to the extent that if a person is a cause, even one of many causes, of water pollution, that person if prosecuted by the Environment Agency was likely to be found guilty of the offence of polluting controlled waters in breach of section 85 of the Water Resources Act 1991 [99], subject to a small number of defences almost usually unavailable.

CONCLUSION

Should the Marine Insurance rule of proximate causation in English law be changed? The discretion in the present system allows an adjudicator to claim the use of intuition or common sense to achieve what is perceived to be a just or equitable outcome. However, there is very little commonsensical or equitable in what can be an all-or-nothing lottery. Moreover, whereas the family of a miner victim of mesothelioma may deserve sympathy from the courts in an hour of need, it is hard to justify a refusal of apportionment between two insurers, or a complete dismissal of a claim against an insurer in respect of a risk which only partially contributed to a loss.

The difficulties of apportionment should not be used to dissuade a legislator from trying to achieve a fair outcome. If apportionment can be achieved in tort in relation to the determination of liability on the basis of causative fault, there is no reason why apportionment of causation cannot be achieved in the context of marine insurance. The Norwegian Plan approach, undoubtedly, solves at least one of the major problems relating to causation in marine insurance law.

REFERENCES

[1] See: Wright, R.W., Causation in Tort Law, 73 California Law Review 1985 1735 at 1737.

[2] (1854) 9 Exch.341. In that case Alderson, B. made the following oft-cited statement: "Where two parties have made a contract which one of them has broken, the damages which the other party ought to receive in respect of such a breach of contract should be such as may fairly and reasonably be considered either arising naturally, i.e. according to the usual course of things, from such breach of contract itself, or such as may reasonably be supposed to have been in the contemplation of both parties, at the time they made the contract, as the probable result of the breach of it."

[3] [2008] UKHL 48.

[4] (6 EDW.7.c.41).

[5] It is to be noted that the preamble to the Marine Insurance Act 1906 specifically states that it is an Act 'to codify the Law relating to Marine Insurance'.

[6] Templeman on Marine Insurance, 6th edition, p. 190.

[7] Pink v. Fleming (1890) 25 QBD 396. In the said case Lord Esher MR stated the following in his judgment in relation to the question of proximate cause: "This question can only arise where there is a succession of causes, which must have existed in order to produce the result. Where that is the case, according to the law of marine insurance,

the last cause only must be looked to and the others rejected, although the result would not have been produced without them.." This approach is no longer followed.

[8] [1918] AC 350, at 369.

[9] id., at pp. 370-371.

[10] Clarke, M.A., The Law of Insurance Contracts (5th Edition, Informa, 2006), p. 785.

[11] [1997] 2 Lloyd's Rep. 440, at p. 458.

[12] Op.cit., §776.

[13] [1918] A.C. 350, at 365.

[14] 1942 A.C. 691

[15] It is to be noted that the term 'warlike operation' is no longer listed in modern marine insurance policies.

[16] 1942 A.C. 691, at p. 706. See also TM Noten BV v. Harding [1990] Lloyd's Rep. 283 at 286-7 (discussed infra)

[17] Chappel v Hart (1988) 195 CLR 232 as cited in The Law of Insurance Contracts by M.A. Clark (5th edition Informa, London, 2006).

[18] loc. cit., clause 4.5.

[19] See above, footnote number 7.

[20] (1890) 25 Q.B.D. 396.

[21] [1914] 3 K.B. 1121.

[22] Id., at p. 1129.

[23] [1918] AC 101, HL.

[24] id., at 111-114.

[25] See also the 2009 version of the Institute Cargo Clauses.

[26] Loc.cit., paragraph 1.1.

[27] Loc.cit., paragraph 1.2.

[28] Loc. Cit., paragraph 4.1.

[29] Loc. Cit., paragraph 5.1.

[30] Loc. Cit., paragraphs 6, 7.1 and 7.3.

[31] Loc. Cit., Clause 7.3.

[32] See The Cendor Mopu [2011] UKSC 5, at §57 per Lord Mance.

[33] [1982] 1 Lloyd's Rep. 369, at 381.

[34] See U.S. case-law cited in Clark, M.A., *The Law of Insurance Contracts* (5th Edition, Informa, London, 2006).

[35] [2011] EWHC 1520.

[36] [2012] EWHC 460 (Comm).

[37] Id., at §46.

[38] Ibid.

[39] See also Clause 24 of IVCH [1995]; see also clauses 32 and 33 of the International Hull Clauses (01/11/02).

[40] Emphasis added. A similar approach to causation has been used in the past in the JC 97/077 Computer Millennium Clause (Cargo): "In no case shall this insurance cover any loss, damage, expense or liability of whatever nature which might otherwise be recoverable under this insurance arising out of or in any way connected with, whether directly or indirectly, the use or operation of any computer, computer system, computer software, programme or process or any electronic system where any such loss, damage, expense or liability arises, whether directly or indirectly, as a consequence of (i) the

date change to the year 2000 or any other date change and/or (ii) any change or modification of or to any such computer, computer system, computer software, programme or process or any electronic system in relation to any such date change."

[41] 01/11/02.

[42] See Clark, M.A., The Law of Insurance Contracts (5th Edition, 2006, Informa), at p. 802 et seq.

[43] See ICC A (1/1/82).

[44] 1921 2 A.C. 41.

[45] id., at pp. 46-47.

[46] 1/12/82 (emphasis added).

[47] [1940] 67 Ll. L. Rep. 484

[48] (1940) 67 Ll. L. Rep. 484, at p. 507.This point is not affected by the appeal from the said judgment which is reported at [1941] 67 Ll. L. Rep. 484.

[49] [1985] 1 Lloyd's Rep. 264; [1987] 1 Lloyd's Rep. 32. See also: Sea Shore Marine v. Phoenix Assurance, The Vergina (Commercial Court, 16 May 2001), [2002] 1 Lloyd's Rep. 50.

[50] [1973] 2 Lloyd's Rep. 237.

[51] [1987] 2 Lloyd's Rep. 32 at 36.

[52] id. See also The Vergina [16 May 2001, Commercial Court]. See Gauci, G., Causation Problems in Maritime Insurance Law: The Vergina, 2001, Shipping & Transport Lawyer International, Vol. 3, Number 1, 14-17.

[53] See Gauci, G., Piracy and its Legal Problems: With Specific reference to the English law of Marine Insurance, 2010, JMLC Vol. 41, No. 4, October 2010, 541—560, at 551.

[54] [2011] UKSC 5.

[55] For the meaning of 'inherent vice, see Soya GmbH v. White [1983] 1 Lloyd's Rep. 122, at p. 126.

[56] Id., at §47.

[57] Loc.cit., §88.

[58] See also §2-16 of the said Plan.

[59] See Det Norske Veritas,, Commentary to the Norwegian Marine Insurance Plan 1996, Version 1999,1999.

[60] (1995 c. 21).

[61] Paragraph (1) of section 1 of the Law Reform (Contributory Negligence) Act 1945 provides: "Where any person suffers damage as a result of his own fault and partly of the fault of any other person or persons, a claim in respect of that damage shall not be defeated by reason of the fault of the person suffering the damage, but the damages recoverable in respect thereof shall be reduced to such extent as the court thinks just and equitable having regards to the claimant's share in the responsibility for the damage..".

[62] See Rogers W.V.H., Winfield and Jolowicz on Tort, Sweet & Maxwell, 17th Edition, London 2006, at §6-423.

[63] See Lunney and Oliphant, Tort Law, Text and Materials (OUP, 2010), p.301.

[64] Ibid. The effects of rule of last opportunity is there described as follows: "This enabled the claimant to recover notwithstanding his own negligence, if upon the occasion of the accident the defendant could have avoided the accident while the defendant could not."

[65] See British Columbia Electric Ry v Loach [1916] 1 A.C. 719. A similar rule was applicable in Roman Law. According to W.A. Hunter, Roman Law (4th Edition), Sweet and Maxwell 1903, pp. 246-7):"Even a person negligently causing an injury is relieved from blame if the damage is accomplished only by the concurrent negligence of the sufferer. Hence there was no remedy when the sufferer had the power to escape from danger, and did not exert himself to do so. He could only claim compensation when he either did not foresee the injury, or could not have helped himself if he had foreseen it. (D. 9, 2, 28, 1.)"

[66] Section 187(1)(a) provides: "Where, by the fault of two or more ships, damage or loss is caused to one or more of those ships, to their cargoes or freight, or to any property on board, the liability to make good the damage or loss shall be in proportion to the degree in which each vessel was in fault."

[67] Steele, J., Tort law – Text, Cases and Materials, 2nd edition OUP 2010, p. 276-7.

[68] [2011] UKSC 5..

[69] Institute Cargo Clauses A (1/1/1982)

[70] [[2009] 2 All ER (Comm) 795 at §33.

[71] [2009] 2 All ER (Comm) 795.

[72] Id., at §111.

[73] [2004] 2 C.L.C. 682.

[74] [2009] 2 C.L.C. 1056 at 1090-1091.

[75] [2011] UKSC 5.

[76] Id., at §, per Lord Saville at §44.

[77] Ibid.

[78] It is to be noted that section 40 (1) of the Marine Insurance Act 1906 provides that 'in a policy on goods or other moveables there is no implied warranty that the goods or moveables are seaworthy'. (See §41 of the Supreme Court judgment [2011] UKSC 5).

[79] See European Group Ltd v Chartis Insurance UK Ltd [2012] EWHC 1245 (QB).

[80] [1990] 2 Lloyd's Rep. 283.

[81] [2011] UKSC 5, at §63.

[82] [1990] 2 Lloyd's Rep. 283., at p. 288.

[83] Id., at p. 289.

[84] [QBD Commercial division (Lexis Library), 30/7/1996]. See also CA [1998] 2 Lloyd's Rep. 8.

[85] ibid. See also [1998] Lloyd's Rep. 8.

[86] 1973 S.C. (H.L.) 37.

[87] Id., at p. 56.

[88] [2002] UKHL 22.

[89] Id., at §168.

[90] Id., at §38-40.

[91] [2006] UKHL 20.

[92] Steele, J., Tort Law: Text, Cases and Materials, 2nd edition, OUP 2010, p. 245.

[93] [2006] UKHL 20, at §46.

[94] id., at §47. Lord Rodger in Barker v Corus (at §90) dissented from the majority decision on the grounds that he found that the desirability of throwing a lifeline to wrongdoers and their insurers was not an obvious one.

[95] Id., at §48.

[96] "3 Mesothelioma: Damages: (1) This section applies where: (a) a person ('the responsible person') has negligently or in breach of statutory duty caused or permitted another person ('the victim') to be exposed to asbestos, (b) the victim has contracted mesothelioma as a result of exposure to asbestos, (c) because of the nature of mesothelioma and the state of medical science, it is not possible to determine with certainty whether it was the exposure mentioned in paragraph (a) or another exposure which caused the victim to become ill, and (d) the responsible person is liable in tort, by virtue of the exposure mentioned in paragraph (a), in connection with damage caused to the victim by the disease (whether by reason of having materially increased a risk or for any other reason).(2) The responsible person shall be liable – (a) in respect of the whole damage caused to the victim by the disease (irrespective of whether the victim was also exposed to asbestos – (i) other than by the responsible person, whether or not in circumstances in which another person has liability in tort, or, (ii) by the responsible person in circumstances in which he has no liability in tort), and (b) jointly and severally with another liable person..." (emphasis added)."See also Sienkiewicz v. Griff (UK) Ltd [2011]UKSC 10.

[97] See, now, the Environmental Permitting (England and Wales) Regulations 2010/675.

[98] [1998] Env. L.R. 396.

[99] See, now, the Environmental Permitting (England and Wales) Regulations 2010/675.

In: Selected Issues in Maritime Law and Policy
Editor: Maximo Q. Mejia, Jr.
ISBN: 978-1-62618-508-1

Chapter 4

DIMENSIONS ON THE CONCEPT OF INHERENT VICE AS AN EXCLUDED PERIL IN MARINE INSURANCE

D. Rhidian Thomas*

Emeritus Professor of Maritime Law and Founder Director of the Institute of International and Trade Law, Swansea University, Swansea, UK

INTRODUCTION

The primary object of this contribution is to address the concept of inherent vice as an excluded peril in marine insurance and, in particular, to engage several aspects of the judicial development of the concept: namely, the association between unseaworthiness of insured cargo and inherent vice, and between defective packaging and inherent vice, and the ever-present question of causation. Interest in this particular area of marine insurance law has been heightened by the recent decision of the UK Supreme Court in *Global Process Systems Inc and Another v Syarikat Takaful Malaysia Berhad (The Cendor Mopu)* [1], the impact of which will be considered over the course of the following exposition.

Before proceeding to analyse these issues, it is first necessary to make a few introductory observations about the concept of inherent vice in the context of marine insurance.

Inherent Vice as an Excluded Peril

Loss proximately caused by inherent vice or nature of the subject-matter insured is invariably identified as an excluded peril in contemporary marine policies, as is also the case in relation to contracts for the carriage of goods by sea. [2]. Marine policies mainly provide protection against external perils which cause loss, not against causes of loss which emanate from within the insured subject-matter itself. This position has a long contractual history, which is reinforced by section 55(1) and (2)(c) of the Marine Insurance Act 1906, which provides,

* rhidianthomas@btinternet.com.

(1) Subject to the provisions of this Act, and unless the policy otherwise provides, the insurer is liable for any loss proximately caused by a peril insured against, but, subject as aforesaid, he is not liable for any loss which is not proximately caused by a peril insured against.

(2) In particular –

(a) …

(b) …

(c) Unless the policy otherwise provides, the insurer is not liable for…inherent vice or nature of the subject-matter insured…

The section indicates how an ordinary marine policy is to be construed; it does not introduce an implied statutory exclusion [3]. By the use of the phrase 'Unless the policy otherwise provides' it also indicates that by its express terms a marine policy may provide cover for losses caused by inherent vice or nature of the insured subject-matter [4]. Such a loss continues to be a fortuity and, therefore, may be insured by an appropriately worded policy [5]. This is a further indication that the exclusion, where it exists, does not arise as a question of law or public policy, but as a matter of contract.

The current standard contacting practice is revealed in the Institute Cargo Clauses (A) – (C), 01/01/2009, clause 4, the general exclusion clause, which provides –

In no case shall this insurance cover

…

4.4 loss damage or expense caused by inherent vice or nature of the subject matter insured

In an 'all risks' cargo policy, even in the absence of an express exclusion, the cover does not extend to loss or damaged caused by inherent vice or nature of the insured subject-matter [6]. This is not because of the absence of a fortuity; it is presumably because the fortuity emanates from within the insured subject-matter itself, rather than from an external source.

With regard to hull and machinery insurance the London market standard forms do not include a similar express contractual exclusion, with the matter consequently governed by section 55(2)(c). But the insurance does customarily cover loss or damage to the subject-matter insured caused by 'any latent defect in the machinery or hull but does not cover any of the costs of correcting the latent defect' [7]. It is probable that there will be circumstances when a latent defect in the hull or machinery will also fall within the words 'inherent vice or nature of the subject-matter', and in that event the standard hull policy may be considered as providing express cover for loss or damage caused by inherent vice or nature of the subject matter, but not for the inherent vice or defect itself.

As is the case with regard to excluded perils generally, the burden of proof is on the underwriter to prove that the loss in respect of which the claimant seeks an indemnity was proximately caused by inherent vice or nature of the insured subject matter [8].

The question of how inherent vice/nature is to be defined has provoked much debate. Despite the familiarity of the exclusion, its full ambit is not always understood: the concept is an evolving phenomenon which embraces much complexity, with its underpinning principles and parameters often ambiguous and, on occasions, contentious. It has already been observed that the source of the peril is both statutory and contractual, and that as an exclusion of liability it is incorporated into a range of different marine covers. Save in exceptional circumstances, it is highly probable that a uniform meaning will be attributed to the peril, whatever its legal source and contractual location, If there is to be any variation, it is likely to be in its application to particular cases, influenced by the nature, characteristics and condition of the insured goods, and the voyage embarked upon [9].

The question of causation occupies a pivotal position in marine insurance law generally, and the legal framework which has been developed over the course of the twentieth century applies equally to instances when inherent vice or nature is pleaded. Although this legal framework is now firmly established, the manner of its application continues to pose difficulties. The exercise is one of fact and degree, with the judgment of the trial judge or arbitrator usually conclusive [10].

To avoid monotonous repetition reference will be made henceforth to 'inherent vice' only and not to the customary wider form of words, 'inherent vice or nature of the subject-matter insured', unless the context requires otherwise. There is also little benefit to be obtained from submitting the full standard wording to close linguistic analysis: for present purposes the focus will be directed to what the words in their generality connote, namely loss arising from the inherent characteristics or intrinsic nature of the insured subject-matter [11].

The Basic Concept

A definition of inherent vice is not proffered in the MIA 1906, but in broad terms it is understood to relate to a peril arising from the internal nature or condition of the subject-matter insured, as distinct from external perils which adversely impact on an insured subject-matter, such as fire or earthquakes or perils of the seas [12]. Inherent vice, in a sense, refers to self inflicted damage or loss, the insured subject matter is the cause of the damage or loss suffered by it. Obvious examples include decay, corruption, decomposition, perishing and spontaneous combustion of the subject-matter [13]. A less obvious example arises from its application to the carriage of live animals, where harm is caused to the animal by its inability to cope with the ordinary conditions of the voyage and takes fright [14]. Beyond listing examples, there is an underpinning principle, namely that the peril derives from the natural behaviour or condition or nature of the insured subject-matter, in the circumstances of its transportation. It is not, however, a necessary precondition that the subject-matter must be in any way defective [15].

There is a predisposition to think of inherent vice as applicable to the insurance of cargo only, but it is not so restricted. It may equally apply to the insurance of ships [16], though in this regard the concept is closely allied to other concepts such as unseaworthiness, debility and latent defect, and where the dividing line is to be drawn may not always be easy to identify [17].

The core idea, as it applies to goods, was expressed by Byles J in *Koebel v Saunders* [18] as -

> A loss of goods which perish by some inherent vice or weakness, as in the case of tender animals unfit to bear the agitation of the sea, gun-cotton, or the like, or in more ordinary instances of fruit, flour, or rice, which are liable to heat or perish on the voyage...

In the same case Willes J explained inherent vice as 'nothing more than the development of the cargo's inherent characteristics'. [19]

More recently in *Soya Mainz Kommanditgesellschaft v White* [20], Lord Diplock was of the opinion that inherent vice

> ...means the risk of deterioration of the goods shipped as a result of their natural behaviour in the ordinary course of the contemplated voyage without the intervention of any fortuitous external accident or casualty [21].

The natural behaviour of the insured subject-matter may manifest itself in many and various ways, according to the nature of the subject-matter and the voyage undertaken, but in all instances what ultimately is of crucial importance is the internal or inherent or intrinsic character of the peril, and also its causal significance [22]. The cargo must have possessed some inherent tendency on shipment which has manifested itself under ordinary conditions of carriage. The critical questions arising out of Lord Diplock's definition have centred on the meaning of 'ordinary course of the contemplated voyage' and 'without the intervention of any fortuitous external accident or casualty'. The latter will be returned to in the later discussion of causation; as for the former, it is now clear that it does not serve to introduce any external precondition into the definition of inherent vice, such as conditions relating to sea and weather [23].

It is now also appreciated that the internal nature, condition or process that causes the loss need not be universally associated with the insured subject-matter, in the sense that the loss would have manifested itself in all circumstances and conditions. It continues to be a case of inherent vice notwithstanding that the internal process of destruction or diminution was initiated or expedited by the precise condition of the goods when shipped and/or the conditions appertaining to the transportation of the goods. This proposition was accepted by Donaldson LJ in *Soya v White* [24] who recognised that external circumstances might influence and affect the natural behaviour of insured property. On the facts of the case, the external conditions related to the conditions in which insured soya bean with a moisture content of between 12% and 13% had been carried [25]. Another obvious example of the validity of this proposition is when animals take fright in the course of transit by sea and injure themselves, which usually occurs in response to the impact of ordinary sea conditions on the carrying vessel [26].

In The Cendor MOPU [27] Lord Mance articulated the principle in the following terms-

> ...inherent vice can embrace a disposition to injury by a train of events that is, firstly, not purely internal and, secondly, depends upon a combination of external events that [are] foreseeable, but by no means certain to occur [28]

Support for this principle is to be found in *T M Noten BV v Harding* [29], a case which concerned the insurance of leather gloves on ICC(A), all risks, terms. The damage to the gloves had been caused because the gloves had been shipped wet and in that condition they deteriorated as a result of their natural behaviour in the ordinary course of the voyage [30]. The decision of the British Columbia Court of Appeal in *Nelson Marketing International Inc v Royal and Sun Alliance Insurance Co of Canada* [31] follows the same approach.

Laminated truck flooring, the insured subject matter, had been shipped with a high moisture content and the subsequent damage suffered by it was attributable to its nature as shipped.

Although this approach to the concept of inherent vice has received wide judicial endorsement [32], it carries within it the seeds of potential difficulties which have yet to be confronted in the authorities. It requires a line to be drawn between external or ambient conditions which in one way or another contribute to the emergence of inherent vice and external or ambient conditions which amount to an independent contributing cause of loss, which could also be identified as the proximate cause of the loss.

The contextual character of inherent vice also serves to reinforce the principle that it does not connote inevitable loss [33]. According to the circumstances, it might be that the consequences are inevitable, but this is not an essential precondition. In most circumstances the consequences are likely to be contingent.

Inherent vice is also to be distinguished from wear and tear and other analogous perils, though drawing the line between them may again be troublesome [34].

Inherent Vice and Fitness of Goods for Carriage

In the recent development of the law an association emerged between inherent vice and fitness of insured goods to withstand the ordinary incidents of the voyage to be embarked upon. Goods which were unfit in this sense and which were lost or damaged in transit were held to have suffered detrimentally by virtue of inherent vice. One effect of this development was to bring the law of marine insurance and the law of carriage of goods by sea into alignment, as to the meaning of inherent vice [35].

This alignment was accepted in the Court of Appeal by Donaldson LJ in *Soya Mainz Kommanditgesellschaft v White* [36], who observed -

> It seems to me to be both right and natural that the concept should be treated similarly in the context of both carriage by sea and marine insurance [37].

Under the law relating to carriage of goods by sea inherent vice relates to 'the unfitness of the goods to withstand the ordinary incidence of the voyage, given the degree of care which the shipowner is required by the contract to exercise in relation to the goods' [38].

Donaldson LJ articulated the proposition, as it applied to marine insurance, in the following terms [39]-

> …a loss is proximately caused by inherent vice if the natural behaviour of the goods is such that they suffer a loss in the circumstances in which they are expected to be carried

Donaldson LJ emphasised further that the test of unfitness was to be applied in the context of the particular voyage on which the goods were being conveyed; it did not apply more widely to any normal voyage of similar duration [40]. An essential first step was, therefore, to determine precisely the reasonably foreseeable conditions likely to be encountered on the carrying voyage, which the insured was presumed to know or to have the means of ascertaining.

This approach was subsequently followed by Moore-Bick J in *Mayban General Insurance Bhd v Alstom Power Plants Ltd* [41], who expressed the principle in the following words [42] –

> Goods tendered for shipment must…be capable of withstanding the forces that they can ordinarily be expected to encounter in the course of the voyage and these may vary greatly depending on the route and the time of year… If…the conditions encountered by the vessel were no more severe than could reasonably have been expected, the conclusion must be that the real cause of the loss was the inherent inability of the goods to withstand the ordinary incidents of the voyage.

On the facts of the case a transformer was insured under a project policy which covered materials and equipment carried as marine cargo to the project site on 'all risks' terms, excluding loss caused by inherent vice or nature of the subject-matter. It was held that heavy seas damage to the transformer, transported in a container, encountered in the Western Approaches on a voyage leg from Rotterdam to Malaysia, had been caused by inherent vice or nature of the subject-matter, because of the packed transformer's inability to withstand the ordinary incidents of the voyage. The seas encountered were very severe with waves in excess of six metres and wind force 8 to 10 recorded, which caused the vessel to roll and pitch violently. Nonetheless, the judge held that the conditions encountered were no more serious than could reasonably have been expected and that consequently the real cause of the loss was inherent vice.

This was, even at first sight, a harsh and contentious decision which raised serious concerns about the direction in which the concept of inherent vice was being judicially developed. It probably surprised the market and raised serious questions about the value of cargo insurance on 'all risks' terms, which was widely assumed to cover rough seas damage. The implication of the decision was that the cover provided was limited to loss caused by seas that were exceptional, extraordinary and unforeseeable [43].

The debate raised by this line of authority was reopened and ultimately settled by the Supreme Court in *The Cendor MOPU* [44], itself an unusual and significant case. It was concerned with the insurance of a jack-up oil rig to be transported from Texas to Malaysia. The rig was towed on a barge by a tug on the terms of a charter party and insured for the period from the commencement of loading until the completion of discharge on 'all risks' terms, under an insurance which incorporated Institute Cargo Clauses A, 1/1/1982, with 'inherent vice and nature of the subject-matter' an excluded peril. The rig was transported with its three legs in place and elevated in the air above the deck of the barge. On the second part of the voyage from Cape Town to Malaysia, when off Durban, the three legs were lost in quick succession. During the course of the preceding voyage across the Atlantic from Galveston to Cape Town, the legs had developed cracks and at the time of the actual loss, when the sea was significantly rougher, further stresses had been placed on the legs by the impact on the carrying barge made by the height and direction of the prevailing waves. Once the first leg had fractured and crashed into the sea, this increased the stresses on the remaining two legs, which were then quickly lost.

The resulting legal dispute centred on the proximate cause of the loss, was it the inherent weak nature of the legs of the rig or perils of the sea, namely the impact of the sea conditions encountered at the time of the loss? Only if it were the latter was the loss insured under the all risks policy. This raised, predominantly, a question of fact. At first instance the judge concluded that "...a developed crack would not, on its own, have been sufficient to cause one of the legs to come off. That required in addition a 'leg-breaking' or 'final straw' stress that finally fractured the weakened steel." [45]. This factual conclusion, which was not challenged in the subsequent appeals, was to prove crucial in the later history of the litigation.

At first instance the judge, addressing the question of causation, held that the loss had been caused by inherent vice of the subject-matter within the meaning of the policy. Following the legal principle laid down in *The Mayban*, the judge held that the legs were not capable of withstanding the normal incidents of the insured voyage, including the weather reasonably to be expected, and on the facts this inherent vice was the proximate cause of the loss. The Court of Appeal took a different view of the proximate cause, identifying it to be the 'leg-breaking wave', which was a peril of the sea [46]. The Court circumvented the principle in *The Mayban* by defining it more narrowly, being of the opinion that it applied only when by common understanding the loss "would be bound to occur as the ordinary incidents of any normal voyage of the kind undertaken" [47]

The Supreme Court agreed with the conclusion of the Court of Appeal but reasoned matters differently. The Court declared *The Mayban* to have been wrongly decided and also rejected the definition of inherent vice proffered by Donaldson LJ in *Soya v White* [48], adding that there was no indication in the subsequent speech of Lord Diplock in the House of Lords that he was in agreement with that definition. The approach adopted in *The Mayban* was also considered not to be supported by authority and Lord Saville went on to express the opinion that "Such a definition pays scant regard as to how and in what circumstances the loss occurred" [49]

A material influence on the reasoning of the Supreme Court was the belief that the acceptance of the definition of inherent vice in *The Mayban* would materially diminish the efficacy of traditional cargo insurance. The cover would extend only to perils of the seas which were exceptional, unforeseen or unforeseeable, and not include perils of the seas which, objectively assessed, amounted to ordinary and foreseeable incidents of the contemplated voyage. This distinction also was not recognised in the concept of perils of the seas, with it clearly established that exceptional sea conditions was not *sine qua non*. A loss might be proximately caused by perils of the seas notwithstanding that the sea conditions were within the range which could reasonably have been anticipated [50].

The approach in *The Mayban* was also viewed as being difficult to reconcile with the position adopted in the Marine Insurance Act 1906 to the impact of unseaworthiness on cover, particularly sections 39 and 40, and also with how this aspect of cover was addressed in practice. In particular, section 40(1) of the 1906 Act, disclaims the existence of an implied warranty that insured goods are seaworthy [51]. The subsection does not further provide a definition of seaworthiness, but presumable the definition provided in section 39(4), in connection with voyage and time policies on ships, applies, thereby indicating that there is no implied warranty that insured goods shall be reasonably fit in all respects to encounter the ordinary perils of the seas of the adventure insured [52] The natural implication of the subsection is that because goods are not reasonably fit in this sense, it does not necessarily deprive the assured of cover under the policy.

The conclusion of the Supreme Court was that *The Mayban* had attributed to inherent vice too wide a meaning and it had unjustifiably narrowed the meaning of perils of the seas. The definition of inherent vice formulated by Lord Diplock was approved [53], with the explanatory rider that the words 'in the ordinary course of the contemplated voyage' did not embrace weather conditions foreseeable on the carrying voyage, but rather drew a contrast with a voyage on which an external accident or casualty occurred [54]. Where such an accident or casualty occurred, which could amount to an event falling within the definition of perils of the seas, it became a factual question of causation in deciding which peril had caused the loss. On the facts of the case, the Supreme Court agreed with the Court of Appeal that the foreseeable sea conditions off Durban, which were properly characterised as a peril of the sea, were the cause of the loss. The ultimate leg-breaking stress was a fortuity caused by a peril of the sea.

Extension of Inherent Vice to Packaging

Beyond the insured goods, it has been judicially affirmed that the concept of inherent vice extends to any packaging that has been utilised, so that a defect or deficiency of the packaging may constitute inherent vice.

Notwithstanding that the early authorities on this question are far from conclusive [55], Donaldson LJ in the Court of Appeal in *Soya Mainz Kommanditgesellschaft v White* [56] gave unqualified approval to the principle. He expressed his reasoning, disagreeing with the contrary opinion expressed in the then current edition of Arnould [57], in the following words [58] –

> I also disagree with their view that to regard the unfitness of the packing of goods as constituting inherent vice is an unjustifiable extension of the concept.
>
> The subject matter of the insurance includes the materials in which the goods are packed. A bagged cargo is wholly different from a bulk cargo, and it would be absurd to contend that where a bagged cargo ends the voyage as a bulk cargo, the subject matter has suffered no loss.

In *The Mayban* [59], Moore-Bick J, accepted the proposition, again without reservation, saying [60]

> ...inadequate packing, where packing is required to withstand the ordinary incidents of the voyage, can properly be regarded as an aspect of inherent vice. The insurer is entitled to assume that the goods as presented for shipment are packed in a way that will enable them to withstand the ordinary incidents of the carriage and, unless he expressly agrees otherwise, does not accept the risk of loss caused by inadequate packing. For some kinds of goods packing may extend to bracing necessary to prevent the movement of internal parts.

This reasoning of Donaldson LJ is relevant to the identification of the subject-matter insured, so determining what has been insured [61], but it is far from convincing with regard to the wider question of the relationship between deficient packaging and inherent vice. Of course, both the goods and packaging may have their respective values, sufficient to make the insured wish to insure both, which may be done separately or in combination, invariably the latter. Even when this is the case, it will rarely be done expressly, and difficult question of construction may arise, when the subject matter has been identified generally, in determining whether the cover extends to include the packaging. When it has been so extended, the goods and packaging are subject to the same insurance terms and conditions, but, nonetheless, they retain their separate identities. If because of some internal condition or characteristic or frailty the packing fails and beyond the packing itself loss or damage results to the goods, it seems fanciful to attribute the loss to inherent vice of the compounded entirety.

The example adopted by Donaldson LJ is also troublesome. Viewed logically the loss has been directly caused by bad packing (on the assumption that an absolute standard of care applies) and not the internal nature or characteristic or condition of the goods. This would appear also to be the common sense view.

The reasoning of Moore-Bick J must also be considered vulnerable in view of the facts that the Supreme Court disapproved of the approach adopted by the judge to the concept of inherent vice [62].

The separateness of packaging is in many contemporary cargo policies recognised by the identification of bad packaging as a conditional exclusion from cover [63]. This is the case in the Institute Cargo Clauses, (A) – (C) (1/1/09), cls.4 and 4.3, which state –

> In no case shall this insurance cover ...
>
> Loss damage or expense caused by insufficiency or unsuitability of packing or preparation of the subject-matter insured to withstand the ordinary incidents of the insured transit where such packing or preparation is carried out by the Assured or their employees or prior to the attachment of this insurance (for the purpose of these Clauses "packing" shall be deemed to include stowage in a container and "employees" shall not include independent contractors)

The exclusion is of a conditional and limited nature, and extends to the packing of containers. It is likely to be resorted to as the first line of defence by insurers when loss or damage to cargo can be attributed to bad packing. The potential relevance of this exclusion was recognised by Moore-Bick J in The *Mayban* [64], but the judge remained of the opinion (which would probably now be recognised as erroneous) that " inadequate packing, where packing is required to enable the goods to withstand the ordinary incidents of the voyage, can properly be regarded as an aspect of inherent vice" [65].

The exclusionary approach represents a much more logical, appropriate and sensible approach to the problem of bad packing, and it would be rare for the exclusion not to be incorporated into a cargo policy. It avoids the conceptual problems associated with the extension of the concept of inherent vice, and it is doubtful if it places insurers in a less advantageous position. It provides an efficient answer to the problem which Donaldson LJ identified when a bagged cargo is delivered as bulk cargo because the bags lacked the requisite sturdiness, when the loss suffered will relate to the cost of re-bagging the cargo [66].

The reservation which the editors of Arnould expressed in the 15th edition does not appear in subsequent editions [67]. Presumably this means that they now accept the premise, or at least feel duty bound to follow the recent judicial dicta. Nonetheless, it is suggested that there continues to exist good reason to question the validity of the extension of inherent vice into the realm of packaging on both logical and practical grounds. It will recalled from the earlier discussion of the relation between inherent vice and unseaworthiness of cargo, that the

Supreme Court in *The Cendor MOPU* disapproved of Donaldson LJ's judgment to the extent it was relevant to that issue and also the decision in *The Mayban* [68]. It may be that the disapproval will also spread to the dicta in both cases relating to the relation between inherent vice and bad packing.

CAUSATION

Whether or not a particular loss is covered by a policy will generally depend on ascertaining the cause of the loss. It is, therefore, not sufficient merely to establish an insured peril, it must be shown that loss has been caused by an insured peril, with the burden of proof on the claimant. The same is true when an excluded peril, such as inherent vice, is pleaded as a defence by an insurer: beyond establishing the existence of inherent vice, the burden of proof is on the insurer to establish that the particular loss was caused by the inherent vice [69]. It follows that in the present context the reference to inherent vice refers to a peril by which loss is caused, and not to the loss implicit in the inherent vice itself [70].

The general position of the law relating to liability and causation is set out in section 55(1) of the Marine Insurance Act 1906, which provides –

> Subject to the provisions of this Act, and unless the policy otherwise provides, the insurer is liable for any loss proximately caused by a peril insured against, but, subject to the aforesaid, he is not liable for any loss which is not proximately caused by a peril insured against

Since the decision of the House of Lords in *Leyland Shipping Co Ltd v Norwich Union Fire Insurance Society Ltd* [71], the test of proximate cause has been interpreted to mean proximate in efficiency, connoting the dominant or principal or real cause. It does not necessarily mean the last contributing cause in point of time, which had been the favoured test in the period preceding the 1906 Act [72]. It is now also clearly established that the test is to be applied to the facts of individual cases by "applying the common sense of a business or seafaring man"; a person whom Bingham L J characterised as 'the hypothetical oracle' [73].

This very practical approach to what is predominantly a question of fact has not necessarily succeeded in making the exercise any more certain. Its effect is to arrogate the question of causation to the virtually unchallengeable judgment of judges and arbitrators, which does not necessarily lead to greater uncertainty [74]. Questions relating to the proximate cause of an insured loss can raise very tricky issues of fact, with the judicial instinct far from being uniformly harmonious, as the authorities well illustrate.

The facts in *Noten v Harding* [75] illustrate as effectively as any the nature of the potential factual difficulties. Insured leather gloves were wrapped and packed in cardboard boxes which were stuffed into standard closed-top box containers. The gloves were shipped wet because they had absorbed moisture from the humid atmosphere of Calcutta, the place of shipment, and once stuffed in the container they quickly equilibrated with the atmosphere in the container. The consignment was discharged at Rotterdam where the temperature was much cooler, which caused the outside of the container to cool, so that there was a significant difference in temperature between the outside and inside of the container. This situation served to generate convection currents within the container, with warm air rising from the stow and circulating around the container. As it did so, the warm air carried moisture from the gloves which condensed on the roof of the container, and the droplets of water which so formed fell on to the boxes stowed below. This caused the boxes and wrappings to become sodden and collapsed, the gloves to become mouldy and mildewed, and they also stank.

What was the proximate cause of the damage to the gloves? Both parties agreed that the gloves had been shipped wet and that this was the source of the moisture. The insurers contended that the loss had been caused by inherent vice. On the other hand, the assured contended that the causal effect of the moisture in the gloves had been broken by the process of convection and condensation within the container, which caused droplets of water to form on the roof of the container, which fell down on the stow and were the actual cause of the damage. This, it was argued, represented an independent and separate cause of loss which was external to the boxes of gloves.

At first instance the judge accepted the contention of the assured [76], but it was rejected on appeal. The Court of Appeal concluded that the loss had been effectively caused by the fact that the gloves had been shipped wet, and accordingly the defence of inherent vice prevailed and the policy was not obliged to pay. This conclusion the appellate court considered to represent the commonsense approach to the facts. In advocating this approach, Bingham LJ (as he then was) said [77] -

> The damage was caused because the goods were shipped wet…I regard it as immaterial that the moisture travelled round the container before doing the damage complained of.

And as for the contention of the assured, the Lord Justice observed,

> He would [i.e. the hypothetical oracle]…regard the distinction based on the intermediate migration of moisture to and condensation of moisture on the roof of the container as owing more to the subtlety of the legal mind than to the common sense of the mercantile [78].

A similar factual circumstance arose in the Canadian case, *Nelson Marketing International Inc v Royal and Sun Alliance Insurance Co of Canada* [79]. Laminated wood flooring had absorbed moisture while waiting shipment in Malaysia and consequently was shipped wet. In the course of the voyage the flooring was exposed to heat which caused moisture to escape from the wood and condense on its surface, under the plastic covering in which it was packed. The flooring had been insured under an 'all risks' policy and a claim made under it for wet damage. At first instance the claim was successful, the judge reasoning that although the moisture emanated from within the laminated wood flooring, the cause of the damage was the external environmental conditions in the holds of the vessel. An appeal, in which the *Noten* case was considered, was successful, with the deterioration attributed to the inherent nature of the insured goods. There had been no external fortuitous occurrence, "the cargo having simply succumbed to the ordinary incidents of the voyage because of the cargo's inherent nature or susceptibility" [80]

A further question arises as to the relation of inherent vice to other proximate causes. It is, of course, possible for there to be concurrent proximate causes of an insured loss, and in response to this possibility several prima facie rules of construction have been developed.

One well established rule provides that where there are two proximate causes, one of which is covered by the policy and the other is specifically excepted, the policy does not pay [81]. This rule is of clear potential relevance to the present discussion where inherent vice is being analysed as an excepted peril [82], and the question arises whether it continues to apply.

The decision of the Supreme Court in *The Cendor MOPU [83]* indicates that the general approach is modified where one concurrent proximate cause is inherent vice. It is said that the root of this qualification is to be found in the definition of inherent vice formulated by Lord Diplock in *Soya v White* [84], which has been previously considered [85], and which concludes with the qualification '*without the intervention of any fortuitous external accident or casualty'*. It is widely assumed that Lord Diplock had 'perils of the seas' immediately to mind when introducing this qualification, but there is no reason to believe that the qualification is so limited, and that it may extending to any external peril[86].

The phrase is construed as formulating the proposition that inherent vice, as an excepted peril, is only available when it is the sole proximate cause of the loss, with the necessary implication that once there exists a concurrent insured peril which is also causative, inherent vice ceases to be available and the concurrent causative peril is identified as the proximate cause. This conclusion appears to be arrived at as an incident of the definition of inherent vice, and not as the product of a factual judgment based on the weight of evidence [87]. Where there is also present an external proximate cause, there can be no pleading of inherent vice. Whether inherent vice is the sole cause is to be judged against the backdrop of the other insured perils identified in the policy; where there is another but uninsured peril, inherent vice remains the sole cause [88]. The clear implication of this line of reasoning is that inherent vice cannot exist as a concurrent proximate cause.

All three judges of the Supreme Court who delivered detailed judgments appear to support the legal analysis outlined above [89], viewing Lord Diplock's definition of inherent vice as consistent with the authorities and the scheme of the 1906 Act. The position is made clearest in the speech of Lord Mance [90] –

> …it is difficult to find in it any place for the weighing exercise that is suggested by the Court of Appeal's approach in The Miss Jay Jay…there is no apparent limitation in Lord Diplock's qualification "without the intervention of any fortuitous external accident or casualty" – in other words, on the face of it, anything that would otherwise count as a fortuitous external accident or casualty will suffice to prevent the loss being attributed to inherent vice…On this basis, it would only be if the loss or damage could be said to be due to uneventful wear and tear (or debility) in the prevailing weather conditions or to inherent characteristics of the hull or cargo not involving any fortuitous external accident or casualty that insurers would have a defence.

The situation which arose in *The Cendor MOPU* was ultimately perceived by the Supreme Court as raising a question of causation: was the loss caused by the weakness of the rig's legs or perils of the seas? In favouring the latter, the claim of inherent vice to be regarded as the proximate cause was erased as a question of definition, it was no longer a question of weighing the evidence and arriving at a conclusion of fact [91]. But even if the traditional position prevailed, Lord Saville was of the opinion that it would have been exceptionally difficulty to identify inherent vice as a concurrent proximate cause [92]

Beyond the immediate issue relating to inherent vice, the Supreme Court affirmed the general rule of construction that when loss has been caused by both an insured peril and an excluded peril under the policy, the exclusion applies and the insurers are not obliged to pay. This rule has been affirmed in judicial dicta in the lower courts on many occasions [93], but interestingly Lord Mance left open the applicability of the rule to the facts of a case such as those before the Court where there are two concurrent causes arising independently of each other but combining to cause loss [94].

CONCLUSION

The analysis undertaken in this contribution to the judicial interpretation of the concept of inherent vice is typical of the approach associated with the most common category of disputes arising under marine policies, namely those relating to cover. Disputes relating to fundamental doctrine and principles are far from exhausted but are many times fewer. Disputes relating to cover are, in their essence, about the proper construction of policy wordings; they are about the meaning of words in their commercial context and against the backdrop of market practice. The language of marine insurance is rich and colourful, and to most, apart from the cognoscente, often puzzling and mysterious. Many of the words have been familiar in the dealings of the market for many centuries but there exists no inevitable correlation between longevity and comprehensibility.

Nonetheless, whatever the nature of the difficulties, a proper understanding of the meaning of the words which constitute the lexicon of marine insurance law and practice is an essential precondition to an understanding of the cover provided by marine policies.

REFERENCES

[1] [2011] UKSC 5; [2011] 1 Lloyd's Rep 560.
[2] eg Hague and Hague Visby Rules art 4(2)(m).
[3] The Cendor MOPU, above, per Lord Clarke at p.587, para 134; Bennett [2007] LMCLQ 315.
[4] Soya Mainz Kommanditgesellschaft v White [1983] 1 Lloyd's Rep 122(HL); European Group Ltd and Others v Chartis Insurance UK Ltd [2012] EWHC 1245(Comm), [2012] Lloyd's Rep IR 603.
[5] infra, under the title, 'The basic concept'.
[6] British and Foreign Marine Ins Co Ltd v Gaunt [1921] 2 AC 41, 57, per Lord Sumner; Mayban General Insurance Bhd v Alstom Power Plants Ltd [2004] 2 Lloyd's Rep 609, 611, per Moore-Bick J.
[7] e.g. International Hull Clauses 2003, clause 2.2.2.
[8] The Cendor MOPU, supra, per Lord Saville, p564 [20].
[9] The Cendor MOPU, supra, per Lord Mance, p.578 [85].
[10] infra, under the title 'Causation'.
[11] The Cendor MOPU, above, per Lord Mance at p.569 [51]; Lord Clarke at p.585 [122].

[12] The Cendor MOPU [2010] 1 Lloyd's Rep 243,264, Carnwarth LJ in the Court of Appeal perceived inherent vice ' to be something inherent in the subject insured, as opposed to the impact of external factors…', citing Arnould's Treatise on the Law of Marine Insurance and Average, 2nd ed (1857) Vol. II, pp 782 and 783. See also The Cendor MOPU, supra, p. 585 [113], per Lord Clarke.

[13] In Soya Mainz Kommanditgesellschaft v White [1982] 1 Lloyd's Rep 136(CA), spontaneous combustion was regarded as a classical example of inherent vice. See also, Boyd v Dubois (1811) 3 Camp 133, where reference is made to cargo with a tendency to 'effervesce and generate fire which consumed it'.

[14] Koebel v Saunders (1864) 17 CBNS (NC) 71; The Cendor MOPU, above, per Lord Mance p.571[60]. Contrast Lawrence v Aberdein (1821) 5 B and Ald 107; Gabay v Lloyd (1825) 3 B and C 793.

[15] T M Noten BV v Harding [1990] 2 Lloyd's Rep 283, 287, Bingham LJ.

[16] The Cendor MOPU, supra, per Lord Mance pp 576-577 [78] and [81].

[17] The Cendor MOPU, supra; J J Lloyd Instruments Ltd v Northern Star Insurance Co Ltd (The Miss Jay Jay) [1987] 1 Lloyd's Rep 32. See also n.7.

[18] (1864) CBNS (NC) 71, 79.

[19] ibid p. 78.

[20] [1983] 1 Lloyd's Rep 122.

[21] ibid p. 126.

[22] infra, under the title 'Causation'.

[23] The Cendor MOPU supra. See also infra, under the title, 'Inherent vice and fitness of goods for carriage'.

[24] [1982] 1 Lloyd's Rep 136 (CA),

[25] ibid p.150.

[26] supra n.14.

[27] supra n. 1.

[28] p.571 [63]. This principle is a deduction from the decision in T M Noten BV v Harding [1990] 2 Lloyd's Rep 283 (CA), see infra n. 29.

[29] [1990] 2 Lloyd's Rep 283 (CA).

[30] ibid p.289, per Bingham LJ. See also infra n.71 et seq.

[31] (2006) 57 BCLR(4th) 27. See also infra n.75 et seq.

[32] eg, Whiting v New Zealand Insurance Co Ltd (1932) 44 Ll.L.R.179, 180, per Roche J, 'Moist atmosphere is not an accident or incident that is covered. It is more or less a natural test or incident which the goods have to suffer and which the underwriter has not insured against'. Also, The Cendor MOPU, supra, Court of Appeal, per Waller LJ [56]; Supreme Court, supra, per Lord Clarke, p.583 [114]; T M Noten BV v Harding [1990] 2 Lloyd's Rep 283 (CA), [70] per Carnworth LJ.

[33] The Cendor MOPU supra, per Lord Mance at p.568 [51], 'By inherent vice, insurers do not mean some characteristic of the rig which was bound to lead to the loss of the legs. Inevitability is not the test of inherent vice…' Also, Soya v White [1982] 1 Lloyd's Rep 135, 150, per Donaldson LJ.

[34] As illustrated by the Cendor MOPU, supra, where the Court of Appeal and Supreme Court were of the opinion that the cracking in the legs, prior to the impact of the leg-breaking wave, amounted to wear and tear and, therefore, would not have been covered by the insurance.

[35] cf. Scrutton on Charterparties (20th edn, 1996) article 111.
[36] [1982] 1 Lloyd's Rep 136.
[37] ibid p. 149. Donaldson LJ disagreed with a statement to the contrary in Arnould, 15th edn, para. 762, note 22.
[38] Scrutton on Charterparties (20th edn 1996) article 111, notes 31 and 32.
[39] ibid p. 150. It is possible to take some support for this proposition from British and Foreign Marine Ins Co Ltd v Gaunt [1921] 2 AC 41.
[40] ibid pp.150 – 151.
[41] [2004] 2 Lloyd's Rep 609.
[42] ibid p.614, para 21. Some support for this principle may also be derived from N E Neter and Co Ltd v Licenses and General Insurance Co Ltd [1944] 1 All ER 341, 343, per Tucker J.
[43] Bennett [2007] LMCLQ 315.
[44] supra n.1.
[45] [2009] 2 Lloyd's Rep 72, 88 [87].
[46] [2010] 1 Lloyd's Rep 243, 262-3 [64] (CA).
[47] ibid p.262 [62].
[48] supra n.39.
[49] supra p.565, [27].
[50] J J Lloyd Instruments Ltd v Northern Star Insurance Co Ltd (The Miss Jay Jay) [1985] 1 Lloyd's Rep 264, 271, per Mustill J (first instance).
[51] section 40(1) provides – 'In a policy on goods or other moveables there is no implied warranty that the goods or moveables are seaworthy'.
[52] cf. E D Sassoon and Co v Western Assurance Co [1912] AC 561; also The Cendor MOPU, per Lord Saville, p. 567 [41].
[53] supra n 21.
[54] The Cendor MOPU, per Lord Mance pp.576 – 577 [80] and [81]; also Lord Saville, p.567 [45], "…what Lord Diplock was saying…was that where goods deteriorated, not because they had been subjected to some external fortuitous accident or casualty, but because of their natural behaviour in the ordinary course of the voyage, then such deterioration amounted to inherent vice or nature of the subject matter insured".
[55] The early authorities which offer support for this proposition are not unassailable because in them the claims failed, in the first place, by virtue of the loss not being, covered, Berk v Styles [1956] 1 QB 180; [1955] 2 Lloyd's Rep 382; Gee and Garnham Ltd v Whittall [1955] 2 Lloyd's Rep 562; and, secondly, because of the way the risk was defined, Traders and General Insurance Association v Bankers and general Insurance Co. (1921) 9 Ll. L.Rep 223.
[56] [1982] 1 Lloyd's Rep 136(CA).
[57] 15th edn, para 762.
[58] ibid p.149 -150.
[59] [2004] 2 Lloyd's Rep 609.
[60] ibid p.614.
[61] With regard to cargo insurance nice questions may arise whether the insurance also covers packaging, see Brown v Fleming (1902) 7 Com Cas 245, F.W.Berk and Co Ltd v Style [1956] 1 Q.B. 180, [1955] 2 Lloyd's Rep 382.
[62] supra

[63] e.g. Cargo Insurance Policy of Antwerp, 20.4.2004, article 11.2.4. (PE 100).

[64] supra p.614 [19].

[65] ibid.

[66] cf. European Group Ltd and Others v Chartis Insurance UK Ltd [2012] EWHC 1245(Comm); [2012] Lloyd's Rep IR 603.

[67] There have been two subsequent editions, with the17th published in 2008.

[68] supra n.46.

[69] The Cendor MOPU, supra, where it was common ground that the burden of proof was on the defendant insurers.

[70] Soya Mainz Kommanditgesellschaft v White [1983] 1 Lloyd's Rep 122,126, per Lord Diplock.

[71] [1918] AC 350.

[72] Thompson v Hopper (1856) 6 El and Bl 172; (1856) 6 El and Bl 937; Dudgeon v Pembroke (1877) 2 App Cas 284.

[73] T M Noten BV v Harding [1990] Lloyd's Rep 283, 286-7, Bingham LJ.

[74] The Cendor MOPU, supra, p.568 [49] per Lord Mance, 'From that moment, the proximate cause became a matter of judgment and less easy to identify with certainty',

[75] [1989] 2 Lloyd's Rep 527, [1990] 1 Lloyd's Rep 283 (CA).

[76] [1989] 2 Lloyd's Rep 527 (Phillips J).

[77] ibid p.288.

[78] ibid p.287.

[79] (2006) 57 BCLR(4th) 27.

[80] ibid per Lowry JA, para 13.

[81] P.Samuel and Co Ltd v Dumas [1924] AC 431, 467; Wayne Tank and Pump Co Ltd [1974] QB 57, 75; J J Lloyd Instruments Ltd v Northern Star Insurance Co Ltd, The Miss Jay Jay [1987] 1 Lloyd's Rep 32, 40; Midland Mainline Ltd v Eagle Star Insurance Co Ltd [2004] 2 Lloyd's Rep 604.

[82] J J Lloyd Instruments Ltd v Northern Star Insurance Co Ltd, The Miss Jay Jay [1985] 1 Lloyd's Rep 264, [1987] 1 Lloyd's Rep 32 (CA).

[83] supra n.44

[84] [1983] 1 Lloyd's Rep 122 (HL).

[85] supra n.21.

[86] The Cendor MOPU, supra, Lord Mance at p. 576 [80].

[87] The Cendor MOPU, supra, Lord Saville p. 566 [31] ; Lord Mance p. 576 [80 – 81] ; Lord Clarke p.583 111].

[88] Lord Clarke p.583, para 114, agreeing with Waller LJ in the Court of Appeal, at p.261, para 56.

[89] Lords Saville, Mance and Clarke (all former judges of the Commercial and Admiralty courts).

[90] pp.576-577 [80 and 81].

[91] cf European Group Ltd and Others v Chartis Insurance UK Ltd [2012] EWHC 1245(Comm), [2012] Lloyd's Rep IR 603, 628-629, per Popplewell J.

[92] p.568 [47].

[93] supra n.81.

[94] p.579 [88].

In: Selected Issues in Maritime Law and Policy
Editor: Maximo Q. Mejia, Jr.
ISBN: 978-1-62618-508-1

Chapter 5

SHIP-SOURCE MARINE POLLUTION AND PUBLIC INTERNATIONAL LAW

Chie Kojima*
Associate Professor of International Law, Musashino University, Tokyo Japan

INTRODUCTION

The 1982 United Nations Convention on the Law of the Sea (hereinafter UNCLOS) [1] obliges its States Parties to take necessary measures to protect and preserve the marine environment. A State may be held liable if damage results from that State's failure to fulfill its international obligations concerning the protection and preservation of the marine environment under UNCLOS. Practical challenges of this public international law approach arise in situations where marine pollution damage results from a private ship and develops into an international conflict but only in a political sense. States normally do not have to bear the cost of pollution damage because of the well-established polluter-pays principle [2] by which the person who caused the pollution should, in principle, bear the cost of pollution. For oil pollution damage, the civil liability and compensation fund conventions make shipowners strictly liable according to this principle and ensure prompt and adequate compensation to victims by making corrective compensation arrangements available at the national and international levels. There is often no necessity for the coastal State that suffered oil pollution damage to invoke State responsibility of the flag State whose vessel caused the pollution to the coastal State, while the flag State could be held liable for the damage when the flag State failed to exercise its due diligence obligations towards its vessels.

The public international law approach to marine pollution, however, remains as useful means in preventing marine pollution and in ensuring compensation for transboundary damage as proved by some international cases. This chapter gives an overview of existing national, international and unilateral strategies for the prevention, reduction and control of ship-source marine pollution as well as means for the restoration of damage caused by ship-source marine pollution. These strategies demonstrate how the international community

* chie.kojima@aya.yale.edu.

utilizes these various strategies to achieve the common goal of protecting and preserving the marine environment.

I. Prevention, Reduction and Control of Ship-source Marine Pollution under International Law

A. General Obligations of States to Protect and Preserve the Marine Environment

Part XII of UNCLOS provides for the most comprehensive set of general obligations of States to protect and preserve the marine environment.

The obligations under UNCLOS Part XII are reiterated or elaborated by other conventions such as the 1972 Convention on the Prevention of Marine Pollution by Dumping of Wastes and Other Matter (London Convention) [3], as amended in 1978, 1980, 1989 and 1993, and supplemented by the 1996 Protocol [4], 1973 International Convention for the Prevention of Pollution from Ships [5], supplemented by the 1978 Protocol [6] (MARPOL 73/78) and a number of regional agreements. These conventions and agreements are independent from UNCLOS technically, but they could be considered as founding, supplemental or implementing agreements of UNCLOS Part XII in a wider sense for those States that are parties to both UNCLOS and those conventions [7].

Article 194, paragraph 1, of UNCLOS provides all States Parties' general obligations to take all measures that are necessary to prevent, reduce and control marine pollution [8] from any source, in accordance with their capabilities. Article 194, paragraph 2, law sets forth the obligation of all States to take all measures necessary to ensure that activities under their jurisdiction or control are so conducted as not to cause damage by pollution to other States and their environment. These obligations apply to all activities resulting in every kind of pollution, i.e., the release of toxic, harmful or noxious substances from land-based sources, from or through the atmosphere, by dumping, from vessels, from installations and devices used in exploration or exploitation of the natural resources of the seabed and subsoil, or from other installations and devices operating in the marine environment [9].

This obligation of States not to cause damage to other States and their environment predates UNCLOS as customary international law [10]. In the *Trail Smelter Arbitration* [11], the Arbitral Tribunal stated that:

> under the principles of international law, as well as the law of the United States, no State has the right to use or permit the use of its territory in such a manner as to cause injury by fumes in or to the territory of another or the properties or persons therein when the case is of serious consequence and the injury is established by clear and convincing evidence [12].

The responsibility of States not to cause damage to the environment is reiterated in Principle 21 of the 1972 Declaration of the United Nations Conference on the Human Environment as follows:

> States have, in accordance with the Charter of the United Nations and the principles of international law, the sovereign right to exploit their own resources pursuant to their own environmental policies, and the responsibility to ensure that activities within their jurisdiction or control do not cause damage to the environment of other States or of areas beyond the limits of national jurisdiction.

When applied in the ocean spaces, the zonal approach taken by UNCLOS, which divides the ocean spaces into internal waters, territorial seas, contiguous zones, exclusive economic zones (EEZs), continental shelf, high seas and the deep seabed, plays an important role in allocating legislative and enforcement jurisdiction over matters concerning the prevention, reduction and control of ship-source pollution.

B. Specific Obligations of States for the Prevention, Reduction and Control of Ship-Source Marine Pollution

1. Legislative Jurisdiction

Legislative jurisdiction of flag, coastal and port States over pollution from vessels is explicitly provided under Article 211 of UNCLOS.

First, all States Parties to UNCLOS are obliged to establish international rules and standards through the competent international organization or general diplomatic conference [13]. In the context of pollution from vessels, MARPOL 73/78 serves as such "international rules and standards", and the International Maritime Organization (IMO) serves as the "competent international organization" [14].

Second, flag States must adopt laws and regulations for their vessels, which "at least have the same effect as that of generally accepted international rules and standards established through the competent international organization or general diplomatic conference" [15].

Third, port States may, without prejudice to the right of innocent passage, establish particular requirements for the prevention, reduction and control of vessel-source pollution, as a condition for the entry of foreign vessels into their ports or internal waters or for a call at their off-shore terminals. Port States adopting special requirements must give due publicity to the requirements and communicate them to the competent international organization [16].

Fourth, coastal States may adopt laws and regulations for the prevention, reduction and control of marine pollution from foreign vessels in the territorial sea, on the condition that such laws and regulations do not hamper innocent passage of foreign vessels [17]. In the EEZs, coastal States may adopt laws and regulations for the prevention, reduction and control of marine pollution from vessels, in accordance with generally accepted international rules and standards established through the competent international organization [18]. Where there is a necessity for a coastal States to adopt special mandatory measures for the prevention of vessel-source pollution due to "recognized technical reasons in relation to its oceanographical and ecological conditions, as well as its utilization or the protection of its resources and the particular character of its traffic", that coastal State may adopt such measures by acquiring approval of the competent international organization [19]. The designation of a Particularly Sensitive Sea Areas (PSSAs) by the IMO is considered to be such an approval of special measures [20].

2. Enforcement Jurisdiction

(1) Enforcement by Flag States

Enforcement jurisdiction of flag States for the prevention, reduction and control of pollution from vessels is provided under Article 217 of UNCLOS. Flag States that are States Parties to UNCLOS are obliged to ensure compliance by vessels flying their flag or of their registry with applicable international rules and standards, established through the competent international organization or general diplomatic conference, and with their own laws and regulations adopted in accordance with UNCLOS for the prevention, reduction and control of pollution of the marine environment from vessels and to take other measures necessary for their implementation [21].

In particular, flag States are responsible for ensuring compliance by vessels flying their flags or of their registry with requirements of the international rules and standards in respect of design, construction, equipment and manning of vessels [22]. In case of a violation of these international rules and standards, the flag State must provide for immediate investigation and, where appropriate, institute proceedings in respect of the alleged violation irrespective of where the violation occurred or where the pollution caused by such violation has occurred or has been spotted [23].

The enforcement by flag States, however, has been found weak due to the widespread practice of flags of convenience. Flags of convenience allow vessels owned by the nationals of other States to register with very few regulations. Flags of convenience "have no requirement for crewing of their ships by nationals of the flag State, offer very low registration fees, low annual tonnage fees, relief from taxation of earnings, and a more relaxed scrutiny of international regulatory safety and crewing requirements, often through lack of administrative resources and expertise" [24]. International conventions [25] do not prescribe any obligatory criterion for the genuine link to be established between the flag State and its vessel [26]. It is the flag State's authority to adopt the requirements for registration of a vessel. It is argued that the effective exercise of jurisdiction and control over vessels by the flag State is one of the ways by which the flag State can show the genuine link [27]. Such effective exercise of jurisdiction and control may be demonstrated by administrative mechanisms for carrying out the necessary surveys of the vessels and checking the certification of the crews, as well as by enforcement mechanisms for applying international safety, labour and pollution standards against the owners and operators of its vessels [28].

(2) Enforcement by Coastal States

Article 220 of UNCLOS provides for enforcement by coastal States for the prevention, reduction and control of pollution from vessels. When there are clear grounds that a foreign vessel navigating in the territorial sea, during their passage, violated laws and regulations of the coastal State relating to the prevention, reduction and control of pollution, that coastal State may take necessary measures including physical inspection of the vessel and may institute proceedings including detention of the vessel [29]. Such laws and regulations must be adopted in accordance with applicable international rules and standards such as MARPOL 73/78.

When such a violation occurs in the EEZ, the coastal State may require the vessel navigating in their territorial sea or EEZ to give information regarding its identity and port of registry, its last and its next port of call and other relevant information required to establish whether a violation has occurred [30]. If there are clear grounds for believing that a violation is committed in the EEZ by a vessel navigating in the territorial sea or the EEZ, and results in a *substantial discharge causing or threatening significant pollution of the marine environment*, the coastal State may undertake physical inspection of the vessel for matters relating to the violation [31]. In the case that there are clear grounds for believing that a violation committed in the EEZ by a vessel navigating in the territorial sea or the EEZ, and results in a *discharge causing major damage or threat of major damage to the coastline or related interests of the coastal States*, the coastal State may institute proceedings, including detention of the vessel [32].

Coastal States usually have incentives to enforce their own environmental rules and standards based on their own exclusive interests over their resources. Coastal State's enforcement is, however, likely to fail when the State does not have a functioning administrative and judicial system as well as resources to implement their own regulations. There is also a tendency that coastal States take unilateral actions to protect their environmental interests. Examples of such a claim include, for instance, the claim to deny innocent passage to vessels carrying ultra-hazardous materials in the territorial sea and the claim to impose inspections on vessels exercising the right of innocent passage, without relying on any conventional arrangements [33].

The first example of unilateral action is that, after the *Prestige* incident of 13 November 2002, Spain and France decided to impose inspections of oil tankers passing through their EEZs and expel these tankers from their EEZs if they were found to be unseaworthy [34]. The second example can be given by the shipping of radioactive materials. A series of shipments of highly radioactive materials - plutonium, high level nuclear wastes (HLW) and mixed plutonium/uranium oxide (MOX) fuel - from France to Japan starting in 1992 made a number of States in Africa, South American and the South Pacific claim their right to deny the passage of the vessels in question in their jurisdictional waters [35]. The *Akatsuki Maru* first transported 2,200 pounds of plutonium from France to Japan in 1992, which was followed by a series of transportation of HLW and MOX fuel by the *Pacific Pintail*, the *Pacific Teal*, and the *Pacific Swan* in the following years [36]. Due to vigorous protests worldwide, the vessels carrying highly radioactive materials eventually avoided passing the exclusive economic zones of those protesting States [37].

It is controversial whether or not these unilateral claims could be justified under the law of the sea. UNCLOS does not permit States to take such unilateral actions explicitly. UNCLOS rather assures the right of innocent passage to all ships including those potentially dangerous ships and requires the flag State to take precautionary measures under Article 23:

> Foreign nuclear-powered ships and ships carrying nuclear or other inherently dangerous or noxious substances shall, when exercising the right of innocent passage through the territorial sea, carry documents and *observe special precautionary measures* established for such ships by international agreements. [emphasis added]

On the other hand, UNCLOS sets forth rules enabling the enforcement by coastal States in Article 220. Paragraphs 2 and 3 of Article 220 state that, where there are clear grounds for believing that a vessel navigating in the territorial sea or in the exclusive economic zone of a State has violated laws and regulations of the coastal State or applicable international rules and standards for the prevention, reduction and control of pollution from vessels, that coastal State may undertake physical inspection and institute proceedings including detention of the vessel.

While UNCLOS is silent about the obligation to give a prior notification by a vessel carrying ultra-hazardous materials, some other international instruments, both binding and non-binding, require the State transporting highly toxic materials to give a prior notification to the potentially affected State. The non-binding international instruments integrating the principle of prior informed consent comprise the 1990 International Atomic Energy Agency Code of Practice on the International Transboundary Movement of Radioactive Waste [38], the 1992 Rio Declaration on Environment and Development [39], and Article 8 of the 2001 ILC Draft Articles on Prevention of Transboundary Harm from Hazardous Activities [40]. The binding international agreements integrating the principle of prior informed consent include the 1989 Basel Convention on the Control of Transboundary Movements of Hazardous Wastes and Their Disposal [41], the 1991 Bamako Convention on the Ban of the Import into Africa and the Control of Transboundary Movement and Management of Hazardous Wastes within Africa [42], the 1996 Protocol on the Prevention of Pollution of the Mediterranean Sea by Transboundary Movements of Hazardous Wastes and their Disposal [43], and the 1998 Rotterdam Convention on the Prior Informed Consent Procedure for Certain Hazardous Chemicals and Pesticides in International Trade [44].

In light of the international instruments enumerated above, it can be argued that the obligation to give a prior notification became a general principle of international environmental law, notably in the context of transboundary movements of ultra-hazardous materials [45]. Such an obligation to give a prior notification is generally called "prior informed consent" and defined as a procedure that requires the exporting State to provide relevant information on a planned transfer of the materials to the importing State as well as transit States [46]. With the provided information, the importing State and transit States must be able to assess the possible environmental impacts of the transport and to take preventive measures [47].

It follows that, according to Article 220 of UNCLOS, if there is a violation of the obligation to acquire prior informed consent under those relevant international environmental instruments by a foreign vessel, the coastal State could use that violation as a justification of its enforcement actions against the foreign vessel. Coastal States, however, cannot legitimately enforce its laws and regulations that explicitly prohibit well-established rules under international law, such as the right of innocent passage.

(3) Enforcement by Port States

Enforcement by port States serves as a means for complementing the weakness of flag State enforcement. Article 218 of UNCLOS stipulates that a port State may undertake investigations against a vessel that is voluntarily within its ports or at its off-shore terminals, and where the evidence so warrants, institute proceedings in respect of any discharge from that vessel *beyond* its jurisdictional waters in violation of applicable international rules and standards established through the competent international organization or general diplomatic conference [48]. If the port State is a party to MARPOL 73/78, that State may enforce stringent rules of MARPOL 73/78 as such applicable international rules and standards upon foreign ships in its ports even if their flag States are not bound by MARPOL 73/78 [49]. Port States must cooperate with any other States requesting for investigation of a discharge violation, irrespective of where the violation occurred [50]. Any proceedings instituted by the port State on the basis of such an investigation may be suspended at the request of the coastal State when the violation has occurred within the internal waters, territorial sea or EEZ of that coastal State, and the evidence and records of the case, together with any bond or other financial security posted with the authorities of the port State, must be transmitted to that coastal State. Such transmittal must preclude the continuation of proceedings in the port State.

The IMO strengthened the rules on port State control and integrated them into a number of its technical conventions and its regional approaches for the prevention, reduction and control of marine pollution. Under the auspice of the IMO, nine regional port State control agreements (Memoranda of Understanding) were concluded as such regional approaches [51]. For instance, the Paris MoU [52] consists of 27 maritime administrations from North America and Europe and aims to eliminate sub-standard vessels in their jurisdictional waters. The participating States in the Paris MoU conduct inspections on board foreign vessels in their ports with regard to their compliance with international safety, security, labor and environmental standards. Such regional approaches appeal to the common interests of the region and, therefore, is likely to bring participating States' adherence.

The trends of strengthening enforcement by a group of regional port States can be also observed in the European Union (EU) law. In 2005, the European Parliament and the Council of European Union issued Directive 2005/35/EC and urged the its Member States to take necessary measures to charge penalties to any person – the shipowner, the master of the ship, the owner of the cargo, the classification society or any other person involved - who causes or contributes to ship-source discharges of polluting substances in the internal waters including ports, the territorial sea, straits used for international navigation, in the EEZ of a EU Member State, and in the high seas "if committed with intent, recklessly or by serious negligence" [53]. The Directive points to the fact that:

> [n]either the international regime for the civil liability and compensation of oil pollution nor that relating to pollution by other hazardous or noxious substances provides sufficient dissuasive effects to discourage the parties involved in the transport of hazardous cargoes by sea from engaging in substandard practices; the required dissuasive effects can only be achieved through the introduction of penalties applying to any person who causes or contributes to marine pollution [54].

The Directive obliges EU Member States to undertake an appropriate inspection, with due regard to the relevant guidelines adopted by the IMO, against a ship which is voluntarily within a port or at an off-shore terminal of the Member States and is suspected of having been engaged in or is engaging in a discharge of polluting substances either within or outside the areas of the Member States' national jurisdiction [55]. In the case that the ship suspected of discharge of polluting substances does not call at a port of the Member States, the Member State which holds the information of the suspected discharge must inform the State of the next port of call about the suspected discharge and request that State to take appropriate measures [56].

Furthermore, the European Union and the Council of European Union adopted Directive 2009/20/EC which urges EU Member States to ensure both shipowners of vessels flying its flags and foreign vessels entering its ports to have insurance and to refuse entry of any ship which does not carry on board such insurance certificates into any of its ports [57]. The importance of insurance for maritime claims is emphasized by relevant international organizations not only for the purpose of ensuring prompt and adequate compensation for victims of marine pollution [58], but also for the purpose of eliminating substandard ships.

The enhanced enforcement actions of EU port States with regard to the refusal of the entry of any vessels without insurance certificates complements the regulatory approach to insurance companies as proposed in the 2002 policy statement by the Organisation for Economic Co-operation and Development (OECD) [59]. In the policy statement, the OECD Maritime Transport Committee points to the fact that the insurance industry serves as a "very effective cover for substandard ships by allowing their risk to be spread over many players in the transportation chain, and ultimately to consumers" and thus urges the insurance industry to identify and target providers and users of substandard ships [60] and to consider *refraining from providing insurance cover unless the deficiencies of the ships are eliminated* [61]. The Maritime Transport Committee, accordingly, recommends the establishment of compulsory insurance by the IMO for all ships, which at the same time prohibits insurers from paying fines for shipowners when prosecuted and found guilty of safety or pollution related offences [62]. In this way, while port State inspections alone cannot eliminate substandard ships completely, insurance companies themselves could be used as a regulatory device to induce incentives for shipping industry to act in an environmental sound way [63]. The Committee further recommends the governments to regulate industry to create economic incentives and rewards – such as reduced classification fees, lower insurance premiums, fewer and less time consuming port state inspections and lower port charges – for shipowners, which are taking serious anti-pollution actions [64].

A series of actions taken by the EU, namely the Directive urging EU Member States to introduce penalties to any person who causes or contributes to ship-source discharges of polluting substances, were challenged by a coalition of shipping industry and some scholars in maritime law. They contend that such actions are not in conformity with provisions under MARPOL 73/78 and UNCLOS [65]. When implementing the port State control for vessel-source pollution, State parties to UNCLOS must observe Article 230 of UNCLOS, which provides that only monetary penalties may be imposed "except in the case of a willful and serious act of pollution in the territorial sea". The wording of the Directive "if committed with intent, recklessly or by serious negligence" needs to be carefully interpreted and applied in light of Article 230 of UNCLOS.

State Responsibility

While there are established compensation frameworks for certain kinds of vessel-source pollution at the international and domestic levels [66], a State itself may be held liable for marine pollution damage caused by a failure of that State to fulfil its obligations under UNCLOS described above. Article 235 of UNCLOS stipulates the responsibility and liability of States as follows:

1. States are responsible for the fulfilment of their international obligations concerning the protection and preservation of the marine environment. They shall be liable in accordance with international law.
2. States shall ensure that recourse is available in accordance with their legal systems for prompt and adequate compensation or other relief in respect of damage caused

by pollution of the marine environment by natural or juridical persons under their jurisdiction.

3. With the objective of assuring prompt and adequate compensation in respect of all damage caused by pollution of the marine environment, States shall cooperate in the implementation of existing international law and the further development of international law relating to responsibility and liability for the assessment of and compensation for damage and the settlement of related disputes, as well as, where appropriate, development of criteria and procedures for payment of adequate compensation, such as compulsory insurance or compensation funds.

Accordingly, the flag State whose vessel caused marine pollution may be held liable, under international law, if there is a probable cause between the pollution and the failure to fulfill its international obligations concerning the prevention, reduction and control of vessel-source pollution under UNCLOS. On this point, the Grand Chamber of the Court of Justice of the European Union stated, in its Judgment in *International Association of Independent Tanker Owners (Intertanko)* v. *Secretary of State for Transport* (Case C-308/06) on 3 June 2008, as follows:

> [I]t is the flag State which, under the Convention[UNCLOS], must take such measures as are necessary to ensure safety at sea and, therefore, to protect the interests of other States. The flag State may thus also be held liable, vis-à-vis other States, for harm caused by a ship flying its flag to marine areas placed under those States' sovereignty, where that harm results from a failure of the flag State to fulfil its obligations [67].

This statement confirms the traditional State to State paradigm under international law in which the injured State may ask for compensation to the violating State. Article 235 of UNCLOS, however, does not clarify whether a mere violation of obligations to prevent marine pollution gives any other State Party to UNCLOS a cause of action. Furthermore, problems remain when a State violated its environmental obligations towards the international community as a whole (obligations *erga omnes*) and caused environmental damage in the areas beyond national jurisdiction, such as on the high seas.

With regard to the question on the damage caused in the areas beyond national jurisdiction, the Advisory Opinion on the *Responsibilities and Obligations of States Sponsoring Persons and Entities with respect to Activities in the Area* can be used as a useful guidance. In the Advisory Opinion, the International Tribunal for the Law of the Sea confirms that UNCLOS does not specify "what constitutes compensable damage or which subjects may be entitled to claim compensation" [68]. The Tribunal continues to state that "[i]t may be envisaged that the damage in question [as referred in UNCLOS Article 139, paragraph [2] would include damage to the Area and its resources constituting the common heritage of mankind, and damage to the marine environment" [69]. By referring to Article 48 of the ILC Articles on State Responsibility [70], the Tribunal concludes that not only the International Seabed Authority but also each State Party to UNCLOS may be "entitled to claim compensation in light of the *erga omnes* character of the obligations relating to preservation of the environment of the high seas and in the Area" [71].

Although the Advisory Opinion is related to the activities in the Area, one could make an analogy to the flag State responsibility and liability for damage caused by their vessels on the high seas. However, it must be noted that Article 194, paragraph 1, of UNCLOS, which considers the best practical measures and the capabilities of the responsible State, weakens the effectiveness of the obligations *erga omnes* to protect the marine environment [72].

II. The Settlement of International Disputes and Remedial Measures in the Prevention, Reduction and Control of Ship-Source Marine Pollution

A. Advisory Roles of the International Courts and Tribunals

One of the advantages of advisory proceedings of the international courts and tribunals, as compared to litigations brought by two conflicting parties, is that international organizations are able to make representations in the proceedings of advisory opinions before international courts and tribunals for the interests of the international community. In this procedure, the nature of proceedings becomes multilateral in the sense that the international organization requesting for an advisory opinion represents not only a group of States but also the international community as a whole. In this regard, although advisory opinions are non-binding, they are often preferred to bilateral formal proceedings in environmental disputes.

With regard to the advisory function of the International Court of Justice (ICJ), Article 96, paragraph 1, of the Charter of the United Nations stipulates that the Security Council and the General Assembly of the United Nations have the competence to seek advisory opinions on any legal question before the ICJ. Other organs of the United Nations and specialized agencies may also request advisory opinions on legal questions arising within the scope of their activities [73]. Accordingly, with regard to questions concerning international environmental law, the Economic and Social Council (ECOSOC), the IMO, the World Health Organization (WHO), the International Atomic Energy Agency (IAEA) and the United Nations Environment Programme (UNEP) have the competence to do so [74]. In the Advisory Opinion on the *Legality of the Threat of Use of Nuclear Weapons*, for instance, the protection of the environment was raised as a part of the arguments by the General Assembly and the WHO [75].

The advisory function of the ITLOS is similar to that of the ICJ, but provided differently in the relevant international instruments. According to Article 159, paragraph 10, and Article 191 of UNCLOS, only the Seabed Dispute Chamber can give advisory opinion upon request by the Assembly or the Council of the International Seabed Authority. The Seabed Dispute Chamber gives such opinions "as a matter of urgency" [76]. Under this procedure, the first advisory opinion was requested by the Council of the International Seabed Authority with regard to the question concerning *Responsibilities and Obligations of States Sponsoring Persons and Entities with respect to Activities in the Area* [77].

UNCLOS, however, is silent about the competency of the ITLOS itself to give advisory opinion as a full court. The ITLOS has later elaborated its Rules in 1996, by which the ITLOS is given the competence to render advisory opinions. Article 138, paragraph 1, of the Rules of the International Tribunal for the Law of the Sea provides:

> The Tribunal may give an advisory opinion on a legal question if an international agreement related to the purposes of the Convention specifically provides for the submission to the Tribunal of a request for such an opinion.

According to this provision, international organizations can make a request for an advisory opinion if they so decide in an international agreement or "States could consider submitting an advisory opinion [...] through an international 'body' such as the Meeting of States Parties to the Convention" [78]. In this way, the proceedings of advisory opinion before the ITLOS can also be characterized as multilateral. The phrase "purposes of the Convention" under Article 138, paragraph 1, of the Rules of the Tribunal includes the issues of marine pollution and the preservation of the marine environment [79].

The role of advisory opinions by international courts and tribunals in the prevention, reduction and control of marine pollution is that such opinions can provide the concerned members of the international community with authoritative interpretations of international agreements before conflicts escalate. Advisory opinions, however, may not induce adherence for a question where interests of the international community are divided or of political nature, as seen in the advisory opinion on the *Legality of the Threat or Use of Nuclear Weapons* [80].

The role of international judicial institutions must be distinguished from other international institutions, which might play a role in the prevention of international conflicts. The IMO, for instance, provides its Member States with multilateral forums where States may discuss potential conflicts with the view of reaching a consensus together with other States sharing the same interests [81]. The establishment of sea lanes and traffic separation schemes in straits used for international navigation and in archipelagoes in consultation with the IMO may serve as an example [82]. Rosalie Balkin positively evaluates the role of the IMO in conflict prevention as follows:

> It is not a court or tribunal but undoubtedly facilitates the resolution of disputes between member States, including on matters of law. It also operates as a forum for the development of treaties and other international instruments whose purpose is to regulate diverse areas of maritime activity. Perhaps most importantly it functions as a forum in which member States regularly meet to discuss and debate issues of importance to them. In this way it acts as a 'safety valve' for the airing of potential disputes and problems and provides a mechanism whereby States are given the opportunity to participate in the development of workable and practicable solutions [83].

B. International Adjudication and Arbitration

The formal international dispute settlement procedures that are available to States include proceedings before the ICJ, ITLOS and arbitral tribunals [84]. The ICJ and ITLOS are typically characterized as formal forums resolving State-to-State disputes. Formal proceedings before the ICJ or ITLOS play a limited role in resolving environmental disputes, because environmental disputes involves large community interests and States are reluctant to harden the rules of international environmental law by a binding judgment. A number of

States consider that rules of international environmental law consist of "soft" obligations and argue that state responsibility cannot result from a violation of such soft obligations.

The ICJ and ITLOS can take into account the multinational nature of environmental disputes by allowing a third State to intervene in a bilateral litigation. The right to intervene in the proceedings is given to third parties by the ICJ (Article 63 of the Statute of the International Court of Justice) and by the ITLOS (Article 32 of the Statute of the International Tribunal for the Law of the Sea). The intervening third party should have "an interest of a legal nature which may be affected by the decision" in the case (Article 62 of the Statute of the International Court of Justice; Article 31 of the Statute of the International Tribunal for the Law of the Sea). The ITLOS has a distinctive feature of being an international tribunal, which allows non-State entities to be a party in "any case expressly provided for in Part XI or in any case submitted pursuant to any other agreement conferring jurisdiction on the Tribunal which is accepted by all the parties to that case" [85]. A wider participation in the proceedings may facilitate environmental disputes to be solved before international courts and tribunals.

The arbitral tribunals play an even more flexible role for disputes concerning the marine environment. Annex VIII of UNCLOS provides for specific provisions regarding disputes arising out of pollution from vessels and by dumping. According to the Annex, disputes relating to the protection and preservation of the marine environment, and disputes relating to navigation, including pollution from vessels and by dumping, may be referred to the special arbitration procedure regulated by that Annex. Under article 2 thereof, the UNEP is designated as the body responsible for maintaining the appropriate list of experts in the field of the protection and preservation of the marine environment, and the IMO is the designated body in the field of navigation, including pollution from vessels and by dumping.

C. International Compensation Fund

International compensation fund is primarily a solution for providing prompt, adequate and effective remedies to those suffered damage in the event of accident or damage arising out of certain lawful activities [86]. Damage to be covered by an international compensation fund generally includes both those caused to persons and/or property and those caused to the environment *per se* with the limitation to the costs of measures of reinstatement which are taken within areas of national jurisdiction. Currently, there is not yet a functioning international liability mechanism for environmental damage that has occurred beyond areas of national jurisdiction, while ideas to protect global commons are evolving in the treaty regime for the Antarctica, that for the deep seabed, and that for the outer space. The need for the development of a liability regime, especially strict liability for harm to vulnerable deep-sea ecosystems from various activities was reiterated by the Ad Hoc Open-ended Informal Working Group to study issues relating to the conservation and sustainable use of marine biological diversity beyond areas of national jurisdiction in 2006 [87].

The *Torrey Canyon* disaster in 1967 triggered the need for the establishment of a liability regime for oil pollution as well as a compensation fund to complement financial security available at the national level. The legislative attempt was made by the IMO and resulted in adopting a civil liability convention for oil pollution damage in 1969. The necessity of liability and compensation for the victims of pollution and other environmental damage was also underlined in Principle 22 of the 1972 Stockholm Declaration and Principle 13 of the 1992 Rio Declaration. The Principles urge States to cooperate to develop further international law regarding liability and compensation for adverse effects of environmental damage caused by activities within the jurisdiction or control to areas beyond their jurisdiction.

There exist two types of a liability regime which serve as a model for further developments of an international liability regime for: (1) damage caused within areas of national jurisdiction and (2) damage caused to the marine environment beyond areas of national jurisdiction [88]. The former can be illustrated by the liability regime for oil pollution damage [89] and the latter can be illustrated by the liability regime for the Antarctic [90].

The liability regime for oil pollution damage imposes strict but limited liability to the shipowner whose ship caused pollution damage in the territory, territorial sea or exclusive economic zone of a State Party to the 1992 CLC. When no liability for damage arises under the 1992 CLC, when the damage exceeds the shipowner's liability under 1992 CLC, or when the owner liable for the damage under the 1992 CLC is financially incapable of meeting his obligations in full and any financial security that may have been provided does not cover or is insufficient to satisfy the claims of compensation, the international fund established by the 1992 Fund Convention will supplement the compensation for the damage up to 203 million Special Drawing Rights including the amount paid under the 1992 CLC to the claimant who is in a State that is a party to the 1992 Fund Convention [91].

The Antarctic Treaty regime imposes strict liability for the costs of a response action to environmental emergencies [92] to both State and non-State operators whose activities in the Antarctic Treaty area, including the marine space of the Antarctic, result in significant and harmful impact on the Antarctic environment. Response action includes reasonable measures to avoid, minimize or contain the impact of the environmental emergency including clean-up in appropriate circumstances and determining the extent of that emergency and its impact [93].

The Parties to the Antarctic Treaty have responsibility for requiring its operators to take prompt and effective response action in cases of environmental emergencies arising from the activities of that operator [94]. If the operator failed to take any such response action, the operator shall be held liable for the costs of the response action taken by Parties [95]. When a State operator or any Party fails to take the response action, the State operator shall pay the costs of the response action that should have been taken into the fund [96]. When it is a non-State operator who failed to take the response the response action, an amount of money that reflects as much possible the costs of the responsible action that should have been made must be paid directory either to the fund, to the Party of that operator, or to the Party that has the enforcement mechanism toward the non-State operator [97]. The fund provides for the reimbursement of the reasonable and justified costs incurred by a Party or Parties in taking response action for environmental emergencies [98].

A compensation fund based on civil liability may bypass the question of State responsibility and provide prompt, adequate and effective remedies to those suffered damage. At the same time, as the awareness of the international community to protect and preserve the marine environment beyond national jurisdiction glows, a combined responsibility of States and non-State actors in the Antarctic Treaty regime might serve as a model for the future international law of the sea regime.

Conclusion

Proshanto K. Mukherjee developed a spectrum of marine pollution conventions where those conventions interface with each other as public, regulatory and private law conventions [99]. He also identified the characteristics of those conventions as being preventive, mitigative and/or remedial. This chapter covers only the public international law of marine pollution in his spectrum, mainly the rights and obligations of States for the prevention, reduction and control of marine pollution from vessels under UNCLOS, State responsibility attached to those obligations, and possible strategies that States could take as remedial measures under international law.

Without a supra-national power enforcing rules of international law, it is eventually the decision-makers who choose to comply or not to comply with international conventions to which they are parties. In other words, decision-makers choose to take either international, national, or unilateral measures for promoting inclusive and/or exclusive interests of States. In response to the EU decision-makers' actions to introduce penalties for anybody who caused ship-source pollution, Proshanto K. Mukherjee wrote:

> [P]ublic authorities charged with law-making mandates and administering law and justice should act with unfailing responsibility casting aside their politically influenced biases and motivations. They should apply the penal law of ship-source pollution with rationality and in compliance with the international law regimes which they themselves have helped to articulate and by which their States are bound. Only then will the laudable vision of universality in promoting and fostering cleaner seas become a reality [100].

This author agrees with Proshanto K. Mukherjee that decision-makers must act in conformity with international conventions that they agreed to, for maximizing the inclusive interests of the international community in the protection of the marine environment. The overview of public international law of marine pollution in this chapter well indicates such universal approaches and the necessity to further develop a common strategy to protect the marine environment not only in the areas within national jurisdiction but also in the areas beyond national jurisdiction. Marine environmental law evolves towards the common goal of protecting and preserving the marine environment for the international community as a whole.

References

[1] United Nations Convention on the Law of the Sea, 10 Dec. 1982, 1833 U.N.T.S. 3. As of 6 November 2012, the number of ratification and accession to the Convention is counted 164.

[2] The "polluter" should bear the expenses of carrying out the measures decided by public authorities to ensure that the environment is in an acceptable state. *See* Org. for Eco. Cooperation & Development [OECD], Guiding Principles Concerning the International Economic Aspects of Environmental Policies, OECD Doc. C(72)128 (26 May 1972).

See also, OECD, The Polluter-Pays Principle: OECD Analyses and Recommendations, Doc. OCDE/GD(92)81, 1992.

[3] Convention on the Prevention of Marine Pollution by Dumping of Wastes and Other Matter, 29 Dec. 1972, 1046 U.N.T.S. 120.

[4] Protocol to the Convention on the Prevention of Marine Pollution by Dumping of Wastes and Other Matter, 7 Nov. 1996, 36 I.L.M. 1.

[5] International Convention for the Prevention of Pollution from Ships, 2 Nov. 1973, 1340 U.N.T.S. 184.

[6] Protocol of 1978 relating to the International Convention for the Prevention of Pollution from Ships, 17 Feb. 1978, 1340 U.N.T.S. 61.

[7] For a general understanding of implementation agreements under international law, see Chie Kojima & Vladlen S. Vereshchetin, Implementation Agreements, in MAX PLANCK ENCYCLOPEDIA OF PUBLIC INTERNATIONAL LAW (Rüdiger Wolfrum ed., 2012).

[8] UNCLOS, Art. 1, para. 1(4) defines pollution of the marine environment as "the introduction by man, directly or indirectly, of substances or energy into the marine environment, including estuaries, which results or is likely to result in such deleterious effects as harm to living resources and marine life, hazards to human health, hindrance to marine activities, including fishing and other legitimate uses of the sea, impairment of quality for use of sea water and reduction of amenities".

[9] UNCLOS, Art. 194, para. 3.

[10] PHILIPPE SANDS, 242 PRINCIPLES OF INTERNATIONAL ENVIRONMENTAL LAW (2nd ed., 2003).

[11] Trail Smelter Case (United States v Canada), III RIAA 1905 (11 Mar. 1941).

[12] Id. at 1965.

[13] UNCLOS, Art. 211, para. 1.

[14] IMO, Implications of the United Nations Convention on the Law of the Sea for the International Maritime Organization: Study by the Secretariat of the International Maritime Organization (IMO), Doc. LEG/MISC.6, 10 Sep. 2008, at 49.

[15] UNCLOS, Art. 211, para. 2.

[16] UNCLOS, Art. 211, para. 3.

[17] UNCLOS, Art. 211, para. 4.

[18] UNCLOS, Art. 211, para. 5.

[19] UNCLOS, Art. 211, para. 6.

[20] IMO, Revised Guidelines for the Identification and Designation of Particularly Sensitive Sea Areas, Doc. A 24/Res.982, 6 Feb. 2006. Any measure pursuant to Article 211(6) of UNCLOS "where existing measures or a generally applicable measure would not adequately address the particularized need of the proposed area" is listed as one of the legal bases of an application for the designation of a PSSA.

[21] UNCLOS, Art. 217, para. 1.

[22] UNCLOS, Art. 217, para. 2.

[23] UNCLOS, Art. 217, para. 4.

[24] JOHN N. K. MANSELL, 76 FLAG STATE RESPONSIBILITY: HISTORICAL DEVELOPMENT AND CONTEMPORARY ISSUES (2009).

[25] *E.g.*, Convention on the High Seas, Art. 5, para. 1; UNCLOS, Art. 91, para. 1; United Nations Convention on the Conditions for Registration of Ships (done 7 Feb. 1986, not yet in force), Preamble, Art. 1.

[26] Robin R. Churchill & Christopher Hedley, The Meaning of the "Genuine Link" Requirement in Relation to the Nationality of Ships, Oct. 2000, *available at*: www.oceanlaw.net/projects/consultancy/pdf/ITF-Oct2000.pdf (last visited 30 Jan. 2013), at 68-70.

[27] Id. at 70.

[28] Id. at 71.

[29] UNCLOS, Art. 220, para. 2.

[30] UNCLOS, Art. 220, para. 3.

[31] UNCLOS, Art. 220, para. 5.

[32] UNCLOS, Art. 220, para. 6.

[33] Stuart Kaye, Freedom of Navigation in a Post 9/11 World: Security and Creeping Jurisdiction, in THE LAW OF THE SEA: PROGRESS AND PROSPECTS 347, 361 (David Freestone et al. eds., Oxford University Press, 2006).

[34] Emma Daly, After Oil Spill, Spain and France Impose Strict Tanker Inspections, N.Y. TIMES, Nov. 27, 2002, at 5.

[35] Jon M. Van Dyke, Sea Shipment of Japanese Plutonium under International Law, 24 OCEAN DEV. & INT'L L. 399 (1993).

[36] Jon M. Van Dyke, The Legal Regime Governing Sea Transport of Ultrahazardous Radioactive Materials, 33 OCEAN DEV. & INT'L L. 77, 78 (2002).

[37] Those protesting States include Antigua and Barbuda, Argentina, Brazil, Chile, Columbia, Dominican Republic, Egypt, Fiji, Guinea, Indonesia, Iran, Haiti, Kiribati, Malaysia, Malta, Nauru, New Zealand, Oman, Papua New Guinea, Peru, The Philippines, Puerto Rico, Saudi Arabia, Singapore, South Africa, Venezuela and Yemen. See Kaye, supra note 33, at 362, citing from Marco Roscini, The Navigational Rights of Nuclear Ships, 15 LEIDEN J. INT'L L. 251 (2002); Jon M. Van Dyke, Balancing Navigational Freedom with Environmental and Security Concerns, 2003 COLO. J. INT'L ENVTL. LAW & POL'Y 19 (2003); Jon M. Van Dyke, The Legal Regime Governing Sea transport of Ultrahazardous Radioactive Materials, 33 OCEAN DEV. & INT'L L. 77 (2002).

[38] One of the basic principles on international transboundary movement in the Code of Practice reads: "Every State should take the appropriate steps necessary to ensure that, subject to the relevant norms of international law, the international transboundary movement of radioactive waste takes place only with the prior notification and consent of the sending, receiving and transit States in accordance with their respective laws and regulations".

[39] Principle 19 of the Rio Declaration reads: "States shall provide prior and timely notification and relevant information to potentially affected States on activities that may have a significant adverse transboundary environmental effect and shall consult with those States at an early stage and in good faith" (U.N. Doc. A/CONF.151/5/Rev.1).

[40] Article 8, paragraph 1, of the ILC Draft Articles reads: "If the assessment referred to in article 7 indicates a risk of causing significant transboundary harm, the State of origin shall provide the State likely to be affected with timely notification of the risk and the assessment and shall transmit to it the available technical and all other relevant information on which the assessment is based".

[41] Basel Convention on the Control of Transboundary Movements of Hazardous Wastes and Their Disposal, *done* Mar. 22, 1989, 1673 U.N.T.S. 57 (May 5, 1992). Article 6,

paragraph 1, of the Basel Convention reads: "The State of export shall notify, or shall require the generator or exporter to notify, in writing, through the channel of the competent authority of the State of export, the competent authority of the States concerned of any proposed transboundary movement of hazardous wastes or other wastes". Article 6, paragraph 2, stipulates the reaction of the importing State: "The State of import shall respond to the notifier in writing, consenting to the movement with or without conditions, denying permission for the movement, or requesting additional information". A number of regional agreements on transboundary movements of hazardous wastes adopted in the 1990s were modelled after the Basel Convention, thus also adopting the rules for prior informed consent.

[42] Bamako Convention on the Ban of the Import into Africa and the Control of Transboundary Movement and Management of Hazardous Wastes within Africa, done Jan. 30, 1991, 2101 U.N.T.S. 177 (Apr. 22, 1998).

[43] Article 6, paragraph 3, of the Protocol reads: "The transboundary movement of hazardous wastes only takes place with the prior written notification of the State of export as specified in Annex IV to this Protocol, and the prior written consent of the State(s) of import and the State(s) of transit".

[44] Rotterdam Convention on the Prior Informed Consent Procedure for Certain Hazardous Chemicals and Pesticides in International Trade, done Sept. 10, 1998, 2244 U.N.T.S. 337 (Feb. 24, 2004). The Rotterdam Convention is build upon the 1985 FAO International Code of Conduct on the Distribution and Use of Pesticides and the 1989 UNEP London Guidelines for the Exchange of Information on Chemicals in International Trade, both of which are ceased on 24 February 2006. See, FAO, International Code of Conduct on the Distribution and Use of Pesticides, F.A.O. Res. 10/85, available at: www.fao.org/docrep/x5562E/X5562e0a.htm (last visited 30 Jan. 2013); UNEP, London Guidelines for the Exchange of Information on Chemicals in International Trade, U.N.E.P. Dec. 15/30 as amended, May 25, 1989, available at: www.chem.unep.ch/ethics/english/longuien.htm (last visited 30 Jan. 2013).

[45] Roscini, supra note 37, at 253; PHILIPPE SANDS, PRINCIPLES OF INTERNATIONAL ENVIRONMENTAL LAW 841 (2nd ed., 2003).

[46] Katharina Kummer Peiry, Prior Informed Consent, in MAX PLANCK ENCYCLOPEDIA OF PUBLIC INTERNATIONAL LAW (Rüdiger Wolfrum ed., 2012).

[47] In the case that such prior informed consent is provided in a multilateral environmental agreement, the right given to transit States is limited to those transit States which are parties to the agreement. E.g., Article 6, paragraph 4, of the Basel Convention.

[48] UNCLOS, Art. 218, para. 1.

[49] This principle is also enshrined under Article 5, paragraph 4, of MARPOL 73/78.

[50] UNCLOS, Art. 218, para. 3.

[51] Europe and the north Atlantic (Paris MOU); Asia and the Pacific (Tokyo MOU); Latin America (Acuerdo de Viña del Mar); Caribbean (Caribbean MOU); West and Central Africa (Abuja MOU); the Black Sea region (Black Sea MOU); the Mediterranean (Mediterranean MOU); the Indian Ocean (Indian Ocean MOU); and the Arab States of the Gulf (GCC MoU (Riyadh MoU)).

[52] E.g., Paris Memorandum on the Understanding of Port State Control, Information available at: www.parismou.org/ (last visited 30 Jan. 2013).

[53] Directive 2005/35/EC, O. J. L 255 (30 Sep. 2005), as amended by Directive 2005/35/EC, O. J. L 280/52 (27 Oct. 2009).

[54] Id. preamble.

[55] Id. Art. 6.

[56] Id. Art. 7.

[57] Directive 2009/20/EC, O. J. L 131/128 (28 May 2009), Arts 4-5.

[58] E.g., IMO, Guidelines on Shipowners' Responsibilities in Respect of Maritime Claims, IMO Res. A.898(21) (25 Nov. 1999).

[59] OECD, Maritime Transport Committee, Policy Statement on Substandard Shipping by the Maritime Transport Committee of the OECD, April 2002, available at: www.oecd.org/dataoecd/18/37/2080990.pdf (last visited 30 Jan. 2013).

[60] Id. In the policy statement, a "substandard ship" is defined as "a vessel, through its physical condition, its operation or the activities of its crew, fails to meet basic standards of seaworthiness and thereby poses a threat to life and/or the environment".

[61] Id.

[62] Id.

[63] ALEXANDRE KISS & DINAH SHELTON, 262 INTERNATIONAL ENVIRONMENTAL LAW (Transnational Publishers, 3rd ed., 2004).

[64] OECD Policy Statement, supra note 59.

[65] See Case C-308/06, International Association of Independent Tanker Owners (Intertanko) v. Secretary of State for Transport (Eur. Ct. Justice, 3 Jun. 2008), available at: http://curia.europa.eu/ (last visited 30 Jan. 2013); Proshanto K. Mukherjee, The Penal Law of Ship-Source Marine Pollution: Selected Issues in Perspective, in LAW OF THE SEA, ENVIRONMENTAL LAW AND SETTLEMENT OF DISPUTES: LIBER AMICORUM JUDGE THOMAS A. MENSAH 463, 492-496 (eds by Tafsir Malick Ndiaye & Rüdiger Wolfrum, 2007).

[66] See the chapter on liability and compensation for ship-source oil pollution damage in this volume.

[67] International Association of Independent Tanker Owners (Intertanko) v. Secretary of State for Transport, supra note 65, at para. 62.

[68] Seabed Disputes Chamber of the International Tribunal for the Law of the Sea, Responsibilities and Obligations of States Sponsoring Persons and Entities with respect to Activities in the Area, Advisory Opinion of 1 February 2011, para. 179.

[69] Id.

[70] Article 48 reads "Any State other than an injured State is entitled to invoke the responsibility of another State … if: (a) the obligation breached is owed to a group of States including that State, and is established for the protection of a collective interest of the group; or (b) the obligation breached is owed to the international community as a whole."

[71] Responsibilities and Obligations of States Sponsoring Persons and Entities with respect to Activities in the Area, supra note 68, para. 180.

[72] Mahnoush H. Arsanjani & W. Michael Reisman, The Quest for an International Liability Regime for the Protection of the Global Commons, in INTERNATIONAL LAW: THEORY AND PRACTICE: ESSAYS IN HONOUR OF ERIC SUY 469, 483-484 (Karel Wellens ed., Nijhoff 1998).

[73] UN Charter, Art. 96, para. 2.

[74] Alan Boyle, Environmental Dispute Settlement, in MAX PLANCK ENCYCLOPEDIA OF PUBLIC INTERNATIONAL LAW (Rüdiger Wolfrum ed., 2012).

[75] Legality of the Threat of Use of Nuclear Weapons, Advisory Opinion, 1996 I.C.J. 226 (July 8), para 27.

[76] UNCLOS, Art. 191.

[77] Responsibilities and Obligations of States Sponsoring Persons and Entities with respect to Activities in the Area, supra note 68.

[78] See ITLOS, Statement by Judge Rüdiger Wolfrum, President of the International Tribunal for the Law of the Sea, to the Informal Meeting of Legal Advisers of Ministries of Foreign Affairs, New York, Oct. 23, 2006, available at: www.itlos.org/ (last visited 30 Jan. 2013).

[79] Tafsir Malick Ndiaye, The Advisory Function of the International Tribunal for the Law of the Sea, 9 CHINESE J. INT'L L. 565, 585.

[80] Legality of the Threat or Use of Nuclear Weapons, Advisory Opinion, 1996 ICJ Rep 226 (Jul. 8).

[81] Rosalie Balkin, The Role of the International Maritime Organization in the Settlement of International Disputes, in NAVIGATIONAL RIGHTS AND FREEDOMS AND THE NEW LAW OF THE SEA 293, 306-313 (Donald R. Rothwell & Sam Bateman eds., Nijhoff 2000).

[82] UNCLOS, Art. 41, para. 4 and Art. 53, para. 9.

[83] Balkin, supra note 81, at 313.

[84] UNCLOS, Art. 287.

[85] Statute of the International Tribunal for the Law of the Sea, Art. 20, para. 2.

[86] Chie Kojima, Compensation Fund, in MAX PLANCK ENCYCLOPEDIA OF PUBLIC INTERNATIONAL LAW (Rüdiger Wolfrum ed., Oxford University Press, 2012).

[87] UNGA, Report of the Ad Hoc Open-ended Informal Working Group to study issues relating to the conservation and sustainable use of marine biological diversity beyond areas of national jurisdiction, U.N. Doc. A/61/65 (Mar. 20, 2006) (prepared by Juan Manuel Gómez-Robledo & Philip D. Burgess), at para. 53.

[88] For detailed discussions on the design of an international liability regime for the global commons, see Mahnoush H. Arsanjani & W. Michael Reisman, The Quest for an International Liability Regime for the Protection of the Global Commons, supra note 72.

[89] International Convention on Civil Liability for Oil Pollution Damage, adopted 29 Nov. 1969 (19 June 1975), as modified by the 1992 Protocol, adopted 27 Nov. 1992, 1956 U.N.T.S. 285 (30 May 1996) [hereinafter 1992 CLC]; International Convention on the Establishment of an International Fund for Compensation for Oil Pollution Damage, adopted Dec. 18, 1971 (16 Oct. 1978), replaced by the Protocol of 1992, adopted 27 Nov. 1992, 1953 U.N.T.S. 373 (30 May 1996) [hereinafter 1992 Fund Convention]. In addition, the 2003 Protocol establishes the third layer of compensation arrangements, i.e. the International Oil Pollution Compensation Supplementary Fund, in cases that the damage surpasses the amount available under the 1992 CLC and the 1992 Fund Convention.

[90] Annex VI to the Protocol on Environmental Protection to the Antarctic Treaty, Liability Arising from Environmental Emergencies, adopted 17 June 2005, not yet in force, 45 I.L.M. 5.

[91] 1992 Fund Convention, Art. 4. For details, see International Oil Pollution Compensation Fund 1992, CLAIMS MANUAL, December 2008 Edition, available at: www.iopcfunds.org/publications/ (last visited 30 Jan. 2013).

[92] Environmental emergencies are defined as "any accidental event that has occurred, having taken place after the entry into force of this Annex, and that results in, or imminently threatens to result in, any significant and harmful impact on the Antarctic environment", Annex VI, Art. 2(b).

[93] Annex VI, Art. 2(f).

[94] Annex VI, Art. 5, para. 1.

[95] Annex VI, Art. 6, para. 1.

[96] Annex VI, Art. 6, para. 2(a).

[97] Annex VI, Art. 6, para. 2(b).

[98] Annex VI, Art. 12, para. 1.

[99] Proshanto K. Mukherjee, *supra* note 65, at 471-478.

[100] Id. at 496.

In: Selected Issues in Maritime Law and Policy
Editor: Maximo Q. Mejia, Jr.
ISBN: 978-1-62618-508-1

Chapter 6

The International Legal Framework Governing Liability and Compensation for Ship-Source Oil Pollution Damage

Jingjing Xu*
Professor of Maritime Law and Economics,
School of Management, Plymouth University, Plymouth, UK

Introductory Remarks

Until recent times, the seas were perceived to be inexhaustible; the only two uses of the oceans known to us were navigation and fishing and they were thought to be harmless to the marine environment. [1] All this changed after oil was discovered in 1860. Ocean navigation had already started moving from the era of sailing ships to steamships; and subsequently, oil came to be used as fuel instead of coal.

As oil became the world's principal source of energy, its transportation by sea in tankers made it the most important cargo. Thus, the advent of the tanker followed by the supertanker and then the VLCC (very large crude carrier) and the ULCC (ultra large crude carrier) marked advancements in marine navigational technology that were phenomenal for the times. However, this dramatic progress in shipping also signalled the dawn of a new menace – pollution of the seas from oil.

During the 1950's some national governments realised that carriage of oil by sea could harm the ocean environment and some effort was thus made to develop international legal regimes to deal with this problem. The International Convention for the Prevention of Pollution of the Sea by Oil, 1954 (OILPOL 1954) was adopted in that context. However, the seriousness of oil pollution damage was still not fully recognised and the international community were not at all prepared for any environmental catastrophe until the unanticipated grounding of the *Torrey Canyon*.

The incident occurred on 18th March 1967 when the Liberian tanker *Torrey Canyon* ran aground on Seven Stones reef off the coast of southwest England. At the time it was carrying

* E-mail: jingjing.xu@plymouth.ac.uk

a cargo of approximately 120,000 tons of crude oil. Following the grounding about 80,000 tons of the cargo spilled into the sea. [2] The incident involved a number of countries. The vessel was owned by Barracuda Tanker Corporation, registered in Monrovia, and was bareboat chartered to Union Oil Company of California, U.S.A., a company that operated out of Bermuda. The master and crew on board were of Italian nationality. [3]

The magnitude of the oil spill was unprecedented up to that time and it rudely awakened the international maritime community. A series of responses were made following the incident. In the same year the Council of the Inter-governmental Maritime Consultative Organization (IMCO) which is now known as International Maritime Organization (IMO) [4] called an extraordinary session and a Legal Committee was established to deal with the legal issues which had arisen from the incident. The law making role of the Organization which was hitherto concerned primarily with technical and regulatory matters, assumed a new function - the development of an international civil liability regime pertaining to damage from oil spills.

In 1969, the IMCO Assembly convened an international conference in Brussels, [5] out of which two important international conventions emerged; one is the Intervention Convention [6] and the other is the International Convention on Civil Liability for Oil Pollution Damage which is normally referred to as the Civil Liability Convention (CLC), 1969.

The CLC 1969 is perhaps the most significant development in the international civil liability regime pertaining to damage from oil spills. As it will be discussed later, the Convention established an international legal regime for liability arisen from pollution damage caused by oil spills from laden tankers. Two years later, a companion regime of the CLC – the Fund Convention 1971 was adopted to provide additional compensation to victims suffering oil pollution damage. Some major amendments were made to the two Conventions in 1992 and the scope of application of the Conventions was extended to include oil spills from non-laden tankers on ballast voyage with oil residues on board.

As the CLC regime mainly applies to oil tankers, there was a significant lacuna in the international regime of liability and compensation for ship-source persistent oil pollution damage before the International Convention on Civil Liability for Bunker Oil Pollution Damage (Bunkers Convention) was adopted in 2001. It must be recognised that some large non-tankers may carry oil in their bunkers up to 10,000 tonnes which is even larger than the oil cargo carried in some tankers. [7] Furthermore, bunker oils are of highly viscous and persistent nature and the chemical composition makes it more harmful than cargo oil. The Bunkers Convention was created to plug the gap; which, in simple terms, provides a liability regime for pollution damage arising from the escape or discharge of bunker oil from ships other than oil tankers.

In any discussion on oil pollution at sea, the International Convention on Liability and Compensation for Damage in Connection with the Carriage of Hazardous and Noxious Substances by Sea (HNS Convention), 1996 must also be addressed. Although the word "oil" is not included in the title of the Convention, the HNS Convention does cover damage caused by oil carried as cargo which falls outside the scope of the CLC regime. For example, pollution damage caused by non-persistent oil or non-pollution damage caused by persistent oil is covered by the HNS Convention.

This paper will present a detailed discussion on the salient features of the international regime of liability and compensation for ship-source oil pollution damage. This includes the

CLC/Fund regime, the Bunkers Convention and the HNS Convention. Two points need to be made at the outset. Firstly, the discussion in this paper will only focus on the liability component of the private law of marine pollution. The private law of marine pollution essentially involves two components; namely, liability for damage caused by pollution and the damages or compensation available for such damage. Liability is a qualitative concept. In law, liability arises when the quality of conduct or standard of behaviour of a person is repugnant to the law because it causes damage or injury to others. In contrast, damages or compensation is a civil remedy, and one that is quantitative in character. It is the qualitative attribute of liability that dictates the quantum of damages that the wrong-doer must pay according to the law to the person who has suffered the damage or injury. [8] This paper will focus on the liability issues in the regime; issues pertaining to compensability will not be discussed.

Secondly, the discussion in this paper will only focus on the current international convention regime which is essentially the prevailing international law on the subject. The applicable law in respect of liability for oil pollution damage in common law or civil law jurisdictions where the convention law does not apply will not be addressed. It should be pointed out that international conventions are the dominant regimes in the field of liability and compensation for marine pollution damage.

Given the international character of marine pollution and the multi-faceted implications of a typical oil spill at sea, [9] there is no doubt that this is an area of maritime law that is best served by international convention law.

1. The CLC/Fund Regime

As mentioned earlier, the *Torrey Canyon* incident engendered human ingenuity and served as a catalyst for the development of international law in the field of pollution from mega oil spills at sea. In 1969, under the auspices of IMCO, the International Convention on Civil Liability for Oil Pollution Damage, 1969 was adopted. The object and purpose of this Convention was to establish a uniform liability and compensation regime for victims of ship-source oil pollution damage.

The CLC regime essentially addresses pollution damage emanating from major oil spills at sea, although it has been suggested that there is nothing in the CLC 1969 or its successor the CLC 1992 that precludes its application in respect of claims for pollution damage caused by operational discharges as distinguished from oil spills. [10]

However, operational discharges, except from tank washings, do not fall within the definition of "oil" in the CLC which is restricted to oil carried as cargo or in the bunkers of a tanker. Bilge and engine room discharges do not contain oil that can be used as cargo or fuel. In practical terms, operational discharges are hardly amenable to private law claims for loss or damage suffered because the source of the discharge cannot be easily identified and linked with the area of contamination except in instances where a polluting vessel is on a continuous or regular short-distance, specific run over an extended period of time. [11] If specificity of polluted area and quantification of damage can be established, it may be possible to advance a claim for compensation under the Conventions but only in respect of pollution from tank washings of a tanker.

1.1. The CLC, 1969

Liability and its attendant remedy in the form of damages or compensation revolves around three major issues; namely, what should be the basis of liability, who should be liable, and whether liability, or rather, the amount of compensation, should be limited by law, and if so, to what extent. At the Brussels diplomatic conference the first issue engendered intense debate. Should liability be based on fault, or should it be strict or even absolute, were the questions under consideration. [12] As might be expected, traditionalists would obviously support the notion of fault based liability. [13] Those of common law persuasion would naturally look to the familiar civil liability regime of torts and the principles embedded in the attendant case law. Those belonging to the continental civil law system would similarly look at their own corresponding regimes. But liability for pollution damage at an international level needed a special kind of legal treatment. [14]

In traditional tort or delict, liability can only be imposed on the defendant polluter if the plaintiff claimant successfully proves on a balance of probabilities that the damage or injury suffered by him was proximately caused by the fault or negligence of the defendant. [15] By contrast, in the strict liability regime, which in terms of English law derives its origin from the law of nuisance, the plaintiff need only prove damage. [16] Once that is done, the defendant is liable regardless of the presence or absence of fault, be it in the form of negligence, nuisance or any other tort.

However, in the strict liability regime, even though it is relatively rigorous, certain exceptions are afforded which enable the defendant to escape liability in prescribed circumstances. Usually, these are extraordinary circumstances beyond the control of the defendant to which the pollution damage is attributable. In maritime law, the notion of *force majeure,* one of which is "act of God", is well recognised in view of the fact that shipping operates in a harsh environment where ships and their crew are exposed to hazards of natural phenomena. Other exceptions to strict liability include situations where a person other than the defendant polluter may have caused the pollution regardless of the fault of that person. In a strict liability regime, the plaintiff's burden of proof is less onerous since only proof of damage or injury is required. In an absolute liability regime the polluter is liable notwithstanding the circumstances. There are no exceptions and therefore no defences. As such, from the defendant's viewpoint absolute liability is the most rigorous.

The question of who should be liable emerged as a highly debated issue at the Brussels conference. Should the owner or operator of the polluting ship be liable, or should it be the owner of the pollutant oil cargo; or, should liability be divided or apportioned between the two? [17] In traditional maritime law, it is the shipowner or operator who is liable for tortious acts committed by the master or crew, or where damage is attributable to the ship itself. The rationale is that the ship that caused the damage was under the navigational control of the shipowner's servants. In juxtaposition to that notion is the application of the so-called "polluter pays" principle. [18] The question arises then as to who is the polluter?

The answer is not straightforward. In the first instance it may be said that the ship is the instrument of the damage because it is the vehicle through which the pollutant is transported; and therefore, the owner or operator of the ship who is vicariously in possession of the pollutant at the time of the incident, should be liable. However, it is also arguable that the owner of the pollutant should be liable since the pollution damage is caused by the pollutant. Indeed, these were the two alternative positions advanced at the diplomatic conference. The former view was consistent with the normal law and practice in the maritime field which worked well with traditional cargoes because they did not pose a threat to the marine environment. But with the advent of the oil tanker the situation changed, and the environment became increasingly vulnerable with supertankers, VLCCs and ULCCs plying the oceans.

With regards to limitation of liability, at the conference the question was centred on whether the limit of liability should be the same as in the prevailing international regime of global limitation or should those limits be raised; or whether a new and separate regime should be created providing considerably higher limits than those provided for in the global limitation regime. [19] It should be mentioned at this juncture that the notion of limitation of liability, which was at one time unique to maritime law and is still a distinctive feature of shipping, is deeply rooted in maritime practice. [20] Where there is limitation of liability, the unsuccessful defendant shipowner is not obliged to pay the whole amount of the damages. He need only pay up to a stipulated amount usually calculated according to the tonnage of the ship; so the plaintiff himself bears the balance of his loss or damage. The practice stems from the original notion that a shipowner should only be liable for the amount that represents the value of his ship regardless of the damages assessed against him. Limitation according to tonnage is based on the premise that the larger the ship, the higher is its value. In modern times that premise is no longer entirely valid; the type and use of a vessel is largely determinative of its value, but size in terms of tonnage is nevertheless a decisive criterion.

The concept of limitation of liability evolved historically as a privilege accorded to shipowners. Its object is to support and sustain shipping, commercial trade being a nation's economic lifeline. It also manifests public recognition of the entrepreneurial and daring spirit of maritime adventurers. Thus, traditionally, it has been granted pursuant to public policy rather than by virtue of a legal right. [21] In the past, therefore, the onus has been cast on the defendant invoking limitation to show that in the given circumstances he is entitled to it. However, under the "conduct barring limitation" provisions of the current convention regimes, the onus is on the plaintiff claimant to show that the defendant shipowner is not so entitled. In effect, the privilege of limitation has been converted to a right. [22]

At the diplomatic conference in Brussels negotiations reached a near deadlock because of the divergent views and interests of the parties. Eventually, the parties did arrive at a compromise that led to the adoption of the Civil Liability Convention. The three principal issues discussed above were resolved, but as the subsequent historical record shows, not everything was conclusive. [23] The legal regime was one of strict liability and that remains as such to this day. The registered shipowner alone was to be liable for pollution damage, but as we shall see, that aspect of the regime was soon to be modified by a complementary companion regime. The limitation amount was set at 2000 poincare francs per ton of limitation tonnage of the vessel with a maximum set at 210 million poincare francs per incident. [24] The amounts in terms of the value of the United States dollar at the time stood at USD 134 per ton and USD 14 million, respectively. [25]

The CLC 1969 came into force in 1975. In addition to the above, there are a number of other salient features in the Convention. The Convention applies only to persistent oil carried in bulk as cargo or in the bunkers of a laden tanker. Thus, the Convention is not applicable in cases of pollution damage from non-persistent oils such as aviation fuel, gasoline, light diesel oil and kerosene. The expression "laden tanker" is not a convention term but is used to describe a tanker loaded with oil cargo in bulk. Notably pollution caused by bunker oil spills from a non- tanker or an un-laden tanker is not covered by the CLC 1969.

As provided in Article II, the Convention is geographical in its application in that it is applicable to any pollution damage occurring within the territorial sea of a state party. [26] In other words, the Convention is still applicable even if the pollution is caused by a ship that flies the flag of a state that is not a party to the Convention. This is quite unique as most maritime conventions are flag state conventions in the sense that the convention applies to every ship of the flag state that is a party to the convention regardless of the ship's location.

The Convention under Article VII(8) provides for all claims to be channelled through the shipowner who is defined in Article I(3) as the registered owner of the vessel at the time of the pollution incident. This provision affords a considerable measure of procedural convenience to small time claimants such as subsistence fishermen. In practice, the ship's third party liability insurer, which is usually the P and I Club, handles the claims.

Article VII(1) requires every vessel carrying over 2000 tons of cargo oil in bulk to provide evidence of financial responsibility. This is usually in the form of liability insurance or other security such as a banker's guarantee for the amount of the applicable limitation for the ship. According to Article VII, every tanker must carry a certificate attesting to compliance with this requirement. A claimant can have direct access to the insurer. Compulsory insurance was first suggested for carriage of passengers by sea around the first quarter of the 20th century. It did not end with any positive result but then appeared in the Convention on the Liability of Operators of Nuclear Ships (Nuclear Ships Convention) adopted in 1962. [27] The Convention, however, has not yet entered into force, and it does not seem that it will in the near future. [28] This makes the CLC 1969 the first international convention that provides detailed provisions on compulsory insurance.

As per Article VI, following a pollution incident, the owner of a vessel to which the Convention applies may invoke limitation by constituting a fund with the forum court in the amount equivalent to the applicable limit. The fund stands as security for pollution claims against the shipowner and precludes any action *in rem* being instituted against the ship in jurisdictions where such actions are possible. [29]

The Convention, under Article V(2) provides that if a shipowner is found to be guilty of actual fault or privity with regard to the pollution incident, he will lose his right to limit liability.

1.2. The Fund Convention, 1971

It has been mentioned earlier that at the diplomatic conference in Brussels there was vigorous debate over whether liability for pollution damage should be borne by the shipowner exclusively, or should it be shared, and if so, how. Under traditional civil liability law in the maritime field there was no precedent for holding any entity other than the owner or operator of the ship liable in law for damage caused by the ship. The damaging agent in the case of an oil spill is the oil cargo which, while it is on board, is a constituent part of the ship and is under the charge of the master who is a servant of the owner or operator of the ship. Where there is an oil spill resulting from a collision or grounding the causative factor lies in the navigation of the ship, faulty or otherwise, which is under the direct control of the master. Thus, on all counts, it is the owner or operator of the ship who is under fire when it comes to civil liability and reparation by way of damages. [30] That, at any rate, is the traditional viewpoint in maritime law given that ship-generated oil pollution is indubitably a maritime tort.

Nevertheless, the "but for" argument can be advanced in reference to the nature of the cargo as a pollutant. It can be reasonably argued that the pollution damage would not have taken place but for the oil. If the cargo was rice or tea or some other organic, non-toxic, biodegradable substance that spilled out of the ship, accidentally or otherwise, there would have been no pollution damage. While the traditional maritime law of liability posed an impediment to imposing civil liability on any entity other than the shipowner or operator, there was no reason why the cargo owners could not bear some functional responsibility for providing supplementary compensation through a suitable mechanism. [31]

At the diplomatic conference it was recognised that oil pollution damage in such mammoth proportions as demonstrated by the *Torrey Canyon* disaster was unprecedented and that causation could at least partially be attributed to the contaminating nature of the cargo. Therefore, the question arose as to whether the owner of the pollutant cargo, the oil, should have something to answer for. Many were of the view that it would be inequitable for the tanker industry to bear the full brunt of the compensation burden. [32] Moreover, by reason of the maximum limitation amount being USD 14 million many claims would not be met in the event of a mega oil spill. As will be seen later in this discussion, the protagonists who were thinking ahead were more than accurate in this regard. Before the conclusion of deliberations, a resolution was adopted which called for another diplomatic conference to be convened by IMCO by the year 1971. This conference would address the issue of how cargo interests should bear some of the burden of reparation for oil pollution damage suffered by victims. In due course, Brussels became the venue for another diplomatic conference in 1971. Out of the deliberations of that conference emanated another landmark convention which was a companion regime to the CLC of 1969. This was the International Convention on the Establishment of an International Fund for Compensation for Oil Pollution Damage, 1971, otherwise known as the "Fund Convention". [33] The Fund Convention came into force in 1978.

The CLC 1969 and the Fund Convention 1971 together provide an integrated scheme and it is designed in the way that a state cannot be a party to the Fund Convention unless it is also a party to the CLC. However, a state can be a party to the CLC without being a party to the Fund Convention.

The object of the Fund Convention through the establishment of the International Oil Pollution Compensation (IOPC) Fund is to provide supplementary or additional compensation to victims of pollution damage beyond what is provided for under the CLC if the compensation under the CLC is inadequate or unavailable. [34] Inadequacy of compensation can arise in three circumstances set out in Article 4 (1) of the Fund Convention. One, if there is no liability under the CLC, if, for example, the shipowner successfully pleads one of the defences under Article III of the Convention. Two, the shipowner may be incapable of paying the required compensation in accordance with the limit of liability under the CLC by reason of insolvency or other financial constraint or impediment. Three, if the totality of damages claimed is in excess of the shipowner's liability pursuant to the CLC. Compensation under the Fund Convention is available in these circumstances subject to the "exoneration" provision set out in Article 4(3). In these circumstances, the Fund will step in to lift the total available compensation up to the limit set out in the Convention, that was 450 million poincare francs amounting to approximately USD 30 million at the time with the first 210 million poincare francs (USD 14 million) being payable under the CLC 1969. [35]

The IOPC Fund is an inter-governmental organisation established to administer the regime of the Fund Convention. It is financed through the exaction of an annual levy imposed on oil cargo owners in state parties to the Fund Convention - Any person who has received in one calendar year more than 150,000 tonnes of crude oil and heavy fuel oil after sea transport in ports or terminal installations of a state party immediately after carriage by sea is obliged to contribute to the Fund. [36] It should be pointed out that the contribution of the oil cargo interests is not in any form of liability recognised at law; it can be characterised as functional responsibility in the nature of an ethical or moral obligation in a sociological context. The Fund is the mechanism devised to accomplish this responsibility.

The Fund has legal personality and the capacity to sue and be sued in its own name. By conferring legal personality on the IOPC Fund through the Convention, the non-legal notion of responsibility has been transformed into legal liability. In a sense the IOPC Fund as an entity is the *alter ego* of the cargo interests who, it was agreed, should bear some responsibility for damage from oil spills. Since the Fund is capable of being sued, it can be liable for payment of compensation under the Fund Convention in the same manner as any other litigant even though it is not the polluter *per se*. Therefore it can be said that in the CLC/Fund scheme the purity of the "polluter pays" principle has been substantially modified through a functional approach to the whole issue of liability and compensation for oil pollution damage.

Originally, another stated object of the Fund Convention, 1971 expressed in Article 2 (1), was to provide relief from the additional financial load faced by shipowners under the CLC. This so-called roll-back relief was intended to be subject to conditions designed to ensure compliance by shipowners of maritime safety requirements in general and other relevant conventions. This provision was removed by Article 3 of the 1992 Protocol to the Fund Convention, 1971. [37]

1.3. Changes to the CLC 1969 and Fund 1971

Amendments have been made to both Conventions over the years through protocols. One of the amendments was made in 1976 where the unit of the limitation amounts was changed from poincare gold to the "unit of account" or "monetary unit" which is the special drawing right (SDR) defined by the International Monetary Fund (IMF). [38] The rationale for this amendment was that the SDR is a stable unit the value of which is pegged to a basket of major currencies by the IMF and this could help avoid the fluctuation and instability in the price of gold to which the poincare franc was pegged. The limitation amount under the CLC then became 133 SDR per limitation ton up to a maximum of 14 million SDR. [39] The limitation amount of 450 million poincare francs under the Fund Convention, which included the CLC limit of liability, became 30 million SDR per incident.

In Article 4(6) of the Fund Convention 1971 there is provision for the Assembly to increase the aggregate amount of compensation to a maximum of 900 million francs. The Assembly is empowered to make such a decision "...having regard to the experience of incidents which have occurred and in particular the amount of damage resulting therefrom and to changes in the monetary values, ..." In April 1979, pursuant to a decision of the

Assembly taken in accordance with this provision, the ceiling was raised to 675 million poincare francs equivalent to USD 50 million approximately, in respect of a single pollution incident.

Some further amendments were made to the two Conventions in 1984. The need for the amendments was triggered by the *Amoco Cadiz* disaster which occurred off the coast of Brittany in March, 1978. The incident surpassed the record of the *Torrey Canyon* and became the worst of its kind up to that point in time. The country that suffered the most from the incident was France and the French Government therefore sought to reconsider adequacy of compensation under the CLC/Fund regime. As the law making machinery moved slowly, nothing much happened until March, 1982, when the Legal Committee at IMCO commenced a review of the Conventions and consideration of proposed amendments. The principal objective of the revision exercise was to enhance and improve the total compensation scheme under the Conventions. Additionally, certain provisions would have to be amended which were incomplete, ambiguous or outdated. At the Legal Committee two divergent views surfaced regarding the fundamental object and purpose of the dual convention regime. The tanker industry contended that the object of the compensation scheme in its totality was to apportion liability between themselves, the carrier interests, and the cargo interests. The oil companies, on the other hand, took the position that the role of the cargo interests in the compensation scheme was to provide through the IOPC Fund, an additional supplementary compensation in cases of catastrophic oil spills. The primary liability for oil damage rested with the shipowners since the carrier was responsible for the environmentally safe and sound transportation of the oil cargo.

A diplomatic conference was eventually convened and protocols to the two Conventions adopted in 1984. The Protocols, however, failed to enter into force. This was mainly because the United States as the world's largest importer of oil transported by sea refused to join the Convention. The United States Government, responding to a staunch national pro-environment lobby favoured a virtually unlimited liability regime for pollution damage. [40] The Protocols were so designed that the scheme consisting of a tiered system of compensation with significantly raised aggregate amounts of compensation could only work meaningfully if the world's largest importers of oil would join the Conventions. Unfortunately, the United States, the world's largest oil importer at the time was a not a party to the CLC or the Fund Convention, and Japan, the second largest importer did not accept the Protocols.

The possibility of the United States ever joining the regime diminished following the *Exxon Valdez* disaster which reinforced the United States' unilateral stance. The mega disaster occurred in Prudhoe Bay, Alaska in 1989; the damage and ensuing claims were far in excess of those associated with the *Torrey Canyon* and *Amoco Cadiz* incidents. The mammoth environmental consequence provided the impetus for the enactment of the United States Oil Pollution Act, 1990.

It was not until 1992 when the issue of adequacy of compensation under the CLC 1969 and Fund 1971 regime was reopened. The international community under the auspices of IMO adopted the 1992 Protocols to the two Conventions. Much of the scheme of the failed 1984 Protocols was maintained with some further revisions and updating. The totality of the revision resulted in virtually two new conventions and provision was made for the denunciation of the old conventions by parties once the requisite number of states accepted the new conventions which were called CLC 1992 and Fund Convention 1992. They both entered into force on 30 May 1996.

The two old conventions are now normally referred to as the "old regime" and the 1992 Conventions are referred to as the "new regime". Many of the provisions in the new CLC and Fund Convention are the same as in their 1969 and 1971 versions, respectively.

1.4. The CLC 1992

The following is a synopsis of the 1992 liability and compensation scheme focusing on its principal features and highlighting the important changes from the old regimes.

As mentioned earlier, the roll-back relief provision in the old scheme no longer exists. It is now truly a scheme that is entirely for the benefit of claimants who are victims of pollution damage. The scheme as a whole is sound and rational both legally and functionally. Among other substantive provisions, whereas the geographical scope of application of the old conventions was limited to the territorial sea, *i.e.,* 12 nautical miles from the baselines of a coastal state, under the 1992 Conventions, this has been increased to 200 nautical miles. In other words, the geographical perimeter is the exclusive economic zone (EEZ) as defined by UNCLOS.

The basis of liability under the new CLC remains strict and it is the registered owner of the polluting ship who is liable. The defences or exceptions to strict liability remain unchanged. The first one is *force majeure, i.e.,* damage resulting from an act of war, hostilities, civil war, insurrection or a natural phenomenon of an exceptional, inevitable and irresistible character. The other defences are damage from sabotage by a third party and damage caused by negligence of a public authority in maintaining aids to navigation. The shipowner may also escape liability, wholly or partially, if he proves that the victim himself intentionally caused the pollution damage. [41] Under the new CLC 1992, all claims in the primary instance must be channelled against the owner. Claimants are precluded from making claims against servants or agents of the owner, crew members, pilot, charterer, salvor or any person taking preventive measures, including servants and agents of all of the above-noted persons, unless it is proved that the damage resulted from "their personal act or omission, committed with the intent to cause such damage, or recklessly and with knowledge that such damage would probably result." [42]

Under CLC 1969, if an owner was found to be actually at fault or was privy to the commission or omission of the act that caused the pollution, he would be precluded from invoking limitation of liability. The so-called actual fault or privity test was a hallmark of previous limitation regimes including the 1957 Global Limitation Convention. In a series of English cases the courts had a tendency to allow limits to be easily broken. [43] As a result, shipowners and their insurers found themselves frequently faced with unlimited liability to the extent that limits of liability established by convention or domestic statutes, made little sense in practical, commercial terms.

The trend was reversed in a series of conventions where the test for conduct barring limitation was fundamentally changed. [44] The new formulation of words made limitation virtually unbreakable and was strongly supported at the international level by the insurance industry. The *quid pro quo* of significantly higher limits turned out, on balance, to be beneficial for all parties concerned and was eventually accepted by most maritime countries. [45] In the CLC regime, the new formulation of the "conduct barring limitation" is provided in Article V(2) of CLC 1992.

The compulsory insurance requirements of CLC 1969 including certification attesting to compliance are carried over into the 1992 regime. The certificate may be required to be produced to the relevant authorities of a state party to the Convention when a ship enters or leaves a port or offshore terminal in that state. The requirement for certification may be imposed by coastal state parties on tankers flying the flag of a non-state party as well. [46]

An important change has been made to the type of ship covered by the Conventions. The old conventions applied to pollution damage from laden tankers only. The notion is manifested in the definition of "ship" in CLC 1969 which is "any sea-going vessel and any seaborne craft of any type whatsoever, actually carrying oil in bulk as cargo." [47] In other words, tankers on a ballast voyage were not covered by the old conventions. By contrast, the 1992 Conventions are applicable to non-laden tankers within certain limits as is apparent from the new definition of "ship" which is –

> …any sea-going vessel and seaborne craft of any type whatsoever constructed or adapted for the carriage of oil in bulk as cargo, provided that a ship capable of carrying oil and other cargoes shall be regarded as a ship only when it is actually carrying oil in bulk as cargo and during any voyage following such carriage unless it is proved that it has no residues of such carriage of oil in bulk aboard. [48]

The new definition thus covers tankers or combination carriers on a ballast voyage after discharging a cargo of oil with residues of the oil cargo on board. The definition would not cover such a vessel after tank cleaning operations have been completed and the vessel is ready to load a non-oil cargo.

In terms of pollutant, the coverage of the original conventions was limited to pollution damage from persistent hydrocarbon mineral oils "whether carried on board a ship as cargo or in the bunkers of such a ship." [49] That has remained in the 1992 regime. [50] When the definitions of "oil" and "ship" are examined together, it is clear that, in addition to pollution caused by oil cargo carried in ships as defined in the CLC, pollution caused by bunker oil of a tanker, laden or unladen, as the case may be according to the definition of "ship", is covered by the Convention, but pollution from bunker oil of a non-tanker such as a dry cargo ship is not. Be that as it may, it is submitted that there is an anomaly. If the material definition of oil is substituted in the definition of "ship", the latter definition would read "ship" means any sea-going vessel … *etc.* … when it is actually carrying oil (as cargo or in the bunkers of such a ship) in bulk as cargo …*etc.*

The definition of "pollution damage" has been changed in the 1992 CLC from what it was in the old 1969 CLC. It now explicitly contains two elements; one is -

> loss or damage caused outside the ship by contamination resulting from the escape or discharge of oil from the ship, wherever such escape or discharge may occur, provided that compensation for impairment of the environment other than loss of profit from such impairment shall be limited to costs of reasonable measures of reinstatement actually undertaken or to be undertaken;

and the other is –

> the costs of *preventive measures* (emphasis added) and further loss or damage caused by preventive measures.

The definition of "preventive measures" has not changed; it refers to "any reasonable measures taken by any person after an *incident* (emphasis added) has occurred to prevent or minimize pollution damage." The definition of "incident" which features in the unchanged definition of "preventive measures" has however been altered in the 1992 CLC. [51] In CLC 1969, "incident" means any occurrence, or series of occurrences having the same origin, which causes pollution damage. In CLC 1992, the new definition is expanded. In it "incident" means any occurrence or series of occurrences having the same origin, which causes pollution damage *or creates a grave and imminent threat of causing such damage.* [52] The upshot of the above observations is that the old conventions applied only to preventive measures taken after oil had escaped or been discharged. Thus, the costs of pure threat removal measures such as those that were so successful as to prevent any actual oil spill were not compensable. By contrast, under the 1992 Conventions, costs of preventive measures are compensable even if there is no oil spill, provided there was grave and imminent threat of pollution damage. [53]

The limits of liability have been increased considerably. Under 1992 CLC Protocol, the limits are as follows-

(a) for a ship not exceeding 5,000 units of gross tonnage, 3 million SDR;
(b) for a ship between 5,000 and 140,000 units of tonnage, 3 million SDR plus 420 SDR for each additional unit of tonnage; and
(c) for a ship of 140,000 units of tonnage and above, 59.7 million SDR. [54]

In October 2000, pursuant to the provisions of Article 15 of CLC 1992 and Article 34 of the Fund Convention 1992, the IMO Legal Committee adopted two resolutions to raise the limits of both Conventions by about 50.37%. The amended limits entered into force on 1 November, 2003. Under the first resolution, the increased limits of shipowner's liability under the CLC became-

(a) for a ship not exceeding 5,000 units of tonnage, 4,510,000 SDR;
(b) for a ship between 5000 and 140,000 units of tonnage 4,510,000 SDR plus 631 SDR for each additional unit of tonnage; and
(c) for a ship of 140,000 units of tonnage and above, 89,770,000 SDR.

1.5. The Fund Convention, 1992

Upon the Fund Convention, 1992 entering into force on 30 May 1996, the IOPC Fund 1992 was established under that Convention. The basic obligations of the 1992 Fund which is to provide compensation under the 1992 scheme remain largely the same as those under the old regime. [55] Specifically the Fund is liable to pay compensation to victims of oil pollution damage in state parties who have not obtained full compensation under the CLC 1992 in circumstances set out in Article 4(1) of the Fund Convention, 1992.

The IOPC Fund is not obliged to pay any compensation in cases where-

(a) the damage has occurred in a non-state party to the Fund Convention;
(b) the pollution damage is attributable to an act of war, hostilities, civil war, insurrection or was caused by a spill from a warship; or
(c) the claimant is unable to prove that the damage resulted from an incident involving a ship as defined in the CLC, or more than one ship. [56]

Pursuant to both the 1992 Conventions, amendments to the Conventions may be effectuated through the convening of a diplomatic conference at the request of not less than one third of the state parties. [57] However, changes to the limits of liability in the case of the CLC, and the compensation limits in the case of the Fund Convention, can be brought about through deliberations within the Legal Committee. A proposal for such a change must be requested by at least a quarter of the state parties to the relevant Convention and must be circulated by the Secretary General six months in advance of it being submitted to the Legal Committee for consideration. Amendments must be adopted by a two-thirds majority present and voting in the Legal Committee. No amendments may be considered before 15 January, 1998 or before the entry into force of the 1992 Conventions. [58]

As per the compensation limits, under the Fund Convention 1992, the aggregate amount of compensation payable for one incident is 135 million SDR inclusive of the amount paid by the shipowner under CLC 1992. The IOPC Fund is liable for the balance. The 1992 scheme has also introduced the two-tier system of compensation pursuant to which the maximum amount of 135 million SDR can be increased to 200 million SDR for an incident that occurs during a period when in respect of three parties to the Convention, the combined amount of contributing oil received in those states was at least 600 million tonnes in the preceding calendar year. [59]

As mentioned earlier, in 2000, the IMO Legal Committee adopted two resolutions to raise the limits of both Conventions by about 50.37%. The amendments to the 1992 Fund Convention under the second resolution brought the aggregate amount of compensation under the 1992 scheme to 203 million SDR.

Meanwhile, the Assembly of the IOPC Fund had established a Working Group to examine the *status quo* and determine whether the total compensation available under the 1992 scheme as it stood was sufficient. The general feeling was that although the scheme had worked reasonably well since the inception of the two Conventions, there were times when the system appeared to be inadequate. Some participants of the Working Group expressed the view that in order for the scheme to continue to work efficiently and maintain its credibility, the maximum levels of compensation must be high enough to cover all claims even in the worst of oil spills. Other states were of the opinion that the ceiling of 203 million SDR reached pursuant to the IMO Legal Committee's decision was sufficient and there was no need for a further increase. The divergent views within the Working Group led to a proposal for the establishment of an optional third tier of compensation; a Supplementary Compensation Fund 2003 (SCF). [60]

The 1992 Fund Assembly adopted a draft protocol relating to the establishment of the SCF in October 2001. Eventually in May 2003, a diplomatic conference was convened. [61] After somewhat protracted negotiations, a Protocol was adopted creating the International Oil Pollution Supplementary Compensation Fund (IOPSCF or Supplementary Fund) which entered into force on 3 March 2005. [62] The salient features of the Protocol are as follows:

(a) The Supplementary Fund established by the Protocol is a new intergovernmental organisation;
(b) States parties to the 1992 Fund Convention can become parties to the Protocol and thus become members of the Supplementary Fund which is to be financed by contributors from oil importers in those state parties (IOPSCF states);
(c) The total amount of compensation available for any one incident is 750 million SDR which includes the maximum amount of 203 million SDR available under the 1992 Conventions;
(d) Compensation from the Supplementary Fund is payable only for incidents occurring after the Protocol has entered into force for the state affected;
(e) The annual contributions to the Supplementary Fund in respect of a IOPSCF state is payable by any person who in a calendar year receives total quantities of contributing oil in excess of 150,000 tonnes after sea transport in ports and terminals in that state;
(f) For contribution purposes there is an assumption that a minimum aggregate quantity of 1 million tonnes of contributing oil is received in each IOPSCF state. [63]

2. The Bunkers Convention

As discussed in the above text, pollution damage caused by bunker oil of a non-tanker is not covered by the CLC regime. This, in fact, was a significant lacuna in the international legal framework governing ship-generated oil pollution at sea as the bunker fuels carried in non-tankers such as dry cargo ships may cause more pollution damage than cargo oil carried on tankers. As mentioned at the beginning of this paper, some large non-tankers may carry oil in bunkers up to 10,000 tonnes which is even larger than the oil cargo carried in some tankers. [64] Moreover, the highly viscous and persistent nature as well as the chemical composition makes bunker oil more harmful than cargo oil. There have been many bunker oil spill incidents which have caused serious environmental problems. The *New Carissa,* a Panamanian-flagged wood chip carrier, ran aground off the Coos Bay, Oregon, United States during a storm in February 1999, and consequently broke apart. As a result, two of the five fuel tanks on the ship began to leak and eventually spilled approximately 70,000 gallons (262,500 litres) of thick bunker oil and diesel onto the beach and into the water. [65] The incident resulted in substantial claims for clean-up and wreck removal costs. [66] In some other incidents, such as the *Fedra,* [67] the spills were of relatively small quantity, but the environmental damage so caused is still devastating.

To address this lacuna in the law, the International Convention on Civil Liability for Bunker Oil Pollution Damage (the Bunkers Convention) was adopted on 23rd March 2001. It entered into force on 21st November 2008 - 12 months following the ratification of 18 States including 5 States each with ships whose combined gross tonnage is not less than 1 million. [68] As of 31 December 2010, there are 58 member states.

The objective of the Convention is to provide uniform international rules and procedures for determining questions of liability and providing adequate, prompt and effective compensation for damage caused by pollution resulting from the escape or discharge of bunker oil from ships that are not covered by the CLC regime. Unlike the CLC/Fund regime which is a two-tier system with the first tier being the liability imposed on the shipowner and the second being the supplementary compensation provided by the IOPC Fund, the Bunkers Convention is a single-tier system and there is no corresponding international fund to accompany it. It was thought, during the negotiations that led to the adoption of the Convention, that this single-tier regime would be sufficient in most cases to ensure full compensation to victims of pollution damage caused by bunker oil spills. [69]

The Bunkers Convention is largely modelled on the CLC 1992 with some provisions being very similar or even identical to the provisions in the CLC. There are, however, a number of differences which are significant and deserve close examination. In the ensuing text, the salient features of the Bunkers Convention will be discussed highlighting the similarities and differences between the CLC and the Bunkers Convention.

The definition of "pollution damage" [70] is almost identical to that in the CLC except for the words "escape or discharge of *bunker oil* (emphasis added) from the ship". In the CLC the corresponding words are "escape or discharge of *oil* (emphasis added) from the ship". Two concepts need to be examined in conjunction with this definition; one is "bunker oil" and the other is "ship".

As defined in Art 1 (5), "bunker oil" means "any hydrocarbon mineral oil, including lubricating oil, used or intended to be used for the operation or propulsion of the ship, and any residues of such oil." There are two notable points in relation to this definition; one is that oil carried on board a ship as cargo is not covered by the Bunkers Convention; the other is that this definition is not restricted to persistent hydrocarbon mineral oil as in the CLC. [71] In other words, the Bunkers Convention covers both persistent and non-persistent oil.

The concept of "ship" relates to several articles in the Convention. Art 1(1) provides a very broad definition which reads "'Ship' means any seagoing vessel and seaborne craft, of any type whatsoever." This broad connotation is then "narrowed down" by a number of "exclusions" provided in Art 4. According to 4(2) and (3), the Convention does not apply to warships or other ships owned or operated by a State and used, for the time being, only on Government non-commercial service although a State Party may decide to apply this Convention to these ships by notifying the Secretary-General of IMO of the terms and conditions of such application.

Another exclusion is provided in Art 4(1) which reads –

> This Convention shall not apply to pollution damage as defined in the Civil Liability Convention, whether or not compensation is payable in respect of it under that Convention.

As provided in Art 1(6), "Civil Liability Convention" here refers to the 1992 CLC. As it may be recalled, the 1992 CLC applies to, in addition to pollution damage caused by spills of persistent cargo oil, bunker oil spills from a laden tanker carrying persistent oil or a non-laden tanker with persistent oil residues on board. Thus, pursuant to Art 4(1), the Bunkers Convention applies to bunker oil spills from non-tankers, laden tankers carrying non-persistent oil and unladen tankers with no persistent oil residues on board.

It is quite apparent that the purpose of this provision is to make these two Conventions mutually exclusive. There are, however, a few gaps that are notable in terms of the integrity of the international legal regimes governing liability and compensation of ship-generated oil pollution at sea. This is mainly caused by the use of the words "… whether or not compensation is payable in respect of it under that Convention". This can be interpreted to the effect that the Bunkers Convention will not apply to a bunker oil spill as long as it is from a ship that falls within the definition of "ship" in the CLC 1992 even if the CLC is not applicable in that case. It is thus submitted that in several situations where an oil spill occurs, no international liability regime will be applicable.

One situation is when bunker oil is spilled from an un-laden tanker with persistent oil residues on board in a country that is a party to the CLC 1969 and the Bunkers Convention but not to the CLC 1992; none of these Conventions will be applicable. The CLC 1992 is not applicable because the country is not a party to it; the CLC 1969 is not applicable because the ship involved is not a laden tanker; the Bunkers Convention is not applicable because the ship involved falls within the definition of "ship" provided in the CLC 1992 and is thus excluded from the Bunkers Convention. Another situation is when bunker oil is spilled from a laden tanker in a country that is a party to the Bunkers Convention but not to any of the CLCs. In this case, neither the CLCs nor the Bunkers Convention will be applicable as laden tanker falls within the definition of "ship" in the CLC 1992. [72]

One may argue that these gaps would disappear when countries all become parties to the CLC 1992. Be that as it may, there is still a lacuna that should be recognised. That is the pollution damage caused by spills of non-persistent bunker oil from a ship as defined in the CLC. This is due to the fact that the CLC does not cover non-persistent oil and the Bunkers Convention does not cover "CLC ships".

As in the CLC 1992, the Bunkers Convention is geographical in its application and the applicability includes the territorial sea and the EEZ of a contracting state. [73] Another similarity between the two Conventions is the basis of liability. In the Bunkers Convention it is also strict. The exceptions afforded to enable the defendant to escape liability are the same as in the CLC as well. [75]

However, it must be noted that the parties on whom strict liability is imposed are different from those in the CLC. Under the Bunkers Convention, the parties who may be liable for pollution damage include the "registered owner, bareboat charterer, manager and operator of the ship". [76] This is much broader than the corresponding parties in the CLC. However, how likely the victims of pollution damage would sue the manager or operator of the ship for compensation is questionable. Notably in the Bunkers Convention a system of compulsory liability insurance is required but the obligation to maintain insurance rest only on the registered shipowner. [77] It may be reasonable to imagine that the financial capability of the manager and operator of the ship may not be guaranteed.

The provision regarding compulsory insurance reads as follows:

> The *registered owner* (emphasis added) of a ship having a *gross tonnage greater than 1000* (emphasis added) registered in a State Party shall be required to maintain insurance or other financial security ... to cover the liability of the registered owner for pollution damage in an amount equal to the limits of liability under the applicable national or international limitation regime, but in all cases, not exceeding an amount calculated in accordance with the Convention on Limitation of Liability for Maritime Claims, 1976, as amended.

The words "the applicable national or international limitation regime" are noteworthy. It has been pointed out that the applicable national regime for this purpose is the law of the flag state. [78] In any case, however, the limits shall not exceed the limits provided in the

LLMC1976 as amended (that is the Protocol of 1996 to amend the Convention on Limitation of Liability for Maritime Claims, 1976), even if according to the applicable law of the flag state the liability is unlimited.

This concerns another important concept in the Convention; namely, limitation of liability. Notably, the Bunkers Convention does not set up its own limits; instead, it refers to "any applicable national or international regimes, such as the Convention on Limitation of Liability for Maritime Claims, 1976, as amended" [79] as the regime for limitation of liability.

As the Convention is geographical in its application, the applicable national regime here, in the normal course, would be the law of the contracting state where pollution damage occurs. In other words, it is the coastal state the law of which would normally determine the amount of the limitation of liability. It should be noted, however, that limitation of liability is a matter for the forum state, that is, the state in whose courts limitation is being invoked which may or may not be the court of the state where the pollution claim is litigated on the merits.

The linkages described above between the Bunkers Convention and the application of national and international regimes may cause a number of uncertainties. One uncertainty is related to the employment of the LLMC and it is caused by the fact that "the LLMC does not explicitly grant the right of limitation of pollution claims". [80] As Jacobsson points out, some categories of claims that arise from oil pollution such as claims for property damage and clean-up costs, may fall within the categories of claim that are subject to limitation under the LLMC, but the situation is unclear with regard to other claims such as claims for pure economic loss suffered by fishermen and the tourism industry. [81]

Another uncertainty may arise due to the fact that some contracting states of the Bunkers Convention are not parties to the LLMC. In that case, it is, of course, the national law of the forum state where the pollution damage claim is litigated that is applicable. If according to the national law, the liability for maritime claims is unlimited, the liability of the "shipowner" (as defined in the Convention) will be unlimited. [82] Some contracting states of the Bunkers Convention are still parties to the LLMC 1976 and have not yet ratified the 1996 Protocol. The limitation of liability in such cases is significantly lower than in the amended Convention. Even if the countries are parties to both the LLMC 1996 and the Bunkers Conventions, in relation to pollution damage caused by bunker spills, they may treat limitation differently. Australia, for example, applies the LLMC directly without amendment and the United Kingdom has enacted the LLMC with additional provisions in its national legislation. [83]

Lack of uniformity in this regard is quite significant which translates into different levels of exposure for shipowners. The uncertainties force shipowners to consider, once involved in a bunker spill incident, not only the Bunkers Convention *per se* but also the limitation regime applicable in the forum state or the state where the pollution damage occurs. Article 6 of the Bunkers Convention where the limitation of liability is provided has therefore been described as "an unusual, and perhaps, unfortunate, provision." [84]

What adds to the complexity of the issue is the compulsory insurance as required in the Convention. As discussed earlier, the shipowner's insurance limit may be determined by the applicable law of the flag state and in any case it will not exceed the limit calculated in accordance with the LLMC 1996. A difficulty may arise when a ship from a state where the limitation of liability is relatively low (for example, the country is a party to the LLMC 1976) spills bunker oil in a country which is not a party to the LLMC and has its own legal regime which provides for much higher limits, or even unlimited liability such as in the United States.

Flowing from the above analysis, it may be concluded that the Bunkers Convention is an important international treaty without which there would be a significant gap in the international legal framework governing ship-generated oil pollution at sea. It, however, has a number of deficiencies not the least of which is that the regime lacks uniformity in providing a system of limitation of liability and compulsory insurance. The exclusivity of the Convention from the CLC is carefully designed but several lacunae may still be found in applying the Conventions.

3. THE HNS CONVENTION

As mentioned earlier, a discussion on the international legal framework governing liability and compensation for oil pollution at sea would not be complete without mentioning the HNS Convention.

The HNS Convention was adopted in 1996 under the auspices of IMO. [85] It aims to ensure adequate, prompt and effective compensation for damage to persons and property, costs of clean-up and reinstatement measures and economic losses caused by the maritime transportation of hazardous and noxious substances (HNS). These substances include various types of oil. In the following text, an analysis will be carried out with regard to the key features and application of the Convention in relation to damage caused by oils.

As provided in Article 1(1), "ship" in the HNS Convention means "any seagoing vessel and seaborne craft, of any type whatsoever" – This of course includes tankers, carrying persistent or non-persistent oil. Article 4(4) then narrows down the concept by excluding warships or other ships owned or operated by a State and used, for the time being, only on Government non-commercial service although, as provided in 4(5) a State Party may decide to apply this Convention to these ships by notifying the Secretary-General of IMO of the terms and conditions of such application. It is worth noting that under Article 5(1) the Convention allows a State to exclude from the application of the Convention, ships which satisfy all these three conditions: (1) not exceeding 200 gross tonnage; (2) carrying hazardous and noxious substances only in packaged form; and (3) while being engaged on voyages between ports or facilities of that State.

The definition of "HNS" as cast in the Convention is very broad including packaged goods, bulk solids, liquids, liquefied gases such as liquefied natural gases (LNG) and liquefied petroleum gases (LPG). [86] The definition of these substances in the Convention is largely based on lists of individual substances that have been previously identified in a number of IMO Conventions and Codes designed to ensure maritime safety and prevention of pollution, *e.g.*, the International Convention for the Prevention of Pollution from Ships, 1973, as amended by the Protocol of 1978 relating thereto (MARPOL 73/78) and the International Maritime Dangerous Goods Code (IMDG Code). [87] The HNS Convention is applicable when ships are carrying these substances as cargo [88] or as residues from the previous carriage. [89] Notably, the Convention does not cover radioactive materials. [90]

The liquids covered by the Convention include both persistent and non-persistent oils. As provided in Article 1(5)(a)(i), oils covered by the HNS Convention are the oils listed in

Appendix I of Annex I to MARPOL 73/78. The oils listed in Appendix I are divided into eight categories and each category includes one or a few substances. A full list of the oils is presented below [91]:

- Asphalt solutions: Blending stocks; Roofers flux; Straight run residue
- Oils: Clarified; Crude oil; Mixtures containing crude oil; Diesel oil; Fuel oil no.4; Fuel oil no.5; Fuel oil no. 6; Residual fuel oil; Road oil; Transformer oil; Aromatic oil (excluding vegetable oil); Lubricating oils and blending stocks; Mineral oil; Motor oil; Penetrating oil; Spindle oil; Turbine oil
- Distillates: Straight run; Flashed feed stocks
- Gas oil: Cracked
- Gasoline blending stocks: Alkylates – fuel; Reformates; Polymer – fuel
- Gasolines: Gasinghead (natural); Automotive; Aviation; Straight run; Fuel oil no.1 (kerosene); Fuel oil no. 1-D; Fuel oil no.2; Fuel oil no.2-D
- Jet fuels: JP-1 (kerosene); JP-3; JP-4; JP-5 (kerosene, heavy); Turbo fuel; Kerosene; Mineral spirit
- Naphtha: Solvent; Petroleum; Heartcut distillate oil

Although it is footnoted in the Appendix that the list of oils "shall not necessarily be considered as comprehensive", [92] it does appear to be an inclusive list of both persistent and non-persistent oils of petroleum origin.

To fully appreciate the applicability of the HNS Convention pertaining to oils, the concept of "damage" as defined in the Convention must be analysed. Under Article 1(6), "damage" means:

(a) loss of life or personal injury on board or outside the ship carrying the hazardous and noxious substances caused by those substances;
(b) loss of or damage to property outside the ship carrying the hazardous and noxious substances caused by those substances;
(c) loss or damage by contamination of the environment caused by the hazardous and noxious substances, provided that compensation for impairment of the environment other than loss of profit from such impairment shall be limited to costs of reasonable measures of reinstatement actually undertaken or to be undertaken; and
(d) the costs of preventive measures and further loss or damage caused by preventive measures.

In comparison with the concept of "pollution damage" as defined in the CLC 1992 and the Bunkers Convention, item (a) above is somewhat unique. In the definition of "pollution damage", loss of life or personal injury on board or outside the ship is not included. Quite understandably, this is due to the hazardous and noxious nature of some the substances that may be fatal to human health.

Article 4(3)(a) further provides that this Convention shall not apply to "pollution damage as defined in the International Convention on Civil Liability for Oil Pollution Damage, 1969, as amended, whether or not compensation is payable in respect of it under that Convention". It may be recalled that pollution damage as defined in the CLC 1992 includes loss or damage caused outside the ship by contamination resulting from the escape or discharge of persistent cargo or bunker oil from laden tankers or unladen tankers with residues on board and the costs of preventive measures and further loss or damage caused by preventive measures. When this is examined together with Article 4(3)(a) in the HNS convention, it may be concluded that loss or damage caused by non-persistent oil and non-pollution damage caused by persistent oil, *e.g.*, loss of life, personal injury or damage caused by fire or explosion, is covered by the HNS Convention.

Notably, due to the use of the words "whether or not compensation is payable in respect of it under that Convention", some pollution incidents may fall outside the scope of the international legal framework governing liability and compensation for ship-source oil pollution damage. When pollution damage is caused by a spill of persistent cargo oil from a ship in the territorial sea of a State which is party to the HNS Convention but not to the CLC 1992, neither of these Conventions will be applicable. The reason for the CLC not being applicable is because the victim State is not a party to the Convention; the HNS Convention is not applicable because the pollution damage falls within the scope of the CLC regime even though the CLC is not applicable in this case. This perhaps could provide more incentives to the states to become parties to the CLC regime.

It is worth pointing out here that the gaps between the CLC and the Bunkers Convention in relation to bunker oil spills as discussed earlier in this paper still exist even with the presence of the HNS Convention. This is simply because the substances covered by the HNS Convention must be carried on board as cargo or residuals, *i.e.,* excluding bunkers.

The geographical scope of the HNS Convention is different from the CLC and the Bunkers Convention. The latter two are applicable to pollution damage occurring within the territory including territorial sea and the EEZ of a State Party. The applicability of the HNS Convention is more complicated in that it varies according to the type of damage, and in some circumstances the Convention is applicable even if the damage has occurred in a non-State Party. The scope of application of the Convention as set out in Article 3 is particularised in terms of four instances.

- Under paragraph (a), the Convention applies to "any damage caused in the territory, including the territorial sea, of a State Party". [93]
- Under paragraph (b), for "damage by contamination of the environment", the Convention is applicable if it is caused in the EEZ, or equivalent, of a State Party. [94]
- Under paragraph (c), for "damage, other than damage by contamination of the environment caused outside the territory, including the territorial sea, of *any State*", the Convention is applicable if this damage is caused by a substance carried on board a ship registered in a State Party.
- Under paragraph (d), the Convention is applicable for preventive measures wherever taken.

A potential confusion exists in relation to the term "to preventive measures wherever taken" in paragraph (d) read in conjunction with the chapeau "[T]his Convention shall apply exclusively". To clearly understand the purport of that expression, one needs to look at the definition of "preventive measures" in paragraph 7 of Article 1 which incorporates the term "Incident"; and then look at the definition of "Incident" in paragraph 8 of that Article.

The expression "wherever taken" in paragraph (d) of Article 3 does not imply place or location in any open-ended sense, *i.e.*, anywhere or everywhere, but rather within the scope of place or location as set out in the preceding paragraphs, namely, paragraphs (a), (b) and (c) of Article 3. If the word "wherever" is construed literally, it can lead to an anomalous situation where the Convention could apply to a ship on the high seas whose flag state is not a party to the Convention. Surely that could not have been intended by the draftsman. Perhaps in formulating the provision, more attention should have been given to specificity, precision and clarity.

In this context, it is notable that the word "damage" appears in paragraphs (a), (b) and (c) but not in paragraph (d). If the definition of "Damage" were to be transposed from Article 1 paragraph 6 into paragraphs (a), (b) and (c) of Article 3, then "cost of preventive measures" would be included in respect of damage mentioned in those paragraphs. It is notable that paragraph (d) of Article 3 refers to "preventive measures" as a practical matter whereas subparagraph (d) of Article 1 paragraph 6 speaks to "cost of preventive measures" characterised as damage of a certain kind. The distinction is important.

With regard to the liability issues, the same as in the CLC, under the HNS Convention liability for damage is channelled through the registered owner [95] of the ship. [96] The liability basis is also strict with certain defences. Most of the available defences provided in the HNS Convention are the same as those in the CLC and the Bunkers Convention with only one exception that is unique in the HNS Convention. This is provided in Article 7(2)(d); it reads –

> … the failure of the shipper or any other person to furnish information concerning the hazardous and noxious nature of the substances shipped either
>
> (i) has caused the damage, wholly or partly; or
>
> (ii) has led the owner not to obtain insurance in accordance with article 12;
>
> provided that neither the owner nor its servants or agents knew or ought reasonably to have known of the hazardous and noxious nature of the substances shipped.

The rationale of this provision is straightforward. Considering there are a huge number of different substances that are defined in the HNS convention, it would be unreasonable to request the shipowner to be familiar with the nature of each of the substances.

Compulsory insurance is also required in the HNS Convention but there is no specific requirement on minimum carriage as in the CLC (2000 tonnes) or minimum gross tonnage of the ship as in the Bunkers Convention (1000 tonnes). [97] Claims for compensation may be brought directly against the insurer or person providing financial security. 98] Under the Convention, shipowner's liability is limited unless "it is proved that the damage resulted from the personal act or omission of the owner, committed with the intent to cause such damage, or recklessly and with knowledge that such damage would probably result". [99] The same as the CLC, the HNS Convention sets up its own limits. Under Article 9(1), the limits are –

> (a) 10 million units of account [100] for a ship not exceeding 2,000 units of tonnage; and
>
> (b) for a ship with a tonnage in excess thereof, the following amount in addition to that mentioned in (a):
>
> for each unit of tonnage from 2,001 to 50,000 units of tonnage, 1,500 units of account
>
> for each unit of tonnage in excess of 50,000 units of tonnage, 360 units of account

> provided, however, that this aggregate amount shall not in any event exceed 100 million units of account.

It must be noted that the HNS Convention, on its own, provides a two-tier system with the first tier being the registered owner paying for his liability and the second tier being the International Hazardous and Noxious Substances Fund (HNS Fund) paying additional compensation. [101] The HNS Fund is financed by contributions based on the quantities of contributing cargo received in the territory of a State Party after sea transport. [102] It provides compensation up to a maximum of 250 million SDR including the amount paid by the shipowner and his insurer. [103] As it is modelled on the IOPC Fund, the working mechanism of this Fund is very similar to that in the CLC/IOPC Fund regime except a unique feature; that is, that the HNS Fund has four separate accounts. The reason for setting up separate accounts was that during preliminary discussion in the Legal Committee of the IMO on the draft HNS Convention in which a single account was designed, it became apparent that such a system would disadvantage those sectors which are relatively safer but likely to transport in large volumes. [104] Having separate accounts would largely avoid cross-subsidising damages.

These are accounts for oil, LNG and LPG and a general account for bulk solids and other HNS. [105] Each account will only meet claims resulting from incidents involving the respective cargoes. Individual receivers in the State Parties shall contribute to the separate accounts in proportion to the quantities of HNS received if the quantities received are above the following thresholds:

Oil account:	*for persistent oil*	150,000 tonnes
	for non-persistent oil	20,000 tonnes
LNG account:		no minimum quantity
LPG:		20,000 tonnes
General account:		20,000 tonnes

It is worth noting that the threshold for persistent oil is the same as that in the CLC/Fund regime; and for those oil receivers who receive oil in excess of this threshold shall contribute to the IOPC Fund and the HNS Fund as well if the state is a party to both the Fund Convention and the HNS Convention. This extra burden imposed on the persistent oil receivers may reduce the incentive of states to become parties to the Convention.

The HNS Convention is complex in many ways; not the least of which is that it covers between 3500 to 5000 different substances at any one time. [106] Consequently, establishment and operation of the HNS Fund is not going to be easy – it is thought that there may be about half a million individual receivers of the substances defined in the Convention. [107] The HNS Convention has not entered into force yet although it was adopted in 1996. This indeed is not surprising considering the complexity and the difficulties in practice.

In order to facilitate ratification and expedite entry into force of the Convention, a Protocol to the HNS Convention was adopted in April 2010 at a diplomatic conference convened by the IMO. The 2010 Protocol aims to address the problems which are thought to be the barriers to ratification of the Convention. Three major issues are dealt with. Firstly, to deal with the difficulties in relation to data collection and setting up a report system on the volumes of packaged goods, the Protocol removes the obligation for receivers of packaged goods to contribute to the HNS Fund. The Fund, however, will continue to pay, where appropriate, the additional compensation to victims of incident involving these cargoes. This of course would increase exposure of bulk cargo receivers. As a remedy to this, the shipowner's limitation of liability is increased by approximately 15%. [108]

Another issue is about the LNG account. Whereas in the other three accounts the person responsible for making contributions is the receiver, in the LNG account the person liable for making contribution is the person who holds title to an LNG cargo immediately prior to discharge. [109] Whilst it may be in line with the unique contractual arrangements for the purchase and transport of LNG, it is very difficult to administer and to enforce payment as the titleholders may not be subject to the jurisdiction of a State Party. [110]To resolve this issue, the Protocol shifts the responsibility for payment to the receiver at the point of discharge, unless there is an agreement for the titleholder to assume the responsibility.

The last issue relates to the obligation of contracting states to report on contributing cargoes. This is part of the requirements when a state ratifies the Convention under Article 43. The past experience, however, has not been very encouraging. To deal with this problem, the Protocol expressly requires states to submit reports on contributing cargos when depositing their instrument of ratification of the Protocol. [111] The Protocol further requires states to submit annual reports thereafter until the Protocol enters into force; failing that will result in temporary suspension of being a Contracting State. If a State Party fails to submit annual report after the Protocol enters into force, its right to claim compensation will be prohibited with only one exception, that is regarding claims for death and personal injury. [112] In the above brief discussion the key features of the HNS Convention are presented with a special focus on the applicability of the Convention in relation to oil pollution at sea. With the adoption of the Protocol, hopefully the Convention will enter into force in the near future.

CONCLUSION

Dealing with marine pollution is not an easy task. It has been recognised that due to the international character of shipping, efforts towards marine pollution abatement must be concentrated at the international level. The legal approaches manifested through international regulatory and private law regimes appear to be the most suitable in the maritime context.

Over the past few decades, in order to deal with liability and compensation issues in relation to oil pollution damage caused by ships, a number of international conventions have been developed including, *inter alia,* the CLC 1969, the Fund Convention 1971, the CLC 1992, the Fund Convention 1992, the Bunkers Convention 2001 and the HNS Convention 1996.

The designs of these conventions have all involved compromises in one way or another and it is therefore quite understandable that there are various weaknesses in these conventions. But nevertheless, over the years they have served their purposes well; and the past experiences have shown that the international maritime community is very capable of responding to new challenges and can act quite promptly in developing appropriate legal regimes.

REFERENCES

[1] In the seventeenth century, the celebrated Dutch jurist Hugo de Groot known by his Latin name Grotius, stated in his famous treatise on mare liberum that "[t]he vagrant waters of the seas are … necessarily free"; and that "[T]he right of occupation … rests upon the fact that most things become exhausted by promiscuous use and that appropriation, consequently, is the condition of their utility to human beings. But this is not the case with the sea; it can be exhausted neither by navigation nor by fishing, that is to say, in neither of the two ways in which it can be used." See Hugo Grotius, *The Freedom of the Seas*, translated by Ralph Van Deman Magoffin, Carnegie Endowment for International Peace, New York: Oxford University Press, 1916.

[2] For more details regarding the incident see British Government document Cmnd. No. 3246 (1967) *Secretary of State for the Home Department, "The Torrey Canyon"* and Edgar Gold, "Pollution of the Seas and International Law", (1971) 3(1) *Journal of Maritime Law and Commerce,* 13 at pp.21-22. See also Proshanto K. Mukherjee and Robert S. Lefevbre, "Fishermen and Oil Pollution Damage: The Regimes of Compensation" in J-L. Chaumel (ed.) *Labour Developments in the Fishing Industry*, Canada: Special Publication Fisheries and Aquatic Sciences 72 at p.74.

[3] Ved P. Nanda, "The *Torrey Canyon* Disaster: Some Legal Aspects", (1967) 44 *Denver Law Journal*, 400 at p.401. See footnote 6 at that page.

[4] The name of IMCO was changed to International Maritime Organization (IMO) in 1982. It is not merely a "consultative" body as its original name implied, but has powers to make law through conventions.

[5] IMO, "Background", available online at http://www.imo.org/OurWork /Environment/PollutionPrevention/OilPollution/Pages /Background.aspx [accessed on 25th Dec 2010].

[6] The full name of the Convention is called the International Convention Relating to Intervention on the High Seas in Cases of Oil Pollution Casualties, 1969.

[7] Måns Jacobsson, "Bunkers Convention in Force", (2009) 15, *Journal of International Maritime Law*, pp.21-36 at p.21.

[8] See generally Proshanto K. Mukherjee, "Liability and Compensation for Environmental Damage Caused by Ship-Source Oil Pollution: Actionability of Claims" in Michael G. Faure, Han Lixin and Shan Hongjun (Eds.) *Marine Pollution Liability and Policy China, Europe and the US,* Alpen aan den Rijn: Kluwer Law International, 2010, pp.75-95.

[9] See Jingjing Xu, "Theoretical Framework of Economic Analysis of Law Governing Marine Pollution", (2006) 5(1) *WMU Journal of Maritime Affairs*, 75.

[10] Gotthard Gauci, *Oil Pollution at Sea: Civil Liability and Compensation for Damage*, Chichester: John Wiley and Sons, 1997, p.32**.** See also Chao Wu, *Pollution from the Carriage of Oil by Sea: Liability and Compensation*, London, The Hague, Boston: Kluwer Law International, 1996, pp.48-49.

[11] See Jingjing Xu, "The Spectrum of the Legal Regime Governing Ship-source Oil Pollution and its Economic Implications", (2007) 12 (6) *Journal of International Maritime Law*, 402.

[12] Mukherjee and Lefevbre, *supra*, note 2, at p.74. See also R. Michael M'Gonigle and Mark W. Zacher, *Pollution, Politics and International Law: Tankers at Sea,* Berkeley and Los Angeles: University of California Press, 1979, at pp.151, 167, 170; Z. Oya Özçayir, *Liability for Oil Pollution and Collisions*, London: LLP, 1998, p.212; and Wu, *supra*, note 10, at p.56 and footnote 114 at that page.

[13] See Oya Özçayir, *ibid.* for positions taken by some delegations and their reasons. See also, M'Gonigle and Zacher, *ibid.* at pp.170-171.

[14] M'Gonigle and Zacher, *ibid.* at pp.151-152.

[15] See in particular Mukherjee and Lefevbre, *supra*, note 2, at p.74, and generally W. V. H. Rogers, *Winfield and Jolowicz on Tort,* 16th Ed., London: Sweet and Maxwell, 2002, Chapter 5.

[16] Gauci, *supra*, note 10, at p.19; Rogers, *ibid.* at p.443.

[17] See generally Wu, *supra*, note 10, at pp.50-54; and Oya Özçayir, *supra*, note 12 and M'Gonigle and Zacher, *supra*, note 12, at pp.167, 170.

[18] It is said that "polluter pays" is a principle of economics rather than of law, at least in terms of its original rationale. The issue is a moot point since it is now also accepted as a legal principle and the legal regime of pollution liability revolves around this principle. See Patricia W. Birnie and Alan E. Boyle, *International Law and the Environment*, 2nd Ed., Oxford: Oxford University Press, 2002, pp.92-94. See also Marie-Louise Larsson, *The Law of Environmental Damage: Liability and Reparation*, The Hague: Kluwer Law International; Stockholm: Norstedts Juridisk, 1999, pp.90-94. The implications are discussed in Chapter 7.

[19] The global limitation regime prevailing at the time was the International Convention on Limitation of Liability for Owners of Sea-Going Ships, 1957 applicable in respect of all maritime claims; hence the term "global".

[20] The term "limitation of liability" is somewhat of a misnomer. The limitation is not in respect of liability which is qualitative, but rather, in respect of the amount of compensation payable which is quantitative. It is the quantum of damages that is limited according to law.

[21] Lord Denning in *The Bramley Moore*, [1963], 2 Lloyd's Rep. 429 at p.437 (CA).

[22] N.J.J. Gaskell, C. Debattista and R.J.S.Swatton, *Chorley and Giles' Shipping Law*, 8th Ed., London: Pitman Publishing, 1988, p.411. See also F.J.J. Cadwallader, "The New Convention on Limitation of Liability" in Edgar Gold (ed.) Proceedings, *New Directions in Maritime Law, 1978,* Dalhousie University, Halifax, pp.10-13.

[23] M'Gonigle and Zacher, *supra*, note 12, at pp.172-174.

[24] Under the CLC 1969, the limitation tonnage was essentially the net tonnage of the ship.

[25] M'Gonigle and Zacher, *supra*, note 12, at p.173.

[26] Under UNCLOS as well as current customary international law the breadth of the territorial sea is 12 nautical miles measured seawards from the baseline. But in 1969, a 3-nautical mile territorial sea was the prevailing norm.

[27] Article III(2).

[28] See Duygu Damar, "Compulsory Insurance in International Maritime Conventions", 2009(15) *Journal of International Maritime Law*, 151 at p.155.

[29] Mukherjee and Lefevbre, *supra,* note 2, at pp.74-75.

[30] Under the International Convention on Civil Liability for Bunker Oil Pollution Damage, 2001 (Bunkers Convention) a bareboat and demise charterer can also be

liable. See Articles 1(3) and 3(1). More discussion on the Bunkers Convention will be carried out later in this paper.

[31] See statement made by Alan Philip, Head of the Danish delegation to the 1969 Brussels diplomatic conference in Committee II, *Official Records*, at p.628 cited in M'Gonigle and Zacher, *supra*, note 12, at p.172, in particular, footnote 77 at that page.

[32] See statement of Mr. Rajwar, Head of Indian delegation at the 1969 Brussels diplomatic conference cited in M'Gonigle and Zacher, *ibid.*

[33] Mukherjee and Lefevbre, *supra,* note 2, at p.75, M'Gonigle and Zacher, *ibid.* at p.182.

[34] See Preamble (fifth clause), Article 2 (1)(a) and Article 4 (1) (chapeau).

[35] M'Gonigle and Zacher, *supra*, note 12, at p.173.

[36] See Måns Jacobsson, "The International Oil Pollution Compensation Fund: Ten Years of Claims Settlement Experience", *Proceedings, 1989 Oil Spill Conference*, American Petroleum Institute, Washington D.C. at p.509.

[37] Gauci, *supra*, note 10, at p.22.

[38] The "unit of account" is applicable to member states of the IMF; for non-member states, the term "monetary unit" is used. Both the expressions have the same definition in terms of the SDR. See Article V of the CLC Protocol of 1976 and Article II of the Fund Protocol of 1976.

[39] The effective limitation, *i.e.*, the amount for which the shipowner is liable under the CLC is lesser of 133 SDR multiplied by the limitation tonnage of the ship and the maximum amount, *i.e.*, 14 million SDR.

[40] Even though the *Amoco Cadiz* disaster took place off the French coast and France was a party to the CLC and Fund Convention, many claimants pursued their claims in the United States courts in the hope of obtaining much higher compensation than was possible under the conventions. The total claims were in excess of USD 2 billion. Wikipedia, "Amoco Cadiz", available at http://en.wikipedia.org/wiki/Amoco_Cadiz [accessed on 3rd Jan 2011].

[41] Article III(3) of CLC 1992.

[42] See Article III(4) of CLC 1992. In the 1969 regime only servants and agents of the owner enjoyed this privilege.

[43] See *The Lady Gwendolen* [1965] P. 294; and *The Marion* [1984] A.C. 563.

[44] Examples are the International Convention on Carriage of Passengers and Their Luggage By Sea, 1974, (PAL), the International Conventional on Limitation of Liability for Maritime Claims, 1976 (LLMC) and the International Convention on Carriage of Goods By Sea, 1978 (Hamburg Rules).

[45] Some common law countries did have misgivings at first because the new test involved a reversal of onus from the shipowner to the claimant and, according to some, made the test akin to the standard of proof required in penal law. The objections were raised in relation to ratification of LLMC 1976. See Cadwallader, *supra*, note 22, at p.6-33.

[46] Måns Jacobsson, "The International Compensation Regime and the International Oil Pollution Compensation Funds", lecture note, World Maritime University, 4 August 2005, at p.2.

[47] Article I(1).

[48] Article I(1) of CLC 1992.

[49] Bunker oil of tankers is covered so long as it is persistent oil. There are some grades of bunker oil that are non-persistent; these would not be covered by the Convention.

[50] These include crude oil, fuel oil, heavy diesel oil and lubricating oil. Whale oil has been deleted. See Article I(5) of CLC 1992.

[51] See Article I(6) for the definition of "Pollution damage", Article I(7) for the definition of "Preventive measures", and Article I(8) for the definition of "Incident".

[52] The italicised words are additional.

[53] See Jacobsson, *supra*, note 46, at p.1.

[54] See Article 6 of 1992 CLC Protocol.

[55] The 1971 Fund continued to exist until 24 May 2002 when it ceased to be in force. See IOPC Funds Annual Report 2005, at p.13.

[56] IOPC Funds Annual Report, 2005, at p.13.

[57] Article 14 of CLC 1992 and Article 32 of the Fund Convention 1992.

[58] See Article 15 of CLC 1992 and Article 34 of the Fund Convention 1992.

[59] See Fund Convention 1992 Protocol Article 6 (3)(c) which is a new provision.

[60] Jacobsson, *supra*, note 46, at pp.12-13.

[61] At the conference there were participants from 51 state parties to the 1992 Fund Convention, 17 non-state parties, 2 inter-governmental organisations and 11 non-governmental organisations (NGOs). See Jacobsson, *ibid.* at p.14.

[62] Jacobsson, *ibid.* at p.12.

[63] Jacobsson, *ibid.*at pp.12-13. It is notable in the foregoing context that during the period 2000 to 2003, when the above-noted developments were taking place, two major oil spills occurred; the *Erika* and the *Prestige* incidents. For both cases, see IOPC Fund, *Annual Report 2005*, pp.73, 99.

[64] Jacobsson, *supra*, note 7, at p.21.

[65] See Environmental Global Issues Map: New Carissa Oil Spill on the Oregon Coast. McGraw-Hill. 1999-03, available at http://www.mhhe.com/biosci/pae/es_map/articles /article_29.mhtml [accessed on 27th Dec 2010].

[66] Jacobsson, *supra*, note 7, at p.21.

[67] The Liberian-flagged bulk-carrier ran aground off Gibraltar on 10th October 2008 spilling some 100 tonnes of bunker oil. The oil contaminated fishing boats, pleasure craft, cruise ships and other commercial vessel and it necessitated the closure of the water intakes to a desalination plant. See Jacobsson, *supra*, note 7, at p.21.

[68] Article 14 (1).

[69] Jacobsson, *supra*, note 7, at p.23.

[70] Artical 1(9).

[71] As defined in the CLC1992, Article I(5), "Oil" means any persistent hydrocarbon mineral oil such as crude oil, fuel oil, heavy diesel oil and lubricating oil, whether carried on board a ship as cargo or in the bunkers of such a ship.

[72] See also Jacobsson, *supra*, note 7, at pp.24-25.

[73] Article 2.

[74] Article 3(1).

[75] Article 3(3) provides – No liability for pollution damage shall attach to the shipowner if the shipowner proves that: (a) the damage resulted from an act of war, hostilities, civil war, insurrection or a natural phenomenon of an exceptional, inevitable and irresistible character; or (b) the damage was wholly caused by an act or omission done with the intent to cause damage by a third party; or (c) the damage was wholly caused by the negligence or other wrongful act of any Government or other authority responsible for

the maintenance of lights or other navigational aids in the exercise of that function. Article 3(4) provides – If the shipowner proves that the pollution damage resulted wholly or partially either from an act or omission done with intent to cause damage by the person who suffered the damage or from the negligence of that person, the shipowner may be exonerated wholly or partially from liability to such person.

[76] Article 1(3).

[77] Article 7(1). It is notable that only the registered owner of a ship having a gross tonnage greater than 1000 is required to maintain insurance or other financial security, whereas in the CLC the minimum carriage is 2000 tonnes.

[78] P. Griggs, "International convention on civil liability for bunker oil pollution damage", (2001) 2 *Il Diritto Marittimo*, 859; M. N. Tsimplis, "The Bunkers Convention 2001: Completing and Harmonising the Liability Regime for Oil Pollution from Ships?" (2005)1 *Lloyd's Maritime and Commercial Law Quarterly*, 83 at p.92.

[79] Article 6.

[80] Jacobsson, *supra*, note 7, at p.29.

[81] *Ibid.*

[82] See *ibid.* See also Tsimplis, *supra*, note 78, at pp.91-92.

[83] Nicholas Gaskell, "The bunker Pollution Convention 2001 and Limitation of Liability" (2009) 15 *Journal of International Maritime Law*, 477 at p. 479.

[84] *Ibid.*

[85] IMO, "HNS Convention", available online at http://www.imo.org/OurWork/Legal/Pages/HNSConvention.aspx [accessed on 20th Jan 2011].

[86] Some bulk solids such as coal and iron ore are excluded because of the low hazards they present. See IOPC Fund, "Draft Guide to the Implementation of the HNS Convention", Prepared by the Secretariat of the IOPC Fund 1992, June 2005.

[87] Article 1(5).

[88] Article 1(5)(a). It should be noted that the HNS Convention does not cover damage caused during the transport of HNS to or from a ship. Cover starts from the time when the HNS enters the ship's equipment or passes its rail, on loading, and the cover ends when the HNS ceases to be present in any part of the ship's equipment or passes its rail on discharge. See Article 1(9).

[89] Article 1(5)(b).

[90] Article 4(3)(b). It provides the HNS Convention shall not apply to "damage caused by a radioactive material of class 7 either in the International Maritime Dangerous Goods Code, as amended, or in appendix B of the Code of Safe Practice for Solid Bulk Cargoes, as amended."

[91] As in MARPOL73/78, 2006 Consolidated Edition.

[92] MARPOL73/78, 2006 Consolidated Edition, p.127.

[93] Article 3(a).

[94] Article 3(b).

[95] Article 1(3).

[96] Article 7(5).

[97] Article 12.

[98] Article 12(8).

[99] Article 9(2).

[100] This is Special Drawing Right. See Article 9(9).

[101] Article 13.

[102] Articles 16-23.

[103] Article 14(5).

[104] R. P. Balkin, "The HNS Protocol", available online at http://www.imo.org/KnowledgeCentre/PapersAndArticlesByIMOStaff/Documents/The%20HNS%20Protocol%20-%20R%20Balkin.pdf [accessed on 2 Feb 2011].

[105] Articles 16-19.

[106] Balkin, *supra*, note 104, at p.4.

[107] IMO LEG\CONF\10\6(A).

[108] 2010 Protocol, Article 9(1). See also Balkin, *supra*, note 104, at p.6.

[109] Article 19(1)(b).

[110] Balkin, *supra*, note 104, at p.7.

[111] *Ibid.* at p.9.

[112] *Ibid.* at p.4.

In: Selected Issues in Maritime Law and Policy
Editor: Maximo Q. Mejia, Jr.
ISBN: 978-1-62618-508-1

Chapter 7

PLACES OF REFUGE: WHO PAYS COMPENSATION WHEN THINGS GO WRONG?

Måns Jacobsson

INTRODUCTION

Ships in distress have been seeking place of refuge since time immemorial. When the only issue was human lives in danger, it was not questioned that a ship in distress was entitled to refuge by coastal States. Likewise, if the purpose of the ship seeking shelter was to preserve property, ships were not normally refused refuge either.

In recent years the issue of the right of a ship in distress to refuge in coastal waters and ports has taken on another dimension in view of the large quantities of oil and other hazardous cargoes carried by sea and the increased importance of environmental issues. Coastal States have increasingly been reluctant to allow ships in distress carrying polluting or otherwise hazardous substances to enter their ports and coastal waters if the entry of the ship would represent a significant risk to the environment of the State concerned.

In a number of cases ships have been refused entry in view of the environmental risks, real or perceived, which the ship represented. The most extreme example is that of the *Castor*, a ship carrying a cargo of gasoline, which developed a major crack on its main deck during a storm in the western Mediterranean off the coast of Morocco in December 2000. As its cargo was non-persistent oil, it did not present a significant pollution risk but it was considered that there was a serious risk of explosion. Requests for permission to enter coastal waters to lighten the ship were refused by seven States, and the ship had to be towed around the Mediterranean for several weeks before a transfer operation could be carried out in Libyan waters. Other examples of cases in which requests for refuge were refused by coastal States are the *Christos Bitas* (United Kingdom, 1978), the *Khark 5* (Morocco, 1989), the *Erika* (France, 1999) and the *Prestige* (Spain, 2002), to mention just a few. [1]

There are two incidents that occurred in 2012 of interest in this context. The *Stolt Valor*, a tanker carrying highly flammable chemicals, exploded and caught fire on 15 March 2012 some 70 kilometres off Saudi Arabia. It appears that requests for access to a place of refuge made to coastal States through a regional organisation were denied and that formal permission to enter a place of refuge was not granted until 25 June 2012, the ship entering a shipyard in Bahrain three days later. As a result of this delay, the removal of the remaining cargo and bunkers had to be carried out at sea in difficult whether conditions. On 14 July 2012 the *Flaminia*, a containership carrying a large variety of products including chemicals, caught fire and exploded in mid-Atlantic on voyage from Charleston (United States) to Antwerp (Belgium). Requests for the ship to be allowed to enter their territorial waters were denied by five European States and two other States were reluctant to commit themselves at short notice. The ship was not given permission to enter German waters until five weeks after the incident and arrived at the port of Wilhelmshafen on 9 September. The delay in granting the ship access to a place of refuge resulted in an increased risk that the ship would break.

There are, however, also cases where requests for refuge have been granted by the coastal State in spite of the fact that allowing the ship entry represented a serious pollution risk. A notable case is the *Sea Empress* (United Kingdom, 1996). The ship, laden with some 130 000 tonnes of crude oil, ran aground on rocks in the entrance to the port of Milford Haven in Wales, resulting in an initial loss of around 2 000 tonnes of crude oil. Although quickly refloated, the tanker grounded again a number of times during persistently bad weather. The ship was finally refloated. Plans to take the ship out to sea were abandoned and the ship was taken alongside a jetty inside the port where the remaining cargo, some 58 000 tonnes, was discharged. It is estimated that 72 000 tonnes of crude oil and a small quantity of bunkers were released as a result of the incident. [2]

Another example, this time in respect of a containership, is the *Napoli* (United Kingdom, 2007). The ship which was carrying over 2 300 containers, some of which contained hazardous substances, and some 3 000 tonnes of bunkers, had been seriously damaged during a storm in the English Channel. The United Kingdom authorities decided that the ship should be beached on the South Devon coast where the bunkers and containers were removed. Although some 100 containers were washed overboard and some of the bunker oil was spilt during the removal operation, the courageous decision to beach the vessel most likely avoided serious environmental damage. [3]

The fact that coastal States in a number of cases have refused refuge to vessels in distress has resulted in a discussion of the conditions under which coastal States are entitled under international law to refuse entry on the grounds that the ship represented a major environmental hazard, and this issue has been dealt with in numerous publications. Consideration has also been given to the liability of a coastal State under public international law for damage resulting from its decision to grant or refuse entry. [4]

This chapter will focus on the possibilities for Governments and other parties in the public and private sectors to obtain compensation under the global regime governing liability and compensation for oil pollution damage caused by oil spills from tankers established by the 1992 Civil Liability Convention, the 1992 Fund Convention and the 2003 Supplementary Fund Protocol. [5] Some observations will also be made on the corresponding questions in relation to spills of bunker oil from non-tankers and spills of hazardous substances other than oil. [6]

RIGHT TO PLACE OF REFUGE UNDER PUBLIC INTERNATIONAL LAW

Various views have been expressed as to the position of international law on the question of the extent to which a coastal State is obliged to allow a ship in distress to enter its coastal waters. An analysis of this question falls outside the scope of the present chapter. Suffice to say that the prevailing view appears to be that if the entry of the ship involves significant environmental risks for the coastal State, there is no legal obligation for that State to grant the ship access to a place of refuge, and the coastal State is in such a case entitled to making such access conditional on additional requirements. It is also considered that there is no general right for a coastal State to refuse access to a ship in distress. The widely accepted view seems to be that any decision whether or not to grant a ship access to a place of refuge is to be taken in the light of the particular circumstances of the case. [7]

It should be noted that a State which refuses a ship in distress access to a place of refuge may incur liability under public international law for pollution damage caused in another State as a result of such refusal. The chapter will however not deal with questions of inter-State liability under public international law in cases of transboundary pollution. [8]

Notwithstanding the limitation of the scope of this chapter, it has been considered appropriate to deal briefly with the work carried out within the International Maritime Organization (IMO) and the European Union (EU) in this field. [9]

IMO GUIDELINES ON PLACES OF REFUGE

In 2003 the IMO Assembly adopted Guidelines on places of refuge for ships in need of assistance. [10] The purpose of the Guidelines, which are not mandatory ("soft law"), is to provide the parties concerned with a framework enabling them to respond effectively and to attempt to set up a common framework for assessing the situation of ships in need of assistance. In the Guidelines it is submitted that there are circumstances under which it is desirable to carry out a cargo transfer operation or other operations to prevent or minimise damage or pollution and that for this purpose it would usually be advantageous to take the ship to a place of refuge. In the Guidelines it is stated that granting access to a place of refuge could involve a political decision which can only be taken on a case-by-case basis with due consideration given to the balance between the advantage for the affected ship and the environment resulting from bringing the ship into a place of refuge and the risk to the environment resulting from that ship being near the coast. [11] Coastal States should establish procedures consistent with the Guidelines by which to receive and act on requests for assistance with a view to authorising, where appropriate, the use of a suitable place of refuge.

The IMO Guidelines do not address liability and compensation issues.

European Union Consideration of Issues Relating to Places of Refuge

The issue of places of refuge has also been dealt with within the European Community/European Union. Directive 2009/17/EC establishing a Community vessel traffic monitoring and information system deals briefly with places of refuge as regards the procedures to be followed by European Union Member States when considering whether to grant a place of refuge, but it does not spell out any criteria to be applied for taking decisions on requests by ships in distress. [12] In the preamble to the Directive (paragraph 14) it is stated that the IMO Guidelines are to form the basis of any plans prepared by Member States in order to respond effectively to the threats posed by ships in need of assistance.

Of relevance for the purpose of the present chapter is the following statement in the Directive (preamble paragraph 18; cf. art. 20d):

> Ports which accommodate a ship should be able to rely on prompt compensation in respect of costs and any damage arising from the operation. To that end, it is important that the relevant international conventions be applied. Member States should endeavour to put in place a legal framework under which they could, in exceptional circumstances and in accordance with Community law, compensate a port or other entity for costs and economic losses suffered as a result of accommodating a ship. Moreover, the Commission should examine existing mechanisms within Member States for the compensation of potential economic loss suffered by a port or a body and should, on the basis of this examination, put forward and evaluate different policy options.

The European Commission has carried out the examination requested in the Directive, resulting in the publication in November 2012 of a Report on liability and compensation for financial damages sustained by places of refuge when accommodating a ship in need of assistance. [13] In the report an assessment is made of the need for an additional mechanism of liability and compensation for the damages suffered by a place of refuge following reception of a vessel in need of assistance. The report contains *inter alia* the following statement (section 5.1):

> International conventions adopted to this date on the subject of liability in the area of maritime transport offer a system of rules ensuring the applicability of liability mechanisms that are satisfactory in the areas covered by these conventions, and also pertinent in the context of reception of a ship in a place of refuge.

The International Compensation Regimes

Regime Relating to Tanker Oil Spills

The international regime relating to tanker oil spills is a compensation system in three tiers. The first tier of compensation is provided under the 1992 Civil Liability Convention and is paid by the registered owner of the ship which causes the oil pollution or his liability insurer. The 1992 Fund Convention provides a second tier of compensation paid by the International Oil Pollution Compensation Fund 1992 (1992 Fund). A third tier was added in 2005 by the creation of a Supplementary Fund set up under the 2003 Protocol to the 1992 Fund Convention. The regime was originally based on two earlier Conventions, the 1969 Civil Liability Convention and the 1971 Fund Convention, which were replaced by the 1992 Conventions. [14]

The liability under the first tier of the 1992 regime is channelled to the registered owner of the ship involved, with the exclusion of certain other parties from liability. Of particular interest for the purpose of this chapter is the exclusion from liability of salvors and persons taking measures to prevent or minimise pollution damage (preventive measures). [15] The shipowner has strict liability for pollution damage, and he is exempt from liability in only a few particular cases, but his liability is normally limited in amount. [16]

The shipowner is obliged to maintain insurance to cover his liability under the Convention up the limitation amount applicable to the ship in question. The victims are entitled to bring legal action directly against the insurer.

Compensation is paid by the 1992 Fund under the second tier when the victims do not get full compensation from the shipowner or his insurer. The maximum amount of compensation payable under the 1992 Fund Convention is 203 million Special Drawing Rights (US$ 304 million), including the amount actually paid under the 1992 Civil Liability Convention. [17] The Supplementary Fund provides additional compensation to that under the 1992 Fund Convention so that the total amount available for compensation for pollution damage in States that have ratified the 2003 Supplementary Fund Protocol is 750 million SDR (US$1 125 million), including the amount payable under the 1992 Conventions.

Each of the Fund Conventions and the Supplementary Fund Protocol established an intergovernmental organisation to administer the compensation regime created by the respective treaty, the International Oil Pollution Compensation Funds 1971 and 1992 (hereinafter referred to as the 1971 Fund and the 1992 Fund, respectively) and the International Oil Pollution Compensation Supplementary Fund (hereinafter referred to as the Supplementary Fund); the three organisations are normally collectively referred to as the IOPC Funds. The organisations, which are administered by a joint Secretariat headed by a Director, have their headquarters in London. The Funds are financed by contributions levied on any person who received in the relevant calendar year more than 150 000 tonnes of crude oil and heavy fuel oil in ports or terminal installations in a State which is a member of the respective Fund after carriage by sea. [18]

The 1992 Conventions have become a truly global regime having been ratified by a large number of States. As at 31 May 2013, the 1992 Civil Liability Convention had been ratified by 130 States and the 1992 Fund Convention by 111 States, among them all EU Member States except three landlocked States (Austria, the Czech Republic and Slovakia). [19] There are 29 States parties to the 2003 Supplementary Fund Protocol, including 19 EU Member States. [20]

Bunkers Convention

Experience shows that the most serious oil spills are caused by oil tankers. However, non-tankers often carry significant quantities of bunker oil. Many such ships have a bunker capacity of 5 000 tonnes and some up to as much as 10 000 tonnes. A stricken non-tanker could therefore constitute a significant pollution risk in a place of refuge situation.

In 2001 a Diplomatic Conference adopted a convention governing liability and compensation for pollution damage caused by spills of bunker oil from ships other than tankers, the International Convention on Civil Liability for Bunker Oil Pollution Damage, 2001 (Bunkers Convention). This Convention, which has been ratified by 68 States, is a one-tier regime with the liability falling on the shipowner as defined in the Convention (which includes not only the registered owner but also the bareboat charterer, manager and operator of the ship), and there is no supplementary compensation from an international fund. There are no channelling provisions protecting salvors and others who take preventive measures against compensation claims.

Since the Bunkers Convention only entered into force in 2008, there is hardly any experience yet of the functioning of this regime. [21]

HNS Convention

In 1996 an international Convention dealing with liability and compensation for damage in connection with sea transport of chemicals and other dangerous cargoes was adopted under the auspices of IMO, but this Convention (normally referred to as the HNS Convention) has not entered into force. [22] The HNS Convention would create a two-tier compensation regime very similar to the regime under the 1992 Civil Liability and Fund Conventions with a first tier of shipowner liability and a second tier providing supplementary compensation from an international fund. The total amount available for compensation under the HNS Convention is 250 million SDR (US$ 375 million), including any amount paid by the shipowner and his insurer. [23]

However, a number of important States had indicated that there were serious obstacles to their ratification of the HNS Convention, and it became clear that it was unlikely that the Convention would enter into force in its original version. In order to remove the obstacles to the entry into force of the HNS Convention, a Protocol to the Convention was adopted in April 2010. It appears that the 2010 Protocol provides appropriate solutions to the problems identified as obstacles to ratification. The question is, however, whether there is a sufficient political will to proceed to ratification of the 2010 Protocol by a sufficient number of States to bring it into force within a reasonable period of time. [24]

As at 31 May 2013, no State had ratified the 2010 Protocol.

Consideration within IMO of Liability Issues in Relation to Places of Refuge Situations

The issue of the applicability of the 1992 Civil Liability Convention and the 1992 Fund Convention when ships are taken to places of refuge was considered by the IMO Legal Committee in 2003 in the aftermath of the *Prestige* incident which occurred in Spain in 2002. [25] The discussion was held mainly on the basis of a document presented by Spain. [26]

The Spanish delegation stated that it had some doubts whether the current liability and compensation regime addressed all situations that might arise in connection with places of refuge and mentioned that it had identified seven situations that should be examined by the Committee in determining whether existing instruments were sufficient. The Legal Committee noted that the situations identified in the document presented by the Spanish delegation raised four general issues:

- Does a State violate its obligations under international instruments if it allows a ship to enter a place of refuge without proper insurance?

- Even if the ship concerned holds the proper insurance, does the State which allows the ship to enter a place of refuge have any liability in the event the insurance cover fails?
- If the shipowner loses the right to limit liability as a result of Civil Liability Convention provisions on breaking the limit, does the State which allowed the ship to enter a place of refuge have any liability?
- Does the current regime permit the payment of so called fixed costs?

During a preliminary discussion in the Legal Committee, the following views were expressed:

- To some extent the questions raised by the Spanish delegation were abstract, theoretical or based on hypothetical conditions and it would be difficult to provide advice in the absence of specific fact situations.
- Application of the existing liability and compensation Conventions did not seem to be unclear, though the interpretations made by national courts might be hard to predict.
- The perception or concern that a gap might exist in the international liability and compensation regime could result from the fact that certain instruments such as the HNS Convention and the Bunkers Convention were not yet in force, and this kind of gap could be closed if States took steps to ratify these instruments.
- The fact that questions were being raised regarding the application or interpretation of the 1992 Civil Liability and Fund Conventions in the context of places of refuge should not be viewed as a sign that these instruments in themselves were insufficient or ineffective.
- The 1992 Fund Convention will apply to ships without insurance, or where insurance proves to be ineffective.

Several delegations expressed the view that they did not consider that the issues raised by Spain gave a proper reflection of the Conventions and the IOPC Fund practice. Further, they held the view that it was clear that the liability Conventions covered ships in distress and the place of refuge situation.

As mentioned above, the IMO Guidelines on places of refuge do not address liability and compensation issues. However when the Guidelines were adopted, the IMO Assembly requested the Legal Committee to consider these Guidelines from its own perspective, including the provisions on financial security to cover coastal state expenses and/or compensation issues.

In 2005 the Legal Committee considered whether there was a need for an additional, legally binding instrument regarding places of refuge. The Committee took the view that at that point in time there was no need for an additional convention on this matter. [27] The Committee stated that the more urgent priority would be to implement all existing liability and compensation conventions and that a more informed decision as to whether such an additional convention was necessary might best be taken in the light of the experience acquired through their implementation. [28]

DRAFT INSTRUMENT PREPARED BY THE COMITE MARITIME INTERNATIONAL

In spite of the position taken by the IMO Legal Committee that there was no need for an additional convention dealing with places of refuge situations, the Comité Maritime International (CMI)[29] prepared a draft instrument on places of refuge intended to supplement the IMO Guidelines. [30] The purpose of the draft instrument was *inter alia* to emphasize the position under customary international law of a presumption of a right of access of a ship in distress, to make that presumption rebuttable by the coastal State if it could show that it was reasonable to refuse access and to strengthen the requirement set out in the Guidelines that access could be refused only on reasonable grounds.

The draft instrument also contains provisions on immunity for a competent authority which reasonably grants access to a ship in need of assistance from compensation claims for loss or damage caused to the ship, its cargo or other third parties and their property. In addition, the draft instrument deals with the liability of public authorities for damage caused as a result of a refusal to grant such access. If, by reason of such refusal, another State, the shipowner, the salvor, the cargo owner or any other party suffers damage, the body that refused access shall under the draft instrument be liable to compensate the party having suffered the damage, unless the authority in question can establish that it acted reasonably. [31]

When the draft instrument was considered by the Legal Committee in 2009, the Committee concluded that there was no need for a new convention at that point in time and that the international regime comprising existing liability and compensation conventions for pollution damage at sea provided a comprehensive legal framework, especially when coupled with the IMO Guidelines on places of refuge. [32]

APPLICATION OF THE INTERNATIONAL COMPENSATION REGIMES TO PLACES OF REFUGE SITUATIONS

Tanker Oil Spills

Since the inception of the international regime in 1978, the International Oil Pollution Compensation Funds (IOPC Funds) have dealt with tens of thousands of compensation claims under the Civil Liability and Fund Conventions and have gained considerable experience in the handling of claims. The overwhelming majority of these claims have been settled amicably and court actions against the Funds have been taken in respect of only a very low number of incidents. There are therefore relatively few court cases on the application and interpretation of these treaties.

The Governments of Fund Member States have through the governing bodies of the organisations developed the international regime in the light of experience gained from major oil spills. [33] The Assemblies of the Funds have adopted certain criteria for the admissibility of compensation claims that are set out in a Claims Manual. [34]

Although the 1992 Civil Liability Convention and the 1992 Fund Convention were not elaborated specifically to address situations relating to places of refuge, the 1992 Conventions do apply to oil spills in such situations in the same way as to any other oil spills.

The discussion below focuses on issues of special interest in places of refuge situations, such as to what extent compensation is available for various types of loss or damage, the effects on the right to compensation of contributory negligence by the claimant, the importance of the channelling provisions in the Conventions and issues relating to recourse actions.

Property Damage

Oil spilt from a ship in a place of refuge situation may cause damage to property, for example in the form of contamination of pleasure craft and fishing gear. Such damage will be compensated under the 1992 Conventions.

Economic Loss in Fishing and Tourism Sectors

Persons whose property has become contaminated by oil spilt in a place of refuge situation may also suffer loss of earnings, for example a fisherman who is unable to fish while his fishing gear is cleaned or replaced, and he will be compensated under the international regime for his economic loss (*consequential economic loss*). However, persons whose property has not been contaminated may also suffer losses. A fisherman whose gear did not get contaminated may have to abstain from fishing for a period of time to avoid having his nets polluted. An hotelier or restaurateur whose premises are close to a public beach may suffer losses because the number of guests decreases during the period of pollution (*pure economic loss*). Both consequential economic loss and pure economic loss are in principle admissible for compensation under the international regime provided there is a sufficiently close link of causation between the contamination and the loss. [35]

Preventive Measures, Including Clean-Up Operations

Under the 1992 Conventions the concept of pollution damage includes costs of any reasonable measures to prevent or minimise pollution damage (*preventive measures*) and further loss or damage caused by such measures (art.I.6 and I.7).

The 1992 Conventions apply to preventive measures wherever taken, also those taken on the high seas, provided the measures were taken to prevent or minimise pollution damage in areas to which the Conventions apply, i.e. the territory, territorial sea or EEZ or corresponding area of a State party (art.II (b)). [36] It has been considered that also measures taken within the territorial waters of a State not party to the Civil Liability and Fund Conventions to prevent pollution damage in a State party fall in principle within the scope of application of the Conventions. [37]

Loss or damage caused by reasonable measures to prevent or minimise pollution is also compensated under the 1992 Conventions. For example, if clean-up operations result in damage to roads, piers and embankments, the cost of the resulting repairs is compensated. [38]

In order for preventive measures to qualify for compensation, the measures must be taken after an incident has occurred. The concept of incident is fairly broad, namely 'any occurrence, or series of occurrences having the same origin, which causes pollution damage or creates a grave and imminent threat of pollution damage'.

Expenses for preventive measures are recoverable even if no spill of oil occurs, provided that there was a grave and imminent threat of pollution damage and the measures were objectively reasonable. If a State or a port authority admits a ship in distress to a place of refuge and no oil is spilt, the costs relating to the ship's entry would nevertheless be compensated, provided there was a grave and imminent threat of pollution damage and admitting the ship was a reasonable step to prevent or minimise oil pollution. The issue of whether in a particular situation there was a grave and imminent threat of pollution could give rise to disputes.

As regards the concept of *reasonableness*, the governing bodies of the IOPC Funds have taken the view that whether or not a measure is reasonable should be determined on the basis of objective criteria in the light of the facts available at the time of the decision to take the measures. It has been emphasized that those in charge of the operations should continually reappraise their decisions in the light of development and technical advice. The fact that a Government or a public authority decides to take certain measures does not, in the view of these bodies, in itself mean that the measures are reasonable for the purpose of compensation under the Conventions. On the other hand the fact that the measures proved to be ineffective is not in itself a reason for rejection of a claim. The governing bodies have further decided that the costs incurred, and the relationship between these costs and the benefit derived or expected, should in their opinion also be reasonable. [39]

In the context of its consideration of a claim by the Spanish Government for costs incurred for removing the oil from the sunken wreck of the *Prestige*, the 1992 Fund Assembly decided not to widen the criteria for the admissibility of claims for the costs of preventive measures so as to include social and/or political considerations. It also decided that when considering the reasonableness of such measures, account should be taken of the potential environmental damage which could be caused if the measures were not taken. [40]

The reception of a ship in a place of refuge would normally fall within the concept of preventive measures, provided it was reasonable to grant the ship access for the purpose of preventing or minimising pollution damage, and in that case the costs incurred by the authorities concerned and the pollution damage resulting therefrom would qualify for compensation. [41] When considering whether the State's/authority's decision was reasonable in the circumstances the IMO Guidelines on places of refuge for ships in need of assistance could be relevant. It is possible that some measures taken by the State in a place of refuge situation could be considered as reasonable whereas other measures would not.

In a place of refuge situation the State concerned will normally take steps to prevent that oil escapes from the ship. If oil is nevertheless spilt the State will take measures to minimise the damage caused, for instance by laying booms to prevent the oil from affecting sensitive areas or by clean-up at sea or on the beaches, and such measures are normally considered as preventive measures. Transferring the oil from the oil tanker involved or removing the oil from a sunken tanker could also be considered as preventive measures. The costs incurred for such operations qualify for compensation provided they are *reasonable*.

The decisions by the authorities in places of refuge situations may well be influenced by a number of considerations other than objective technical factors. It is submitted, however, that also in such cases the question of whether the measures taken by the authorities were reasonable and therefore qualify for compensation as preventive measures should be decided on the basis of objective technical criteria. It should be recognised that the authorities concerned and the parties involved in the operations will often have to decide rapidly, and without full knowledge of the circumstances, in the taking preventive measures, and it appears therefore that when the test of reasonableness is to be applied, they should be allowed a certain margin of error in their judgement. [42]

Salvage Operations

Bringing a ship in distress to a place of refuge will in many cases involve salvage operations. An important question is therefore to what extent operations normally considered as salvage will be considered as preventive measures under the 1992 Conventions. [43] It should be noted that salvage operations can be carried out not only by professional salvors but also for instance by a public authority.

The Funds' governing bodies have decided that salvage operations qualify for compensation under the 1992 Conventions if their primary purpose was the prevention of pollution (the 'primary purpose test'). [44] If the operations have another purpose, e.g. to salvage hull or cargo, they would not, in the view of these bodies, fall within the definition of 'preventive measures' and would not therefore qualify for compensation. It is however often difficult to ascertain the primary purpose of a salvage operation. A salvage operation may well have the dual purpose of preventing or minimising pollution damage and salvaging ship and cargo ('dual purpose test′), and the Funds have decided that for the purpose of compensation the cost of the operation should in such a case be apportioned between these two activities. [45]

Also salvage operations carried out even if no oil spill occurs may qualify for compensation as preventive measures provided there was a grave and imminent threat of oil pollution damage.

The question of whether a salvage operation was objectively reasonable should be determined in the light of the facts available at the time of the decision to take the measures and not with hindsight. This means that also an unsuccessful salvage operation could be considered as a reasonable preventive measure in the circumstances.

The Funds have decided that compensation relating to salvage operations considered to be 'preventive measures' should not be assessed in the same way as salvage awards but would only cover costs incurred by the salvor and a reasonable profit margin. [46]

Compensation For Fixed Costs

During the above-mentioned discussions in the IMO Legal Committee in 2003, the question was raised whether the regime established by the 1992 Conventions covered compensation for so-called *fixed costs*.

Preventive measures, including clean-up operations at sea or on shore, are often carried out by public authorities which use permanently employed personnel, or vessels, vehicles and equipment owned by those authorities. The authorities may then incur *additional costs*, i.e. expenses which arise solely as a result of the incident and which would not have been incurred had the incident and related operations not taken place, for instance overtime payments to personnel involved in clean-up operations. Reasonable *additional costs* are accepted by the IOPC Funds.

The authorities may also incur costs which would have arisen for the authorities concerned even if the incident had not occurred, such as normal salaries for permanently employed personnel and capital costs of vessels owned by the authorities, so called *fixed costs*. The Funds accept a reasonable proportion of *fixed costs*, provided that these costs correspond closely to the clean-up period in question and do not include remote overhead charges. [47]

Damage to the Environment

In the 1992 Conventions and the Supplementary Fund Protocol, 'pollution damage' is defined as 'damage caused by contamination'. The definition contains a proviso to the effect that compensation for impairment of the environment (other than loss of profit from such impairment) is limited to costs of reasonable measures of reinstatement actually undertaken or to be undertaken (art.I.6 and art.1.2, respectively). This implies that these treaties limit compensation to economic losses and do not provide compensation for damage to natural resources as such or for other damage of a non-economic nature. [48]

If, in a place of refuge situation, spilt oil causes damage to the environment which results in, for instance, economic losses for fishermen or businesses in the tourism industry such economic losses qualify for compensation under the 1992 Conventions, whereas ecological damage, loss of image or moral damage do not.[49] Compensation is not paid on the basis of an abstract quantification of damage calculated in accordance with theoretical models. [50]

The authorities of the State affected by an oil spill in a place of refuge situation may wish to take measures to restore the damaged environment. As already mentioned, costs of reasonable measures to reinstate the environment are compensated under the international regime. With respect to the criterion of reasonableness, reference is made to what is stated above in respect of preventive measures, i.e. that the reinstatement measures should be reasonable from an objective point of view. The purpose of any reasonable measures of reinstatement should be to bring the damaged site as closely as possible back to the same ecological condition as if the oil spill had not occurred. [51]

Grounds of Exoneration and Contributory Negligence

As mentioned above the shipowner has strict liability for pollution damage and is exempt from liability only in a few particular cases.

If a ship is allowed to enter a place of refuge and oil pollution damage occurs as a result of an act of war, hostilities, civil war or insurrection, or was wholly caused by an intentional act of a third party, e.g. an act of terrorism, the shipowner would be exonerated from any liability (art.III.2.a). However the Funds would be exempt only if the pollution damage resulted from an act of war, hostilities, civil war or insurrection but not if the damage was otherwise caused by the intentional act of a third party (art. 4.2). [52]

Furthermore, the shipowner would be exonerated if the pollution damage resulted from a natural phenomenon of an exceptional, inevitable and irresistible character (e.g. a major tsunami), whereas the Funds would not be exonerated in such a case.

The shipowner would also be exempt from liability if in a place of refuge situation an oil spill were to occur and the incident was wholly caused by negligence of a public authority in the maintenance of lights or other navigational aids in the exercise of that function, whereas again the Funds would not (art.III.2b). [53]

It should be noted that in order for the shipowner to be exonerated from liability in cases of intentional acts of a third party or negligence of a public authority in the maintenance of navigational aids the pollution damage must have been *wholly caused* by such act. The expression *wholly caused* may give rise to difficulties in interpretation. [54]

An important issue is the effect of contributory negligence on the liabilities of the shipowner and the Funds. As regards the shipowner, this issue is dealt with in Article III.3 of the 1992 Civil Liability Convention which reads:

> "If the owner proves that the pollution damage resulted wholly or partially either from an act or omission done with intent to cause damage by the person who suffered the damage or from the negligence of that person, the owner may be exonerated wholly or partially from his liability to such person."

If a State or a port authority in a place of refuge situation was negligent in carrying out clean-up operations or taking other preventive measures and as a result pollution damage occurred, the shipowner might be wholly or partially exonerated from his liability vis-à-vis that State or authority. It is also conceivable that if a State were to direct a ship in distress to a clearly unsuitable place of refuge and as a consequence thereof pollution damage occurred, this could be considered as contributory negligence. [55] It appears that the same would apply if, as a result of a manifestly unreasonable refusal by a State to permit a ship access to a place of refuge, that State were to suffer pollution damage. It would be for the competent courts to decide whether and, if so, to what extent, the shipowner would be exonerated vis-à-vis the State in such cases. When considering whether the State's decision was reasonable, the courts may take into account the IMO Guidelines on places of refuge for ships in need of assistance. The shipowner would however in such a case not be exonerated from liability to other persons having suffered pollution damage.

As regards pollution damage in States parties not only to the 1992 Civil Liability Convention but also to the 1992 Fund Convention, Article III.3 in the former Convention is of limited importance, since the 1992 Fund could not invoke contributory negligence as grounds for total or partial exoneration in respect of preventive measures (Article 4.3 last sentence of the 1992 Fund Convention). Consequently, if, in order to prevent or minimise pollution damage, a State has taken measures for a ship to enter a place of refuge within its jurisdiction or for the ship to leave its waters but through negligence contributed to pollution damage being caused, the Funds would not be entitled to invoke contributory negligence as grounds for reduction of the compensation to be paid to that State for the costs of clean-up and other preventive measures, provided that the measures themselves were reasonable in the sense set out above. Should the measures not be reasonable from an objective point of view, they are not preventive measures for the purpose of the 1992 Conventions, and the ensuing costs would not qualify for compensation under 1992 Conventions. [56]

Channelling of Liability

As mentioned above, the liability for oil pollution under the 1992 Civil Liability Convention is channelled to the registered shipowner, and claims for compensation for pollution damage may not be made against the owner otherwise than in accordance with that Convention (art. III.4).

Subject to the provisions relating to recourse actions by the shipowner, no claim for compensation for pollution damage under the 1992 Civil Liability Convention or otherwise may be made against *inter alia* the following persons (art.III.4):

any person performing salvage operations with the consent of the shipowner or on the instructions of a competent public authority;

any person taking preventive measures;

any servant or agent of these persons.

A salvor who takes a ship to a place of refuge cannot therefore be held liable for pollution damage caused in connection with the salvage operations. The same applies to a person who takes other preventive measures, for example carries out clean-up of oil which has been spilt in a place of refuge situation, but the protection against compensation claims will in that case apply only if the measures were reasonable in the circumstances, because if they were not objectively reasonable they are not preventive measures within the meaning of the 1992 Civil Liability Convention. The protection given to salvors and other parties taking preventive measures is often referred to as 'responder immunity'.

It could happen that a salvage operation involving a stricken oil tanker carried out by a public authority is unsuccessful, resulting in pollution damage. In such a case the channelling provisions would apply to the authority concerned in its capacity of salvor. If, however, the salvage operations were not carried out by the public authority itself but only directed and controlled by the authority the question would arise whether the authority and the State concerned could be liable for the damage. It is possible that in such a case the authority could, depending on the circumstances, be considered as a person taking preventive measures and the State/authority would then be protected against compensation claims by the channelling provisions, provided the measures were objectively reasonable. If, on the other hand, the measures were not objectively reasonable they would not qualify as preventive measures.

It should be noted that the protection against compensation claims for pollution damage which the Convention gives persons falling within the scope of the channelling provisions does not apply if the damage resulted from the personal act or omission of the person concerned, committed with the intent to cause such damage, or recklessly and with knowledge that such damage would probably result (art. III.4). A salvor or a person taking preventive measures, including a public authority, who as a result of such recklessness causes pollution damage could therefore be held liable for the damage caused.

Total Admissible Claims Exceeding the Maximum Amount Available for Compensation

If the total amount of the established claims exceeds the total amount of compensation available under the treaties applicable to the incident in question, the compensation paid to each claimant will be reduced proportionally. [57]

Experience shows that a major oil pollution incident can cause pollution damage exceeding the total amount available under the 1992 Civil Liability and Fund Conventions, US$ 304 million. [58] In such a case States and other public bodies that have incurred expenses and private bodies and individuals who have suffered economic losses may not in a place of refuge situation obtain full compensation for their losses and expenses.

Difficulties have arisen in some incidents involving the 1971 Fund and/or the 1992 Fund where the total amount of the claims arising from the incident exceeded the amount available for compensation under the applicable Conventions or where there was a risk that this would occur. The Funds have therefore had to limit payments to victims to a percentage of the agreed amount of their claims (so called "pro-rating"). In most cases it eventually became possible to increase the level to 100%, once it had been established that the total amount of admissible claims would not exceed the amount available for compensation, but the delay in payment of part of the compensation has in some cases caused financial hardship to victims, for instance to fishermen and small businesses in the tourism industry.

The situation is different, however, for States that are parties to the Supplementary Fund Protocol, since the very high amount available, US$ 1 125 million, should be sufficient for all compensation claims to be paid in full from the outset in practically all cases.

Recourse Actions

A special question is whether and, if so, to what extent, the shipowner/insurer and the 1992 Fund can in a place of refuge situation recover from third parties amounts paid by them in compensation under the international regimes. [59]

The 1992 Civil Liability Convention gives the shipowner an extensive right of recourse. It is provided that nothing in that Convention shall prejudice any right of recourse by the shipowner against third parties (art. III.5). The shipowner is therefore entitled to pursue claims for recovery of the amounts paid by him in compensation by way of recourse against any third person who has caused or contributed to the incident or the resulting pollution, including those covered by the channelling provisions, e.g. salvors and persons taking preventive measures. [60] Any recourse action will however not be an action under the Civil Liability Convention but on the basis of the applicable national law.

The 1992 Fund's right to take recourse action is significantly narrower than that of the shipowner.

The 1992 Fund Convention provides that the Fund shall in respect of any amount of compensation it has paid acquire by subrogation the rights that the person so compensated may enjoy under the 1992 Civil Liability Convention against the shipowner or his insurer (art. 9.1). Subject to the shipowner's right to limit his liability, the Fund would therefore be entitled to take recourse action against the shipowner/insurer to recover the amounts that the Fund has paid in compensation to claimants.

It is further provided that nothing in the 1992 Fund Convention shall prejudice any right of the 1992 Fund of recourse or subrogation against persons other than the shipowner and his insurer, and the Fund's right of subrogation against such persons shall not be less favourable than that of an insurer of the person compensated by the Fund (art. 9.2 and 9.3). As regards recourse actions against any third parties other than the shipowner and his insurer, the Fund would therefore be subject to the same restrictions as the persons compensated by it.

It appears therefore that as regards amounts paid by the 1992 Fund in compensation to the shipowner/insurer, the Fund would be entitled to bring recourse action also against persons protected by the channelling provisions, since the shipowner would be entitled to do so. With respect to compensation payments made by the Fund to persons other than the shipowner/insurer, the Fund would not be entitled to bring recovery actions against persons protected by the channelling provisions since the person compensated would not be entitled to take such actions. The Fund would, however, be entitled to take recourse action in respect of subrogated claims against persons not protected by the channelling provisions, for example the owner of a colliding ship.

As is the case for recourse actions by the shipowner, recovery actions by the 1992 Fund will not be actions under the Conventions but will be based on national law.

An important issue is whether recourse actions may be pursued by the shipowner/insurer or the 1992 Fund against a State or other public body which has refused a ship in distress access to a place of refuge and this refusal has caused pollution damage. It is submitted that such an action could in principle be brought if the refusal to grant access was objectively unreasonable.

The IOPC Funds have so far not brought recourse action against a State in places of refuge situations.

Insurance Requirements and Requests for Security

As mentioned above, the question was raised in the IMO Legal Committee as to the consequences from the point of view of compensation if a State permits a ship in distress to enter a place of refuge within its jurisdiction although the ship does not have the liability insurance required under the 1992 Civil Liability Convention, or the shipowner had taken out the required insurance but the insurer could revoke cover or the insurer would be unable to fulfil his obligations. [61]

It is submitted that the State could not in such cases be held liable for the absence of insurance cover. Should the shipowner in such cases be unable to pay compensation the Funds would pay all admissible compensation claims in full. [62]

In many cases a coastal State or port authority has made it a condition for allowing a ship in distress access to a place of refuge that the shipowner provides security for the damage that may be caused. With regard to States parties to the 1992 Civil Liability Convention, it should not be necessary to request security for oil tankers carrying more than 2 000 tonnes of persistent oil as cargo, because such ships must under that Convention have liability insurance for pollution damage up to the limitation amount applicable to the vessel (art. VII.1). For States parties also to the 1992 Fund Convention there is additional protection since the 1992 Fund would cover also the shipowner's/insurer's liability in case they are unable to fulfil their obligations (art.4.1b). There may however be grounds for a State to request security for damage not falling within the definition of pollution damage laid down in 1992 Conventions.

Moreover, the question arises whether a State respects its obligations under the 1992 Civil Liability Convention if it makes it a condition for allowing such an oil tanker in distress entry to a place of refuge in its waters that the shipowner gives a guarantee covering also damage to which that Convention applies. It is submitted that although such a request is not specifically prohibited by that Convention, the requesting State would nevertheless not respect the spirit of the Convention, namely that the shipowner and his insurer should not for pollution damage to which the Convention applies together be held liable for an amount exceeding the ship's liability limit under that Convention. An insurance certificate issued by the flag State in accordance with that Convention evidences the existence of insurance for pollution damage up to that amount, and such a certificate issued by one State party to the Convention shall be accepted by other States parties (art. VII.7). It is in any event very unlikely that the P&I Clubs would give such a guarantee providing for additional compensation for such damage above the limitation amount applicable to the ship in question. [63]

In order to avoid discussion of the wording of a security delaying the ship's entry in a place of refuge, the International Group of P&I Clubs has developed a standard form of a letter of guarantee covering claims outside the compensation regimes under the international Conventions that are in force up to a maximum amount to be set in view of the circumstances of the particular case but not exceeding the limitation amount applicable to the ship in question. It is understood that the International Group Clubs use this standard letter and that such a letter of guarantee is normally accepted by the State concerned.

It has been suggested that States could, as a condition for giving an oil tanker access to a place of refuge, require that the shipowner waives his right to limitation of liability. It appears questionable whether such a condition respects the provisions on limitation of liability laid down in the Civil Liability Convention.

Bunkers Convention

The liability provisions of the 2001 Bunkers Convention are very similar to those of the 1992 Civil Liability Convention, but there are some major differences. A difference of particular importance in relation to places of refuge situations is that the Bunkers Convention does not contain any channelling provisions. This means, for instance, that salvors and persons taking measures to prevent or minimise pollution damage are not protected against compensation claims.

States are free, however, to introduce channelling in their national legislation. To meet the concerns expressed by a number of States and by the industries concerned, the 2001 Diplomatic Conference which adopted the Bunkers Convention also adopted a Resolution inviting States to consider, when implementing the Convention, the need to introduce in their national legislation provisions for the protection for persons taking preventive measures. In the Resolution the Conference recommended that persons taking preventive measures be exempt from liability except when the liability resulted from a conduct which under the Civil Liability Convention would not entitle those persons to protection against compensation claims. [64] It is already clear that the Resolution has not lead to uniformity in respect of channelling of liability between the States parties.

Contrary to what is the case under the Civil Liability Convention and the HNS Convention, there is no special limitation regime under the Bunkers Convention, but the issue of limitation is to be resolved pursuant to the applicable national or international regime (art. 6). The most likely international regime to be applied is the 1976 Convention on Limitation of Liability for Maritime Claims (LLMC), either in its original version or as revised by the 1996 Protocol thereto. In States parties to that Convention, claims under the Bunkers Convention relating to spills of bunker oil from ships other than oil tankers in place of refuge situations will therefore have to compete in the limitation amount with other types of claim. [65]

As mentioned above, the Bunkers Convention is a one-tier regime with the liability falling on the shipowner as defined in the Convention (which under Article 1.3 includes not only the registered owner but also the bareboat charterer, manager and operator of the ship), and there is no supplementary compensation from an international fund. If, in a place of refuge situation involving a non-tanker, the admissible claims for oil pollution damage exceed the limitation amount applicable to the ship in question, there are no additional funds available. It is expected, however, that the situation will improve for those States that are parties to the 1996 Protocol to the LLMC, as at 31 May 2013 47 States. The IMO Legal Committee decided in April 2012, by application of a special procedure laid down in the LLMC (the "tacit acceptance procedure") to increase the limitation amount set out in the 1996

Protocol by 51%. The amendments will enter into force on 19 April 2015, unless not less than one fourth of the States parties object to the amendments by 19 October 2013. [66]

HNS Convention

The HNS Convention will, once it has entered into force, apply to places of refuge situations in a very similar way to the international regime established by the 1992 Civil Liability and Fund Conventions. It should be noted that whereas the 1992 Conventions apply only to pollution damage and do not cover damage caused by fire and explosion, such damage would be covered by the HNS Convention for all ships, including oil tankers.

Wreck Removal Convention

The international regimes dealt with above do not apply to removal of wrecks, unless the removal is considered as preventive measures, i.e. reasonable measures to prevent or minimise oil pollution damage, or in the case of the HNS Convention damage caused by hazardous substances.

In this regard reference should be made to the 2007 International Convention on the Removal of Wrecks which is not yet in force. This Convention will impose strict liability on the shipowner, charterer and operator for the costs of removing wrecks which pose a threat to navigation or the marine environment and imposes a system of compulsory insurance to cover such costs. The Convention will however only apply to wrecks located in the exclusive economic zone of the States parties, i.e. outside the territorial waters, unless the State concerned has extended its application to its territory and territorial waters.

European Community Directive on Environmental Liability

In this context reference should be made to European Community Directive 2004/35/EC on environmental liability with regard to prevention and remedying environmental damage which in principle could apply to places of refuge situations. [67]

The Directive does not create a proper civil liability regime and gives only right to compensation to public authorities. It imposes strict liability or liability based on fault, depending on the type of activity involved, on the person who operates or controls the activity causing environmental damage.

Unlike the international conventions discussed in this chapter, the Directive does not deal with traditional damage such as damage to property and economic loss. It applies to certain types of environmental damage caused by various activities such as the transport by sea of dangerous and polluting goods, namely to damage to protected species and habitats, to contamination of land and to damage to waters covered by the so-called Water Framework Directive. [68] No distinction is made between owned and un-owned natural resources. The Directive also applies to *preventive measures*, i.e. measures taken after an event with a view to prevent or minimise environmental damage. It further applies to *remedial measures*, viz.

actions to restore the damaged natural resources to the condition that would have existed had the environmental damage not occurred ("baseline condition"), or to provide an equivalent alternative to those resources.

The Directive does not apply, however, to environmental damage arising from incidents in respect of which liability or compensation falls within the scope of the 1992 Civil Liability Convention, the 1992 Fund Convention, the 2003 Protocol to the 1992 Fund Convention, the Bunkers Convention or the HNS Convention, including any future amendments thereto, which is in force in the EU Member State concerned. If a particular incident falls within the scope of any of these Conventions, any type of environmental damage arising from such an incident is therefore excluded from the application of the Directive, provided the Convention is in force and applies to the incident. The Directive also provides that it shall be without prejudice to the right of the person operating or controlling the activity in question to limit his liability in accordance with national legislation implementing the 1976 LLMC, including any future amendments thereto. [69]

Since all EU Member States having a coastline are parties to the 1992 Conventions [70] the Directive will not apply to tanker oil spills in places of refuge situations in European waters, so there will not be any conflict between these Conventions and the Directive.

As regards spills of bunker oil from non-tankers, the Directive will in places of refuge situations apply only in respect of Portugal and Sweden, being the only coastal EU Member States not yet being parties to the Bunkers Convention; however, Sweden is expected to ratify the Bunkers Convention during the summer of 2013. Since the HNS Convention is not in force, the Directive will apply in places of refuge situations to damage caused by hazardous and noxious substances carried by sea. Considerable problems could arise in cases of bunker spills or, once the HNS Convention has entered into force, damage caused by hazardous and noxious substances, if damage is caused in several EU Member States which are not all parties to the relevant treaty. [71]

Action for Compensation Against a State or Public Authority for Damage Caused in Places of Refuge Situations

In places of refuge situations, it is possible that a State or public authority will incur liability for pollution damage or damage caused by hazardous substances, and such liability would be based on the applicable national law. [72] The condition for such liability to arise may, dependent on national law, be for instance that the damage was caused by negligence on the part of the State/authority or by the State/authority not having acted with due diligence. However, as regards incidents to which the 1992 Civil Liability Convention or the HNS Convention applies, the channelling provisions would normally protect the State or authority against compensation claims if its action fell within the concept of preventive measures, i.e. reasonable measures to prevent or minimise damage of the kind covered by the respective Convention. As regards the interpretation of the concept of *reasonableness* reference is made to what is stated above in relation to preventive measures in general. Likewise, the channelling provisions in these Conventions would normally protect a State or public authority having performed salvage operations. It should be noted that the Bunkers

Convention does not give any protection to a State or authority in such cases, since there are no channelling provisions in that Convention.

It is conceivable that a State/public authority could be held liable if it directed a ship in distress to a clearly unsuitable place of refuge or if its the refusal to permit a ship access to a place of refuge was manifestly unreasonable and as a consequence thereof damage occurred. [73] When considering whether the State/authority had acted reasonably, the courts may, as in the case where contributory negligence by the State/authority is alleged, take into account the IMO Guidelines on places of refuge for ships in need of assistance. [74]

It can probably be assumed, however, that those having suffered damage in places of refuge situations would, except in rare cases, rather pursue their claims under the applicable international regimes based on strict liability than take legal action against a State or public authority.

The *Prestige* incident (Spain, 2002) gives an example of an action against a State relating to an oil pollution case. The Spanish State had taken legal action before the District Court of first instance in New York against the ship's classification society, American Bureau of Shipping (ABS), requesting compensation for all damage caused by the incident, on the grounds that ABS had been negligent and reckless in its inspection of the *Prestige*. ABS denied the allegation and took in its turn legal action in the same court in the form of a counter-claim against the Spanish State, arguing that if the State had suffered damage, this was caused in whole or in part by its own negligence, *inter alia* by unreasonably refusing the ship entry into the port of La Coruña. ABS requested that that the Spanish State should be ordered to indemnify it for any amount it may have to pay in compensation pursuant to a judgement relating to that incident. The case came after appeal before the Court of Appeals in New York which held that the State had not produced sufficient evidence to establish that ABS had acted in a reckless manner and rejected the State's claim. Since that claim was rejected, the counter-claim of ABS was not considered by the Court of Appeals. [75]

Proposals for Development of International Law Relating to Compensation in Place of Refuge Situations

In recent years discussions have taken place on the possibilities to develop the present legal principles for the purpose of facilitating for coastal States to grant access to places of refuge.

It has for instance been suggested that a new treaty instrument be prepared which would address a number of issues relating to places of refuge, including provisions on liability and compensation. It has been proposed that the Civil Liability and Fund Conventions should be revised for the purpose of improving the possibilities for those suffering damage in places of refuge situations to be compensated.

The suggestion has been made that ports should be treated as salvors and be given the right to salvage rewards which would act as an incentive for them to give a ship in distress access to a place of refuge. It has been suggested that the insurers, i.e. the P&I Clubs, should on a voluntary basis agree not to invoke the right of limitation in places of refuge situations or to undertake to indemnify a State for liabilities and losses resulting from place of refuge operations.

It has been proposed that the provisions on channelling of liability in the 1992 Civil Liability Convention should be amended so as to include public authorities granting a ship access to a place of refuge. It has also been suggested that, instead of that Convention being amended, the 1992 Fund Assembly could adopt a resolution on the interpretation of the 1992 Conventions in relation to places of refuge situations to the effect that measures taken by a coastal State in such situations would generally be considered as preventive measures.

A discussion of these proposals falls outside the scope of the present chapter. [76]

CONCLUSION

When a tanker or other ship in distress carrying oil or other hazardous cargoes requests to be granted a place of refuge, the Government, port authority or other public body involved is often reluctant to permit the ship to enter, for fear that this could result in major damage of various kinds, for example costs for clean-up of polluted beaches, costs of salvage operations, loss of income for fishermen and fish farmers and losses for businesses in the tourism sector. There may be fears that it will be difficult or impossible to get compensation for the damage caused. It may also be feared that those suffering pollution damage may sue the State in negligence for the damage they have suffered. These concerns are understandable. It should in any event be recognised that a refusal to grant access to a place of refuge may also result in significant damage, as was amply illustrated by the *Prestige* incident. [77]

It is submitted that as regards oil tankers these fears are exaggerated, since the international compensation regime relating to spills from such ships, which applies also in places of refuge situations, has in general functioned well. In most cases compensation has been paid promptly and without claimants having to resort to court actions. The fact that the shipowner has strict liability for pollution damage, that his liability is covered by insurance and that the 1992 Fund will step in and pay compensation if the total damage exceeds the amount payable by the shipowner and his insurer results in those suffering pollution damage in a place of refuge situation normally being compensated without major difficulties. In addition, the channelling provisions providing responder immunity to salvors and those carrying out clean-up operations or taking other preventive measures should result in removing hesitation on the part of these groups to intervene rapidly also in difficult circumstances. Although the shipowner may sometimes be exonerated from liability, totally or against a particular claimant on the grounds of contributory negligence, the 1992 Fund would very rarely be exonerated from liability. In particular the Fund may not invoke contributory negligence in respect of preventive measures. It is suggested, therefore, that those having suffered pollution damage would, except in rare cases, rather pursue their claims under the international regime than take legal action against a State or public authority where normally negligence or failure to act with due diligence on the part of the defendant would have to be established.

Problems have mainly arisen in cases where the amount available for compensation was or could have been insufficient to compensate all claimants in full under the 1992 Conventions or their predecessors, and admittedly it could occur also in the future in places of refuge cases that the total amount of the damage exceeds the amount available under the 1992 Conventions, US$304 million. This problem is however largely overcome for States which are members of the Supplementary Fund, as a result of the very high amount available for compensation, US$1 125 million, which should allow all admissible claims to be paid in full from the outset in practically all cases.

Concerns have been expressed that a State having granted an oil tanker in distress a place of refuge may be exposed to recourse action by the shipowner/insurer and the IOPC Funds. Although this cannot be ruled out, experience of the application of the Civil Liability and Fund Conventions shows that the risk of such recourse actions is fairly small.

The above analysis shows, in the author's opinion, that when a State or other public body has to decide whether to allow an oil tanker in distress to proceed to a place of refuge in its waters, this decision can be taken in the knowledge that the international compensation regime established by the 1992 Conventions and the 2003 Supplementary Fund Protocol gives good financial protection in case a major oil spill were to occur, which should make it easier for such a request to be granted.

With respect to places of refuge situations involving spills of bunker oil from ships other than oil tankers, the main weaknesses of the regime created by the Bunkers Convention is the uncertainty as to the limitation amount that will apply and the portion thereof available for pollution damage claims when non-pollution claims are also taken into account, the absence of channelling provisions and the absence of a second layer of compensation. The Bunkers Convention represents nevertheless a considerable improvement in the possibilities for public bodies and others to obtain compensation for pollution damage caused by a bunker oil spill from a ship having entered a place of refuge. Since spills of bunker oil seldom are of the same magnitude as a major tanker oil spill, the Bunkers Convention gives a fairly good financial protection for coastal States in places of refuge situations. The increased limitation amounts in the 1996 Protocol to the LLMC which are expected to enter into force in 2015 will greatly improve the situation as regards the States parties to that Protocol, and the increased amounts should normally be sufficient to cover any pollution damage caused in such situations. [78]

Until the HNS Convention enters into force, there is no international regime providing for strict liability for ships in distress carrying hazardous cargoes other than oil. Liability issues will be decided in accordance with the applicable national law, and the shipowner and any other potentially liable party will normally be liable only if negligence on their part is proven. In addition the shipowner may be entitled to limit his liability to an amount which is insufficient to provide full compensation to the public authorities and other claimants, and there is no second layer of compensation provided by an international fund.

Once the HNS Convention has entered into force, the situation will be largely the same for ships in distress carrying other hazardous cargoes than oil as for oil tankers, with the caveat that the total amount available for compensation under that Convention (US$375 million) will be significantly lower than that under the Supplementary Fund Protocol. According to information given by the International Group of P&I Clubs there has, however, not been any case where the damage caused by hazardous and noxious substances carried by sea has exceeded that amount. [79]

Concerns have been expressed that ships not falling within the scope of the Conventions in force may not have liability insurance. These concerns should have been greatly reduced as regards the EU Member States as a result of Directive 2009/20/EC on the insurance of shipowners for maritime claims which should have been implemented by Member States by

31 December 2011. [80] Under that Directive any ship of 300 gross tonnage or more flying the flag of an EU Member State or entering a port in such State shall have insurance to cover maritime claims up to the limitation amount laid down in the 1976 LLMC as amended by the 1996 Protocol thereto. [81] It cannot be ruled out, however, that a ship flying the flag of a non-EU Member State without insurance would have to be granted access to a place of refuge in a EU Member State.

It should be recognised that there are certain types of damage which are not covered by the international compensation regimes discussed above. These regimes do not for instance allow compensation for non-economic consequences of damage to the environment. In addition the international regimes do not cover damage to port installations and costs of wreck removal unless the removal falls within the definition of preventive measures, i.e. reasonable measures to prevent or minimise oil pollution damage, or in the case of the HNS Convention reasonable measures to prevent or minimise damage caused by hazardous substances.

It should also be noted that, as mentioned above, the report published by the European Commission in November 2012 contains *inter alia* a statement to the effect that the International conventions on the subject of liability in the area of maritime transport offer a satisfactory system in the areas covered by these conventions pertinent in the context of reception of a ship in a place of refuge.

The financial protection which the international compensation regimes give in places of refuge situations is of course only available in respect of damage in States that have ratified the relevant Conventions, and States should therefore have an incentive to become parties to these treaty instruments, if they have not already done so.

REFERENCES

[1] For details of these cases and for further examples see Colin de la Rue and Charles B. Anderson, *Shipping and the Environment,* 2nd ed (2009) at p. 541, 905-916; *Annual Reports of the International Oil Pollution Compensation Funds* 1999 at p. 118 for the *Erika* incident and 2002 at p. 116 for the *Prestige* incident (hereinafter Annual Reports). See also Richard Shaw: Places of Refuge, International Law in the Making, *Journal of International Maritime Law* 2003 at p. 161-163; Proshanto K. Mukherjee: Refuge and Salvage, in *A. Chirop and O. Linden (Ed.), Places of Refuge for Ships, Emerging Environmental Concerns of a Maritime Custom* p. 271.

[2] Annual Report 1996 at p.94.

[3] Concerning this incident, see de la Rue and Anderson note 1 supra at p. 914. The decision to beach the vessel was taken by the Secretary of State's Representative (SOSREP), a post created after the *Sea Empress* incident; see de la Rue and Anderson note 1 supra at p. 915.

[4] See for example Eric van Hooydonk: *Places of Refuge, International Law and the CMI Draft Convention*, Lloyd's List, London, 2010.

[5] International Convention on Civil Liability for Oil Pollution Damage, 1992, International Convention on the Establishment of an International Fund for Compensation for Oil Pollution Damage, 1992, and the Protocol of 2003 to the

International Convention on the Establishment of an International Fund for Compensation for Oil Pollution Damage, 1992.

[6] Some authors have dealt with these issues in some detail. See Erik Røsæg and Henrik Ringbom: *Liability and Compensation with Regard to Places of Refuge*, Study EMSA/RES/001-2004 prepared for the European Maritime Safety Agency, 2004 (available at: www.emsa.europa.eu/implementation-); Stuart Hetherington: Civil liability and monetary incentives for accepting ships in distress, in *Comite Maritime International (CMI) Yearbook 2003, Vancouver I, Part II, documents for the Vancouver Conference*, p. 457-467; Henrik Ringbom: You are welcome, but....Places of refuge and environmental liability and compensation, with particular reference to the EU; in *CMI Yearbook 2004* p. 208-233; Mukherjee note 1 supra at p. 2.

[7] For a detailed discussion of this issue see Erik van Hooydonk: The obligation to offer a place of refuge to ships in distress, *CMI Yearbook 2003*, part II, p. 403; Stuart Hetherington: *Prestige* – Can the law assist? *CMI Yearbook 2003*, part I p. 361-374. Agustin Blanco-Bazán: The Law of the Sea: Places of refuge, in *Canadian Council of International Law, Globalism, People, Profits and Progress,* Kluwer Law International 2002 p. 65; R.R. Churchill and A.V. Lowe, *The Law of the Sea*, 3rd ed, 1999 at p. 61-65; Henrik Ringbom and Malgorzata Nesterowicz: Places of Refuge and Environmental Liability and Compensation in the EU – an Update in *Environmental Liabilities in Ports and Coastal Areas, Institute of Maritime and Commercial Law,* Åbo Akademi University 2011 p. 82-84.

[8] Articles 194(2), 195 and 232 of the United Nations Convention on the Law of the Sea (UNCLOS). See James Crawford: *Brownlie's Principles of Public International Law* (8thed. 2012) Chapter 25; Philippe Sands and Jaqueline Peel: *Principles of international environmental law (*3rd ed. 2012) Chapter 17; Patricia Birnie, Alan Boyle and Catherine Redgwell: *International Law and the Environment* (3rd ed. 2009) at p. 430-434.

[9] Work relating to places of refuge has also been carried out within the framework of regional environmental protection organisations; see Ringbom and Nesterowicz note 7 supra at p. 82.

[10] Resolution A.949 (23).

[11] For an analysis of the Guidelines see Mukherjee, note 1 supra at p. 279; Shaw note 1 supra at p. 163.

[12] The 2009 Directive constitutes a revision of an earlier Directive 2002/59/EC.

[13] COM(2012) 715 final, dated 30.11.2012.

[14] There are however still 36 States parties to the 1969 Civil Liability Convention; no EU Member State is party to that Convention. The 1971 Fund Convention ceased to be in force in 2002.

[15] This exclusion also covers the servants or agents of the shipowner, the members of the crew, the pilot and the charterer, manager or operator of the ship.

[16] The shipowner is deprived of the right to limit his liability if it is proven that the pollution damage resulted from his personal act or omission, committed with the intent to cause such damage, or recklessly and with knowledge that such damage would probably result.

[17] The unit of account in the 1992 Conventions and the Supplementary Fund Protocol as well as in the HNS Convention is the Special Drawing Right (SDR) as defined by the

International Monetary Fund. The figures given in US dollars in this chapter have been arrived at by using the rate of exchange applicable on 31 May 2013, i.e. 1 SDR = 1.496770...

[18] For details of the international regime reference is made to the IOPC Funds' Annual Report 2012 and to the Funds' website at www.iopcfund.org. See also Måns Jacobsson: The International Liability and Compensation Regime for Oil Pollution from Ships – International Solutions for a Global Problem, (2007) 32 *Tulane Maritime Law Journal* p. 1; de la Rue and Anderson note 1 supra at p. 81-174.

[19] Romania has ratified the 1992 Civil Liability Convention but not the 1992 Fund Convention.

[20] The United States have not ratified any of these treaties but adopted their own legislation in the form of the Oil Pollution Act 1990 (OPA-90). For the main differences between the international regime and OPA-90 see Jacobsson note 18 supra at p. 19.

[21] Måns Jacobsson: The Bunkers Convention in force, *Journal of International Maritime Law*, 2009 p. 21; Måns Jacobsson: La Convención Bunker en vigor, in *Analisis de 10 años de vigencia de las leyes marítimas venezolanas*, Academia de Ciencias Políticas y Sociales, Universidad Central de Venezuela, Serie Eventos 28, 2012, p. 407; de la Rue and Anderson note 1 supra at p. 255-266.

[22] International Convention on Liability and Compensation for Damage in Connection with the Carriage of Hazardous and Noxious Substances by Sea, 1996 (HNS Convention).

[23] For a detailed analysis of the HNS Convention see Måns Jacobsson: The HNS Convention and its 2010 Protocol, in *Pollution at Sea: Law and Liability*, Chapter 3, B. Soyer and A Tetterborn (ed), Lloyds List 2012; de la Rue and Anderson note 1 supra at p. 269-293; Magnus Göransson: The HNS Convention (1997) *Uniform Law Review* at p. 249.

[24] Måns Jacobsson: Diplomatic Conference adopts Protocol to the 1996 HNS Convention, Shipping and Transport International 2010 Number 2 at p. 8.

[25] IMO document LEG 87/17, paragraphs 150-161.

[26] IMO document LEG 87/7/1.

[27] The policy of the IMO is that the IMO bodies will entertain proposals for new conventions or amendments to existing conventions only on the basis of clear and well-documented demonstration of compelling need; IMO Assembly Resolution A.500(XII) adopted in 1981, and reiterated by Resolution A.177(18) adopted in 1993.

[28] IMO document LEG 90/15 p. 49; Rosalie Balkin: The IMO position with respect to places of refuge, in *CMI Yearbook 2005-2006* at p. 154; Richard Shaw: IMO Legal Committee, Report on meetings 18-29 April 2005, *Journal of International Maritime Law* 2005 p. 160.

[29] The Comité Maritime International (CMI) is an international non-governmental organisation the object of which is to contribute to the unification of maritime law.

[30] IMO document LEG 95/9.

[31] For the work of the CMI relating to places of refuge see www.comitemaritime.org.

[32] IMO document LEG 95/19, section 9(a).

[33] Joseph Nichols, Admissibility of claims: development of the IOPC Funds' policy, in *The IOPC Funds' 25 years of compensating victims of oil pollution incidents*, Canterbury 2003, at p. 103.

[34] Claims Manual published by the International Oil Pollution Compensation Fund 1992 (December 2008 edition); a revised edition will be published in 2013 to reflect amendments adopted in October 2012. See also Guidelines for presenting claims in the fisheries, mariculture and fish processing sector and Technical Guidelines for assessing fisheries sector claims, issued by the International Oil Pollution Compensation Fund 1992 (December 2008 editions); similar Guidelines for claims in the tourism sector are expected to be published in 2013.

[35] As regards claims for economic losses in these sectors see de la Rue and Anderson note 1 supra at p. 415-430; Jacobsson note 18 supra at p. 25; Nichols note 33 supra at p. 106-111; Claims Manual p. 27-34.

[36] A State that has not declared an EEZ may for the purpose of the application of the 1992 Conventions and the Supplementary Fund Protocol declare an area beyond and adjacent to its territorial sea determined by that State in accordance with international law and extending not more than 200 nautical miles from the baselines from which the breadth of its territorial sea is measured.

[37] 1971 Fund Executive Committee in the *Kihnu* case (Estonia, 1993); document 71FUND/EXC.49/12, paragraph 3.4.6.

[38] Claims Manual p. 23.

[39] For a detailed analysis of the concept of reasonableness see Måns Jacobsson: How clean is clean? The concept of 'reasonableness' in the response to tanker oil spills, in *Scritti in Onore di Francesco Berlingieri*, special issue of *Il Diritto Marittimo* 2010 p. 565; See also Claims Manual p. 23-25; de la Rue and Anderson note 1 supra at p. 383-390, 998.

[40] Fund document 92FUND/A.11/24, paragraphs 3.3-3.5; Jacobsson note 39 supra at p. 575-580.

[41] In the 2012 Report from the European Commission it is stated that it could be useful to obtain all relevant clarifications at the IMO level in order to confirm that reception of a vessel in a place of refuge could, in principle, be considered a preventive measure (COM(2012) 715 final, section 5.1 paragraph 3). It is submitted that, in the light of what is stated above, there is no need for such a clarification.

[42] Cf. Måns Jacobsson and Norbert Trotz: The definition of pollution damage in the 1984 Protocols to the 1969 Civil Liability Convention and the 1971 Fund Convention; *Journal of Maritime Law and Commerce* 1986 at p. 462.

[43] For a detailed discussion of salvage and places of refuge see Mukherjee note 1 supra; Røsæg and Ringbom note 6 supra at p. 25.

[44] Annual Report 1988 p. 32 (*Patmos* incident; Italy, 1985).

[45] Annual Report 1991 p. 45 (*Rio Orinoco* incident; Canada, 1990) and 1992 p. 54 (*Agip Abruzzo* incident; Italy, 1991); for an analysis of the application by the Funds of the dual purpose test see de la Rue and Anderson note 1 supra at p. 400-404.

[46] Claims Manual p. 26.

[47] Claims Manual p. 25-26.

[48] For an analysis of the decisions by the Funds' governing bodies in respect compensation claims relating to damage to the environment see Nichols note 33 supra

at p. 114-117; Måns Jacobsson: L'indemnisation des dommages résultant des atteintes à l'environnement dans le cadre du régime international CLC/FIPOL, *Le Droit Maritime Français,* 2010 p. 469-480; de la Rue and Anderson note 1 supra at p. 477. WIth respect to the situation in the United States in this regard see de la Rue and Anderson at p.515.

[49] It should be noted that the 1992 Civil Liability Convention only governs the liability of the registered owner and that the liability of others is governed by the applicable national law, except if the person in question is entitled to benefit from the protection of the channelling provisions in the Convention. In a judgement in the *Erika* case rendered by the French Court of Cassation in September 2012 four defendants other than the registered owner were held jointly and severally liable by application of French law for *inter alia* ecological damage, loss of image, moral damage and damage to reputation; document IOPC/APR13/8/1 paragraphs 3.3.4-3.3.12.

[50] Resolution adopted by the 1971 Fund Assembly in October 1980 (document FUND/A/ES.1/13, Annex I). In the *Volgoneft 139* case (Russian Federation, 2007) the Russian authorities had submitted a claim for environmental damage based on a mathematical formula, in accordance with national legislation. The claim was however rejected by a Russian court which referred to the above-mentioned proviso in the 1992 Civil Liability Convention (document IOPC/OCT10/3/9, section 10).

[51] As for the policy of the IOPC Funds in respect of reinstatement measures and post spill studies see Nichols note 33 supra at p. 116; Claims Manual p. 35-37.

[52] The Funds would not be liable if the oil originated from a warship or other ship owned or operated by a State and used, at the time of the incident, only on government non-commercial service (art. 4.2.a).

[53] in the *Tsesis* case (Sweden, 1977) the Swedish Supreme Court held that the shipowner was not liable for the pollution damage, since the incident had been wholly caused by negligence on the part of the Swedish Government in its failure to mark a shoal on the maritime chart and to adjust the white sector from a lighthouse; for the facts of the case see de la Rue and Anderson note 1 supra at p. 101. If the 1971 Fund Convention had been in force at that time the 1971 Fund would probably have had to compensate the Swedish Government for the costs of the clean-up operations.

[54] With respect to the interpretation of that expression see Jacobsson note 23 supra at p. 33; de la Rue and Anderson note 1 supra at p. 100.

[55] It could be argued that if a ship were to be directed to a place of refuge and grounds on an uncharted rock resulting in oil pollution, the shipowner would be exonerated from liability under Article III.2.c of the 1992 Civil Liabiiity Convention; cf the *Tsesis* case note 53 supra.

[56] In the *Patmos* case (Italy, 1985) compensation to the Italian Government was reduced on the grounds of contributory negligence by the Port of Messina in the application of dispersants (Court of Appeal judgement January 1994, Annual Report 1994 p. 36-38). In the *Aegean Sea* case (Spain, 1992) the master of the ship and the pilot were held jointly and severally liable for the incident, each of them on a 50% basis (Court of Appeal judgement June 1997); consequently the Spanish State was only entitled to recover 50% of its established claim (Annual Report 1997 p. 54-56 and 2007 p. 5).

[57] Article V.4 of the 1992 Civil Liability Convention, Article 4.5 of the 1992 Fund Convention and Article 4.2 of the Supplementary Fund Protocol.

[58] This has been the case in respect of the *Erika* incident and will be the case in respect of the *Prestige* and *Hebei Spirit* (Republic of Korea, 2007) incidents.

[59] For a detailed discussion of recourse actions see de la Rue and Anderson note 1 supra at p.165-168, 590-596 (salvors), 607-649 (charterers), 667-690 (colliding ships), 658-704 (maritime authorities).

[60] De la Rue and Anderson note 1 supra at p. 109.

[61] The main providers of shipowners' third party liability insurance are the Protection and Indemnity Associations (P&I Clubs), which are mutual insurers. In the great majority of major oil pollution cases, the third party liability insurer is member of the International Group of P&I Associations, a group of 13 mutual insurers that collectively provide liability insurance for approximately 90 per cent of the world's ocean-going tonnage and for some 95 per cent of the world's ocean-going tanker tonnage.

[62] In the preamble to European Community Directive 2009/17/EC (paragraph 21) it is stated: "The absence of financial insurance does not exonerate a Member State from its obligation to perform a preliminary assessment and to decide on the acceptance of the ship in a place of refuge. Though the competent authorities may verify whether the ship is covered by insurance or some other effective form of financial security permitting appropriate compensation for costs and damages associated with its accommodation in a place of refuge, the act of requesting such information must not delay the rescue operation." It is further provided (Article 20c) that the absence of an insurance certificate within the meaning of Directive 2009/20/EC on the insurance of shipowners for maritime claims shall not exonerate a Member State from the preliminary assessment and decision referred to above, and shall not in itself be considered as sufficient reason for a Member State to refuse to accommodate a ship in a place of refuge.

[63] This issue is discussed in Ringbom note 6 supra at p. 229-230.

[64] Conference Resolution 3 on 'Protection of persons taking measures to prevent or minimize pollution damage'.

[65] Since the LLMC does not explicitly grant the right of limitation for pollution claims, there is uncertainty as to whether claims for certain types of pollution damage fall within the scope of that Convention. See P. Griggs R.Williams J. Farr *Limitation of Liability for Marime Claims* (4th edn Informa 2005) at p. 19-25; Jacobsson: Bunkers Convention in force, note 21 supra at p. 29; Ringbom and Nesterowicz note 7 supra at p. 87; Norman A Martínez Gutiérez: *Limitation of Liablity in International Maritime Conventions, The relationship between global limitation conventions and particular liability conventions*, IMLI Studies in Maritime Law, Routledge, 2011.

[66] IMO Resolution LEG.5(99).

[67] For an analysis of the Directive see Edward H.P. Brans: Liability for Damage to Public Natural Resources under the 2004 EC Environmental Directive, *Environmental Law Review* 2005 p. 90; M.A. Nesterowicz: The third legislative package for maritime safety – the liability projects, *Annuaire de Droit Maritime et Océanique* 2007 p. 281; Gerd Winter Jan H Jans Richard Macrory Ludwig Krämer: Weighing up the EU Environmental Liability Directive, *Journal of Environmental Law* 2008 p. 163.

[68] Directive 2000/60/EC establishing a framework for Community action in the field of water policy.

[69] As regards the relationship between the EU Directive and the international maritime compensation regimes see Ringbom and Nesterowicz note 7 supra at p. 87-90; Måns Jacobsson: Perspective of the global compensation regimes; the relationship between EU legislation and maritime liability conventions, *European Journal of Commercial Contract Law* 2012 p. 63..

[70] As mentioned above, Romania is party only to the 1992 Civil Liability Convention.

[71] With respect to possible conflicts between the international liability regimes and Directive 75/442/EC on waste reference is made to Jacobsson note 69 supra at p. 67.

[72] As stated above, this chapter does not deal with questions of inter-state liability under public international law in cases of transboundary pollution.

[73] It could be argued that if a ship were to be directed to a place of refuge and ground on an uncharted rock resulting in oil pollution, the shipowner would be exonerated from liability under Article III.2.c of the 1992 Civil Liability Convention; cf the *Tsesis* case referred to in note 53 supra.

[74] Cf UNCLOS art. 232 and 235.2 as well as the 1969 Convention relating to intervention on the high seas in cases of oil pollution casualties (art. VI) and the 1973 Protocol thereto; de la Rue and Andersen note 1 supra at p. 899-905.

[75] Document IOPC/OCT12/3/6/1, section 2.

[76] These and other proposals are discussed in Ringbom note 6 supra at p. 221-232; van Hoydoonc note 7 supra at p. 437-445; Archie Bishop: Places of refuge – Environmental salvage in *Serving the Rule of International Law – Essays in Honour of Professor David Joseph Attard,* Mare Nostrum Publications 2009 2nd vol. p. 352.

[77] The weaknesses of the international compensation regimes in the context of places of refuge situations are discussed in Røsæg and Ringbom note 6 supra at p. 67-71.

[78] Cf. IMO document LEG 99/4/6 submitted by the International Group of P&I Associations to the session of the IMO Legal Committee held in April 2012, containing data on incidents involving bunker spills for the period 2000-2011.

[79] Cf. IMO document LEG/CONF.17/6, submitted by the International Group of P&I Associations to the 2010 Diplomatic Conference which adopted the Protocol to the HNS Convention, containing data on incidents involving hazardous cargoes durng the period 2000-2010.

[80] Cf. IMO Assembly Resolution A.898(21) on Guidelines on shipowners' responsibilities in respect of maritime claims.

[81] The Directive shall be without prejudice to the regimes established by the 1992 Civil Liability Convention, the Bunkers Convention and the HNS Convention if in force.

In: Selected Issues in Maritime Law and Policy
Editor: Maximo Q. Mejia, Jr.
ISBN: 978-1-62618-508-1

Chapter 8

THE "INTERNATIONAL" ASPECT OF THE CONFLICT OF LAWS: DEFINITIONS, PERSPECTIVES AND REGIMES

F. Mikis Manolis[*,1]
Associate, Hungerford Tomyn Lawrenson and Nichols

The "conflict of laws" as a turn of phrase was first coined by the American jurist Joseph Story in 1834 and is generally referred to synonymously as "private international law" to describe the body of principles and rules applicable to trans-boundary interactions and relationships between private entities.[2] At base, a conflict of laws arises where there is at one least one relevant "foreign" element connecting a matter or transaction with more than one legal unit or jurisdiction.[3] The existence of this foreign element gives rise to one or more of three basic and essential questions: which forum or fora in the relevant legal units has the requisite authority or power to resolve a dispute arising in respect of the transaction at hand?; which of the laws of the relevant legal units will be applied to resolve the dispute?; and will a judgment obtained in a particular forum be recognized and enforced in the other relevant legal units or fora? To wit, jurisdiction, choice of law and recognition and enforcement are the three primary constituent parts of the conflict of laws.[4]

---

[*] E-mail: mmanolis@htln.com.

[1] Dr. Manolis had the singular pleasure and opportunity to be supervised in his doctoral studies by Prof. Proshanto K. Mukherjee whose guidance, wise counsel and friendship will always be greatly appreciated and to whom this piece is dedicated.

[2] William Tetley, Q.C., *International Conflict of Laws: Common, Civil and Maritime* (Montreal: Blais International Shipping Publications, 1994), p. 9; Jean-Gabriel Castel and Janet Walker, *Canadian Conflict of Law* (Markham: LexisNexis Canada, 2003), p. 1.4; and Joseph Story, *Conflicts of Law: Commentaries on the conflict of laws, foreign and domestic, in regard to contracts, rights, and remedies, and especially in regard to marriages, divorces, wills, successions, and judgments, 3rd ed.* (Boston: C. C. Little and J. Brown, 1846).

[3] See, *inter alia*, Castel and Walker, p. 1.1.

[4] William Tetley, Q.C., "Jurisdiction Clauses and *Forum Non Conveniens* in the Carriage of Goods by Sea" in Martin Davies (ed.), *Jurisdiction and Forum Selection in International Maritime Law: Essays in Honor of Robert Force* (The Hague: Kluwer Law International, 2005) at 205. In this vein, Tetley notes that "[e]ach side of the triangle is as important as the other, there being no complete solution to conflict of laws if the proper choice of law is not made in the proper jurisdiction and the decision taken cannot be properly recognized elsewhere." Tetley, *International*, p. 861.

Unlike public international law, which seeks to regulate relations between sovereign States, international organizations or a combination thereof, that is in theory the same everywhere, private international law does not always or necessarily imply a body of principles or rules that are universal in character.[5] Stated another way, private international law can be characterized as a domestic response to the fact that the world is made up of distinct and separate legal systems or units and that two or more distinct bodies of law and two or more distinct court systems may apply to and have jurisdiction over a single trans-boundary transaction.[6] As a feature of domestic law, private international law, despite the "international" moniker varies from country to country.[7] In more cerebral terms, private international is a means by which to address what John Gerard Ruggie refers to as the "paradox of absolute individuation" which flows as a natural consequence from the establishment of the Westphalian system of nation states – having established territorially fixed state formations, having insisted that these territorial domains are disjointed and mutually exclusive, and having accepted these conditions as the constitutive base of international society, what means are left for dealing with problems of that society that cannot not be reduced to territorial solutions?[8]

With this in mind, this paper attempts to examine the international aspect of conflict of laws and the role played by international regimes in its development of private international law. To this end, the paper is divided into three parts. The first section explores the nature of private international law and various perspectives as to its internationality both as a defining characteristic and potential source of norms, principles and rules. In this effort, an attempt is made to identify various shared values, ideals or goals relating to the conflict of laws. The second part examines in the role that international treaties and conventions play in the development of private international law. Within that rubric, the third section explores the general characteristics of three of the primary international regimes relating to matters of choice of law, jurisdiction and recognition and enforcement.

I. Conflict of Laws and "International" Law

While many commentators identify private international law as a branch of domestic law and rightly point out that there is a lack of uniformity in the rules relating to the conflicts of law, private international law is somewhat analogous to public international law in the sense

---

[5] That is, private international law is not "international" in the public international law sense of the word.

[6] Castel and Walker, p. 1.3.

[7] In this vein, Abla J. Mayss comments as follows:

> There are obvious differences between conflict of laws, or private international law, and public international law. The latter is primarily concerned with the rules that govern relations between sovereign States in their interrelations. The former, however, is designed to regulate disputes of a private nature. Conflict of laws is that part of municipal law which only comes into play when a dispute has a connection of some kind with one or more foreign legal systems. Every modern legal system has its own rules of private international law, and they differ from one another as much as any other branch of domestic law.

See Abla J. Mayss, *Principles of Conflict of Laws, 3rd ed.* (London: Cavendish Publishing Ltd., 1999), p. 2.

[8] John Gerard Ruggie, "Territoriality and Beyond: Problematizing Modernity in International Relations" 47(1) *International Organization* 139. The nation state is not, of course, the only "legal unit" of relevance in that conflict of laws issues often arise in federal states as there may be and often are conflicts of law between the laws of the various states, provinces or territories as regards matters falling with the legislative competence of such entities. In other words, conflicts of law may also be national in character. See Castel and Walker, p. 1.2.

that it can be viewed as a system that assigns judicial competence and legislative competence as amongst the courts and legislatures of the world.[9] Such considerations are clearly evident in decisions relating to the assumption of jurisdiction, the determination of the applicable law and *ex post facto* in decisions as to whether a foreign judgment will be recognized and enforced. All such decisions and determinations, although they may be based in national law, have an international objective, i.e. the ordering of international society.[10]

It is generally recognized that private international law rests on and arises in response to the principle of territoriality or sovereignty that itself derives from and is a basic tenet of public international law – that is, States have the exclusive right to regulate activities and persons within their territories and, conversely, do not have the right to regulate activities or persons beyond their borders.[11] As a consequence of this territorial origin, the preoccupation of many commentators has been to explain the origins of the principles and rules that compromise private international law and which principles and rules allow and, in some cases, require courts to abandon a strictly national or territorial view of the world.[12]

So-called "internationalists" source the principles and rules underlying private international law in the law of nations and among the international customary rules or norms that all civilized nations accept as binding upon them.[13] In other words, principles and rules underlying private international law are seen as a form of customary international law, which is external and ostensibly more important than and above the law of any particular state.[14] The attraction of locating conflict of law principles and rules in a source law that has no particular national basis appears in the main to stem from the fact that such an approach to some extent provides a neutral basis on which decision-makers when determining, *inter alia*, choice of law and jurisdiction issues may step outside the policy preferences of the contending States and laws.[15]

As Lea Brilmayer points out, sourcing conflict of laws principles and rules in a normative system external to and more important than the authority of any particular state suffers from two principal shortcomings. First, if there are indeed international customary rules or norms in the sphere of private international law their precise content is difficult to ascertain. Second, even assuming a set of rules or norms can be identified and are logically persuasive, the extent to which these rules or norms can be regarded as authoritative is questionable.[16]

---

[9] See Marvin Baer, Joost Blom, Elizabeth Edinger, Nicholas Rafferty, Geneviève Saumier and Catherine Walsh, *Private International in Common Law Canada: Cases, Texts and Materials* (Toronto: Edmond Montgomery Publications, 1997), pp. 8-9.

[10] Castel and Walker, p. 1.11.

[11] Baer et al. p. 8.

[12] Baer et al. p. 8. In this vein, Lord Mance commented that private international law is the area "par excellence where no national legal system can maintain insular attitude." See Lord Mance, "The Future of Private International Law" (2005) 1(2) J. of P.I.L. 185 at 185.

[13] Castel and Walker, p. 1.11.

[14] Lea Brilmayer, *Conflict of Laws: Foundations and Future Directions* (Boston: Little Brown, 1991), p. 2; Castel and Walker, p. 1.11.

[15] See Brilmayer, pp. 1-2.

[16] See Brilmayer, pp. 2 and 13. Even assuming that such universalized principles and rules can be said to exist, issues will remain at the domestic level as to the extent to and the manner in which such principles and rules form part of or are incorporated or adopted into domestic often remains a live issue. In this regard, a myriad of issues may arise such as whether such principles and rules automatically form part of domestic law, whether there must be express adoption, whether such adoption may occur unless there is an express derogation, whether such principles ought to merely aid in the interpretation of domestic law, and so on. See, for instance, David Ginn, The Domestic Legal Status of Customary International Law in the United States: Lessons from the Federal Courts' Experience with General Maritime Law, (2008) 4 J. Int'l L & Int'l Rel. 105 and *R. v. Hape*, 2007 SCC 26, [2007] 2 SCR 292, paras. 36-39.

In addition to these shortcomings, the notion that conflict of laws principles are in the nature of international customary rules or norms is at odds with the patent diversity of national and intra-national systems relating to the conflict of laws, which itself is clear evidence of the absence of universalized customs.[17] Even taken to the more generalized level of legal traditions there can be marked differences in approach, methodology and emphasis with respect to private international law issues.[18]

The obvious counter-point to the "internationalist" approach is one that identifies conflict of laws principles and rules exclusively as a branch of domestic law, i.e. the "territorialist" approach.[19] This approach avoids the authoritative source issue by focusing exclusively on positive law whose authoritative nature cannot be disputed.[20] In this approach, the task is limited to asking to what are the authoritative laws of the forum that apply to the case at hand. There is an obvious force of consistent practice behind such an approach in that courts and practitioners often do precisely that and no more. This approach too is not without its shortcomings. First, it assumes at the outset, particularly as regards choice of law, that the forum is entitled to determine conflict of laws issues from the perspective of its own chosen rules and interests.[21] Second, this approach limits the role played by critical commentary, normative recommendations and policy arguments as to what domestic law ought to be with respect to the conflict of laws.[22] Of course, "internationalist" and "territorialist" approaches are as described in their strictest forms caricatures that fail to describe the nuances of most existing approaches to private international law, which generally combine elements of both approaches and perspectives.[23] In this vein, despite the fact that it may be difficult to divine

---

[17] Castel and Walker, p. 1.11.

[18] In this respect, Aude Fiorini neatly summarizes the broad differences in approach to private international law as between common law and civilian legal systems as follows:

Unlike in civil law systems the emphasis in common law systems has always been on jurisdiction as against choice of law. The area of jurisdiction in private international law…[marks]…great divide between the common law and the civil law models. Even where aims are shared, methodology differs greatly, notably as a result of the profound difference about how courts should behave.

It is well known that, put simply, civilian systems focus on the structure of the law as opposed its operation while common law systems are based on experience rather than logic, and that traditionally common law judges have been guided by pragmatism and a strong commercial sense and very much 'placed on a pedestal', while their civil law counterparts have been the object of mistrust and been seen as playing a rather mechanical role. Further, the achievement of justice in concrete cases is the focus of common law, while across the channel it is essentially the application of the just rule that seems to count. These opposite attitudes have imprinted particular marks in the field jurisdiction in private international law.

On the continent, jurisdiction is afforded on the basis of clear, rigid, strict and obvious rules which leave little room, if any, for judicial discretion while in European common law systems jurisdiction is assumed on the basis of wide, flexible rules with courts having discretion in the exercise of their jurisdiction. Once seised…a court on the continent will have to exercise [its] jurisdiction even if it not the most appropriate forum and this even if the most appropriate court has subsequently been seized of the same dispute. By contrast, in a similar situation, a common law court would have the power under the *forum non conveniens* doctrine decline jurisdiction even if no other court has yet been seised. In case of parallel litigation, common law courts have developed a weapon that is unknown to civilian courts: anti-suit injunctions, whereby a party can be restrained from instituting, or proceeding with, an action abroad. While it is accepted in both traditions that the parties themselves designate the court which will have jurisdiction to adjudicate on their dispute, choice of court agreements are traditionally given exclusive effect in civil law countries but not in common law countries.

See Aude Fiorini, "The Codification of Private International Law in Europe: Could the Community Learn from the Experience of Mixed Jurisdictions?" (2008) 12(1) E.J. of Comp. L. 1, pp. 9-10.

[19] Castel and Walker, pp. 1.2 and 1.11; Baer et al. p. 8.

[20] Brilmayer, p. 2.

[21] Brilmayer, p. 3.

[22] Brilmayer, p. 3.

[23] For a similar discussion focused on choice of law principles and rules, see Brilmayer, p. 3. In this vein, the British Columbia Court of Appeal in *Furlan v. Shell Oil Co.*, 2000 BCCA 404 noted that jurisdictional issues

the precise content of conflict of laws norms, principles and rules of general or universal application, it is at least arguable that there are a number extant shared values, ideals or goals that permeate most approaches to private international law issues, whether they be domestic or international in character. Specifically, most approaches to private international law place considerable value on the promotion of certainty and predictability.[24] Further, most private international law regimes espouse the notion that the courts and laws of other nations ought to in some fashion be respected. In common law systems this sentiment is usually expressed as a form of comity.[25] A similar attitude is expressed in notions of "mutual trust" underlying the jurisdictional regime established in the European Union under the *Convention on Jurisdiction and the Recognition of Foreign Judgments*, Brussels, 27 September 1968, J.O. L 299/32 (1972) (the "Brussels Convention")[26] and EC Regulation 44/2001 of 22 December 2001 (the "Brussels I Regulation")[27] pursuant to which the legal systems and judicial institutions in member States are to trusted and respected.[28] Moreover, it might be said there is at least some recognition that parties to an international transaction ought to varying degrees be allowed to agree on the law governing the transaction and the location in which disputes arising from the transaction will be resolved.[29] Whether these shared values or goals necessarily amount to international customary law is clearly up for debate. Leaving that question aside, it is clear international law in its conventional and public sense plays an important role in the development of private international law.[30]

---

generally involve a consideration of the "reasonable expectations of national and international legal communities." See *Furlan*, para. 2.

[24] This is particularly the case in respect of international commercial transactions. See, for instance, Charles R. Calleros, "Towards Harmonization and Certainty in Choice-of-Law Rules for International Contracts: Should the U.S. Adopt the Equivalent of Rome I?" (2011) Wisconsin Int'l L.J. (639) available at http://www.bepress.com/charles_calleros/1 and Jean-Gabriel Castel, "The Uncertainty Factor in Canadian Private International Law" (2007) 52 McGill L.J. 555.

[25] Comity, in this sense, was described many years ago by the United States Supreme Court in *Hilton v. Guyot*, 159 U.S. 113 (1895) in the following terms:

"Comity" in the legal sense, is neither a matter of absolute obligation, on the one hand, nor of mere courtesy and good will, upon the other. But it is the recognition which one nation allows within its territory to the legislative, executive or judicial acts of another nation, having due regard both to international duty and convenience, and to the rights of its own citizens or of other persons who are under the protection of its laws.

See also the decision of the Supreme Court of Canada in *Morguard Investments Ltd. v. De Savoye*, [1990] 3 S.C.R. 1077, 1990 CarswellBC 283, which adopted the above definition and disavowed earlier approaches to conflict of laws issues and, in particular, the recognition and enforcement of foreign judgments, that appeared to based on "an unstated assumption that the administration of justice in other countries was inferior." See *Morguard*, paras. 9 and 31.

[26] As amended by O.J. L 304/77 (1978), O.J. L 388/1 (1982) and O.J. L 285/1 (1989).

[27] Council Regulation (EC) No. 44/2001 of 22 December 2001 on jurisdiction and the recognition and enforcement of judgments in civil and commercial matters, O.J. No. L. 012, 16/01/2001 P. 0001 – 0023. The Brussels I Regulation replaced the Brussels Convention and came into force in all Member States except Denmark on 1 March 2002.

[28] In *Turner* v. *Grovit (Case C-159/02)*, [2004] ECR I-3565, the European Court of Justice commented on the Brussels Convention and "mutual trust" as follows at paragraph 24:

24 At the outset, it must be borne in mind that the Convention is necessarily based on the trust which the Contracting States accord to one another's legal systems and judicial institutions. It is that mutual trust which has enabled a compulsory system of jurisdiction to be established, which all the courts within the purview of the Convention are required to respect, and as a corollary the waiver by those States of the right to apply their internal rules on recognition and enforcement of foreign judgments in favour of a simplified mechanism for the recognition and enforcement of judgments (Case C-116/02 *Gasser* [2003] ECR I-0000, paragraph 72).

[29] In this respect, Calleros notes that "states and nations have nearly universally adopted and applied choice-of-law rules that designate application of foreign contract in appropriate circumstances." See Calleros, p. 22. See also Jan-Jaap Kuipers, "Party Autonomy in the Brussels I Regulation and Rome I Regulation and the European Court of Justice" (2009) 10(11) German L.J. 1505.

[30] See, *inter alia*, Tetley, *International Conflict of Laws*, pp. 27-34.

II. TREATIES, CONVENTIONS AND THE CONFLICT OF LAWS

International treaties and conventions can and do affect the development of the conflict of laws in a number of significant ways. First, there are a number of international conventions and instruments, which along with attempting to harmonize or unify the substantive law in specific issue-area, also elaborate various conflict of laws rules applicable to that issue-area. A recent example of such an approach is found in the newly-minted *United Nations Convention on Contracts for the International Carriage of Goods Wholly or Partly by Sea*, Rotterdam, 23 September 2009 (the "Rotterdam Rules") regarding the carriage of goods by sea, which contains detailed provisions of optional application dealing with jurisdiction, arbitration, choice of court agreements, arbitration agreements and the recognition and enforcement of judgments and arbitral awards.[31]

Second, an ancillary consequence or by-product of substantive harmonization or unification can be to mute the difficulties posed by the conflict of laws by effectively eschewing the differences between substantive national laws and, therefore, the conflict between such laws that may apply to a particular transaction. In this vein, Alexander von Ziegler comments as follows:

> ...one could think that in the field of harmonized law, have the disputes arising under that law be decided by a particular court should not be a matter of significance, since, at least from a theoretical point of view, it should not make a difference which court deals with the harmonized law, as the result must always be the same.[32]

---

[31] See Rotterdam Rules, Arts. 66-78. See also the *United Nations Convention on the Carriage of Goods by Sea*, Hamburg, 30 March 1978, Arts. 21 and 22.

[32] Alexander von Ziegler, "Jurisdiction and Forum Selection Clauses in a Modern Law on Carriage of Goods by Sea" in Martin Davies (ed.), *Jurisdiction and Forum Selection in International Maritime Law: Essays in Honor of Robert Force* (The Hague: Kluwer Law International, 2005), p. 86. In this vein, Arthur Rosett, among others, maintains that functionally the harmonization of substantive legal outcomes allows those engaged in international transactions to have a higher level of confidence in the world-wide market. Arthur Rosett, "Unification, Harmonization, Restatement, Codification, and Reform in International Commercial Law" (1992) 40 Am. J. Comp. L. 683, p. 683. On the topic of substantive harmonization or unification, a corollary point arises with respect to the use of choice of law and court agreements in international commerce. Traditionally, among the most favoured approaches for dealing with the diversity of national law in international commercial transactions has been to contractually stipulate a particular national substantive law to govern the transaction and designate of a specific forum in which disputes that may arise in respect of the transaction will be adjudicated with a view to obtaining a modicum of certainty. While this approach may have its advantages, it, to a large extent, merely displaces uncertainty and predictability concerns existing at the substantive level to the conflict of laws category. As noted above, national conflict of laws rules often and usually differ from one jurisdiction to another. In this regard, a reference to a particular substantive law or forum may only be conducive to certainty where such a reference is recognized and enforceable in the forum adjudicating the dispute. Further, whether the reference to a particular law and forum is categorically enforceable can itself be subject to a large measure of uncertainty. "Uniform" or "harmonized" substantive law may also mitigate these uncertainties by way of elaborating a substantive regime that, at least theoretically, ought to give rise to uniform or similar substantive results regardless of the jurisdiction or fora. See A.N. Yiannopolous, "The Unification of Private Maritime Law by International Conventions" (1965) L.C.P. 370, pp. 370-371. In this vein, the conflict of laws system has been characterized as the counter-point to "uniform" law as it in a sense allows for and accommodate for the specific differences on which it based. See Marc Ancel, "From the Unification of Law to its Harmonization" (1976) 51 Tul. L.R. 108, p. 109.

It should be noted, nonetheless, that the ostensible certainty that such "uniform" or "harmonized" laws may bring about can be and is often diminished by divergent treaty interpretation as among various national courts.[33]

Third, there are a number of international instruments and international organizations that take direct aim at and specifically seek to harmonize domestic law regarding the conflict of laws. Among the international organizations most directly involved in harmonization and unification of private international law is the Hague Conference on Private International Law (the "Hague Conference").[34] The Hague Conference, which held its first meeting in 893 and became a permanent inter-governmental organization in 1955, has as its specific mandate "the progressive unification of the rules of private international law."[35] Since 1951 the Hague Conference has adopted 38 international conventions, which have with varying degrees of

---

[33] See Michael F. Sturley, "International Uniform Laws in National Courts: The Influence of Domestic Law in Conflicts of Interpretation" (1987) 27 Va. J. Int'l L. 729, esp. pp. 736-745. This phenomenon is often pointed in objection to the development and adoption of uniform law conventions with the primary argument being that the development of such conventions generally overlooks the fact these conventions must be interpreted against the backdrop of domestic law that would otherwise be applicable. See Malcolm Evans, "Uniform Law: A Bridge Too Far" (1994) 3 Tul. J. Int'l & Comp. L. 145, pp. 149-150 and J.S. Hobhouse, (1990) "International Conventions and Commercial Law: The Pursuit of Uniformity" 106 L.Q.R. 530 where the author comments as follows at page 533:

...[T]o contemplate that conventions for world-wide adoption in all countries is illusory. The courts of each country will approach the resolution of any dispute from a point of view of its own legal and commercial culture and the divergent influences will be far stronger than the influence of any convention.

Further, a court when interpreting domestic legislation can rely on methods of interpretation and established principles that do not vary significantly, if at all, within that legal system. However, when confronted with an instrument that has been prepared and agreed upon at the international level, interpretation becomes more uncertain and problematic as there is rarely an equivalent frame of reference. See John Felegemas, "The United Nations Convention on Contracts for the International Sale of Goods: Article 7 and Uniform Interpretation" in Pace International Law Review (ed.), *Review of the Convention on Contracts for the International Sale of Goods (2000-2001)* (Dordrecht, The Netherlands: Kluwer Law International), fn. 423-fn. 424.

[34] In this context, the terms "unification" or "harmonization" are often used interchangeably. See, for instance, Patrick J.S. Griggs, "Uniformity of Maritime Law – An International Perspective" (1999) 73 Tul. L.R. 1551; Francisco Berlingieri, "Uniformity in Maritime Law and Implementation of International Conventions" (1987) 18(3) J.M.L.C. 317. There is, however, a subtle difference that is often overlooked but bears mentioning. Generally speaking, it may be more accurate to describe "unification" as an attempt to make the laws across various jurisdictions the same, which effort usually contemplates the universal application of a single convention, code or rule, and and "harmonization" as an attempt to make such laws and the outcomes associated with them similar on the understanding that a certain level of local or domestic variation cannot be controlled. See, *inter alia*: Marc Ancel, "From the Unification of Law to its Harmonization" (1976) 51 Tul. L.R. 108, p. 109; John Goldring, "Unification and Harmonisation of the Rules of Law" (1978) 9 Fed. L. Rev. 284, p. 289; Hannu Honka, "Harmonization of Contract Law through International Trade: A Nordic Perspective" (1996) 11 Tul. Euro. Civ. L.F. 111, pp. 113-120; Hannu Honka, "The Legislative Future of Carriage of Goods by Sea: Could it not be the UNCITRAL Draft?" (2004) 46 Scand. St. L. 94, p. 95; George A. Zaphirou, "Unification and Harmonization of Law Relating to Global and Regional Trading" (1994) 14 N. Ill. U. L. Rev. 407, p. 407; Sandeep Gopalan, "New Trends in the Making of International Commercial Law" (2004) 23 J. L. & Com. 117, pp. 120-121 and Troy Keily, "Harmonisation and the United Nations Convention on Contracts for the International Sale of Goods" (2003) 1 Nord. J. Int'l L. 1, p. 14 and Stephen Zamora, "NAFTA and the Harmonization of Domestic Legal Systems: The Side Effects of Free Trade" (1995) 12 Ariz. J. Int'l & Comp. L. 401, pp. 403-405.

[35] See *Statute of the Statute of the Hague Conference on Private International Law*, The Hague, 31 October 1951, Art. 1. For a general overview of the background and history of the organization, see Hague Conference's website at http://www.hcch.net/. Along similar lines, the International Institute for the Unification of Private International Law ("UNIDROIT") and the United Nations Commission on International Trade Law also have among their primary functions the promotion of the harmonization and unification of private international commercial law, which they seek to achieve by way of promoting wider participation in existing international conventions and the acceptance of existing model uniform laws as wells as preparing new international conventions and model uniform laws.

success sought to fulfill the mandate of the organization. Among the most widely ratified of the Hague Conference conventions are those dealing with service of process, the taking of evidence abroad, conflicts of laws relating to the form of testamentary dispositions, international adoption and abduction, and maintenance obligations.[36]

Despite these successes and the important work done by the Hague Conference, those general conventions developed by the Conference, which go to the very heart of the conflict of laws and which seek to more generally regulate the core matters of jurisdiction, choice of law and recognition and enforcement have failed to garner widespread global support. For instance, the Hague Conference's *Convention on Choice of Court Agreements* of 2005[37] and its predecessor[38] have not gained significant international acceptance. Similarly, the 1955 *Convention relating to the Settlement of the Conflicts between the Law of Nationality and the Law of Domicile*,[39] the 1958 *Convention on the Jurisdiction of the Selected Forum in the Case of International Sales of Goods*,[40] and 1971 *Convention on the Recognition and Enforcement of Foreign Judgments in Civil and Commercial Matters*[41] and 1986 *Convention on the Law Applicable to Contracts for the International Sale of Goods*[42] have either not entered into force or have failed to gain widespread international acceptance.[43]

III. Regimes of Particular Note

A. Choice of Law: Rome I and Rome II

While globally accepted regimes relating to jurisdiction, choice of law and recognition and enforcement are rare in nature, there are, nonetheless, a number of international instruments of particular significance and stature. Perhaps first among these instruments is the *Convention on the Law Applicable to Contractual Obligations*, Rome, 19 June 1980, 19 I.L.M. 1492 (the "Rome Convention"), which entered into force on 1 April 1991.[44] The Rome Convention has been touted "as one of the most important single developments in the history

[36] See "Overview" at http://www.hcch.net/index_en.php?act=text.display&tid=26.

[37] *Convention on Choice of Court Agreements*, The Hague, 30 June 2005, 44 I.L.M. 1294 (2005). This convention would not likely, in any event, have an overly significant impact on maritime cargo claims as article 2(g) of this convention stipulates that the convention does not apply to "marine pollution, limitation of liability for maritime claims, general average, and emergency towage and salvage."

[38] *Convention on Choice of Court Agreements*, The Hague, 25 November 1965.

[39] *Convention relating to the Settlement of the Conflicts between the Law of Nationality and the Law of Domicile*, The Hague, 15 June 1955.

[40] *Convention on the Jurisdiction of the Selected Forum in the Case of International Sales of Goods* The Hague, 15 April 1958.

[41] *Convention on the Recognition and Enforcement of Foreign Judgments in Civil and Commercial Matters*, The Hague, 1 February 1971.

[42] *Convention on the Law Applicable to Contracts for the International Sale of Goods*, The Hague, 22 December 1986.

[43] For specific information as to the status of the various Hague Conference conventions see http://www.hcch.net/upload/statmtrx_e.pdf. In this respect, Tetley posits that, despite the fact that a variety of the Hague Conference conventions have not been adopted, they are, nonetheless of "great authority and influence, attaining at times, even the stature of customary international law." Tetley, *International*, p. 30.

[44] As is discussed further below, the Rome Convention has now been replaced by the European Union Regulation (EC) No 593/2008 of the European Parliament and of the Council of 17 June 2008 on the law applicable to contractual obligations (Rome I) the Rome I Regulation 593/2008.

of private international law in Europe and elsewhere."[45] In broad terms, the Rome Convention establishes within the European Union as regards contracts with a foreign element a choice of law regime that is designed, subject to two "escape hatches" or exclusions,[46] to apply uniformly to commercial, consumer and employment contracts. As regards general commercial contracts, the Rome Convention provides that, in the absence of a contractual choice of law provision, the applicable law is the law of the country with which the contract is "most closely connected" with the primary presumption being that the most closely connected country is the home country of the party "who is to effect the performance which is characteristic of the contract."[47] In general terms, consumer contracts will under the Rome Convention be governed by the law of the country in which the consumer resides,[48] while employment contracts are governed by the law of the country in which the employee "habitually" works when performing the contract.[49]

The Rome Convention was updated and replaced in 2008 by the European Union's Regulation (EC) No 593/2008 of the European Parliament and of the Council of 17 June 2008 on the law applicable to contractual obligations (Rome I) (the "Rome I Regulation"), which applies to contracts made after 17 December 2009. The Rome I Regulation maintains the main features of the Rome Convention and sets out more particular default rules applicable to a wide variety of contracts in addition to consumer and employment contracts including, inter alia, contracts for the sale of goods, contracts for the provision of services, franchise contracts, distribution contracts, insurance, contracts for the sale of goods by auction and multilateral contracts for the buying and selling of financial instruments.[50]

A companion piece to the Rome I Regulation is the European Union's Regulation (EC) No 864/2007 of the European Parliament and of the Council of 11 July 2007 on the law applicable to non-contractual obligations (Rome II) (the "Rome II Regulation").[51] As its name suggests, the Rome II Regulation seeks to regulate the choice of law with respect to certain non-contractual matters including tort and delict and various areas outside the area of tort including unjust enrichment, negotiorum gestio or liability accruing when a party without any mandate or authority assumes to take charge of the affairs or concern of another and pre-contractual liability or culpa in contrahendo.[52] Within the field of torts, the general rule established by the Rome II Regulation is the lex loci damni rule such that the applicable law

[45] Tetley, *International Conflict of Laws*, p. 30.

[46] These exclusions are set out in Articles 4(5) and 16, which respectively allow for a departure from certain of the convention's default choice of law rules where "from the circumstances as a whole that the contract is more closely connected with another country" and, more generally, for the non-application of law that is "manifestly incompatible" with the public policy or *ordre public* of the forum.

[47] See Rome Convention, Arts. 4(1) and (2) and Calleros, p. 57.

[48] That is, in the absence of a contractual choice of law. See Rome Convention, Art. 5(3) and Calleros, p. 58.

[49] If the employee does not habitually work in any one country, then the employment contract will be governed by the law of the country in which the place of business through which the employee was engaged is situated. See Rome Convention, Art. 6(2) and Calleros, p. 58.

[50] Rome I Regulation, Arts. 4 and 7.

[51] Like the Rome I Regulation, the Rome II Regulation seeks to promote "the compatibility of the rules applicable in the Member States concerning the conflict of laws and of jurisdiction..." and identifies a "need...for the conflict-of-law rules in the Member States to designate the same national law irrespective of the country of the court in which an action is brought. See Rome I Regulation, Preamble, paras. 2 and 6 and Rome II Regulation, Preamble, paras. 2 and 6. See also Rome II Regulation, Preamble, para. 8, which provides it "should apply irrespective of the nature of the court or tribunal seised."

[52] See Rome II Regulation, Arts. 10-12 and Ministry of Justice, *Guidance on the law applicable to non-contractual obligations (Rome II)*, United Kingdom, 22 January 2009, para. 33. See also *Black's Law Dictionary, 6th ed.* (St. Paul: West Publishing Co., 1990), p. 1036.

will be the "law of the country in which the damage occurs irrespective of the country in which the event giving rise to the damage occurred and irrespective of the country or countries in which the indirect consequences of that event occur."[53] In the realm of torts, the Rome II Regulation also elaborates a further break-down of specific choice of law rules applicable to product liability claims, unfair competition claims, environmental damage, intellectual property rights and certain claims relating to industrial actions such as strikes, lock-outs and the like.[54]

B. Jurisdiction: The Brussels Regime

As regards jurisdictional and recognition and enforcement components of private international law, amongst the most advanced and notable international instruments is one that is again European – the Brussels Convention.[55] Like the Rome Convention, the Brussels Convention has been replaced by subsequent European Union regulation, specifically the Brussels I Regulation.[56] As regards allocating judicial competence, the Brussels Convention and the Brussels I Regulation give primary importance to the domicile of the defendant. In this regard, Article 2 of the Brussels Convention and the Brussels I Regulation provide, subject to the other provisions of these instruments, that persons domiciled in a member or contracting State shall, whatever their nationality, be sued in the courts of that State.[57] The

---

[53] Rome II Regulation, Art. 4(1). This rule, of course, contrasts the traditional *lex loci delicti* approach taken in many jurisdictions, including many in Europe, which, in general terms, provides that the applicable law is law of the place where the tortious occurred, which may or may not be where the injury or damage is suffered. See Mo Zhang, "Party Autonomy in Non-Contractual Obligations: Rome II and its Impacts on Choice of Law" (2009) 39 Seton Hall L. Rev. 861, pp. 864-877. As might be expected, there are exceptions to this general rule, which are set out in, *inter alia*, Articles 4(2) and (3), which provide as follows:

However, where the person claimed to be liable and the person sustaining damage both have their habitual residence in the same country at the time when the damage occurs, the law of that country shall apply.

Where it is clear from all the circumstances of the case that the tort/delict is manifestly more closely connected with a country other than that indicated in paragraphs 1 or 2, the law of that other country shall apply. A manifestly closer connection with another country might be based in particular on a preexisting relationship between the parties, such as a contract, that is closely connected with the tort/delict in question.

Further, the Rome II Regulation provides some latitude to the parties to a dispute to agree to the application of the law of their choice after the fact and allows, subject to certain restrictions, for the application of pre-event or ex ante choice of law agreements "where all the parties are pursuing a commercial activity" and the agreement is freely negotiated." See Rome II Regulation, Art. 14 and Zhang, pp. 892-904.

[54] See Rome II Regulation, Arts. 10-12 and Ministry of Justice, paras. 13-29.

[55] See also the nearly identical convention extant in the European Free Trade Association, i.e. the *Convention of 16 September 1988 on jurisdiction and the enforcement of judgments in civil and commercial matters*, Lugano, 16 September 1988 and its replacement, the *Convention on jurisdiction and the recognition and enforcement of judgments in civil and commercial matters*, Lugano, 30 October 2007 (the "Lugano Convention").

[56] For a good discussion and assessment of the harmonization of private international law in Europe, see Peter Stone, *EU Private International Law: Harmonization of Laws* (Cheltenham: Edward Elgar Publishing, 2006).

[57] Of particular note with respect to Article 2 is its impact on the common law doctrine of *forum non conveniens* as applied by English courts. Pursuant to this doctrine and the principles set out in, *inter alia*, the House of Lords in *Spiliada Maritime Corp.* v. *Cansulex Ltd.*, [1987] 1 A.C. 460, English courts may, despite having jurisdiction *simpliciter*, decline jurisdiction in favour of a more appropriate fora elsewhere. In situations where the competing fora are both members States Article 2 has precluded the application of the forum non conveniens doctrine. See Donald A. Brand and Scott R. Jablonski, *Forum Non Conveniens: History, Global Practice, and Future Under the Hague Convention on Choice of Court Agreements* (Oxford: Oxford University Press, 2007), p. 26 and *Viking Line ABP v. The International Transport Workers' Federation*, [2005] EWHC 1222 (Comm). It was thought, however, that this discretion afforded by the doctrine could, nevertheless, be exercised where the competing forum was a non-member State. See *In Re Harrods (Buenos Aires) Ltd.*, [1992] Ch. 72, [1991] 3 W.L.R. 397 (C.A.). This situation, however, has changed dramatically

Brussels Convention and the Brussels I Regulation do not, however, provide a general definition of the term "domicile" and leave the determination as to whether a party is domiciled in a particular member State to the domestic law of the State in which the matter is being litigated, i.e. the lex fori,[58] although some guidance is found with respect to companies, firms and similar associations.[59] In like fashion, domestic law is applicable to the determination of whether a court has jurisdiction in circumstances where a defendant is not domiciled in a member State.[60]

Another core feature of the Brussels regime is its approach to *lis alibi pendens* – that is, situations where there are two or more proceedings in different countries between the same parties arising out of the same dispute.[61] Pursuant to Article 27 of the Brussels I Regulation,[62] in cases of *lis alibi pendens*, the second court seised of a matter must stay the proceedings before it and must decline jurisdiction if the jurisdiction of the court first seised of the matter is established.[63] An extension of this "first seised rule" as it has been interpreted by the courts

---

with the decision of the European Court of Justice in *Owusu* v. *Jackson (Case C-281/02)*, [2005] 1 Lloyd's Rep 452, [2005] 2 All ER (Comm) 577, [2005] ECR I-1383, which involved a claim by a claimant who was severely injured while on holiday in Jamaica. The claimant along with the first defendant was domiciled in England. The other five defendants were limited liability companies domiciled in Jamaica. Four of the six defendants applied to have the matter stayed pursuant to the doctrine of *forum non conveniens* on the basis that Jamaica was a more appropriate forum as the accident occurred in Jamaica, five of the six defendants were Jamaican and most of the relevant witnesses were located in Jamaica. On a reference from the English Court of Appeal, the European Court of Justice was called upon to determine, *inter alia*, whether the application of the *forum non conveniens* doctrine was inconsistent with the Brussels Convention where jurisdiction was founded on Article 2 and jurisdiction of no other member was is in issue. In the result, the European Court of Justice held that Article 2 of Brussels Convention precluded the application of the doctrine of *forum non conveniens* in the circumstances on the basis that the application of the doctrine would undermine the predictability and legal certainty that the Brussels regime and Article 2 engender and might undermine the uniform application of the regime. While the *Owusu* decision has not been warmly received in the United Kingdom, it is clear that this decision has significantly curtailed the authority of English courts to stay proceedings on forum non conveniens grounds. See, for instance, Edwin Peel, "*Forum non conveniens* and European ideals" [2005] L.M.C.L.Q. 273; Adrian Briggs, "*Forum non conveniens* and ideal Europeans" [2005] L.M.C.L.Q. 378; and C.J.S. Knight, "*Owusu* and *Turner*: The Shark in the Water?" (2007) 66(2) Camb. L.J. 288.

[58] In the regard, Article 59 of the Brussels I Regulation provides: Article 59

In order to determine whether a party is domiciled in the Member State whose court are seised of a matter, the court shall apply its internal law.

If a party is not domiciled in the Member State whose courts are seised of the matter, then, in order to determine whether the party is domiciled in another Member State, the court shall apply the law of that Member State.

[59] Article 60 of the Brussels I Regulation provides: Article 60

For the purposes of this Regulation, a company or other legal person or association of natural or legal persons is domiciled at the place where it has its:

statutory seat, or

central administration, or

principal place of business.

[60] See Brussels I Regulation, Art. 4. This determination, however, is subject to the Brussels I Regulation's rules relating to choice of court agreements and those areas in which certain courts are to have exclusive jurisdiction. See Brussels I Regulation, Arts. 22 and 23.

[61] See, for instance, Abla J. Mayss, *Principles of conflict of law, 3rd ed.* (London: Cavendish Publishing Ltd., 1999), pp. 33 and 79.

[62] See also Brussels Convention, Art. 21.

[63] Article 27 of the Brussels Regulation provides:

Where proceedings involving the same cause of action and between the same parties are brought in the courts of different Member States, any court other than the court first seised shall of its own motion stay its proceedings until such time as the jurisdiction of the court first seised is established.

Where the jurisdiction of the court first seised is established, any court other than the court first seised shall decline jurisdiction in favour of that court.

and, in particular, the European Court of Justice, is the notion that the second court seised may not rule on its own jurisdiction or itself examine the jurisdiction of the court first seised, regardless of the basis on which jurisdiction of the first court may be contested.[64] This approach, for most intents and purposes, precludes the granting of anti-suit injunctions in respect of a proceeding in the court of another member State,[65] which approach has brought with it a significant adjustment for English courts and their relatively robust approach to issuing such injunctions.[66]

As the decisions of the European Court of Justice alluded to above indicate, a significant and in many ways unique feature of the Brussels regime is that a supranational body, the European Court of Justice, is empowered to authoritatively opine on questions of interpretation.[67] As far as private international law goes, there is really no equivalent template elsewhere in the world. This distinctive feature is complemented by an important modification precipitated by the transition from the Brussels Convention to the Brussels I Regulation. Specifically, article 57 of the Brussels Convention, which provided that it did not "affect any conventions to which the Contracting States are or will be parties and which, in relation to particular matters, govern jurisdiction or the recognition or enforcement of judgments" has been modified such that under the Brussels I Regulations this relationship with other international instruments continues but only with respect to existing international instruments.[68] By virtue of this amendment and the administrative rules of the European Union, member States no longer independently negotiate rules relating to jurisdiction in international fora.[69] Accordingly, the European Commission itself has been an integral part of the development of the jurisdictional provisions that are found in various international conventions.[70]

As the above indicates, for this provision to be operative three requirements must be met: are: (1) there must be two concurrent proceedings that share the same cause of action, (2) those proceedings must involve the same parties, and (3) one of the two actions must have been initiated before the other. See also Fabrizio Marongiu Buonaiuti, "Lis Alibi Pendens and Related Actions in Civil and Commercial Matters with the European Judicial Area (2009) Yearbook of Private International Law 511, p. 519.

[64] See *Gasser GmbH* v. *MISAT Srl (Case C-116/02)*, [2003] ECR I-14693 (E.C.J.), paras. 41-54 and *Overseas Union Ltd. v New Hampshire Insurance Co. (Case C-351/89*, [1991] ECR 1991 I-03317.

[65] See also *Turner* v. *Grovit (Case C-159/02)*, [2004] ECR I-3565 and the European Court of Justice's decision in *Allianz SpA (formerly Riunione Adriatica Di Sicurta SpA) and Others* v. *West Tankers Inc., (Case C-185/07).*

[66] See See Nigel Meeson, Q.C., "Comparative Issues in Anti-Suit Injunctions" in Martin Davies (ed.), *Jurisdiction and Forum Selection in International Maritime Law: Essays in Honor of Robert Force* (The Hague: Kluwer Law International, 2005); William Tetley, Q.C., "Jurisdiction Clauses and *Forum Non Conveniens* in the Carriage of Goods by Sea" in Martin Davies (ed.), *Jurisdiction and Forum Selection in International Maritime Law: Essays in Honor of Robert Force* (The Hague: Kluwer Law International, 2005); and Nikiforos Sifakis, "Anti-suit injunctions in the European Union: a necessary mechanism in resolving jurisdictional conflicts" (2007) 13 J.I.M.L. 100, p. 102. As Jonathan Harris points out, this has not stopped English courts from seeking innovative ways to limit the effect of such pronouncements. See Jonathan Harris, "The Brussels I Regulation and the Re-Emergence of the English Common Law" (2008) 4 European Legal Forum I-181.

[67] See, *inter alia*, the consolidated version of the Treaty on the Functioning of the European Union, O.J. C. 83/164, Article 267 and the consolidated version of the *Protocol on the interpretation of the 1968 Convention by the Court of Justice*, O.J. C. 27/01, 26.1.98. As regards the Rome Convention, see the consolidated version of the *First Protocol on the interpretation of the 1980 Convention by the Court of Justice*and the *Second Protocol conferring on the Court of Justice powers to interpret the 1980 Convention*, O.J. C. 27/02, 26.1.98.

[68] In this respect, Article 71(1) of the Brussels I Regulations provides that it will not "affect any conventions to which the Member States are parties and which in relation to particular matters, govern jurisdiction or the recognition or enforcement of judgments."

[69] See, for instance, Rolf Herber, "Jurisdiction and arbitration – should the new Convention contain rules on these subjects?" (2002) L.M.C.L.Q. 405, p. 408.

[70] *Ibid.*

C. Recognition and Enforcement: The Brussels Regime and the New York Convention on Arbitration

With respect to the recognition and enforcement of foreign judgments, the regime established under the Brussels Convention and the Brussels I Regulation is one of the most important and comprehensive.[71] As between European Union member States, this regime provides for and secures the free circulation of most judgments by replacing traditional domestic rules for recognition and enforcement.[72] This is done by, *inter alia*, elaborating uniform recognition and enforcement rules,[73] relatively simple and expeditious procedures for recognition[74] and enforcement and limiting the number of defences available in respect of such procedures.[75] Among the key elements of this recognition and enforcement regime are that foreign judgments[76] covered by the regime are to be recognized in the member States "without any special procedure being required..."[77] and that reviews of the originating court's jurisdiction and the substance of the foreign court's judgment are generally prohibited.[78] This prohibition generally precludes and avoids challenges founded on mistake of law or fact by the foreign court.[79]

Among the defences to recognition and enforcement are two general defences which are not specifically set out in the Brussels I Regulation, i.e. that the Brussels I Regulation does not apply to the judgment at issue and the foreign judgment is enforceable under the law of the State in which it was issued.[80] More specific grounds are set out in Article 34 of the Brussels I Regulation, which provides, *inter alia*, that a judgment will not be recognized where: such recognition is "manifestly contrary" to the public policy of the recognizing State; there has been a denial of natural justice by way of the granting of default judgment when the defendant was not duly served; the judgment at issue is irreconcilable with a judgment given in a dispute between the same parties in the recognizing State or with an earlier judgment given in another member State or a non-member State involving the same cause of action and parties provided that this judgment qualifies for recognition.[81]

As regards respect to recognition and enforcement one of the most successful international regimes is also one of the oldest. The *Convention on the Recognition and Enforcement of Foreign Arbitral Awards*, New York, 10 June 1958, 330 U.N.T.S. 38 (the "New York Convention"), which entered into force 7 June 1959, is among the most successful international conventions with 145 contracting parties. [82] The New York Convention, which

---

[71] Tetley, *International Conflict*, p. 848.

[72] Tetley, *International Conflict*, p. 848 and the Brussels I Regulation, Arts. 32-56.

[73] Brussels I Regulation, Arts. 32-38.

[74] Brussels I Regulation, Arts. 38-56.

[75] Brussels I Regulation, Arts. 34 and 35.

[76] "Judgment" in this context means "any judgment given by a court or tribunal of a Member State, whatever the judgment may be called, including a decree, order, decision or writ of execution, as well as the determination of costs or expenses by an officer of the court." See Brussels I Regulation, Art. 32.

[77] Brussels I Regulation, Art. 33(1).

[78] Brussels I Regulation, Arts. 35(3) and 36. In the limited circumstances where a review of the originating court's may be reviewed, the court or authority reviewing this jurisdiction is bound by the findings of fact made by the originating court. See Brussels I Regulation, Arts. 35(1) and (2).

[79] Tetley, *International Conflict*, p. 849.

[80] Tetley, *International Conflict*, p. 849.

[81] Brussels I Regulation, Art. 34(1)-(4).

[82] For more specific information as to the status, ratification, acceptance and approval of the New York Convention see the United Nations Commission on International Trade Law's website at "Status: 1958 - Convention on the

was developed under the auspices of the International Chamber of Commerce and the United Nations Economic and Social Council,[83] imposes two primary obligations. First, it imposes a general duty on courts in contracting States to give effect to arbitration agreements unless they are "null and void, inoperative or incapable of being performed."[84] Second, the New York Convention obliges contracting States to recognize foreign or "non-domestic" arbitral awards[85] as binding and enforce them "in accordance with the rules of procedure of the territory where the award is relied upon…."[86]

Like the Brussels regime, the New York Convention sets out a limited number of grounds or defences with respect to recognition and enforcement.[87] These include circumstances where:

- a party to the arbitration agreement was under some incapacity or the agreement itself was invalid under its governing law;[88]
- a party was unable to present his or her case as a consequence of, inter alia, not being given proper notice of the appointment of the arbitrator or of the arbitration proceedings, i.e. where there has been a denial of natural justice.[89]
- the arbitral award is *ultra vires* the dispute submitted to arbitration or the arbitration agreement;[90]
- the composition of the arbitral tribunal or the arbitral procedure was not in accordance with the arbitration agreement or, in the absence of an agreement on such issues, the law of the place where the arbitration took place, i.e. the *lex loci arbitri*;[91]
- the award lacks binding effect as a consequence of having not yet become binding upon the parties or having been set aside or suspended by a competent authority;[92]
- the subject matter of the dispute was not capable of resolution under the laws of the country in which recognition and enforcement recognition is sought;[93] and
- recognition and enforcement would be contrary to the public policy of the country in which recognition and enforcement is sought.[94]

Recognition and Enforcement of Foreign Arbitral Awards" at http://www.uncitral.org/uncitral/en/uncitral_texts/arbitration/NYConvention_status.html.

[83] To access the travaux prépatoires of the New York Convention see the United Nations Commission on International Trade Law's website at "Travaux préparatoires: 1958 - Convention on the Recognition and Enforcement of Foreign Arbitral Awards" at http://www.uncitral.org/uncitral/en/uncitral_texts/arbitration/NYConvention_travaux.html.

[84] New York Convention, Art. II(3).

[85] As to the distinction between foreign and non-domestic arbitral, see Albert Jan van den Berg, "An Overview of the The New York Convention of 1958" (2008), International Council for Commercial Arbitration at http://www.arbitration-icca.org/media/0/12125884227980/new_york_convention_of_1958_overview.pdf, p. 2-3.

[86] New York Convention, Art. III. Unlike the Brussels regime, the New York Convention does not specifically set out procedures for recognition and enforcement. In this regard, the lack of universal enforcement procedures has been identified as one of the main shortcomings of the New York Convention. See Robert Briner, "Philosophy and objectives of the Convention" in *Enforcing Arbitration Awards under the New York Convention: Experience and Prospects* (New York: United Nations, 1999), p. 9 and the Brussels I Regulation, Arts. 38-56.

[87] As van den Berg points out, the use of the words "only if" in Article V(1) indicate that the listed grounds do not comprise a non-exhaustive list. See van den Berg, p. 13.

[88] New York Convention, Art. V(1)(a).

[89] New York Convention, Art. V(1)(b) and III and Tetley, *International Conflict*, p. 860.

[90] New York Convention, Art. V(1)(c) and III and Tetley, *International Conflict*, p. 860.

[91] New York Convention, Art. V(1)(d) and III and Tetley, *International Conflict*, p. 860.

[92] New York Convention, Art. V(1)(e) and III and Tetley, *International Conflict*, p. 860.

[93] New York Convention, Art. V(2)(a) and III and Tetley, *International Conflict*, p. 860.

[94] New York Convention, Art. V(2)(b) and III and Tetley, *International Conflict*, p. 860.

While there are some similarities between the New York Convention and the Brussels regime as regards recognition and enforcement, there are, over and above the obvious difference as to the subject-matter upon which they operate, i.e. judicial pronouncements as opposed to arbitral awards, at least two other marked differences between the two instruments that bear mentioning.

First, the New York Convention is a global regime whereas the Brussels regime is by its nature limited in its application to its European Union constituents.[95] A corollary of this is the Brussels regime is not akin to domestic legislation that has quasi-international stature as a result of being copied by other regional bodies or national legislatures or by being consciously referred to by courts in other countries.[96] In other words, the Brussels regime is in many ways *sui generis*. In North America, for instance, the harmonization of conflict of laws rules and principles, to the extent it occurs by legislative means, is often less formal in its inception and proceeds primarily by the drafting of model laws by non-governmental bodies for adoption by national, state or provincial legislatures.[97] Second, unlike the Brussels regime there is no supranational body that, like the European Court of Justice, is empowered to make binding and authoritative pronouncements on the interpretation on the New York Convention. This is not to say, however, that there is not persuasive and noteworthy commentary as to how the provisions of the New York Convention ought to be interpreted, but that such commentary is not binding on the parties to the New York Convention.[98]

CONCLUSION

While private international law may be rightly identified as a branch of domestic law, it is to a certain degree analogous to public international law in the sense that assigns judicial and legislative competence as amongst the various courts and legislatures of the world. In this regard, it is generally recognized that private international law rests on and arises in response to the principle of territorial sovereignty but also embodies principles and rules that allow and, in some cases, require courts to abandon a strictly national or territorial view of the

[95] In this respect, it should be pointed that, while the European Free Trade Association's counterpart to the Brussels, the Lugano Convention, is technically open for accession by non-member states of European Union and the European Free Trade Association, including non-European States, no such accession has occurred with the exception of Poland, which acceded to the Lugano Convention prior to its subsequent entry into the European Union on 1 May 2004. See Lugano Convention, Article 70(1)(c) and Tristan Baumé, "Competence of the Community to Conclude the New Lugano Convention on Jurisdiction and the Recognition and Enforcement of Judgments in Civil and Commercial Matters: Opinion 1/03 of 7 February 2006" (2006) 7(8) German L.J. 681, p. 682.

[96] An example of a statute with such stature is the United Kingdom's Marine Insurance Act, 1906. See, William Tetley, Q.C., "Uniformity of International Private Maritime Law – The Pros, Cons and Alternatives to International Conventions – How to Adopt an International Convention", (2004) 24(2) Tul. Mar. L.J. 775.

[97] See, for instance, the *Uniform Transfer of Litigation Act* drafted and promulgated in 1991 by the United States National Conference of Commissioners on Uniform State Law and the model *Court Jurisdiction and Proceedings Transfer Act* drafted and promulgated in 1994 by the Uniform Law Conference of Canada, which has been adopted and enacted into legislation by some but not all of Canada's provinces, including British Columbia, Nova Scotia and Saskatchewan.

[98] See, for instance, the *Recommendation regarding the interpretation of article II (2) and article VII (1) of the Convention on the Recognition and Enforcement of Foreign Arbitral Awards (New York, 1958)* adopted by the United Nations Commissions on International Trade Law on 7 July 2006 and the International Council for Commercial Arbitration's Guide to the Interpretation of the 1958 New York Convention (The Hague: International Council for Commercial Arbitration, 2011).

world. With respect to the sources of private international law, internationalists consider the principles and rules underlying private international law to be a form of customary international law, while others identify conflict of laws principles and rules exclusively as a branch of domestic law. Both approaches are not without their respective shortcomings and generally fail to describe the nuances of most existing approaches to private international law, which usually combine elements of each approach. As regards the shared values, ideals or goals in private international law issues, the notion that certainty and predictability ought to be fostered and that the courts and laws of other nations ought to in some fashion be respected along with the concept that parties to an international transaction ought to varying degrees be allowed to agree on the law governing the transaction and the location in which disputes arising from the transaction will be resolved arguably permeate most approaches to private international law, be they national or international in nature.

International treaties and conventions can affect the development of the conflict of laws in a variety of ways. Some international conventions and instruments, while seeking to harmonize or unify the substantive law in specific issue-area, also elaborate various conflict of laws rules. A further consequence of such substantive harmonization or unification can be to mute the difficulties posed by the conflict of laws by effectively eschewing the differences between substantive national laws and, therefore, the conflict between such laws that may apply to a particular transaction. Moreover, a number of international instruments and international organizations take direct aim at harmonizing domestic law regarding the conflict of laws. Notable among such organizations is the Hague Conference, which has authored a variety of widely ratified conventions dealing with, *inter alia*, service of process, the taking of evidence abroad, conflicts of laws relating to the form of testamentary dispositions, international adoption and abduction, and maintenance obligations. Despite these successes, however, the more generalized conventions dealing with core issues in the conflict of laws have not garnered widespread international acceptance. Nevertheless, there are a number of international regimes of particular importance that have influenced the development of the private international law significantly.

As regards the choice of law, the Rome Convention and the subsequent European Union instruments, Rome I and Rome II, are of particular significance and stature. In this respect, the Rome Convention has been touted as one of the most important developments in the history of private international law. In broad terms, the Rome Convention establishes within the European Union a uniform choice of law regime applicable to commercial, consumer and employment contracts. In the absence of a contractual choice, the Rome Convention generally provides that the applicable law is the law of the country with which the contract is "most closely connected" in the commercial contract context. Consumer contracts will generally be governed by the law of the country in which the consumer resides, while employment contracts are governed by the law of the country in which the employee "habitually" works. The Rome Convention has now been updated and replaced by the Rome I Regulation, which maintains the main features of the Rome Convention and sets out more particular default rules applicable to a wide variety of contracts in addition to consumer and employment contracts including, *inter alia*, contracts for the sale of goods, contracts for the provision of services, franchise contracts, distribution contracts, insurance, contracts for the sale of goods by auction and multilateral contracts for the buying and selling of financial instruments. The companion piece to the Rome I Regulation, the Rome II Regulation, regulates choice of law matters with respect to certain non-contractual matters including tort and delict, unjust enrichment, *negotiorum gestio* and pre-contractual liability. The general choice of law rule set out in the Rome II Regulation with respect to torts is the *lex loci damni* rule, which provides that the applicable law will be the law of the country in which the damage occurred. The Rome II Regulation also elaborates a further break-down of specific choice of law rules applicable to specific categories of claims, including product liability claims, unfair competition claims, environmental damage and intellectual property rights.

The Brussels regime, consisting of the Brussels Convention and the Brussels I Regulation, is among the most advanced and notable international regimes in the realm of jurisdiction and recognition and enforcement. As regards jurisdiction, the Brussels regime is founded on the concept of mutual trust between European Union member States and places primary importance to the domicile of the defendant. Another distinctive feature of the Brussels regime is the "first seised" rule it employs to resolve situations of *lis alibi pendens* whereby a second court seised of a matter must stay the proceedings before it and must decline jurisdiction if the jurisdiction of the court first seised of the matter is established. The Brussels regime also provides for and secures the free circulation of judgments in the European Union by replacing traditional domestic rules for recognition and enforcement with uniform recognition and enforcement rules and elaborating simple and expeditious procedures for recognition and enforcement. The Brussels regime is also exceptional in that a supranational body, the European Court of Justice, is empowered to authoritatively opine on questions of interpretation.

The New York Convention is one of the most successful and widely adopted international regimes relating to recognition and enforcement. The New York Convention imposes a general duty on courts in contracting States to give effect to arbitration agreements and obliges contracting States to recognize and enforce foreign arbitral awards subject to a limited number of defences. Unlike the Brussels regime, the scope and application of the New York Convention is global. A further difference between the two is that there is no supranational body, like the European Court of Justice, with the authority to make binding pronouncements on the interpretation on the New York Convention. While there is persuasive and noteworthy commentary as to how the provisions of the New York Convention ought to be interpreted, such commentary is not binding in nature.

APPENDIX

Case Law

Allianz SpA (formerly Riunione Adriatica Di Sicurta SpA) and Others v. West Tankers Inc., (Case C-185/07).

Furlan v. Shell Oil Co., 2000 BCCA 404.

Gasser GmbH v. MISAT Srl (Case C-116/02), [2003] ECR I-14693 (E.C.J.).

Hilton v. Guyot, 159 U.S. 113 (1895).

In Re Harrods (Buenos Aires) Ltd., [1992] Ch. 72, [1991] 3 W.L.R. 397 (C.A.).

Morguard Investments Ltd. v. De Savoye, [1990] 3 S.C.R. 1077, 1990 CarswellBC 283.

Overseas Union Ltd. v New Hampshire Insurance Co. (Case C-351/89, [1991] ECR 1991 I-03317.

Owusu v. *Jackson (Case C-281/02)*, [2005] 1 Lloyd's Rep 452, [2005] 2 All ER (Comm) 577, [2005] ECR I-1383.

R. v. Hape, 2007 SCC 26, [2007] 2 SCR 292.

Spiliada Maritime Corp. v. Cansulex Ltd., [1987] 1 A.C. 460.

Turner v. Grovit (Case C-159/02), [2004] ECR I-3565.

Viking Line ABP v. The International Transport Workers' Federation, [2005] EWHC 1222 (Comm).

Treaties, Conventions and Statutory Materials

Statute of the Statute of the Hague Conference on Private International Law, The Hague, 31 October 1951.

Convention relating to the Settlement of the Conflicts between the Law of Nationality and the Law of Domicile, The Hague, 15 June 1955.

Convention on the Jurisdiction of the Selected Forum in the Case of International Sales of Goods The Hague, 15 April 1958.

Convention on the Recognition and Enforcement of Foreign Arbitral Awards, New York, 10 June 1958, 330 *U.N.T.S.* 38.

Convention on Choice of Court Agreements, The Hague, 25 November 1965.

Convention on the Recognition and Enforcement of Foreign Judgments in Civil and Commercial Matters, The Hague, 1 February 1971.

United Nations Convention on the Carriage of Goods by Sea, Hamburg, 30 March 1978.

Convention on the Law Applicable to Contracts for the International Sale of Goods, The Hague, 22 December 1986.

Convention of 16 September 1988 on jurisdiction and the enforcement of judgments in civil and commercial matters, Lugano, 16 September 1988.

Council Regulation (EC) No. 44/2001 of 22 December 2001, O.J. No. L. 012, 16/01/2001.

Protocol on the interpretation of the 1968 Convention by the Court of Justice, O.J. C. 27/01, 26.1.98.

Protocol on the interpretation of the 1980 Convention by the Court of Justice and the *Second Protocol conferring on the Court of Justice powers to interpret the 1980 Convention, O.J. C.* 27/02, 26.1.98.

First Convention on jurisdiction and the recognition and enforcement of judgments in civil and commercial matters, Lugano, 30 October 2007.

Convention on Choice of Court Agreements, The Hague, 30 June 2005, 44 *I.L.M.* 1294 (2005).

Regulation (EC) No 593/2008 of the European Parliament and of the Council of 17 June 2008 on the law applicable to contractual obligations (Rome I).

Regulation (EC) No 864/2007 of the European Parliament and of the Council of 11 July 2007 on the law applicable to non-contractual obligations (Rome II).

United Nations Convention on Contracts for the International Carriage of Goods Wholly or Partly by Sea, Rotterdam, 23 September 2009.

Literature

Ancel, Marc, "From the Unification of Law to its Harmonization" (1976) 51 *Tul. L.R.* 108.

Baer, Marvin, Blom, Joost, Edinger, Elizabeth, Rafferty, Nicholas, Saumier, Geneviève and Walsh, Catherine, *Private International in Common Law Canada: Cases, Texts and Materials* (Toronto: Edmond Montgomery Publications, 1997).

Baumé, Tristan, "Competence of the Community to Conclude the New Lugano Convention on Jurisdiction and the Recognition and Enforcement of Judgments in Civil and Commercial Matters: Opinion 1/03 of 7 February 2006" (2006) 7(8) *German L.J.* 681.

Berlingieri, Francisco, "Uniformity in Maritime Law and Implementation of International Conventions" (1987) 18(3) *J.M.L.C.* 317.

Black's Law Dictionary, 6th ed. (St. Paul: West Publishing Co., 1990).

Brand, Donald A. and Jablonski, Scott R., *Forum Non Conveniens: History, Global Practice, and Future Under the Hague Convention on Choice of Court Agreements* (Oxford: Oxford University Press, 2007).

Briggs, Adrian, "*Forum non conveniens* and ideal Europeans" [2005] *L.M.C.L.Q.* 378.

Brilmayer, Lea, *Conflict of Laws: Foundations and Future Directions* (Boston: Little Brown, 1991).

Briner, Robert, "Philosophy and objectives of the Convention" in *Enforcing Arbitration Awards under the New York Convention: Experience and Prospects* (New York: United Nations, 1999).

Buonaiuti, Fabrizio Marongiu, "Lis Alibi Pendens and Related Actions in Civil and Commercial Matters with the European Judicial Area (2009) Yearbook of Private International Law 511.

Calleros, Charles R., "Towards Harmonization and Certainty in Choice-of-Law Rules for International Contracts: Should the U.S. Adopt the Equivalent of Rome I?" (2011) *Wisconsin Int'l L. J.* 639.

Castel, Jean-Gabriel, "The Uncertainty Factor in Canadian Private International Law" (2007) 52 *McGill L. J.* 555.

Castel, Jean-Gabriel and Walker, Janet, *Canadian Conflict of Law (*Markham: LexisNexis Canada, 2003).

Evans, Malcolm, "Uniform Law: A Bridge Too Far" (1994) 3 Tul. *J. Int'l & Comp. L.* 145.

Felegemas, John, "The United Nations Convention on Contracts for the International Sale of Goods: Article 7 and Uniform Interpretation" in *Review of the Convention on Contracts for the International Sale of Goods (2000-2001)* (Dordrecht, The Netherlands: Kluwer Law International).

Felegemas, John, *Review of the Convention on Contracts for the International Sale of Goods (2000-2001)* (Dordrecht, The Netherlands: Kluwer Law International).

Fiorini, Aude, "The Codification of Private International Law in Europe: Could the Community Learn from the Experience of Mixed Jurisdictions?" (2008) 12(1) *E. J. of Comp. L.* 1

Ginn, David, The Domestic Legal Status of Customary International Law in the United States: Lessons from the Federal Courts' Experience with General Maritime Law, (2008) 4 *J. Int'l L & Int'l Rel.* 105.

Goldring, John, "Unification and Harmonisation of the Rules of Law" (1978) 9 *Fed. L. Rev.* 284.

Gopalan, Sandeep, "New Trends in the Making of International Commercial Law" (2004) 23 *J. L. & Com.* 117.

Griggs, Patrick J. S., "Uniformity of Maritime Law – An International Perspective" (1999) 73 *Tul. L. R.* 1551.

Harris, Jonathan, "The Brussels I Regulation and the Re-Emergence of the English Common Law" (2008) 4 European Legal Forum I-181.

Herber, Rolf, "Jurisdiction and arbitration – should the new Convention contain rules on these subjects?" (2002) L.M.C.L.Q. 405.

Hobhouse, J. S., (1990) "International Conventions and Commercial Law: The Pursuit of Uniformity" 106 L.Q.R. 530.

Honka, Hannu, "Harmonization of Contract Law through International Trade: A Nordic Perspective" (1996) 11 Tul. Euro. Civ. L.F. 111.

Honka, Hannu, "The Legislative Future of Carriage of Goods by Sea: Could it not be the UNCITRAL Draft?" (2004) 46 Scand. St. L. 94.

International Council for Commercial Arbitration's Guide to the Interpretation of the 1958 New York Convention (The Hague: International Council for Commercial Arbitration, 2011).

Keily, Troy, "Harmonisation and the United Nations Convention on Contracts for the International Sale of Goods" (2003) 1 *Nord. J. Int'l L.* 1.

Knight, C. J. S., "*Owusu* and *Turner*: The Shark in the Water?" (2007) 66(2) *Camb. L.J.* 288.

Kuipers, Jan-Jaap, "Party Autonomy in the Brussels I Regulation and Rome I Regulation and the European Court of Justice" (2009) 10(11) *German L.J.* 1505.

Mance, Lord, "The Future of Private International Law" (2005) 1(2) *J. of P.I.L.*

Mayss, Abla J., *Principles of Conflict of Laws, 3rd ed.* (London: Cavendish Publishing Ltd., 1999).

Meeson, Nigel Q. C., "Comparative Issues in Anti-Suit Injunctions" in Martin Davies (ed.), *Jurisdiction and Forum Selection in International Maritime Law: Essays in Honor of Robert Force* (The Hague: Kluwer Law International, 2005).

Ministry of Justice, *Guidance on the law applicable to non-contractual obligations (Rome II)*, United Kingdom, 22 January 2009.

Peel, Edwin, "*Forum non conveniens* and European ideals" [2005] *L.M.C.L.Q.* 273.

Rosett, Arthur, "Unification, Harmonization, Restatement, Codification, and Reform in International Commercial Law" (1992) 40 *Am. J. Comp. L.* 683.

Ruggie, John Gerard, "Territoriality and Beyond: Problematizing Modernity in International Relations" 47(1) *International Organization* 139.

Sifakis, Nikiforos, "Anti-suit injunctions in the European Union: a necessary mechanism in resolving jurisdictional conflicts" (2007) 13 *J.I.M.L.* 100.

Stone, Peter, *EU Private International Law: Harmonization of Laws* (Cheltenham: Edward Elgar Publishing, 2006).

Story, Joseph, *Conflicts of Law: Commentaries on the conflict of laws, foreign and domestic, in regard to contracts, rights, and remedies, and especially in regard to marriages, divorces, wills, successions, and judgments, 3rd ed.* (Boston: C. C. Little and J. Brown, 1846).

Sturley, Michael F., "International Uniform Laws in National Courts: The Influence of Domestic Law in Conflicts of Interpretation" (1987) 27 *Va. J. Int'l L.* 729.

Tetley, William Q. C., "Jurisdiction Clauses and *Forum Non Conveniens* in the Carriage of Goods by Sea" in Martin Davies (ed.), *Jurisdiction and Forum Selection in International Maritime Law: Essays in Honor of Robert Force* (The Hague: Kluwer Law International, 2005).

Tetley, William Q. C., "Uniformity of International Private Maritime Law – The Pros, Cons and Alternatives to International Conventions – How to Adopt an International Convention", (2004) 24(2) *Tul. Mar. L.J.* 775.

Tetley, William Q. C., *International Conflict of Laws: Common, Civil and Maritime* (Montreal: Blais International Shipping Publications, 1994).

United Nations Commission on International Trade Law, *Recommendation regarding the interpretation of article II (2) and article VII (1) of the Convention on the Recognition and Enforcement of Foreign Arbitral Awards (New York, 1958)*, 7 July 2006.

van den Berg, Albert Jan, "An Overview of the The New York Convention of 1958" (2008)), International Council for Commercial Arbitration.

von Ziegler, Alexander, "Jurisdiction and Forum Selection Clauses in a Modern Law on Carriage of Goods by Sea" in Martin Davies (ed.), *Jurisdiction and Forum Selection in International Maritime Law: Essays in Honor of Robert Force* (The Hague: Kluwer Law International, 2005).

Yiannopolous, A. N., "The Unification of Private Maritime Law by International Conventions" (1965) *L.C.P.* 370.

Zamora, Stephen, "NAFTA and the Harmonization of Domestic Legal Systems: The Side Effects of Free Trade" (1995) 12 *Ariz. J. Int'l & Comp. L.* 401.

Zaphirou, George A., "Unification and Harmonization of Law Relating to Global and Regional Trading" (1994) 14 *N. Ill. U. L. Rev.* 407.

Zhang, Mo, "Party Autonomy in Non-Contractual Obligations: Rome II and its Impacts on Choice of Law" (2009) 39 *Seton Hall L. Rev.* 861.

In: Selected Issues in Maritime Law and Policy
Editor: Maximo Q. Mejia, Jr.

ISBN: 978-1-62618-508-1

Chapter 9

THE LEGAL FRAMEWORK FOR ELECTRONIC INTERNATIONAL TRADE: THE ROTTERDAM RULES IN PERSPECTIVE

Abhinayan Basu Bal *

Department of Law, School of Business,
Economics and Law, University of Gothenburg, Sweden

1. INTRODUCTION

The benefits of electronic commerce (e-commerce) are now well established and modern day internet technology allows commercial entities to move away from traditional means to conduct business. One of the objectives behind the creation of a new sea carriage convention instrument called the "United Nations Convention on Contracts for the International Carriage of Goods Wholly or Partly by Sea"[1], otherwise referred to as the "Rotterdam Rules" is to facilitate e-commerce by providing a framework for electronic equivalents of transport documents.[2] The Rules also have three separate chapters[3] dealing with delivery of the goods, rights of the controlling party and transfer of rights, which are the key to solving the problem of how to provide for negotiable electronic transport records[4] thereby facilitating international trade.

Traditional commercial lawyers are not readily open to paradigm shifts where one's way of seeing the world is replaced by another.[5] Kuhn developed his theory to describe scientific revolutions in which scientists in a given field collectively change their perspective. Though one of the drafters of the Rotterdam Rules considers the Rules to be evolutionary and not revolutionary, some of the provisions in the Rules do create a revolution in the minds of traditional legal scholars.[6] The three chapters of the Rules on delivery, control and transfer

---

* Assistant Professor, Department of Law, School of Business, Economics and Law, University of Gothenburg, Sweden. The author attended the 19th, 20th and 21st sessions of the UNCITRAL Working Group III (Transport Law) and the 41st UNCITRAL Commission Session in New York and Vienna during the period 2007-2008 as an observer representing the World Maritime University. The opinions expressed in this article are entirely that of the author and are not attributable to any institution or organization with which the author may be associated in any capacity.

require fresh perspectives on the transport law structure. This paper attempts to break free the inertia of traditional legal scholarship and investigate the justification for the inclusion of the controversial provisions in the Rules.

Following this introduction the paper examines some of the provisions on transport documents and electronic transport records in the Rotterdam Rules. It also probes into some of the controversial provisions of the three chapters in the Rules on delivery of the goods, rights of the controlling party and transfer of rights, which are the key to solving the problem of how to provide for negotiable electronic transport records.

2. Transport Documents and Electronic Transport Records under the Rotterdam Rules

The Rotterdam Rules codifies the contractual relations between the parties to a contract of carriage regardless of the type of document issued or even if no document has been issued. The uncoupling of the law related to bills of lading and the use of a document is a significant feature of the new regime and has been done to facilitate e-commerce. The use of electronic bills of lading by the shipping industry has existed for sometime now but uncertainty remains over their legal recognition in many jurisdictions. Indeed, the desirability of a new transport convention emanated from the deliberations of UNCITRAL Working Group IV on Electronic Commerce. In the mid nineties, one item in the agenda of Working Group IV was to develop electronic equivalents of documents of title. It was concluded that, generally speaking, the virtualization of documents of title was not a feasible proposition because of the formal function of the paper document. Instead, it was viewed that the material functions of documents of title can be incorporated into a structure of electronic messages.[7]

The emphasis of the Rotterdam Rules is on the contract of carriage and not on the document. The proponents of the contractual approach advocated the adoption of a regime that would be more systematic than the existing Hague, Hague-Visby regimes. In their view, the instrumentality of contract is an integral part of the *lex mercatoria*; the basic principles of which are similar in all jurisdictions.

In the Rotterdam Rules there is no specific reference to the bill of lading; the term used is ‘transport document’. There are provisions governing equivalent ‘electronic transport records’.[8] Two types of documents are addressed in the Rules, namely, negotiable transport documents[9] and non-negotiable transport documents.[10]

Notably, the existing carriage of goods regimes do not have any provisions on electronic commerce because at the time when these regimes were negotiated, there was no commercial need to address the topic. The Rotterdam Rules has made an effort to establish a legal framework which will enable the maritime industry to participate in electronic commerce.

Chapter 3 of the Rotterdam Rules deals with electronic transport records. Article 8 of the Rules emphasises the necessity for consent when the parties use an electronic transport record. The drafters of the Rules have tried to avoid imposition of electronic transport records on a party who will need a paper document for legal reasons, such as, where one of the parties to the carriage contract is from a state which is not a party to the new convention and whose law does not recognise the effect of electronic communications. Article 9 of the Rules further emphasises the role of the parties in setting up a system that allows electronic recording and communication of data constituting the transport record. It lays down the minimum requirements for procedures for the use of negotiable electronic transport records and leaves the rest to the parties. Both articles 8 and 9 are medium and technology neutral leaving the exact standard to be determined under national law or by commercial parties.[11] All types of systems, including any new ones that may be developed in the future, whether or not based on a registry system, will be recognised as having the desired effect so long as the minimum requirements stated in articles 8 and 9 are satisfied.[12]

Chapter 8 of the Rotterdam Rules deals with transport documents and electronic transport records. Article 35 provides for the issue of a transport document or electronic transport record by the carrier[13] or performing party.[14] Such issuance is mandatory upon delivery of the goods for carriage unless the shipper and the carrier have agreed not to use a transport document or electronic transport record, or unless it is the custom, usage or practice in the trade not to use one. Article 36 of the Rules lists the contract particulars[15] which must be included in the transport document or electronic transport record referred to in article 35. Details are given in article 40 as to how the description of goods in the contract particulars may be qualified by the carrier, in such a way that the carrier does not assume responsibility for the accuracy of the information furnished by the shipper. Article 38 deals with signature. Electronic signature is not separately defined.[16]

Article 41 deals with the evidentiary value of the transport document or electronic transport record. It provides that it is always *prima facie* evidence of the carrier's receipt of the goods as described in the contract particulars, but proof to the contrary by the carrier in respect of any contract particulars is not admissible when they are included in a negotiable transport document or a negotiable electronic transport record that is transferred to a third party acting in good faith. This is so unless the contract particulars contain a qualifying clause that complies with the requirements of article 40. In such case, the transport document or electronic transport record does not constitute *prima facie* or conclusive evidence to the extent that the description of the goods is qualified by the clause. Thus, the provisions of chapter 8 of the Rotterdam Rules preserve the receipt function of a paper bill of lading in a negotiable transport document or electronic transport record.

To retain the character of the bill of lading as a document of title the Rotterdam Rules deals with symbolic or constructive possession in articles 47 and 51. Article 47 is discussed in detail later in this paper under section 3. The issue of transfer of title to the goods from transferor to transferee of the negotiable document or electronic transport record is not addressed by the Rules. The United States delegation once mentioned that the Rules should not be further complicated as the instant issue is not a matter for transport law but for the law of sale, which is better dealt with under national law. The author subscribes to this viewpoint, as an attempt to address the issue of transfer of title would have led to more controversy.

In the view of one commentator the Rotterdam Rules provides an excellent legal foundation for development of electronic trading systems, by laying down minimum requirements and providing freedom and flexibility to the international maritime community to develop systems for transfer and negotiations that are suited to their needs. Certainty in the law respecting electronic commerce can be achieved by parties to a carriage contract making the law of the Rotterdam Rules applicable to the contract regardless of whether or not the convention itself eventually enters into force.[17]

Considering the international character of the contract of carriage it is submitted that the acceptance of the Rotterdam Rules will be the first step towards harmonization in the field of electronic alternatives to paper bills of lading.

3. DELIVERY OF GOODS

Chapter 9 deals with delivery of goods. Despite the fact that delivery is one of the main obligations of the carrier, the existing carriage regimes do not specifically deal with that obligation. In order to avoid the current practical problems that can result from a lack of such rules, the Rotterdam Rules contain quite extensive rules on delivery. While the rules are not exhaustive, they aim to provide a substantial improvement in terms of the legal certainty surrounding delivery. The discussion below will not deal with all the seven articles in that chapter but instead focus on article 47 which has been one of the most controversial provisions.

Article 47 deals with delivery when the carrier issues a negotiable transport document or negotiable electronic transport record. Pursuant to article 47(2) the carrier can issue a negotiable transport document and has the right to deliver the goods without surrender of that document or an equivalent electronic record. The object of this provision is to solve the practical problems faced by carriers in situations where the cargo owner turns up without the requisite documentation, or does not appear at all. The critics of this provision have pointed out that the intended remedy undermines the function of a negotiable transport document as a document of title. The system envisaged in this provision allows carriers to seek alternative delivery instructions from the original shipper or the documentary shipper thereby removing the requirement to deliver on the production of a bill of lading.

A bill of lading holder has the exclusive right to claim delivery of the goods when they arrive at destination. The bill of lading enables the carrier to verify whether the person presenting it is entitled to receive the goods, relieving the carrier from its obligation to make delivery under the contract of carriage. This purpose of a negotiable transport document to establish the legitimacy of the holder forms an essential part of the security that the bill of lading system aims to provide dating from the medieval times.[18] It is on the basis of this practice that the transport document could develop into a document of title. The bill of lading, which evolved from the register maintained on board ships, was in its early days a non-negotiable document. With the growth in international sea borne trade, increase in complexity of business, concern for speed and the need for transferring property in the goods before they arrived at destination gave rise to the practice of transferring ownership of goods by endorsing the bill of lading to the buyer. Thus, the negotiable bill of lading came into existence which by the eighteenth century became a well established mercantile practice.[19] In contemporary times a negotiable document ensures that the seller may receive from the carrier a document "controlling the disposition of the goods", which is now incorporated in article 58(2) of the CISG.[20] Clause A8 of the INCOTERMS 2000 also requires the seller to provide the buyer with a bill of lading or a sea waybill as proof of delivery when a sale is concluded under a CFR (cost and freight) or a CIF contract.[21] However, article 47(2) of the Rotterdam Rules diverges from the centuries old mercantile practice by providing the carrier with the right to deliver goods without surrender of the negotiable transport document or an equivalent electronic record.

Before analysing this provision, a brief discussion of its legislative history will be useful. During the UNCITRAL Commission session the Australian delegation along with several other delegations severely criticized article 47(2)(a) expressing the view that the provision will increase the risk of fraud which will impact banks and others that rely on the security offered by negotiable transport documents. The Australian delegation also criticized the statutory indemnity in article 47(2)(c) expressing concern that it will create problems for cargo insurers. The delegation went on to explain that in case of a CIF (cost, insurance and freight) shipment, the seller arranges insurance and the policy is assigned to the buyer when the risk of shipment is transferred. If the seller unwittingly provides an indemnity to the carrier by providing alternative delivery instructions, it will impact on any recovery action the insurer might have had against the carrier. This will result in the loss of one avenue for cargo claimants recovering for misdelivery. The delegation went further to state that the combined result of paragraph 2, subparagraphs (a)-(c) of article 47 will be such that a carrier who seeks alternative delivery instructions from a shipper or documentary shipper will be relieved of liability to the holder. Yet the shipper has to give an indemnity to the carrier, a party who has no liability.[22]

During the Commission session half of the Working Group wanted to delete the text of article 47(2) while the other half preferred its retention. The Chairman explained that in such a case, it is the practice of the Commission to retain the text. Nevertheless, a small drafting group was established to come up with a revised compromise text but even then the critics remained unsatisfied. After the revision, the final text of article 47(2) provides two variants of negotiable transport documents. One is truly negotiable and the other is said to be negotiable but in fact is not, because it will contain a statement to the effect that the goods can be delivered without the surrender of the negotiable document.[23]

In response to these criticisms, the Dutch delegation emphasized that the regime under article 47 is aimed at reducing or eliminating the abuses caused by fraudulent practices that exist under the current system such as, issuing of multiple bills of lading, forgery of bills of lading and the continued circulation and sale of bills of lading even following delivery. The new regime sets up a system aimed at removing risk for bankers by restoring the integrity of the bill of lading system, which, however, may require some change in the current practices of banks and commodity traders. Furthermore, the new regime will provide relief to consignees by drawing an end to the expensive and slow process of obtaining letters of indemnity and bank guarantees.

The Dutch delegation emphasized that the purpose of the bill of lading to establish the legitimacy of the holder has come under pressure over the past few decades. Often a bill of lading is unavailable for presentation upon arrival of the goods at its destination. Such unavailability can be divided in three main categories.[24]

First, the bill of lading is held up due to inadvertent causes, such as genuine delays in the documentary process. This can be settled through better business control, practical or *ad hoc* solutions satisfying the parties involved.

The second cause relates to the underlying sale contract. The buyer/consignee may wish to reject the goods, or has not taken up documents from the bank issuing credit because an envisaged resale of the goods is yet to be concluded.

The third category of non-availability of a bill of lading relates to the structure of the trade prevalent while dealing in such goods. This may be due to the credit terms under the sale contract which lasts longer than the time taken to transport the goods. It may also be usual in a particular trade that long chains of buyers and sellers prevent the timely availability of the bill of lading. These chains can also include pre-shipment sales and may even include pre-production sales. In such cases, the bill of lading usually no longer plays a role in respect of the transfer of title to the goods. As between buyer and seller, title may pass on the basis of a series of letters of indemnity. In these letters sellers guarantee to their buyers that they have title to the goods, while they all know that the bill of lading is in the hands of a seller earlier in the chain who is holding it to secure payment of the goods. Whether the title actually passes or not will depend on the wording of the letter of indemnity and the law applicable to the transfer of title, which may not be the law applicable to the contract of sale but the law of the place where the property is situated. Moreover, once a bill of lading has been issued, it is doubtful as to how title will pass without the subsequent use of that bill of lading. It is equally doubtful whether title will pass upon transfer of a bill of lading relating to goods which have already left the carrier's custody.

The English courts have held that a holder of a bill of lading had no claim against the carrier after delivery without production of the bill of lading.[25] Therefore, when a bill of lading is used in trade transactions undermining its function to establish the legal right of the holder to take delivery of the cargo, various uncertainties are created in respect of other roles of the bill of lading which are outside the contract of carriage *per* se.

The second and third causes of non-availability of the bill of lading during delivery mentioned above are intentional in nature and developed through practice of tradesmen without any legal foundation.[26] One commentator estimates the frequency of non-availability of bills of lading after arrival of goods at their destination to be quite high. In the liner trade, a bill of lading is not presented in 15 per cent of all cases where such presentation is necessary. Matters are much worse in the bulk trade where it is estimated to be 50 per cent, while in oil and related trades the figure is close to 100 per cent.[27]

Article 47(2)(a) of the Rotterdam Rules was drafted assuming that a carrier knows or ought to know the trade and its participants. The carrier may often know or at least may have a reasonable suspicion about the whereabouts of the bill of lading. In such a case the carrier must ask the holder of the bill of lading for delivery instructions, or, if that is not possible, seek instruction from the shipper. When such instructions are forthcoming and the carrier delivers the goods accordingly, pursuant to article 47(2)(b) the carrier is discharged from the obligation to deliver the goods to the holder of the bill of lading, irrespective of whether this document has been surrendered to the carrier.[28]

This arrangement is suitable for the carrier provided the shipper is reasonably able to give proper instructions.[29] Article 47(2) is intended to take away the commercial pressure from carriers who are forced to act as indefinite guarantors of the purchase price of the goods carried. The new situation will require some vigilance from banks while accepting a bill of lading as security. When they accept the bill of lading prior to delivery, and are not mentioned as consignee or notify party in the bill of lading, they may be well advised to get hold of the carrier in order to become a notify party. When banks accept the bill of lading after delivery, they run the risk that the document does not provide collateral security as intended which exists under the current system bill of lading practice too. In the view of one commentator, article 47(2) is an attempt to lift the traditional anonymity of the bill of lading holder, which devalues the very purpose of the bill to establish the legitimacy of its holder.[30] The advancement in communication technology forms the basis of such law reform. Furthermore, article 47(2)(a)-(c) is in line with current practice under certain charterparties where the carrier is obliged to follow the instructions of the charterer with regard to the delivery of the goods.

Since bills of lading are issued in sets of three, as a consequence of article 47(2)(a) and (b) it is possible that there may still be bills of lading in circulation where the carrier has already been discharged of the obligation to deliver the goods. The legal value of such a bill of lading is dealt with in article 47(2)(d). In case of an inadvertent delay in the process of transferring the bill of lading, namely, when the goods are, or are arranged to be, purchased or pledged prior to the delivery, and the transfer of the bill of lading to the buyer or the bank takes place after delivery, the document may represent certain claims against the carrier,[31] but it no longer represents the right to obtain delivery of the goods. This rule of subparagraph (d) implies that in other cases the holder of a bill of lading that still circulates after delivery no longer has a claim against the carrier under the contract of carriage. Article 47, however, provides one exception to this rule, which can be found in subparagraph (e). It protects the innocent holder of a bill of lading who did not and could not reasonably have had knowledge of the delivery at the time of becoming a holder, is protected. However, such innocence needs adequate proof.

One commentator submits that article 47(2) deviates from the established principles of law, reflecting more on actual practices and, as such, is experimental in nature. He continues to explain that the chapeau of article 47(2) includes a possible escape and a caveat for the carrier. The phrase 'without prejudice to article 48, paragraph 1' in the chapeau can be construed as the carrier not being obliged to look out for the bill of lading holder but is entitled to make use of the rights under article 48, thus allowing an escape for the carrier. The caveat is that the system of article 47(2) only applies if the bill of lading includes some warning that the document does not necessarily need to be surrendered in order to obtain delivery of the goods.[32]

The author submits that the deviation from established international law with respect to article 47(2) can be called a functional approach[33] which is allied in nature to the notion of problem solving in management theory. The strict legalistic approach to a problem may end up being counterproductive or defeating the purpose for which the law was created in the first place. In such circumstances one must look to all the considerations in the sideline and if necessary, deviate from the established path prescribed by traditional law. Thus, a functional approach is necessary to serve as an alternative to achieve the desired goals.

As noticed during the preparation of the Rotterdam Rules, the route to achieve an optimal solution was not straight. The drafters had to wade through a maze of relevant, or even irrelevant, considerations. At the end of the day an optimum solution was arrived at by way of consensus.[34] Thus, where the approach to the resolution of a problem is a function of the goal or objective to be reached it is a functional approach, in contradistinction to the legalistic approach characterized by inherent rigidity. In this approach, the legal solutions proposed must take into account and be compatible with numerous other related interests and issues.[35]

It is further submitted by the author that the functional approach taken in the Rotterdam Rules with respect to article 47(2) may be exemplified by the evolution of the law of equity within the English legal system. It was the rigidity and inflexibility of the common law system of writs that led to the evolution of the law of equity when common folks frustrated by the strictness of procedure and formalities turned to the clergy for the resolution of their disputes. The Courts of Chancery adopted a functional approach, though unaware of such terminology at that time, to provide solutions based on ecclesiastical principles and created a body of law that came to be known as equity. Eventually, equity merged with the common law and an overall better legal product evolved.[36]

Article 47(2) which generated a lot of debate at the Working Group sessions and criticised by scholars for undermining the existing functions of a bill of lading seems to be an useful provision, but lacks the ability to solve the problem of unavailability of the bill of lading under every circumstance. The chapeau of the provision creates gaps and the shipper may not always be able or willing to provide proper delivery instructions.

This author, amidst some concerns, recognizes the that functional approach taken in article 47(2) to diverge from the centuries old mercantile practice by providing the carrier with the right to deliver goods without surrender of the negotiable transport document or an equivalent electronic record may be helpful in ending the malpractice, and lawmakers need to show no mercy to such practices. In the view of the author the benefits of this functional approach taken in article 47(2) can be fully reaped only when the purpose of the bill of lading to establish the legitimacy of its holder is resolved through the development of suitable electronic trading systems.[37]

4. Rights of the Controlling Party

Chapter 10 of the Rotterdam Rules deals with rights of the controlling party and Chapter 11 which include only two articles deal with transfer of rights in quite a rudimentary fashion. The existing maritime conventions have no provisions dealing with controlling parties or the concept of the right of control. The present law is thus found in domestic law, and may therefore be somewhat different in every jurisdiction although the broad principles are in fact fairly uniform. The drafters of the Rotterdam Rules submit that the new instrument will not tend to change existing law on this subject in any significant way, but will instead provide a solid and uniform legal basis for issues that have in many legal systems been left to unpredictable practices, particularly when there is no negotiable bill of lading in the transaction. The provisions on transfer of rights are based on non-contentious parts of the general law of documents of title and each of the two provisions deals with matters that in bill of lading practice have created difficulties. Perhaps, the transfer of rights deserved more elaborate treatment in an international instrument, but discussions within UNCITRAL revealed widely diverging views which led the Working Group to restrict that chapter to its bare minimum.

As pointed out in the introduction, the concepts of the controlling party, the right of control and the transfer of rights are the key to solving the problem of how to provide for negotiable electronic transport records. Furthermore, the establishment of rules in these areas will enhance certainty in respect of the validity of the security interest that financial institutions may have in the goods. For example, the right to provide instructions to the carrier in respect of the goods during the carriage allows an owner to dispose of the goods during the transport, or allows a financing institution to maintain control over the goods in which it has a security interest. Since the existing law in respect of these matters is largely domestic, changes brought about by the Rotterdam Rules through chapters 10 and 11, will vary from jurisdiction to jurisdiction, although the broad principles adopted are fairly standard. The Rotterdam Rules aims to achieve uniformity in this area of the law by providing a predictable legal basis for what has previously been left to industry practice and local laws. The remaining of this section will focus on the different provisions related to rights of the controlling party.

4.1. Rights of the Controlling Party and Law of Sale of Goods

The Rotterdam Rules, unlike its predecessors, do not confine itself to the contract of carriage of goods and immediately associated matters but reaches out to deal with related topics, such as rights of the controlling party, which in view of some commentators may be considered as a sale and not a carriage concept.[38] Therefore it is important to investigate if there is any potential conflict of rules between the sale of goods law and the Rotterdam Rules with respect to right of control. It is pertinent to note that the drafters of the Rules, mindful of this problem were careful to avoid any apparent inconsistency between the CISG and the Rules.[39]

The application of the Rotterdam Rules is contractual which is defined by the contract of carriage itself.[40] The transport document issued under the contract of carriage plays an important role in international trade and there are certain rights under sale of goods law which are closely entwined with bills of lading, such as the right of disposal of goods, the right of stoppage in transit and the right of control. These are discussed briefly below.

It is common practice in international documentary sales to delay the passing of property beyond the delivery of the goods to the carrier. This is accomplished by the seller retaining control of the bill of lading after the shipment of goods. One of the functions of a bill of lading is that it serves as the document of title. The rule of intention in the passing of property is reinforced by domestic legislation in many jurisdictions.[41] Section 19(1) of the UK Sale of Goods Act 1979 provides that the rule of intention in the passing of goods subsequently appropriated to the contract, the seller by the terms of the contract or of the appropriation may reserve the right of disposal in respect of the goods. Furthermore, despite delivery to the buyer or to the carrier, this reservation will remain effective until the conditions imposed by the seller are fulfilled. Section 19(2) goes on to state that when goods are shipped under the terms of the bill of lading calling for delivery to the order of the seller or agent of the seller, that is *prima facie* a reservation by the seller.

Stoppage in transit is a remedy aimed at securing the payment of the price of goods and protecting the interests of unpaid sellers. It was originally developed by the English Chancery Courts, and was based on the equitable doctrine under which a beneficial owner was allowed to trace the property held by a fiduciary, including a bailee, even where the property had been transferred. An unpaid seller has the right to issue directions to the carrier to stop the goods in transit to their destination when the buyer becomes insolvent. This right was originally based on the principle of privity of contract, under which only the shipper and the carrier had the right of contractual claims against one another. The consignee might have the right of suit only if title passed to him upon or by reason of an endorsement. In that case, the transfer of a document of title has the effect of transferring contractual rights to a transferee, so that he becomes a party to the contract of carriage with the carrier, having the same rights and duties, as contained in the bill of lading, as the transferor. Since title normally will not pass to the buyer unless he pays the price, the shipper retains the right to give instructions to the carrier even after the transfer of a negotiable document to the buyer.[42] This right, though insignificant in modern commercial conditions, is eliminated when the buyer transfers the goods for valuable consideration and the bill of lading has been endorsed to a third party in good faith.[43] Most civil law jurisdictions do not recognize stoppage in transit but do recognize the principle of contracts for the benefit of third parties. Under this principle, the transfer of a negotiable document has the effect of transferring contractual rights to a transferee, as a third party to the contract between the shipper and the carrier.[44] In certain jurisdictions, the seller has the right of stoppage even after the transfer of bill of lading to the buyer.[45]

The right of stoppage in transit under the contract of sale is closely related to the right of control under transport law. The person who has control over the goods in transit, i.e., the controlling party is in the position to give orders to the carrier, including the order of stoppage of goods in transit.[46] Generally, the shipper has the right of control over the goods during transit which includes the right to give orders to the carrier, to change the destination or the consignee, although the burden is on him to show that he still retains this power, which requires presenting a full set of bills of lading. The right of control enables the seller to prevent delivery to a buyer who failed to pay the price and this right resembles stoppage in transit under common law, or the right of retention in civil law. The consignee is deprived of the right of control unless this right was transferred to him before the goods were delivered for carriage. This means that the consignee does not have any right to the goods until he receives them, and he cannot resell them during the voyage.[47]

The parties are free to decide on who will have the right to control the goods during their carriage. In the event the goods have been paid for and ownership has been transferred to the consignee upon loading of the goods, the transport document may state that the right of control is in the hands of the consignee.

When a carrier issues a negotiable transport document, the right of control is exercised through such transport documents and the carrier is obliged to deliver the goods to the holder of the document upon presentation of an original negotiable document. Only the holder of that document is entitled to demand delivery and he may do so only upon presentation of an original document. The right to demand the goods from the carrier is thus transferable by transfer of the document. Even where the document is made out to the order of a named consignee, the shipper as controlling party may, nevertheless, be entitled to redirect the carrier to deliver the goods to another person.[48] The shipper may delete the name of the consignee and either leave this portion of the document blank or insert the name of another consignee, provided that he has retained the right of disposal of the goods.[49] This right is lost, however, once the shipper transfers at least one original to the consignee, who, by becoming the lawful holder of the document, acquires the right to demand delivery of the goods.[50] Once the shipper has transferred all originals to a transferee, the right of control is also transferred to the transferee.

In the case of a non-negotiable document the seller can retain control over the goods in transit by having the right to give instructions to the carrier as to the delivery of the goods. The seller is entitled to give such orders up until the moment the goods arrive at the destination and the named consignee is notified. At that point, control over the goods passes to the named consignee.[51]

There are a few similarities and dissimilarities between stoppage in transit and the right of control. In terms of similarities, both serve as a kind of security.[52] The differences between stoppage in transit and the right of control lie in the difference in the nature of the basis of these rights. Stoppage in transit is based on the contract of sale, which serves to transfer the property rights in a specific object to the buyer in return for the latter's payment of the purchase price to the seller. If the buyer fails to pay the purchase price, the stoppage in transit right aims to restore the property to the seller. On the other hand, the right of control has its basis in the rights derived from the contract of carriage, particularly the rules governing the negotiability of transport documents, which determine the right of control over the goods. This right is only indirectly related to the property right in the sense that the contract of carriage is an instrument which enables the seller to perform his main duty under the contract of sale, *i.e.*, delivery of the goods.

The right of control is useful in situations where the seller does not trust the buyer, whereas stoppage in transit is a 'reservation' needed where the seller has shown trust in the buyer by granting him credit, but the buyer turns out to be unable to live up to that trust. The seller may retain the right of control and exercise stoppage in transit as long as he is the controlling party. Once this right is transferred to the buyer, the seller is no longer in a position to exercise his right of stoppage in transit.

Non-maritime transport conventions include specific provisions on right of control.[53] So far international maritime law conventions have been silent on this matter, probably because the customary practice relating to bills of lading was regarded as sufficient. The only explicit provision on right of control in maritime law is Rule 7 of the CMI Rules for Electronic Bills of Lading 1991.

From the above discussion it is clear that the right of control is not based on property rights because the controlling party may not be the owner of the goods. The controlling party is in the position to give orders to the carrier, either because he is the holder of a negotiable document or because he was given the right of control under the contract of carriage. By issuing a negotiable document, the carrier neither certifies property rights over the goods, nor has the authority to do so. The carrier simply confirms receipt of the goods as described in the document and undertakes to deliver them to the lawful holder of the document. The act of delivery of a negotiable document may have the effect of transferring title. From a carriage law standpoint, the ownership issue is not relevant to the exercise of the right of control, or the right to receive the goods. The only issue that matters under a contract of carriage is who has the right to take delivery of the goods.

The potential conflict between the CISG and the Rotterdam Rules arises from the co-existence of the right of stoppage under sales law and the right of control under carriage of goods law, so that the exercise of one of these two rights affects the other. Under article 71(2) of the CISG, the seller is allowed to intercept the cargo before actual delivery to the buyer, even where the seller has lost control over the goods. Under the Rotterdam Rules, if the shipper has transferred the negotiable document to the consignee, then he cannot prevent delivery of the goods to the consignee. The seller would have no right to make any orders to the carrier when he designates the consignee as the controlling party under article 51(1)(a), when he transfers a non-negotiable document to the consignee without endorsement under article 51(2)(a), or when the consignee is the holder of a negotiable document under article 51(3)(a). Therefore, under the Rotterdam Rules, the carrier would be in breach of his duties toward the controlling party if he were to obey the seller's orders related to stoppage in transit, regardless of whether the purchase price has already been paid in accordance with the applicable sales law.

It is submitted that the right of control under the Rotterdam Rules is based on well settled principles of transport law. The right of stoppage in transit, embodied in article 71(2) of the CISG to protect unpaid sellers, is outdated and has lost its importance in the modern system of international sales due to widespread use of letters of credit and retention of title clauses. Therefore from a practical perspective, there is very little potential for litigation related to this conflict.

4.2. Rights of the Controlling Party under the Rotterdam Rules

The terms 'right of control'[54] and 'controlling party'[55] are defined in the Rotterdam Rules.[56] The term controlling party is defined in a way that allows any person to be a controlling party, regardless of whether it is a party to the contract of carriage. But the Rules do not cover the issue of whether a controlling party may become a party to the contract of carriage by exercising the right of control, although in many jurisdictions, pursuant to national law such parties will be bound by the terms of the contract of carriage when exercising this right.

Article 50 sets out when and to what extent the controlling party can exercise right of control over the goods. The chapeau of paragraph 1 provides that the controlling party is the person entitled to exercise right of control. Subparagraph (a) refers to the ordinary instructions under a contract of carriage which are mainly of operational significance and inherent to any carriage contract.[57] However, the instructions may also relate to situations where the seller does not sufficiently trust the buyer.[58] The exercise of the right of control under subparagraphs (b) and (c) relates to varying the contract of carriage to primarily facilitate enforcement of the right of stoppage in transit and the right of disposal.[59] Paragraph 2 pertains to the connection between the period of right of control of the controlling party and the period of responsibility of the carrier under the contract of carriage. Since parties are free to determine by agreement who will have the right to control the goods during their carriage, the actual custody of the goods with the carrier is not always the decisive factor as to whether the right of control can still be exercised or not. It is important to note here that the right of control of the goods is not terminated due to the reason that the consignee has claimed delivery of the goods. This provision in the Rotterdam Rules protects the seller from an insolvent buyer as the insolvent buyer cannot frustrate an instruction of the seller unilaterally by claiming delivery of the goods.[60]

Article 51 enumerates in detail the identity of the controlling party in different situations and the transfer of the right of control. Paragraph 1 is applicable when a non-negotiable transport document is issued by the carrier or where no document is issued at all.[61] Subparagraph (b) provides that the right of control is transferable and is only effective, in relation to the carrier, if and when it has been notified to the carrier. The manner in which such transfer must take effect is not mentioned in the Rules, and is left to applicable national law. In most jurisdictions, transfer of rights is based on agreement and when the goods are in the hands of a third party, the transfer of rights has to be notified to that third party. Most jurisdictions also allow transfer of rights between the transferor and the transferee to be done electronically.[62] Article 3 of the Rotterdam Rules provides that notification of the transfer to the carrier by the transferor may be made electronically. Consequently, when transfer of the right of control and notification thereof to the carrier may be made electronically, the entire document of title function of the negotiable transport document can be performed electronically.[63]

In such a case, the purpose of a bill of lading to establish the legitimacy of its holder may be possibly solved through the development of electronic trading systems, which will do away with the requirement of a negotiable transport document to control the goods during carriage. Exercise of rights in the goods may be fulfilled through the possession and transfer of the right of control. In such a case the existing payment mechanism against documents under a sale contract will be replaced by payment against transfer of control. The two other functions of a transport document, namely receipt and evidence of the contract of carriage can be performed electronically by creating a platform similar to that of the electronic banking system.[64]

Article 51, paragraphs 2, 3 and 4 relates to the issuance of a specific type of transport document and are exceptions to the main rule contained in paragraph 1. Paragraph 2 applies to a non-negotiable transport document[65] made out to a named person and indicates that it should be surrendered to obtain delivery of the goods.[66] Paragraph 3 applies to negotiable transport documents issued by following the existing bill of lading practice and paragraph 4 applies to negotiable electronic transport records.

Article 52 provides for carrier's execution of instructions which are referred to in article 50. Taking a cue from article 50, this provision is based on the principle that the controlling party may exercise the right of control unilaterally, even in the case of an early delivery or change of consignee that must be regarded as a variation of the contract of carriage. A carrier is, however, only obliged to execute the instructions subject to the conditions laid down in this article. Article 52(1)(b) allows the carrier to ignore the instructions of the controlling party where they cannot "reasonably be executed according to their terms at the moment they reach the carrier", which obviously leave room for disagreement. Moreover, by virtue of article 52(1)(c), the carrier may refuse the controlling party's instructions where they "interfere with the normal operations of the carrier, including its delivery practices". This may give rise to disputes, for example, when a carrier refuses an instruction of the controlling party to offload at a scheduled port where it normally calls only to collect goods.

Article 52 also provides that the additional costs and expenses incurred by the carrier have to be compensated by the controlling party, and the carrier may request security for those amounts. The carrier is held liable only for loss of or damage to the goods or for delay in delivery. The Rules does not deal with situations where a carrier may be held liable for any loss or damage other than loss or damage to the goods resulting from non-compliance of any instruction rightfully given by the controlling party and is left to be determined by the applicable national law. In such a case where the carrier is made liable under national law, in the opinion of one commentator the limitation of liability as prescribed in article 59 of the Rules will apply, because such liability arises from a breach of the carrier's obligation under the Rules.[67]

Articles 54 and 55 which deal with 'variations to the contract of carriage' and 'providing additional information, instructions or documents to carrier', respectively, complete the concept of the controlling party as envisaged in the Rules. Though the Rules do not specify whether the controlling party is or may become a party to the contract of carriage and is left to applicable national law; the Rules envisages that the controlling party is always the party interested in the goods during carriage, but, unless the controlling party is also the shipper, may not be a party to the contract of carriage. Therefore, the rights and obligations of the controlling party are specifically provided for in the Rules, including those in articles 54 and 55. This allows the controlling party to complement the carrier during transport.

Article 54(1) allows the controlling party to agree with the carrier any variation to the contract of carriage during the carriage, such variations being beyond those referred to in article 50(1)(b) and (c). Article 54(2) requires variations to the contract of carriage to be stated on the transport document because instructions given to the carrier pursuant to article 50(1)(b) and (c) may amount to variation of the contract of carriage. In the opinion of one commentator such requirement will be difficult to be accommodated into existing international trade practice, particularly to that of letters of credit.[68]

Article 55(1) puts the controlling party under an obligation to provide instructions relating to the goods upon being requested by the carrier or the performing party. The reasoning behind this provision is that the carrier, who has a general duty of care with respect of the cargo,[69] must, under certain circumstances, protect the interests of the controlling party. The advancement of communication technology has made it possible for the carrier to contact the controlling party for instructions relating to the goods and therefore, the controlling party is put under an obligation to provide such instructions. Article 55(2) allows the carrier to communicate with the shipper when the carrier does not know the controlling party, or when the controlling party is unable to provide adequate instructions. The Rules does not make it obligatory for the carrier to carry out any instruction given under article 55.

Article 56 provides that parties to the contract of carriage may agree that no variations to the contract of carriage will be unilaterally imposed on the carrier and that the right of control itself, including its transferability may be restricted or excluded.

From the above discussion it can be concluded that the relevant provisions on rights of the controlling party serve to fill a lacuna in the law of many jurisdictions and help in harmonizing and modernizing the international law in this field. Because these provisions are most important when the carrier does not issue a physical piece of paper qualifying as a negotiable bill of lading, which is exactly the situation in an electronic commerce transaction, chapter 10 constitutes an important part of the Rules' indirect facilitation of electronic commerce.

CONCLUSION

The inclusion of chapters on delivery of the goods, rights of the controlling party and transfer of rights in the Rotterdam Rules have been criticised by several scholars. One legal commentator expressed scepticism over these chapters as "innovations" which are "obvious risks".[70] Another legal scholar is of the view that the "topics are addressed with surprising and possibly a dangerous degree of detail".[71] Some are also of the view that "it would have been preferable to omit altogether the [three] chapters".[72] The supporters of the inclusion of these chapters emphasize that "these chapters address practical difficulties in maritime transport and, therefore, deserve a place in the Rotterdam Rules".[73]

It is submitted that the legal framework of the Rotterdam Rules can be used to create a platform which will facilitate e-commerce for international sale transactions in conjunction with its transport and financing. It is also submitted that the legal framework required for creating such a platform has to be open and technology-neutral and capable of catering to the needs of companies, large or small, in both developed and developing nations.[74] The platform should also be able to facilitate international transactions through the simplification and harmonization of processes, procedures and information flows; provide information on the right of control over the goods throughout the transaction process by identifying the controlling party; streamline the various administrative procedures at border crossings related to customs, health, safety and security; integrate the various credit and payment systems; and improve trust assessment through a better exchange of information. In summary, the objective of this platform will be to create a simple, transparent and effective process for global business through the standardization of e-business processes and data in the context of global trade facilitation and maritime transport. It is envisaged that once such a platform is effectively in place, it will improve efficiency and reduce transaction costs. An electronic trading platform will provide various actors in the transportation business a common place for exchanging information which is necessary to create a backbone for facilitating international trade transactions in the twenty-first century. The Rotterdam Rules provides a legal foundation for development of electronic trading systems, by laying down minimum requirements and providing freedom and flexibility to the international maritime community to develop systems for transfer and negotiations that are suited to their needs.

Once electronic commerce comes into vogue more extensively in the maritime industry, the physical location and possession of a bill of lading will no longer be important for concluding a carriage contract. The physical possession of a title document will no longer be the only means through which title may be transferred. The three chapters addressing practical difficulties existing in maritime transport thus deserve a place in the Rotterdam Rules. The provisions also pave the way for future of carriage of goods without documents, through electronic transfer of the right of control.

The Rotterdam Rules which seeks to achieve harmonization in the field of carriage of goods law recognizes delivery of goods as one of the key obligations of the carrier under the contract of carriage. The absence of any specific provision on delivery in the earlier carriage regimes created divergent laws in different jurisdictions and many practical difficulties. Moreover, the chapter on right of control when supplemented by national law, as and when needed, will ensure that in all cases where legal consequences are connected to the holding or a transfer of a negotiable transport document, similar legal consequences will follow from the possession or transfer of the right of control. Generally speaking, a right is much easier to transfer electronically than by the physical transfer of a negotiable transport document. It is envisaged that the parties to an international trade transaction can achieve certainty in the law for e-commerce by making the law of the Rotterdam Rules applicable to the carriage contract regardless of whether or not the convention itself eventually enters into force.[75]

End Notes

[1] The creation of this Convention was initiated by the Comité Maritime International (CMI) and was subsequently passed on to the United Nations Commission on International Trade Law (UNCITRAL) Working Group III (Transport Law). The final text of the Convention is annexed to General Assembly Resolution 63/122, UN Doc A/RES/63/122. It was also annexed to the "Report of the United Nations Commission on International

Trade Law on the work of its forty-first session", UN Doc A/63/17 (2008), Annex I. In this research proposal, the subject instrument is referred to as the "Rotterdam Rules".

[2] Indeed, the desirability of a new transport convention emanated from the deliberations of UNCITRAL Working Group IV on Electronic Commerce. In the mid nineties, one item in the agenda of Working Group IV was to develop electronic equivalents of documents of title. It was concluded that, generally speaking, the virtualization of documents of title was not a feasible proposition because of the formal function of the paper document. Instead, it was viewed that the material functions of documents of title can be incorporated into a structure of electronic messages. See "Possible Future Work on Transport Law", UN Doc A/CN.9/497, at p. 3.

[3] Chapters 9, 10 and 11 of the Rotterdam Rules.

[4] The Rotterdam Rules uses the term "electronic transport record" to refer to electronic bills of lading. Article 1(18) of the Rules defines "electronic transport record" as information in one or more messages issued by electronic communication under a contract of carriage by a carrier, including information logically associated with the electronic transport record by attachments or otherwise linked to the electronic transport record contemporaneously with or subsequent to its issue by the carrier, so as to become part of the electronic transport record, that: (a) Evidences the carrier's or a performing party's receipt of goods under a contract of carriage; and (b) Evidences or contains a contract of carriage.

[5] Paradigm shift (or revolutionary science) is the term first used by Thomas Kuhn in his influential book *The Structure of Scientific Revolutions* in 1962 to describe a change in basic assumptions within the ruling theory of science. It is in contrast to his idea of normal science.

[6] See Michael Sturley, "The UNCITRAL Carriage of Goods Convention: Changes to Existing Law", CMI Yearbook 2009, at p. 255.

[7] See "Possible Future Work on Transport Law", UN Doc A/CN.9/497, at p. 3.

[8] Article 1(18) of the Rotterdam Rules defines "electronic transport record" as information in one or more messages issued by electronic communication under a contract of carriage by a carrier, including information logically associated with the electronic transport record by attachments or otherwise linked to the electronic transport record contemporaneously with or subsequent to its issue by the carrier, so as to become part of the electronic transport record, that: (a) Evidences the carrier's or a performing party's receipt of goods under a contract of carriage; and (b) Evidences or contains a contract of carriage.

[9] Article 1(15) of the Rotterdam Rules defines "negotiable transport document" as a transport document that indicates, by wording such as "to order" or "negotiable" or other appropriate wording recognized as having the same effect by the law applicable to the document, that the goods have been consigned to the order of the shipper, to the order of the consignee, or to bearer, and is not explicitly stated as being "non-negotiable" or "not negotiable".

[10] Article 1(16) of the Rotterdam Rules defines "non-negotiable transport document" as a transport document that is not a negotiable transport document.

[11] Medium and technology neutral means that the new convention must be able to adapt to all types of systems, not only those such as the Bolero which is a registry based system. It must be suited to systems operating in a closed environment (such as an intranet), as well as those operating in an open environment (such as the internet). The drafters of the Rotterdam Rules have been careful not to limit the scope of the text to what technology or medium is presently in use, keeping in mind that technology evolves rapidly and that what appears impossible today is probably already on the current agenda of software developers. See CMI Draft Instrument on Transport Law, CMI Yearbook 2001, at p.533.

[12] For a detailed discussion see Miriam Goldby, The performance of the bill of lading's functions under UNCITRAL's draft Convention on the Carriage of Goods: unequivocal legal recognition of electronic equivalents, (2007) 13 JIML, at pp162-163. See also, Jose Angelo Estrella Faria, "Electronic Transport Records" in Alexander von Ziegler, Johan Schelin and Stefano Zunarelli (eds.), *The Rotterdam Rules 2008: Commentary to the United Nations Convention on Contracts for the International Carriage of Goods Wholly or Partly by Sea*, Wolters Kluwer (2010), at pp. 51-69; Michael F. Sturley, Tomotaka Fujita and Gertjan van der Ziel, *The Rotterdam Rules*, Sweet & Maxwell (2010), at pp. 47-57.

[13] Article 1(5) of the Rotterdam Rules defines "carrier" as a person that enters into a contract of carriage with a shipper.

[14] Article 1(6) of the Rotterdam Rules defines "performing party" as a person other than the carrier that performs or undertakes to perform any of the carrier's obligations under a contract of carriage with respect to the receipt, loading, handling, stowage, carriage, care, unloading or delivery of the goods, to the extent that such person acts, either directly or indirectly, at the carrier's request or under the carrier's supervision or control. It further

states that a "performing party" does not include any person that is retained, directly or indirectly, by a shipper, by a documentary shipper, by the controlling party or by the consignee instead of by the carrier.

[15] Article 1(23) of the Rotterdam Rules defines the term "contract particulars" as any information relating to the contract of carriage or to the goods (including terms, notations, signatures and endorsements) that is in a transport document or an electronic transport record.

[16] See UN Doc A/CN.9/WGIII/WP.56, footnote 147 at p. 34 where a reference is made to the definition of electronic signature in the United Nations Model Law on Electronic Signatures 2001.

[17] See Goldby, *supra* note 12, at p. 163.

[18] It is interesting to note that a bill of lading type document had been in existence some two thousand years ago. The modern day word charterparty is derived from the Latin phrase *carta partita*. The receipt issued by the carrier (*carta*) was torn in two pieces (*partita*). One piece was carried on board together with the goods and the other piece went overland through the Roman mail system to the discharge port. The merchant in possession of the piece that fitted to the part carried on board was entitled to receive the cargo. Thus the essence of a bill of lading as a document which identifies the person to whom a carrier may pass the goods in order to be discharged of his delivery obligation under the contract of carriage is a millennia old mercantile practice. See Stewart C. Boyd *et al.*, *Scrutton on Charter Parties and Bills of Lading*, Sweet & Maxwell, 20th edition (1996), at p.3, footnote 19.

[19] See W.E. Astle, *The Hamburg Rules*, Fairplay Publications, 1981 at p. 5.

[20] Article 58(2) of CISG provides that "If the contract involves carriage of the goods, the seller may dispatch the goods on terms whereby the goods, or documents controlling their disposition, will not be handed over to the buyer except against payment of the price."

[21] See ICC INCOTERMS 2000, Yearbook of the United Nations Commission on International Trade Law, 2000, vol. XXXI, at p.605.

[22] See "Comments received from Governments and intergovernmental organizations – States – Australia – 14 April 2008", UNICTRAL 41st session, New York, 16 June - 3 July 2008, UN Doc A/CN.9/658, para. 50, at p.10.

[23] See UNCITRAL 41st Commission Session Report, UN Doc A/63/17, at p. 31.

[24] Prof. Gertjan van der Ziel, who was member of the Dutch delegation, also explained this in a published article. See Professor G J van der Ziel, "Delivery of the goods, rights of the controlling party and transfer of rights", (2008) 14 JIML, at p. 600.

[25] See for example, *The Future Express* [1992] 1 Lloyd's Rep 79 (*per* Diamond J) and on appeal [1993] 2 Lloyd's Rep 542 and *The Delfini* [1990] 1 Lloyd's Rep 252.

[26] Prof. Gertjan van der Ziel in a colloquium in 2004 questioned this practice. According to him, "[s]uch may have genuine business reasons indeed, but it has never been the intention of the bill of lading system that this document would act as a sort of promissory note without a maturity date, as some people seem to believe. No bank would ever issue such a document of title, so why a carrier should be put under such an obligation?" See Gertjan van der Ziel, "Survey on History and Concept", TranspR 7/8-2004, at p. 278.

[27] See Gertjan van der Ziel, *supra note* 24, at p. 601.

[28] *Ibid*, at p. 604.

[29] For example, various bulk trades are structured so that charterers/shippers are in such a position to give proper instructions.

[30] See Gertjan van der Ziel, *supra note* 24, at p. 605.

[31] An example of such a right is claim for damages if the goods are delivered damaged or the delivery is short.

[32] See Gertjan van der Ziel, *supra note* 24, at p. 605.

[33] See in general Ralf Michaels, "The Functional Method of Comparative Law" in Mathias Reimann and Reinhard Zimmermann (eds.), *The Oxford Handbook of Comparative Law*, Oxford University Press (2006). See also Douglas M. Johnston and Phillip M. Saunders (eds.), *Ocean Boundary Making: Regional Issues and Developments*, Croom Helm, pp. 54-57; 320-321; 330-332 for explanation and examples of functionalism and the functional approach as applied to theories of maritime boundary delimitation. Another striking example of functional approach being adopted in the maritime law field is in the international marine pollution conventions, namely, the Civil Liability Convention (CLC) and the International Convention on the Establishment of an International Fund for Compensation for Oil Pollution Damage (Fund Convention). In the CLC/Fund scheme, the purity of the "polluter pays" principle is substantially modified through a functional approach to the issue of liability and compensation for oil pollution damage. For a detailed discussion on the subject see, Jingjing Xu, *The Law and Economics of Ship-Generated Oil Pollution*, unpublished Ph.D. thesis, University of Wales Swansea, May 2006, Chapter 2.

[34] See Hannu Honka, "Scope of Application, Freedom of Contract", CMI Year Book 2009, at p. 270.

[35] Gleaned from personal discussions with Prof. Proshanto K. Mukherjee, while he was explaining the functional approach taken in the Fund Convention.

[36] See Henry Maine, *Ancient Law,* London: Humphrey Milford, Oxford University Press, 1931, at pp.23, 36. See also Proshanto K. Mukherjee, *Maritime Legislation*, Malmo: World Maritime University, 2002, at pp.5, 6.

[37] For a brief discussion on electronic trading systems, see the discussion on article 51 of the Rotterdam Rules below.

[38] D. Rhidian Thomas, "And then there were the Rotterdam Rules", (2008) 14 JIML 189.

[39] See Report of Working Group III (Transport Law) on the work of its eleventh session (New York, 24 March to 4 April 2003), UN Doc A/CN.9/526, para 131.

[40] See Rotterdam Rules, definition of "contract of carriage", article 1(1).

[41] For example, see section 19 of the UK Sale of Goods Act 1979.

[42] This right has now been codified; for example, see section 39(1) of the UK Sale of Goods Act 1979; section 2-705 of the American Uniform Commercial Code.

[43] For example, see section 10 of the UK Factors Act 1889 and section 47(2) of the UK Sale of Goods Act, 1979.

[44] For example, Section 364(1) of the German Commercial Code provides that "the effect of the endorsement is that all rights under the endorsed instrument are transferred to the endorsee." Handelsgesetzbuch [HGB] [Commercial Code] May 10, 1897, Bundesgesetzblatt, Teil I [BGBl. I] 17, as amended, § 364(1) (F.R.G.), as discussed in Caslav Pejovic, "Stoppage in Transit and Right of Control: 'Conflict Of Rules'?", 20 Pace Int'l L. Rev. 129, at p. 135 and footnote 22.

[45] The Norwegian Maritime Code provides: The right of a seller in the event of breach of contract to prevent delivery of the goods to the buyer...or to demand their return, shall apply even though the bill of lading has been passed on to the buyer. The right of stoppage can not be asserted against a third party who has acquired an order or bearer bill of lading in good faith. See, Norwegian Maritime Code § 307, available at http://folk.uio.no/erikro/WWW/NMC.pdf. Other Scandinavian Maritime Codes contain similar provisions.

[46] See Alexander von Ziegler, "The Right of Suspension and Stoppage in Transit", 25 J. L.& Com. 353 (2005), at p. 367, available at http:// www.uncitral.org/pdf/english/CISG25/von%20Ziegler.pdf.

[47] See Caslav Pejovic, *supra* note 44, at p. 144.

[48] See von Ziegler, *supra* note 46, at p 369.

[49] *Ibid.*

[50] *Ibid.*

[51] For a detailed discussion, see Hugo Tiberg, "Legal Qualities of Transport Documents", 23 Tul. Mar. L.J. 1, 36 (1998).

[52] Stoppage in transit is the right of a seller who is entitled, under certain conditions, to exercise this right even where he is not the legal owner of the goods. Right of control also protects the seller, and does so even more effectively by allowing the seller to retain control over the goods until the price is paid. Typically, the right of control will be transferred to the buyer against the payment of the price under a letter of credit.

[53] Montréal Convention 1999 article 12; CMR Convention 1956 articles 12, 14-16; COTIF/CIM Convention 1999 articles 18-22; CMNI Convention 2001 articles 14, 15.

[54] Article 1(12) of the Rotterdam Rules defines "right of control" of the goods as the right under the contract of carriage to give the carrier instructions in respect of the goods in accordance with chapter 10.

[55] Article 1(13) of the Rotterdam Rules defines "controlling party" as the person that pursuant to article 51 is entitled to exercise the right of control.

[56] See article 58 of the Rotterdam Rules which deals with this matter in relation to the holding of a negotiable transport document.

[57] Such instructions may include the temperature at which the goods must be kept as in the case of refrigerated goods, or time of delivery of the goods.

[58] The carrier may be instructed to contact the seller before making delivery. Such an instruction may be given by a shipper/seller when, upon shipment, there is no certainty that the purchase price of the goods will be paid in time and the shipper/seller wants to be sure that the goods will not be delivered prior to receipt of the money.

[59] Such rights can also be exercised to instruct a carrier to change the name of the consignee when the goods are resold to a new buyer. These rights may also be useful for a bank which wants to enforce its rights as the pledgee of the goods.

[60] The position in other non-maritime transport conventions such as the Montreal Convention, CMR, COTIF-CIM, etc. is remarkably different.

[61] Generally no documents are issued in short haul ferry transport or in certain e-commerce business models where the electronic data relating to the carriage do not qualify as an electronic transport record as defined in Article 1 (18) of the Rotterdam Rules.

[62] In earlier versions of the draft convention there was an express provision that transfer of rights could be made electronically. See ACN 9/WG IIIIWP 56, article 63(c)(i). There were some contentious items in this article which resulted in the deletion of the entire article, including this non-contentious part. See Gertjan van der Ziel, *supra note* 24, footnote 32 at p. 606.

[63] For a detailed discussion see Gertjan van der Ziel, *supra note* 24, at pp. 606-607.

[64] *Ibid.*

[65] No-negotiable is defined in the Rules; see Rotterdam Rules, articles 1(15) and 1(16).

[66] This provision was created to cater to the functions of a "nominative bill of lading" or "recta bill of lading". The word "recta" looking from its Latin meaning is linguistically similar to the English "straight bill" of lading. In the US it is established that such a document need not be surrendered. German bills of lading become "recta" by being made out to a named person, while the Scandinavian Maritime Codes require recta bills of lading to have a specific "recta" clause i.e., "not to order" or "non-negotiable." In many jurisdictions such a transport document is distinguished from a sea waybill. See generally Hugo Tiberg, "Transfer of Documents" [2002] LMCLQ 539.

[67] See Gertjan van der Ziel, *supra note* 24, at p. 603.

[68] Professor Charles Debattista expressed this view at a conference in Rotterdam. The Conference, Rotterdam Rules Appraised, was held at Erasmus University, Rotterdam on 24-25 September 2009.

[69] See Rotterdam Rules, article 13(1).

[70] See Jan Ramberg, "UN Convention on Contracts for International Carriage of Goods wholly or partly by Sea", CMI Yearbook 2009 at p.280.

[71] See Thomas, *supra* note 38.

[72] See Anthony Diamond, "The Next Sea Carriage Convention", [2008] 2 LMCLQ 138, at pp. 140-141.

[73] See Gertjan van der Ziel, *supra note* 24, at p. 607.

[74] It is notable in this context that the maritime and banking industry has already taken up initiatives such as the Bolero which is a closed registry system to facilitate electronic international trade. However, it is not sufficient and an open registry system based platform is highly desirable.

[75] The Rotterdam Rules has so far received 24 signatures and 2 ratifications which present a mix of developing and developed countries, including strong seafaring and trading nations, as well as traditional carrier and shipper nations. See Status of the Rotterdam Rules at http://www.uncitral.org/uncitral/en/uncitral_texts/transport_goods/rotterdam_status.html. Pursuant to article 94 of the Rules, the Convention requires ratification or accession by at least 20 states to enter into force and achieve elevation to the status of international law. Pursuant to article 90, no reservations are permitted except that the provisions relating to jurisdiction and arbitration are subject to express affirmation. The states subscribing to it must denounce earlier conventions on the subject.

In: Selected Issues in Maritime Law and Policy
Editor: Maximo Q. Mejia, Jr.
ISBN: 978-1-62618-508-1

Chapter 10

International Legal Framework (UNCLOS, SUA, and UN Resolutions): How Adequate are They in Tackling Piracy?[1]

Samuel Pyeatt Menefee*

Center for Oceans Law & Policy, University of Virginia School of Law, US
Center for National Security Law, University of Virginia School of Law, US

In discussing the legal and judicial frameworks for piracy and crimes at sea, this chapter will review the existing international legal framework, including UNCLOS, SUA, and UN Resolutions, and consider how adequate these responses are in tackling piracy. Discussion and consideration of another important element of the current legal framework for maritime security – the International Ship and Port Facility Security (ISPS) Code – has been intentionally omitted from this chapter.[2]

I. "All Balled Up"; Some Preliminary Thoughts on the International Legal Framework

As recently as December 16, 2008, the United Nations Security Council reaffirmed "that international law, as reflected in the United Nations Convention on the Law of the Sea of 10 December 1982 (UNCLOS), sets out the legal framework applicable to combating piracy and

[1] The author would like to thank Taylor Fitchett, University of Virginia Law Librarian, and Ben Doherty of the University of Virginia Law Library for their help in obtaining sources. A version of this paper was presented as "International Legal Framework (UNCLOS, SUA, and UN Resolutions: How Adequate Are They in Tackling Piracy?" on the Legal Issues Panel at the Kuala Lumpur Conference on Piracy and Crimes at Sea, organized by the Government of Malaysia, May 18, 2009. The views expressed herein are those of the author and do not reflect the public or private position of any organization.

[*] spmenefee@msn.com

[2] For information on the ISPS Code, see the IMO website at www.imo.org. There are publications that discuss and assess the ISPS Code within the context of sea piracy. *See*, for instance, Maximo Q. Mejia Jr., *The ISPS Code, Security Culture, and the Campaign Against Piracy and Other Crimes at Sea*, 104 BIMCO BUL (2009), 42-46.

armed robbery at sea ...."[3] It all sounds *so* simple. If one squints one's eyes, this statement might even appear to be *accurate* (if somewhat superfluous). After further consideration, however, deficiencies begin to appear, suggesting the danger of allowing even such an august body as the Security Council to interpret treaty law. The term "armed robbery at sea" appears *nowhere* in UNCLOS but seems to derive from a later General Assembly Resolution (53/32 (1998)),[4] which also mentions "armed robbery against ships."[5] The search is still on for a source defining the former phrase, but the IMO MSC's Draft Code of Practice for the Investigation of Crimes of Piracy and Armed Robbery Against Ships of 2000[6] has characterized "[a]rmed robbery against ships" as "any unlawful act of violence or detention or any act of depredation, or threat thereof, other than an act of 'piracy', directed against a ship or against persons or property on board such a ship, within a State's jurisdiction over such offences,"[7] so that one has been nailed down. Those who have been following piracy over the years may recall the objections made by some States to the I.C.C.- International Maritime Bureau's use of the term "piracy" for, well, *piracies* which occurred in their waters. These countries were presumably behind the introduction of the two terms in question, one of which still seems to be undefined. This is noted so that it will be understood that a *full* explanation of the legal context for piracy is not on the cards in the space available here.

What this work *does* hope to do is to summarize *several* of the international legal *frameworks* for piracy and related crimes at sea. This seems a more accurate description, as we are dealing with a *series* of systems – some connected, some separate - rather than one purposefully-designed superstructure. In doing this, the general source of each component will be quickly indicated before its adequacy in fighting piracy and maritime crimes of violence is considered. These frameworks – and no claim is made that they are exhaustive - include a) customary international law, b) the Convention on the High Seas (1958) and Convention on the Law of the Sea (1982), c) the original SUA Convention (1988) and Protocol, d) relevant multilateral and bilateral conventions treaties, and arrangements, and e) relevant United Nations resolutions.

The "impressionistic tour" which follows will hopefully stimulate the reader to think harder about the international legal framework – or framework*s* – of the crime.

II. Customary International Law

The role of customary international law, of course, is based on the *practice* of States, but it is a difficult concept to grasp because of its slippery nature. While there is general agreement that customary practice over the years may eventually result in the *codification* of international law, uncodified practices may still be argued to represent valid customary law. This is an area of great controversy – not least as to what should be included under its rubric. While it has suffered from a general lack of study, customary law is one area which offers the

[3] United Nations Security Council Resolution 1851, S/RES/1851 (2008). *See also* United Nations Security Council Resolution 1816, S/RES/1816 (2008) (which speaks of "armed robbery, as well as other ocean activities" and *elsewhere* of "armed robbery against vessels").

[4] United Nations General Assembly Resolution 53/32, A/RES/53/32 §22 (1999).

[5] *Id.*, §23.

[6] Draft Code of Practice for the Investigation of the Crimes of Piracy and Armed Robbery Against Ships, MSC/Circ.984 (20 December 2000).

[7] *Id.*, Annex 2.2.

possibility of future advances, the legal equivalent of "wonder drugs from the jungle." Consider just three examples.

First, while piracy as defined by codified international law has *not* been held to include "descents from the sea," i.e., attacks by pirates on land-based targets, there is good argument from Scandinavian legal sources that this might constitute piracy (think *Vikings*!). Analogous examples might be drawn from other regions, such as the September, 1985 raid on Lahad Datu, Sabah, by individuals who stole $82,000 from a bank and airline office, and killed ten before fleeing by sea.[8] A good argument might be made for including incidents such as these as a form of piracy under international law even if they would not qualify under the Convention on the High Seas (1958) or the Convention on the Law of the Sea (1982).

Second, while the aforementioned two Conventions are generally held to require an attack from *another* vessel for piracy to have occurred, there is historical precedent for classifying at least some *passenger seizures* of vessels as piracy. These range from Confederate takeovers of ships during the American Civil War, to Portuguese views of the hijack of the *Santa Maria* in the early 1960's, to American characterizations of the *Achille Lauro* hijacking. This question has been treated at some length in a contribution made to Professor Natalino Ronzitti's *Maritime Terrorism and International Law*.[9]

Third, there is the interesting insert in several recent Security Council Resolutions concerning piracy off Somalia which "underscores in particular that this resolution shall not be considered as establishing customary international law ...."[10] Say what? While the Security Council is a powerful organization, and while statements such as this may *weaken* the customary force of its resolutions, what we have here is something akin to trying to *legislate* a typhoon out of existence. With all due respect, someone needs to tell the Security Council that it *does not control* customary international law; in the end, words cannot trump actions. While such statements can *retard* the coalescing of rules, but they cannot *prevent* this from occurring. Does anyone truly think that ten or twenty such resolutions, even if each contained this wording, would not represent a prospective *trend* in customary international law?

III. Piracy Provisions of the United Nations Convention on the Law of the Sea (1982) and its Predecessor, the Convention on the High Seas (1958)

These two conventions may be considered together as their wording is almost identical. Both derive from an international desire to codify the laws relating to the sea, including those dealing with piracy. The greatest difference between the two conventions lies in the geographic area they cover; the advance in national jurisdictions means that a smaller area is governed by the 1982 Convention than by its 1958 counterpart. This discussion will

[8] *The IMB Chronology of Pirate Attacks on Merchant Vessels 1981-1987*, ERIC ELLEN, ED., PIRACY AT SEA 265 (1989).

[9] S. P. Menefee, *Piracy, Terrorism, and the Insurgent Passenger: A Historical and Legal Perspective*, in NATALINO RONZITTI, MARITIME TERRORISM AND INTERNATIONAL LAW 43-68 (1990).

[10] United Nations Security Council Resolution 1816, *supra* note 2, §9.

concentrate on the wording of the 1982 Convention which most would concur, is the more relevant.

The adequacy of these conventions in dealing with piracy is open to some question. First, there are problems with *geographical coverage*. Basically, the conventions limit their definition of piracy to areas of the high seas or "place[s] outside the jurisdiction of any State."[11] Piratical attacks in *internal waters* and *territorial seas* are clearly outside convention coverage, while it may be debated whether the State control allowed under art. 33 places the *contiguous zone* within the jurisdiction of a State,[12] or how arts. 55 and 56, dealing with the *exclusive economic zone*, impact the piracy articles.[13] While article 86 appears to limit the application of Part VII's High Seas provisions in this area, article 58 (2) states that "[a]rticles 88-115 and other pertinent rules of international law apply to the exclusive economic zone in so far as they are not incompatible with this Part."[14]

As has been noted before, the piracy articles (100-107 in the 1982 Convention) are also unclear as to what constitutes an "illegal act," how to define the "private ends" which are required for the crime to have occurred, and whether piracy may occur on board a single vessel.

> In considering "acts of violence or detention," are these to be defined and tested under *municipal* or *international* law? If the latter, it is clear that many actions could remain unpunished because of a lack of the necessary "universality." Should we worry if different countries apply different interpretations? To what degree would it even be *possible* to prosecute the crime before an international tribunal? Now, "private ends." The Conventions require this for piracy to have been committed. Not only do we have the same question as to whether this is to be determined by State or by international law, but on it hangs whether some forms of maritime terrorism may be covered by the Conventions.
>
> The ... problem occurs if a "political act" falls outside the definition's requirement of "private ends." But an act or crime is hardly deemed "political," simply because the perpetrator so characterizes it. Nor is it logical that a person once labeled an "insurgent" could never commit acts "for private ends." .... Similarly, an act may have *both* a political and private nature. What appears to be needed, therefore, is a balancing test, in which actions are *strictly* weighed against political objectives. .... Nor should the fulcrum of the decision be the mind of the terrorist; it should be the mind of the judge weighing the facts.[15]
>
> A particular problem under this is how do we treat *ecologically-inspired* violence? Some of you may recall the activities of Sea Shepherd against pirate whalers, but let's not forget that Greenpeace itself has been found guilty of actions falling under the definition of "piracy."[16] If the Somalis, as some of them claim, are reacting against depredations inflicted on their fishing resources, does that make their acts any less piratical?[17]

---

[11] Convention on the Law of the Sea, Montego Bay, Jamaica, December 10, 1982, art. 101(a) (i) and (ii).
[12] *See id.*, art. 33.
[13] *See id.*, arts. 55, 56.
[14] *Id.*, art. 58 (2).
[15] S.P. Menefee, *supra* note 8, at 60.
[16] *See generally* Samuel Pyeatt Menefee, *The Case of the Castle John, or Greenbeard the Pirate?: Environmentalism, Piracy and the Development of International Law*, 24 CAL. W. Int'l L.J. (1993), 1-16.
[17] Samuel Pyeatt Menefee, "Piracy 101: A 'Nuts and Bolts" Approach to the Subject" (paper delivered on January 8, 2009 at 2009 Annual Meeting of the American Association of Law Schools, San Diego, California).

The "One Ship/Two Ships Controversy" I mentioned refers to Article 101 of the 1982 Convention, which states that illegal acts of violence committed for private ends are piracy when directed,

i. on the high seas, against *another* ship or aircraft, or against persons or property on board such ship or aircraft;
ii. against a ship, aircraft, persons, or property in a place outside the jurisdiction of any State.[18]

The two parts of this are not entirely parallel; the first suggests the necessary presence of *two* vessels (so that mutinies without an outside vessel assisting could not be piracy), while the second does not. While it has been argued that the second part was meant to cover Antarctica and perhaps a few unclaimed drying reefs, it seems obvious that the "high seas" is also a place "outside the jurisdiction of any state," and that the clear meaning of part two could cover single sip mutinies on the high seas. Any other reading would mean that seizures such as that of the *Santa Maria* or the *Achille Lauro* could not be considered piracy.[19]

External factors have also undercut the conventions' usefulness. Sometimes, necessary "enabling legislation" has not been put in place. In the case of the *Alondra Rainbow* hijacking, a problem noted by Prof. P.K. Mukherjee was, "that even though India is a party to the [1982] Convention, it had not given effect to it through national legislation that it is bound to do being a dualistic state."[20] On other occasions, there appears to have been a *stretch* to place actions under the Convention's piracy provisions; it was successfully used, for example by a Belgian court, to find *Greenpeace* guilty of piracy in its protests aboard the *Castle John*.[21]

III. The Convention for the Suppression of Unlawful Acts Against the Safety of Maritime Navigation (1988) [SUA Convention] and Protocol

The SUA Convention of 1988 and its Protocol, dealing with fixed platforms, was one result of the hijack of the *Achille Lauro* in 1985. Rather than including unlawful acts against the safety of maritime navigation within the concept of international piracy, it followed what Prof. Tullio Treves has called a "sectorial approach," "identifying particular offenses … and working out specific international instruments for their suppression."[22] Rear Admiral Baumgartner of the USCG has described the agreement as "designed to ensure that appropriate action is taken against persons committing unlawful acts against ships, including, among other acts, the seizure of ships by force; acts of violence against persons onboard

[18] Convention on the Law of the Sea, *supra* note 10, art. 101 (emphasis added).
[19] Samuel Pyeatt Menefee, "Piracy 101," *supra* note 16.
[20] Proshanto K. Mukherjee, *A legal commentary on the Alondra Rainbow judgment*, MAXIMO Q. MEJIA, JR. AND JINGING XU EDS., COASTAL ZONE PIRACY AND OTHER UNLAWFUL ACTS AT SEA 272 (2007).
[21] Samuel Pyeatt Menefee, *supra* note 15, at 1-16.
[22] SAMUEL PYEATT MENEFEE, CONTEMPORARY PIRACY AND INTERNATIONAL LAW 46 (1995).

ships; and the placing of devices on board a ship which are likely to destroy or damage it."[23] While the Convention was focused on the problem of maritime terrorism rather than piracy, its act-specific nature covers both areas. A revision, which added additional acts, was a response to the attack on the World Trade Center, but it did not materially affect coverage of problems related to piracy.

More recently, the prosecute or extradite provisions of SUA have proved particularly useful in connection with piracies off the Horn of Africa; it has been noted that, except for Ethiopia, Eritrea, and Somalia, all States within a thousand nautical miles of the Gulf of Aden are signatories to the Convention.[24]

IV. Relevant Bilateral and Multilateral Treaties, Conventions, and Arrangements Dealing with Piracy

Other treaties and conventions have also arguably played a role in piracy frameworks. First, research into historical bilateral treaties which touch *directly* on piracy appears show some which are still in force with applicable provisions on the subject. Equally useful are those agreements which *indirectly* relate to the crime; elsewhere the connection between hostage-taking and agreements dealing with the slave trade has been discussed.[25] These have been underutilized to date, but appear to be important tools in the fight against piracy.

A regional trans-boundary agreement with importance for the field covers the Straits of Malacca.[26] This appears to be a useful model for other areas fighting the problem. Also relevant in this regard is the Regional Cooperation Agreement on Combating Piracy and Armed Robbery Against Ships in Asia (ReCAAP), which came into force in 2006 and which has been evaluated and critiqued elsewhere.[27] Finally there is the Djibouti Code of Conduct, adopted on January 29th, 2009, which deals with piracy and armed robbery against ships in the Western Indian Ocean and Gulf of Aden.[28] Spatial constraints prevent a more in-depth discussion of these, but they are clearly important legal frameworks which should be taken into consideration.

---

[23] "Statement of RADM William Baumgartner on International Piracy on the High Seas before the Subcommittee on Coast Guard & Maritime Transportation, Committee on Transportation & Infrastructure, U.S. House of Representatives, February 4, 2009," <<http://www.findthatdoc.com/search-74230188-hPDF/download-documents-hoa-testimony-radm-william-baumgartner-uscg-pdf.htm>> (visited February 3, 2013).

[24] *Id.*

[25] Samuel Pyeatt Menefee, *Terrorism and the slave trade: an analogy*, MAXIMO Q. MEJIA, JR. and JINGJING XU, *supra* note 18, at 61-78.

[26] *See* SAMUEL PYEATT MENEFEE, *supra* note 21, at 60-62.

[27] Samuel Pyeatt Menefee, *A Recap of RECAAP*, in MAXIMO Q. MEJIA, ED., MARITIME SECURITY AND CRIME, at 187-99 (2010).

[28] IMO Council Doc. C 102/14 Annex (2009). See also <http://oceansbeyondpiracy.org/matrix/activity/djibouti-code-conduct> (visited 27 Jan 2013).

V. RELEVANT UNITED NATIONS RESOLUTIONS

Finally, something must be said about some of the relevant UN resolutions. Piracy initially came before the United Nations General Assembly in 1954, when the Soviet Bloc complained about Republic of China (Taiwanese) searches of vessels bound for Mainland (PRC) ports, which they deemed "piratical" in nature. The final result was a resolution on "freedom of navigation"[29] which passed the problem on to the International Law Commission and eventually resulted, several years down the road in the piracy provisions of the Convention on the High Seas.[30] The problem of piracy again came to the fore with piratical attacks against the Vietnamese Boat People.[31] On December 14, 1981, United Nations General Assembly Resolution 36/125 called for "greater international efforts in the suppression of piracy on the high seas, in accordance with their international obligations, and to take appropriate action to protect asylum seekers from acts of violence at sea."[32] In 1985, after the hijack of the *Achille Lauro*, General Assembly Resolution 40/61 included a paragraph requesting the IMO "to study the problem of terrorism on board or against ships 'with a view to making recommendations on appropriate measures,'"[33] which led in turn to the 1988 SUA Convention and Protocol.[34]

By the late 1990's, in part because of the actions of IMO, piracy came to feature more commonly in resolutions, routinely appearing in those dealing with oceans and the law of the sea. In General Assembly Resolution 53/32 (1999), for example, sections 22 and 23:

> 22. *Urges* all States, in particular coastal States in affected regions, to take all necessary and appropriate measures to prevent and combat incidents of piracy and armed robbery at sea and to investigate or cooperate in the investigation of such incidents wherever they occur and bring the alleged perpetrators to justice, in accordance with international law;
> 23. *Calls upon* States to cooperate fully with the International Maritime Organization to combat piracy and armed robbery against ships, including by submitting reports or incidents to that organization ....[35]

This was followed by a Resolution in 2000, which built upon the former sections, and urged "regional cooperation,"[36] as well as calling for States

> to implement the International Maritime Organization guidelines on preventing attacks of piracy and armed robbery and to cooperate with the International Maritime Organization Correspondence Group, established to draw up standard guidelines for Governments in investigating attacks against ships and prosecuting offenders, and with other initiatives of the organization in this area ....[37]

---

[29] United Nations General Assembly Resolution 821 (IX) (1954).

[30] *See infra*; SAMUEL PYEATT MENEFEE, *supra* note 21, at 9-26.

[31] *See generally*, Samuel Pyeatt Menefee, *Piracy and the Vietnamese Boat People: A Retrospective*," in MAXIMO Q. MEJIA, ED., *supra* note 26, at 49-104.

[32] United Nations General Assembly Resolution 36/125, A/RES/36/125 (1981); SAMUEL PYEATT MENEFEE, *supra* note 21 at 39-40.

[33] United Nations General Assembly Resolution 40/61, A/RES/40/61 (1985); SAMUEL PYEATT MENEFEE, *supra* note 21, at 43.

[34] *See infra*.

[35] United Nations General Assembly Resolution 53/32, A/RES/53/32 (1999), §22, 23.

[36] United Nations General Assembly Resolution 54/31, A/RES/54/31, §22 (2000). *See also id*., §20.

[37] *Id*., §21.

Additionally, it urged "States to become parties to the Convention for the Suppression of Unlawful Acts against the Safety of Maritime Navigation and its Protocol, and to ensure its effective implementation ...."[38] Resolution 55/7 of the following year reiterated most of these points,[39] as did 56/12 (2001), under a section on piracy and armed robbery.[40] In 2003, the relevant materials were placed under maritime safety and security,[41] and they have generally been filed under similarly less-controversial titles since.[42]

As early as May 10, 2006, the United Nations Security Council expressed concern over "the increasing incidents of piracy and armed robbery against ships in waters off the coast of Somalia, and its impact on security in Somalia ...."[43] A similar worry was detailed in Resolution 1801 (2008),[44] which encouraged

> Member States whose naval vessels and military aircraft operate in international waters and airspace adjacent to the coast of Somalia to be vigilant to any incidents of piracy therein and to take appropriate action to protect merchant shipping, in particular the transportation of humanitarian aid, against any such act, in line with relevant international law, and *welcomes* the contribution made by France to protect the World Food Programme naval convoys and the support now provided by Denmark to this end ....[45]

Both of these resolutions considered piracy as one of several factors in the "situation in Somalia."[46]

Resolution 1816, of June 2, 2008, was the first Security Council action to concentrate *exclusively* on piracy and armed robbery at sea. Based on authority granted by Chapter VII of the Charter, this:

> 1. *Condemns and deplores* all acts of piracy and armed robbery against vessels in territorial waters and the high seas off the coast of Somalia;
> 2. *Urges* States whose naval vessels and military aircraft operate on the high seas and airspace off the coast of Somalia to be vigilant to acts of piracy and armed robbery and, in this context, *encourages*, in particular, States interested in the use of commercial maritime routes off the coast of Somalia, to increase and coordinate their

[38] *Id.*, §23.

[39] *See* United Nations General Assembly Resolution 55/7, A/RES/55/7, §§33-35 (2001).

[40] *See* United Nations General Assembly Resolution 56/12, A/RES/56/12, §§29-32 (2001).

[41] *See* United Nations General Assembly Resolution 57/141, A/RES/57/141, §§26-29 (2003).

[42] *See* United Nations General Assembly Resolution 58/240, A/RES/58/240, §§36-38 (2004) (safety of navigation and flag state implementation); 59/24, A/RES/59/24, §§47-48, 50-51 (2005); 60/30, A/RES/60/30, §§50-53 (2006) (maritime safety and security and flag state implementation); 61/222, A/RES/61/222, §§57-60 (2007); 62/215, A/RES/62/215, §§61-68 (2008); 63/111, A/RES/63/111, §§61-71, 73-75 (2009); 64/71, A/RES/64/71, §§68-90 (2010); 65/37, A/RES/65/37, §§74-75, 81-103 (2011), and 66/231, A/RES/66/231, §§72-74, 80-105 (2012).

[43] United Nations Security Council Resolution 1676, S/RES/1676 (2006).

[44] United Nations Security Council Resolution 1801, S/RES/1801 (2008), which stressed concern "at the upsurge in piracy off the Somali coast described in paragraph 22 of the Secretary-General's report, and *recalling* the joint communiqué of the International Maritime Organization and the World Food Programme of 10 July 2007 ...."

[45] *Id.*, §12.

[46] *See also* United Nations Security Council Resolution 1814, S/RES/1814, §11 (2008), which reiterated the Security Council's support "for the contribution made by some States to protect the World Food Programme maritime convoys" and called upon States and regional organizations, "to take action to protect shipping involved with the transportation and delivery of humanitarian aid to Somalia and United Nations-authorized activities ...."

efforts to deter acts of piracy and armed robbery at sea in cooperation with the TFG [Transitional Federal Government];

3. *Urges* all States to cooperate with each other, with the IMO and, as appropriate, with the relevant regional organizations in connection with, and share information about, acts of piracy and armed robbery in the territorial waters and on the high seas off the coast of Somalia, and to render assistance to vessels threatened by or under attack by pirates or armed robbers, in accordance with relevant international law;
4. *Further urges* States to work in cooperation with interested organizations, including the IMO, to ensure that vessels entitled to fly their flag receive appropriate guidance and training on avoidance, evasion, and defensive techniques and to avoid the area whenever possible;
5. *Calls upon* States and interested organizations, including the IMO, to provide technical assistance to Somalia and nearby coastal States upon their request to enhance the capacity of these States to ensure coastal and maritime security, including combating piracy and armed robbery off the Somali and nearby coastlines;
6. *Affirms* that the measures imposed by paragraph 5 of resolution 733 (1992) and further elaborated upon by paragraphs 1 and 2 of resolution 1425 (2002) do not apply to supplies of technical assistance to Somalia solely for the purposes set out in paragraph 5 above which have been exempted from those measures in accordance with the procedure set out in paragraphs 11 (b) and 12 of resolution 1772 (2007);
7. *Decides* that for a period of six months from the date of this resolution, States cooperating with the TFG in the fight against piracy and armed robbery at sea off the coast of Somalia, for which advance notification has been provided by the TFG to the Secretary-General, may:

a) Enter the territorial waters of Somalia for the purpose of repressing acts of piracy and armed robbery at sea, in a manner consistent with such action permitted on the high seas with respect to piracy under relevant international law; and
b) Use, within the territorial waters of Somalia, in a manner consistent with action permitted on the high seas with respect to piracy under relevant international law, all necessary means to repress acts of piracy and armed robbery;

8. *Requests* that cooperating states take appropriate steps to ensure that the activities they undertake pursuant to the authorization in paragraph 7 do not have the practical effect of denying or impairing the right of innocent passage to the ships of any third State;
9. *Affirms* that the authorization provided in this resolution applies only with respect to the situation in Somalia and shall not affect the rights or obligations or responsibilities of member states under international law, including any rights or obligations under the Convention, with respect to any other situation, and underscores in particular that shall not be considered as establishing customary international law, and affirms further that this authorization has been provided only following receipt of the letter from the Permanent Representative of the Somalia Republic to the United Nations to the President of the Security Council dated 27 February 2008 conveying the consent of the TFG;
10. *Calls upon* States to coordinate their actions with other participating States taken pursuant to paragraphs 5 and 7 above;
11. *Calls upon* all States, and in particular flag, port and coastal States, States of the nationality of victims and perpetrators of piracy and armed robbery, and other States with relevant jurisdiction under international law and national legislation, to

cooperate in determining jurisdiction, and in the investigation and prosecution of persons responsible for acts of piracy and armed robbery off the coast of Somalia, consistent with applicable international law including international human rights law, and to render assistance by, among other actions, providing disposition and logistics assistance with respect to persons under their jurisdiction and control, such victims and witnesses and persons detained as a result of operations conducted under this resolution;

12. *Requests* States cooperating with the TFG to inform the Security Council within 3 months of the progress of actions undertaken in the exercise of the authority provided in paragraph 7 above;
13. *Requests* the Secretary-General to report to the Security Council within 5 months of adoption of this resolution on the implementation of this resolution and on the situation with respect to piracy and armed robbery in territorial waters and the high seas off the coast of Somalia;
14. *Requests* the Secretary-General of the IMO to brief the Council on the basis of cases brought to his attention by the agreement of all affected coastal states, and duly taking into account the existing bilateral and regional cooperative arrangements, on the situation with respect to piracy and armed robbery;
15. *Expresses* its intention to review the situation and consider, as appropriate, renewing the authority provided in paragraph 7 above for additional periods upon the request of the TFG;
16. *Decides* to remain seized of the matter.[47]

Resolution 1838, which followed on October 7th, called on States to deploy naval vessels and military aircraft "on the high seas off the coast of Somalia,"[48] and called for them to "continue to take action to protect the World Food Programme maritime convoys, which is [sic; are] vital to bring humanitarian assistance to the affected populations in Somalia …."[49] It further urged States "to issue to ships entitled to fly their flag, as necessary, advice and guidance on appropriate precautionary measures to protect themselves from attack or actions to take if under attack or the threat of attack when sailing in waters off the coast of Somalia …."[50] While Resolution 1844 (November 20, 2008) only touched on piracy,[51] Resolution 1846 of December 2nd, extended for one year the period that States and regional organizations could enter into Somali waters to repress piracy,[52] and urged use of the SUA Convention in prosecuting the offenders.[53] Security Council Resolution 1851, which was adopted on December 16, 2008, "[*f*]*urther encourages* all states [sic] and regional organizations fighting piracy and armed robbery at sea off the coast of Somalia to consider creating a centre in the region to coordinate information relevant to piracy and armed robbery at sea off the coast of Somalia …."[54]

---

[47] United Nations Security Council Resolution 1816, *supra* note 1.
[48] United Nations Security Council Resolution 1838, S/RES/1838 (2008), §2.
[49] *Id.*, §5.
[50] *Id.*, §6.
[51] United Nations Security Council Resolution 1844, S/RES/1844 (2008).
[52] United Nations Security Council Resolution 1846, S/RES/1846 (2008), §10.
[53] *Id.*, §15.
[54] United Nations Security Council Resolution 1851, *supra* note 1, §5.

In 2009, Resolution 1897, passed on November 30, "[r]*enews* its call upon States and regional organizations" to participate in the fight against piracy by "deploying naval vessels, arms and military aircraft and through seizures and dispersion of boats, vessels, arms and other related equipment used in the commission of piracy and armed robbery at sea off the coast of Somalia, or for which there are reasonable grounds for suspecting such use ...."[55] Specifically it invited:

> ...all States and regional organizations fighting piracy off the coast of Somalia to conclude special agreements or arrangements with countries willing to take custody of pirates in order to embark law enforcement officials ("shipriders") from the latter countries, in particular countries in the region, to facilitate the investigation and prosecution of persons detained as a result of operations conducted under this resolution for acts of piracy and armed robbery at sea off the coast of Somalia, provided that the advance consent of the TFG [Transitional Federal Government] is obtained for the exercise of third state jurisdiction by shipriders in Somali territorial waters and that such agreements or arrangements do not prejudice the effective implementation of the SUA Convention ...[56]

The role of outside states and organizations in anti-piracy operations in Somali waters was again renewed,[57] and a specific call was made "to bring to justice those who are using Somali territory to plan, facilitate, or undertake criminal acts of piracy and armed robbery at sea," noting "that any measures undertaken pursuant to this paragraph shall be consistent with applicable international human rights law ...."[58]

In April of 2010, Resolution 1918 dealt with the prosecution of individuals charged with piracy, affirming that "the failure to prosecute persons responsible for acts of piracy and armed robbery at sea off the coast of Somalia undermines anti-piracy efforts of the international community,"[59] and calling "*on* all States, including States in the region, to criminalize piracy under their domestic law and favourably consider the prosecution of suspected, and imprisonment of convicted, pirates apprehended off the coast of Somalia, consistent with applicable international human rights law ...."[60] November of that year saw, among other actions, a resolution reaffirming interest in several options for prosecuting suspected pirates.[61]

The year 2011 saw several Security Council resolutions dealing with piracy. In April, Resolution 1976 encouraged States and regional organizations "to assist Somalia and other States of the region in strengthening their counter-piracy law enforcement capacities, including implementation of anti-money-laundering laws, [and] the establishment of Financial Investigation Units and strengthening forensic capacities ...."[62] There was also increased emphasis on court-related activity. The resolution welcomed "the readiness of the national and regional administrations of Somalia to cooperate with each other and with States who have prosecuted suspected pirates with a view to enabling convicted pirates to be

[55] United Nations Security Council Resolution 1897, S/RES/1897 (2009), §3.
[56] *Id.*, §6.
[57] *Id.*, §7.
[58] *Id.*, §11.
[59] United Nations Security Council Resolution 1918, S/RES/1918 (2010), §1.
[60] *Id.*, §2.
[61] United Nations Security Council Resolution 1950, S/RES/1950 (2010), §14 (citing S/2010/394).
[62] United Nations Security Council Resolution 1976, S/RES/1976 (2011), §17.

repatriated back to Somalia under suitable prisoner transfer agreements,"[63] urged the construction of additional prisons in Puntland and Somaliland,[64] "[r]*equests* the TFG, with the assistance of UNODC, to elaborate and adopt a complete set of counter-piracy laws,"[65] and decided "to urgently consider the establishment of specialized Somali courts to try suspected pirates both in Somalia and in the region, including an extraterritorial Somali specialized anti-piracy court ...."[66] An October 24th Resolution (2015) appears to have been spurred both by the continuing problem of hostage-taking and by the general failure to prosecute captured pirates.[67] *Inter alia* this:

> 7. *Reiterates* its request, as a matter of urgency, to the TFG and relevant Somali regional authorities to elaborate, with the assistance of UNODC and UNDP, and adopt a complete set of counter-piracy laws, including laws to prosecute those who illicitly finance, plan, organize, facilitate or profit from pirate attacks, with a view to ensuring the effective prosecution of suspected pirates and those associated with piracy attacks in Somalia, the post-conviction transfer of pirates prosecuted elsewhere to Somalia, and the imprisonment of convicted pirates in Somalia, as soon as possible, and *strongly urges* the TFG and regional authorities of Somalia to expeditiously address any other existing obstacles that impede progress in this regard ....
> 8. *Calls upon* UNODC, UNDP and other international partners to further their efforts to support the development of domestic legislation, agreements and mechanisms that would allow the effective prosecution of suspected pirates, and the transfer and imprisonment of convicted pirates ....[68]

Security Council Resolution 2020, passed on November 22nd, 2011, in addition to reiterating many of the measures it had previously called for, stressed the need "for a comprehensive response to repress piracy and tackle its underlying causes by the international community ...."[69] Most recently, the matter was again addressed on November 21, 2012, by Resolution 2077.[70]

CONCLUSION

What may be gleaned from this quick tour of some of the international legal frameworks of piracy law? First, that they are *frameworks*, rather than a single superstructure; time should not be wasted trying to uselessly fit everything into one neat puzzle, but we should take advantage of what each of these legal tools has to offer.

---

[63] *Id.*, §21.
[64] *Id.*, §22.
[65] *Id.*, §23.
[66] *Id.*, §26. *See also id.*, §25, which supports "the ongoing efforts by regional States in the development of anti-piracy courts or chambers in the region ...."
[67] *See* United Nations Security Council Resolution 2015, S/RES/2015 (2011). *See also* United Nations Security Council Resolution 2020, S/RES/2020 (2011) ("*Further recognizing* that pirates are turning increasingly to kidnapping and hostage-taking, and that these activities help generate funding to purchase weapons, gain recruits, and continue their operational activities ....").
[68] United Nations Security Council Resolution 2015, *supra* note 66, §§7-8. *See also id.*, §§16-17.
[69] United Nations Security Council Resolution 2020, *supra* note 66, §2.
[70] United Nations Security Council Resolution 2077, S/RES/2077 (2012).

Customary law is perhaps the most underutilized area of those we have considered. Scholars need to put more effort into evaluating national and regional rules and practices dealing with piracy which may provide evidence of custom and then publicize the results of their studies for further discussion.

The 1958 and 1982 Conventions provide a universal, if limited, approach to the problem of piracy. Here, emphasis should be placed not only on ratifications, but on adoption into national law where this is necessary. Where appropriate, State parties should be urged to use these provisions as a cause of action for prosecuting pirates.

The SUA Convention and its Protocol on Fixed Platforms are essentially involved with vessel control and hostage-taking situations rather than piracy. This does not mean that they are inapplicable, but rather that their emphasis is on specific *acts* rather than categories such as piracy. The recent problems off the Horn of Africa suggest an area in which greater utilization of these agreements might play a major role in the struggle against piracy and maritime violence.

Several bilateral and multilateral treaties, conventions, and other arrangements have relevance for piracy's international legal frameworks, although more historical research remains to be done on this matter. There is no question, however, that the trans-boundary agreement for the Straits of Malacca sets an example for other regions under threat, or that the ReCaap Agreement might be replicated in African contexts. Similarly, agreements concerning suppression of the slave trade might find applicability in some of today's maritime hostage situations.

The General Assembly and the Security Council have a mixed history of dealing with piracy. There is no question, however, that their activities have resulted in increasing involvement with the topic, a trend which may be expected to continue. The recent Security Council resolutions concerning the situation in Somalia might, at first glance, appear to be a remedy specifically tailored to a single regional situation. The lack of control which Somalia has over its own territory and maritime waters is probably unique in today's world, while the temporal restrictions in the resolutions, not to mention the attempts to prevent them from becoming customary international law might suggest that they are a "one-off," whose only bearing is on the current situation in Somalia. This, however, too quickly dismisses their impact. Certainly those who inserted the "non-customary international law" language did not see the resolutions' potential as limited. A better analogy might be to raindrops running down a car's windscreen. While they land on different areas of glass, many subsequently course down the same channels as their predecessors. Similarly, while each World Court case is decided on its own facts, it is hard to believe that the judges do not use similar *methods of evaluation* for similar matters. If this is the case, it makes sense that, with this "Raindrop Approach," the Somali Resolutions will serve as a starting point – even if an *unacknowledged* one – for future Security Council actions dealing with piracy. Similarly, there has been a tendency for those sections of Security Council resolutions dealing with maritime piracy to become longer and more comprehensive over time to more accurately focus on the evolving problem. This "Snowball Approach" suggests that future international regulation in the area will continue to accrete, creating a larger corpus of regulation.

Finally, mention should be made of the Comité Maritime International's draft law on piracy and maritime crimes of violence.[71] This is an NGO attempt to influence *national* legislation on the subject which represents a move toward the *standardization* of State responses toward these crimes, and it, too, may be the beginning of something bigger.

[71] "Maritime criminal acts – draft guidelines for national legislation," submitted by the Comité Maritime International to the International Maritime Organization, 15 August 15, 2007," <<http://www.comitemaritime.org/Uploads/LEG93-12-1%20(2).pdf >> (accessed February 3, 2013).

In: Selected Issues in Maritime Law and Policy
Editor: Maximo Q. Mejia, Jr.

ISBN: 978-1-62618-508-1

Chapter 11

ECONOMIC DEVELOPMENT, POLITICAL STABILITY, AND MARITIME PIRACY: EXPLORING THE LINKAGES*

Maximo Q. Mejia Jr.†
Professor, Maritime Law and Policy, World Maritime University

1. INTRODUCTION

Nam pirata non est ex perduellium numero definitus, sed communis hostis omnium; cum hoc nec fides debet nec ius iurandum esse commune.

- Marcus Tullius Cicero, De officiis, 44 BC [1]

Except for brief interregna, piracy has been the *bête noire* of shipping since the inception of seaborne commerce – a constant criminal challenge to efficient maritime trade. Throughout the ages, it has taken different shapes and forms and threatened different seas and coastlines. The modern phenomenon of piracy at sea can be surveyed as different types and modus operandi starting with, *inter alia*, the pirate attacks against the boat people of Vietnam in 1970s, the Lebanese deviations of the 1980s, South China Sea piracy in the 1980s and 1990s, the Malacca Straits and Indonesian waters in the 1990s and 2000s, Latin American container theft in the 2000s, and finally Somalia and West Africa in the current decade.

Between January 1991 and December 2012, more than 6,000 robberies and violent attacks against merchant vessels have been reported to the International Maritime Bureau (IMB) of the International Chamber of Commerce (ICC) [2]. IMB publishes data and information relating to piracy attacks four times a year – a first quarter report, a second quarter report, a third quarter report, and an annual report [3].

---

* This chapter is an updated and slightly modified version of a report prepared by the author for the Swedish Maritime Administration, to which the author retains copyright against future publication.

† Email: mm@wmu.se

An analysis of the IMB data shows an increasing trend in the number of incidents against ships worldwide since 1991. Though there are peaks and valleys throughout the more than twenty years of reports, it can be said that the annual numbers have remained within the range of 200 to 500. That the early 1990s show only a low level of reporting does not necessarily mean that there were significantly less attacks in the past. One could speculate that it was a period when shipping had yet to get used to the idea of reporting attacks to a piracy-reporting centre. One can only hope that we have since arrived at a point where the statistics offer more meaningful information.

The data also shows how the centre of gravity has shifted in terms of the number of attacks reported, from Southeast Asia to the Horn of Africa. From the mid-1990s to the 2000s, piracy and armed robbery against ships were concentrated in the Far East, particularly the waters of the South China Sea, the Straits of Malacca, and the littoral states. Between 2006 and 2007, just when the number of Southeast Asian incidents started to wane, the number of reports relating to Somali piracy began to rise dramatically.

The increasing number of incidents off the coast of Somalia is alarming and disturbing. The *modus operandi* employed by Somali pirates differs markedly from those found in the Far East. In Southeast Asia, the principal motive of piracy and armed robbery against ships has been to steal personal valuables, cart away supplies and equipment, and to plunder the cargo – whether on a relatively small or a grand scale. Southeast Asian pirates did not hesitate to use violence when necessary. In comparison, historically, the object of Somali pirates has been to exert some effort to keep the ship's condition, the crew's health, and the cargo intact in order to retain a strong bargaining position when negotiating for the ransom payment. However, the annual IMB reports for 2011 and 2012 reveal that Somali pirates have become increasingly aggressive and violent towards their captives in the past two years.

1.1. Use of the Word *Piracy* in this Chapter

Academics tend to discuss the definition of piracy *ad infinitum*. It is, as Murphy writes, "a slippery concept [4]" that defies accurate and incontestable definition. There is a definition under the Law of the Sea Convention, a marine insurance definition, domestic law definitions, a customary international law definition, etc. For purposes of this chapter, unless specifically otherwise qualified, the word piracy is used in its broadest layman's connotation, i.e., an act of robbery or criminal violence against ships, crew, or passengers.

1.2. Objective of this Chapter

The objective of this chapter is to explore piracy's linkages and the challenges it presents to development and security. After the introductory part, this chapter is followed by three more parts: Part II which examines the nexus between piracy, security, and development, by looking at issues such as the millennium development goals, the concept of failed states, fishery resources, and effects on emergency-relief and development aid; Part III which briefly surveys select international and regional issues related to piracy such as the cost to seaborne trade, legal aspects, regional security, United Nations (UN) and International Maritime

Organization (IMO) initiatives, and the Djibouti Code of Conduct; and, finally, Part IV which contains the concluding remarks.

2. The Piracy-Security-Development Nexus

> For those who now live in more stable neighbourhoods, it may seem incomprehensible how prosperity in high-income countries and a sophisticated global economy can coexist with extreme violence and misery in other parts of the globe. The pirates operating off the coast of Somalia who prey on the shipping through the Gulf of Aden illustrate the paradox of the existing global system. How is it that the combined prosperity and capability of the world's modern nation-states cannot prevent a problem from antiquity?
>
> - The World Bank, 2011 [5]

It is widely accepted that only a combination of a multitude of factors – rather than any isolated reason – can begin to fully explain why piracy occurs. Among these many factors, writers invariably include the level of poverty, economic hardship, and socio-political instability as common features explaining the incidence of piracy in affected areas [6]. Nincic writes, for instance, "Maritime piracy frequently has its roots in weak or fragile states, where humanitarian conditions are dire and economic opportunities are limited [7]." According to Baird, "The economic hardship in Somalia and absence of an effective legal regime or enforcement agency has meant anyone who could get their hands on a boat could become a pirate, and many have done so [8]."

Perhaps because the link between economic development, socio-political stability/security, and piracy is seen as self-evident, there does not seem to be a great deal of effort into investigating the connection. One such study, by Mejia, Cariou, and Wolff [9], inquires into this potential relationship by observing changes in the economic and socio-political situations attending 152 countries during the period 1996-2008 using the following indicators: (a) the real GDP per capita in 2005 dollars, from the Economic Research Service of the US Department of Agriculture; and (b) political rights and civil liberties indicators reported by Freedom House [10], an independent watchdog organization that supports the expansion of freedom around the world. Figure 18.6 in that study represents the relationship between the real GDP per capita and the number of attacks reported within a particular country's waters from 1996 to 2008. The chart "suggests that a strong, decreasing relationship exists between the economic development of a country expressed in GDP per capita and the number of attacks reported in a given year [11]."

This finding is reinforced by an associated calculation (Figure 18.7 in Mejia et al. [12]) where the 152 countries were divided into three groups according to the number of attacks reported in a given year: (a) no attacks, (b) 1-5 attacks, and (c) more than 5 attacks. According to this calculation, the mean GDP per capita from 1996 to 2008 for countries with no attacks is USD 10,885, with 1-5 attacks is USD 4,430, and for countries with more than 5 attacks is USD 1,836.

Table 1. Mean score for political rights and civil liberties indicators for countries with either 0, or more than 5, piracy attacks

	Mean score		
	Political rights	**Civil liberties**	**Freedom status**
Countries with no piracy attacks	3.01	3.02	1.71
Countries with more than 5 piracy attacks	3.67	3.96	2.19

Tabulated from data in Mejia, Cariou, Wolff, "Piracy in shipping," p. 363.

To test the relationship between piracy and political rights and civil liberties indicators, Mejia et al. compared the mean for two extremes categories, i.e., countries with 0 and countries with more than 5 attacks. The analysis showed a tendency for countries of the former category to score better in the indicators than countries of the latter category, as presented in Table 1.

To complement the above, Mejia et al. compared the trend in the number of attacks (divided by 100), real GDP per capita (divided by 1,000), political rights, civil liberties, and freedom status (divided by 10) for four locations that showed the highest number of piracy attacks during the period 1996-2008, namely Indonesia, Bangladesh, Nigeria, and Somalia. In the case of Indonesia, the analysis shows that the reduction in the number of attacks over time coincided with improvements in per capita GDP as well as political rights and civil liberties indicators, thus confirming the potential relationship between economic and socio-political conditions and the likelihood of piracy attacks.

This is reinforced in the case of Bangladesh, exhibiting a potential negative relationship between economic and socio-political factors and piracy, though mitigated in the case of Nigeria where the indicators and number of attacks seem to move together. Finally, Somalia represents a situation where attacks are increasing dramatically as the already undesirable levels of economic and socio-political development remain stagnant from 1996 to 2008. The study by Mejia, Cariou, and Wolff supports what has long been postulated by a number of writers – the link between the incidences of piracy attacks on the one hand, and economic and socio-political instability on the other.

2.1. MDGs and Piracy

The millennium development goals (MDGs) are the world's time-bound and quantified targets for addressing extreme poverty and basic human rights in their many dimensions. They consist of eight international development goals with 21 measurable targets that all 193 United Nations member states and at least 23 international organizations have agreed to achieve by the year 2015. The MDGs were officially established following the Millennium Summit in 2000, where all world leaders present adopted the United Nations Millennium

Declaration. The MDGs are designed to encourage development by improving social and economic conditions in the world's poorest countries [13]. The eight MDGs are:

- Goal 1: Eradicate extreme poverty and hunger
- Goal 2: Achieve universal primary education
- Goal 3: Promote gender equality and empower women
- Goal 4: Reduce child mortality rates
- Goal 5: Improve maternal health
- Goal 6: Combat HIV/AIDS, malaria, and other diseases
- Goal 7: Ensure environmental sustainability
- Goal 8: Develop a global partnership for development

According to the World Bank, "No low-income fragile or conflict-affected country has yet achieved a single MDG [14]." Indeed, four of the six countries worst affected by the problem of piracy – Bangladesh, Somalia, Tanzania, and Yemen – are low-income fragile countries [15].

In its 2010 report on MDG progress, Somalia declares that it is unlikely to meet all but one of the eight goals [16]. In its conclusions, the report mentions that, "There is insufficient data to plot progress of Somalia's MDGs, but the country is predicted to be seriously off track in them. With the current political instability it is unlikely that Somalia will reverse this pattern in the near future [17]."

In a separate MDG report, the Somali regional government of Puntland notes "constraints for generating productive and decent work for youth due to lack or limited skills, education and low income opportunities" which in essence "discourage some of them in joining community peace building and country reconstruction but rather cause more youth to participate in clan conflicts, pirate groups or joining illegal militia forces." The Puntland report indicates "Attraction of many youth to piracy activities in the high seas for earning quick wealth and money" as one of the major challenges in meeting the region's MDGs [18]. The situation is not alleviated by the fact that some in the local community are willing to cash in on piracy operations. Local elites share in ransom revenues and therefore leave pirates undisturbed as they negotiate payment. Other inhabitants are hired to provide guard or catering services to hijacked crews. Local commerce can only but welcome the increased spending brought about by the influx of millions of dollars after every successful negotiation. Since they flaunt money, power, and influence in the community, pirates have become the role model for unemployed, underemployed, or plain adventurous [19].

The World Development Report (WDR) 2011 shows how the lack of employment opportunities and other productive activities is the most significant factor attracting people to join criminal gangs or rebel groups [20]. This is reinforced by other studies that also reveal a connection between violence, MDGs, and development in general. Gates et al. employ econometric techniques to test the development consequences of internal armed conflict and state fragility, and conclude that conflict and fragility are undoubtedly major obstacles to development for several MDG indicators (see Table 2) [21].

Table 2. Effect of civil conflict on MDGs

MDG	Label	Indicator	Effect of conflict		Effect of fragility	
			Cross-section	**Fixed-effects**	**Cross-section**	**Fixed-effects**
MDG 1	Ending poverty and hunger	Undernourishment	Detrimental	Detrimental	Detrimental	Unclear
MDG 1		Poverty headcount	Detrimental	Detrimental	Detrimental	No effect
MDG 1		Life expectancy	Detrimental	Detrimental	Detrimental	Detrimental
MDG 1		GDP per capita	Detrimental	Detrimental	Detrimental	Detrimental
MDG 2	Universal education	Prim sch enrolmnt	Detrimental	Detrimental	Detrimental	Beneficial?
MDG 2		Sec sch attainmnt	Detrimental	Unclear	Detrimental	Unclear
MDG 3	Gender parity	Primary sch ratio	Detrimental	Beneficial?	Detrimental	No effect
MDG 3		Life expctncy ratio	No effect	Unclear	No effect	No effect
MDG 4	Child mortality	Infant mortality	Detrimental	Detrimental	Detrimental	Detrimental
MDG 4		Under-5 mortality	Detrimental	Detrimental	Detrimental	Detrimental
MDG 5	Maternal mort	Birth attendance	No effect	Unclear	Detrimental	Beneficial?
MDG 6	Combat AIDS	% HIV positive	Beneficial?	Beneficial?	Beneficial?	No effect
MDG 7	Environmental sustainability	Access to water	Detrimental	Detrimental	Detrimental	Detrimental
MDG 7		Access to sanitatn	No effect	Unclear	No effect	No effect

Source: Gates et al., "Consequences of civil conflict," p. 1.

Another study included in WDR 2011 reveals the detrimental effect of violence on poverty levels in certain weak, fragile, or failed states. It shows that "poverty is declining for much of the world, but countries affected by violence are lagging behind. For every three years a country is affected by major violence (battle deaths or excess deaths from homicides equivalent to a major war), poverty reduction lags behind by 2.7 percentage points [22]."

It has been mentioned that low-income fragile states are still a great distance from achieving the MDGs. Nevertheless, the situation is not hopeless. WDR 2011 notes that "countries that have managed to reduce violence have also produced some of the fastest development gains... Countries emerging from severe violence have made striking development gains, often with strong assistance from the international community [23]."

So far, only isolated incidents of Somali pirates killing fellow gang members or rivals have been reported [24]. On the other hand, there have been clashes between pirates other groups. For instance, there is an animosity between pirates and islamists that seems to be motivated just as much by religion [25] as it is by economics [26]. Violence at sea has occasionally spilled over to the shore and Somalis who could help rebuild the legitimate economy flee instead to escape the violence [27].

One of the conclusions in WDR 2011 is that "Violence is the main constraint to meeting the MDGs [28]." Younger men and even children are being recruited into piracy, to join a new generation of pirates that do not hesitate to use greater violence against hijacked seafarers. Unless legitimate and attractive opportunities are offered in town, there is a great risk that the piracy phenomenon could turn into a vicious cycle of violence [29].

2.2. Weak, Fragile, and Failed States

The literature on MDGs and development use different terms to describe states of varying levels of economic development and socio-political stability. Some of the labels used are weak, fragile, least developed, failed, and collapsed. What the literature makes plain is that there is no universal agreement as to the exact definitions and uses of these terms. Some are used to describe relative levels of development while others are used interchangeably.

According to Hastings, for example, *weak states*

> meet something approaching the Weberian definition of the state. They retain a monopoly on the legitimate use of violence over their territory, and provide political and economic goods, if highly imperfectly. They might have high levels of corruption, crime, and social problems, and few fiscal or administrative resources, but the states soldier on. Indonesia, for example, has some of the highest levels of corruption in the world, and occasional ethno-religious unrest, but the government does function somewhat effectively (if inefficiently) over the vast majority of its territory [30].

Andersen has the following to say in regard of the term *fragile states* [31]:

> There is no authoritative definition of state fragility, nor is there an agreed list of fragile states...
>
> In recent years, 'fragile states' has become the catch-all phrase for states at the low end. In the development community, it has replaced labels such as 'poor performers',

'low-income countries under stress' and 'difficult partnership'. In academia and security circles, terms such as 'failed states' and 'collapsed states' remain common. Sometimes these terms indicate differences in degrees of state weakness: a fragile state has not yet failed, and a failed state has not yet collapsed. Frequently, however, they are just used as different words for problems that are seen as related to the state's lack of will or capacity to perform core state functions.

As for *failed states*, Brooks describes them as those that have lost "control over the means of violence, and cannot create peace or stability for their populations or control their territories. They cannot ensure economic growth or any reasonable distribution of social goods. They are often characterized by massive economic inequities, warlordism, and violent competition for resources [32]."

The World Bank seems to avoid using the label *failed state*, referring instead to *fragile states*. Under the Glossary in WDR 2011, state *failure* is not defined whereas *fragility* and *fragile situations* are [33]. On the other hand, *least developed country* (LDC) is the term preferred by the UN when describing states at the lowest end of the development scale. The following three criteria set by the Committee for Development Policy of the United Nations Economic and Social Council are used in characterising LDCs:

A) A "low-income" criterion, based on a three-year average estimate of the gross national income (GNI) per capita, with a threshold of USD 905 for possible cases of addition to the list, and a threshold of USD 1,086 for graduation from LDC status;
B) A "human assets weakness" criterion, involving a composite index (the Human Assets Index) based on indicators of (i) nutrition (percentage of the population that is undernourished); (ii) health (child mortality rate); (iii) school enrolment (gross secondary school enrolment rate); and (iv) literacy (adult literacy rate); and
C) An "economic vulnerability" criterion, involving a composite index (the Economic Vulnerability Index) based on indicators of (i) natural shocks (index of instability of agricultural production, share of the population made homeless by natural disasters); (ii) trade shocks (an index of instability of exports of goods and services); (iii) exposure to shocks (share of agriculture, forestry and fisheries in GDP; index of merchandise export concentration); (iv) economic smallness (population in logarithm); and (v) economic remoteness (index of remoteness) [34].

State failure, weakness, or fragility does not necessarily result in piracy-infested waters. The condition might facilitate criminality, but the causality is by no means automatic. Murphy offers the following elucidation:

> The most piracy-prone waters between 1991 and 2006 were those of Indonesia. Although Somali waters currently host more recorded incidents, the problem in Indonesia is a continuing one and, although it is a *weak* state where governmental authority does not run throughout its territory, it is not one that has *failed*. The same description can be applied to the Philippines, which also has a significant and long-standing piracy problem. Moving along the spectrum from weakness to strength, India and Brazil are not merely *strong* states but regional powers yet they too suffer piracy attacks along parts of their coastlines and in particular ports. Nor is the state *failure* sufficient to cause piracy. The

2008 Failed States Index lists Bangladesh and Nigeria in its most *failed* category, both of which have serious difficulties with piracy yet also lists several other coastal states where piracy is not a noteworthy problem including Côte d'Ivoire, Pakistan, Guinea and Burma [35] (italics supplied).

In his study, Hastings examines the geographies of state *failure* to explain why pirate behaviour, particularly in terms of sophistication, varies between *failed* and *weak* states. His analysis suggests that less sophisticated attacks are prevalent in *failed* states while more sophisticated attacks prevail in *weak* states. This is explained by the fact that "because they do not have to worry about enforcement, pirates in *failed* states can engage in time-intensive kidnappings for ransom, while only *weak* states provide the markets and transportation infrastructure necessary for operations where ships and cargo are seized and sold for profit." As a result, Hastings' concludes that in the long run, "*weak* states might actually be more problematic for international security in some respects than *failed* states [36]" (italics supplied).

Rotberg expounds on one more category that he refers to as an extreme version of the *failed* state: the *collapsed* state.

> A *collapsed* state is a mere geographical expression, a black hole into which a *failed* polity has fallen. Dark energy exists, but the forces of entropy have overwhelmed the radiance that hitherto provided some semblance of order and other vital political goods to the inhabitants embraced by language affinities or borders. When a state such as Somalia *collapses* (or Lebanon and Afghanistan a decade ago and Sierra Leone in the late 1990s), sub state actors take over. They control regions and sub regions, build their own local security apparatuses, sanction markets or other trading arrangements, and even establish an attenuated form of international relations. By definition, they are illegitimate and unrecognized, but some may assume the trappings of a quasi-state, such as Somaliland in northern Somalia. Yet, within the collapsed state prevail disorder, anomic behaviour, and the kinds of anarchic mentality and entrepreneurial pursuits – especially gun and drug running – that are compatible with networks of terror [37]" (italics supplied).

As far as state *failure* goes, Rotberg assigns Somalia *sui generis* status. "This decade's *failed* states are Afghanistan, Angola, Burundi, the DRC (Democratic Republic of Congo), Liberia, Sierra Leone, and Sudan. These seven states exemplify the criteria of state *failure*. Beyond those states is one *collapsed* state: Somalia [38]."

2.3. Local Fishery Resources

There seems to be sufficient evidence to suggest that the Somali piracy phenomenon can trace its roots to the plunder of Somalia's fishery resources and the dumping of toxic wastes off its coast. However, whether this lends legitimacy to the hijacking of ships as retaliation for alleged injuries to the Somali coast is a separate question altogether.

In its report to the UK government, the Marine Resources Assessment Group (MRAG) shows that Somalia was second only to Guinea in terms of being victimized by illegal, unreported and unregulated (IUU) fishing [39]. The United Nations estimates Somalia's annual loss due to IUU fishing at USD 95 million per annum [40].

In its 2006 report, the UK High Seas Task Force estimated that IUU fishing off Somalia's 3,300 km coastline was being carried out by 700 foreign-owned vessels from as close as Kenya, Pakistan, Saudi Arabia, Sri Lanka, and Yemen to as far as Belize, France, Honduras, Japan, South Korea, Spain, and Taiwan [41].

Concerns that the "uncontrolled nature of foreign poaching, coupled with unsustainable fishing practices such as bottom-trawling undertaken by these vessels" were pushing Somali fish stocks on the verge of collapse gave early Somali would-be pirates "a fig-leaf justification for their actions, leading them to style themselves 'coastguards [42].'" In the early 1990s, these enforcers used the self-styled appellation to force ships to slow down and stand by for boarding [43]. Somali anger towards the foreign fishing fleet morphed into two business models – the sale of fishing and waste-dumping licenses on the one hand and piracy/ship hijacking for ransom on the other.

Nevertheless, piracy soon outgrew the sale of fishing and waste-dumping licenses in terms of profitability. Revenue from licenses declined from USD 600,000 per annum in 1998 to about USD 300,000 in 2002. This decrease in revenue led Mohamed Abdi Hassan "Afweyne" to engage the Somali Marines of Harardhere, and become the first warlord to set up a piracy organization [44]. Numerous other gangs followed suit. Ransom payments grew from barely USD 100,000 per vessel in the early 2000s to a record USD 13.5 million for the oil tanker *Irene SL* in 2011 [45].

Whatever legitimate grievances there may have been on the part of local fishermen have quickly dissolved in the face of local warlords "complicit in the foreign ransacking of Somali fisheries [46]" and the Somali seizure of foreign shipping for profit, rather than to address allegations of uncontrolled fishing. Statistics show that whether in the 1980s or the 2010s, Somali pirates have always preferred to hijack ships that lie low in the water, move with low speed, and carry high value cargo – not fishing vessels [47]. Because of the piracy threat, there has virtually been no poaching by foreign trawlers or dumping of waste off Somalia in the last five years [48]. Local warlords clearly played upon otherwise legitimate concerns, turned "communal fears into animosities," and dubbed pirates the "*guardians* of clan interests [49]." The words, "We will keep attacking on foreign vessels until illegal fishing and toxic dump is stopped [50]" is nothing more than a mantra of excuses.

In the meantime, the development of the Somali fishing industry is retrogressive. With the low level of fishing activity in the past five years, one could even speculate that fish stocks might be recovering. There is in fact testimony from "several of the large fishing companies in Puntland… that 'the fishing is good [51].' Ironically, fishing boats and fishing crews are difficult to assemble and launch either for fear of being attacked by pirates or because both manpower and vessels have been co-opted by pirates [52]. Professional competence in fisheries management has all but disappeared. Shore-side, skilled managers and workers are necessary to run what remaining cold storage and processing facilities have survived both civil conflict and tsunami [53]. Somali fisher folk, one of the most important fishery resources, are being lost to piracy and criminality.

While historically representing only a small fraction of Somali GDP, a modern fishing industry has the potential to contribute to wider economic development in the country. To illustrate this point, the volume of fish landed in Somalia grew from 6,000 tonnes in 1950 to

29,800 tonnes in 2002 [54]. In spite of political instability and recurring violence in the country.

2.4. Emergency-Relief Aid

The humanitarian crisis in Somalia continues to persist. As of 2010, 42% of the population or around 3.2 million people are still in need of emergency humanitarian assistance [55]. In fact, in 2009, the whole Horn of Africa – Somalia, Kenya, and Ethiopia – was beset with its worst humanitarian crisis since the mid-1980s. A total of 16 million people in the region were in need of emergency food and nutrition assistance, most of which would have to be delivered by sea [56].

In response to the situation, the UN established the Central Emergency Response Fund (CERF) to enable more timely and reliable humanitarian assistance to those affected by natural disasters and armed conflicts. 51 countries benefited from CERF funding in 2009, and 34 percent of the total funding benefitted the Horn of Africa. The amount granted to Somalia, USD 60.5 million, was the most in nominal terms any one country has ever received in a single year [57].

The vast majority of food aid for Somalia, around 80-90%, arrives by sea mostly under the auspices of the World Food Programme (WFP). Pirate attacks against WFP ships in 2005 caused the suspension of deliveries to the country, further aggravating the crisis. The increasing threat meant that by 2007, only half the usual number of ships was willing to enter Somali waters to deliver emergency-relief. That year, "the WFP had over 2,400 tons of food supplies waiting on a dock in Tanzania ready for delivery and was having difficulty finding ships to hire. Ship owners feared their vessels would be seized by pirates and their crews held for ransom." In March the following year, "some 40 relief agencies including World Vision and Oxfam said they were unable to help millions of Somalis due to dangers and other impediments to their work [58]." Without the arrival of naval escorts to protect WFP ships, the shipment of crucially needed aid could not have resumed. Even then, the initial lack of coordination among naval escort vessels during the early days of the campaign meant that there were weeks when no aid ships could sail into Somalia [59].

WFP emergency-relief shipments are not the only ones being victimized by pirates. Even commercial shipments of foodstuffs are being hijacked, driving up the prices of food in the country significantly. In 2010, for instance, as many as nine trading vessels came under the control of pirates and most likely used as piracy mother ships. Local traders complain that shipowners in the region refuse to carry their goods, thereby creating "shortages of basic goods, such as rice, flour and sugar [60]." As if to add insult to injury, the very same pirates causing the increase in prices because they have hijacked the vessels meant to carry the cargo, come ashore awash with money that further inflate the economy.

2.5. Development Aid

When it comes to development aid, WDR 2011 mentions quite a few issues as being relevant to fragile, failed, or collapsed states such as Somalia. One is that the international system "is ill-equipped to navigate repeated cycles of violence or the blurred boundaries between political conflict and criminal violence [61].” In this connection, a critical gap was emphasized between focussing on building national capacity instead of addressing security and criminal justice issues. WDR 2011 further regrets that today’s international architecture for cooperation favours recovery rather than prevention [62].

In the last two decades, development aid programmes have neither been consistent nor effective in targeting countries like Somalia. Countries with extended periods of fragility, violence, or conflict experienced more volatility in the aid they received [63]. The lack of flexibility in the application of standard procedures (procedural conformism) for the administration of development programmes in certain areas meant that mobilization has been slow and best-fit institutional approaches ignored [64].

Also relevant in the Somali context, Andersen explains that:

> the 1990s saw a major shift in aid flows towards the so-called ‘good performers’. The obvious flip-side was a tendency to abandon states that performed poorly, i.e. states with weak institutions and a lack of reform-friendly elites. It is this group of states that is now being re-invented as fragile and – precisely because of their fragility – being seen as both needy and worthy of international support. The predicament for donor agencies, however, is that the aid flow cannot simply be shifted towards fragile states. The mechanisms for delivering long-term aid do not work in fragile states: budget support, sector programmes and alignment behind government policies make little sense in settings where the authority, effectiveness and legitimacy of national governments are severely limited [65].

International assistance programmes, MDR 2011 concludes, should exert effort to break the repeated cycles of violence in fragile states. Such programmes will need to refocus “assistance on preventing criminal and political violence through greater, and more integrated, support for security, justice, and jobs; reforming the procedures of international agencies; responding at a regional level; and renewing cooperative efforts among lower-, middle-, and higher-income countries [66].”

Stepping over to the receiving end of the aid programme divide, many writers have speculated on the probability that elements in Somalia may not be in any hurry to resurrect government institutions or the socio-economic infrastructure. In his investigation of the impact of anarchy on Somali development, Leeson finds that “while the state of this development remains low, on nearly all of 18 key indicators that allow pre- and post-stateless welfare comparisons, Somalis are better off under anarchy than they were under government. Renewed vibrancy in critical sectors of Somalia’s economy and public goods in the absence of a predatory state are responsible for this improvement [67].”

Powell et al. took a “comparative institutional approach to examine Somalia’s performance relative to other African countries both when Somalia had a government and during its extended period of anarchy.” What their study found was that although poor, Somalia’s relative economic performance actually improved during its period of statelessness, i.e., at least until 2005, the extent of data covered by this study. Standards of living in Somalia improved as a result of some basic law and order and currency reforms. Powell et al. observe, “Somalia has been relatively peaceful for most of the period since becoming stateless, and living standards have not collapsed [68].”

Coyne argues that Somalis have adapted to their situation. The private sector has apparently developed coping mechanisms to fill the void created by the absence of a central government. He observes that these "have proven to be more effective in generating widespread order than attempts by foreign occupiers to impose a self-sustaining liberal state [69]."

Powell et al. speculate that some sectors in Somalia view the restoration of a state as a high stakes zero-sum game. Their only experience with an established central government has been that clans that "gain control over a central government will use it to appropriate economic resources at the expense of others, and will use the law, patronage, and the monopoly of legitimate use of violence to protect this advantage [70]." On the other hand, Menkhaus thinks that the Somali elite probably would not mind a state, as long as power is not consolidated fully in the centre. At the very least, the elite will most likely appreciate the security and opportunities for prosperity attendant with having an internationally-recognized nominal or "paper" state [71]. According to Mubarak, while the "no-government situation has proven to be far better than the repressive government institutions and policies of Barre's era…, the economic expansion is chaotic and there is a strong new demand for an accountable and effective government that could provide essential public goods for sustainable economic development [72]." Menkhaus attributes the hesitation among political and economic actors to the fear of "a change in the operating environment which, though far from ideal, is one in which they have learned to survive and profit [73]."

3. International and Regional Issues

Piracy: orchestrating the response is a timely and important initiative. We need to assess what is working, what is missing, and what needs to be improved.

- Ban Ki Moon, 2011 [74]

This section examines selected international and regional issues that are relevant to piracy, development, and security. First are the impact and costs arising out of pirate attacks against shipping. Second is an overview of the piracy provisions in the Law of the Sea Convention and some of the challenges attending the legal aspects of counter-piracy efforts. Next is a review of some implications that the current piracy phenomenon may have in terms of regional security. The fourth subsection is a survey of some of the measures undertaken by the UN and the IMO, including an introduction to the Djibouti Code of Conduct.

3.1. Impact and Costs for International Seaborne Trade

There are now a number of studies that attempt to quantify the financial cost and impact of piracy on global seaborne trade. The study by Bowden is the pioneering work and probably the most frequently cited one today. It was the result of a large-scale study commissioned by the One Earth Future (OEF) Foundation to quantify the cost of piracy as part of its Oceans Beyond Piracy project.

The study's calculations estimate that maritime piracy is costing the international economy between USD 7 to USD 12 billion, per year. The study focuses on direct (first) order costs, but also includes some estimates of secondary (macroeconomic costs), where data is available. It concentrates on the supply-side costs to both industry and governments. The study set out to analyze the cost of piracy to the Horn of Africa, Nigeria and the Gulf of Guinea, and the Malacca Straits. The focus is inevitably on the costs of Somali piracy because this is the region where contemporary piracy is most highly concentrated and is the greatest source of current data and information. Table 3 presents the main cost factors and their equivalent values in USD [75].

Table 3. Estimated total costs of maritime piracy, per annum

Cost factor	Value (dollars)
Ransoms: excess costs	USD176 million
Insurance premiums	USD460 million to 3.2 billion
Re-routing ships	USD2.4 to 3 billion
Security equipment	USD363 million to 2.5 billion
Naval forces	USD2 billion
Prosecutions	USD31 million
Piracy deterrent organizations	USD19.5 million
Cost to regional economies	USD1.25 billion
TOTAL ESTIMATED COST	USD7 to 12 billion per year

Source: Figure 13 in Bowden, "The economic costs of maritime piracy," p. 25.

The next study is one conducted by the international consultancy group Geopolicity. The study's self-stated aim is to contribute to "what remarkably little work has been conducted on the economics of piracy." In contrast to the study by OEF, which focuses on calculating direct and indirect costs, the Geopolicity study adds to the analysis an assessment of the benefits accruing to pirates, financiers, sponsors, and other major stakeholders, who reap more revenue from piracy than pirates themselves. According to the Geopolicity study, piracy has emerged as a market in its own right, valued at between USD 4.9-8.3 billion in 2010 alone [76], as summarized and presented in Table 4.

Table 4. Estimated costs related to maritime piracy

Low/high pirate income (2010): using 1,500 pirates	USD33,000-79,000/year
Potential lifetime earnings (2010) : using 1,500 pirates	USD168,000-394,000
Next best alternative	USD500/year
Pirate incomes compared to average income	67-157 higher
Number of pirates could double by	2016
Total cost of piracy 2010	USD4.9-8.3 billion
Projected increase by 2014	USD13-15 billion
Major stakeholders	Financiers, sponsors, officials, pirates, maritime insurers, security companies, navies, merchant marine

Source: Geopolicity, "The economics of piracy."

Geopolicity developed a global economic model for assessing the costs and benefits of international piracy: adding significantly to the debate on the causes and consequences of piracy. The model provides a comprehensive, independent framework of trend analysis, while also highlighting across the *Pirate Value Chain* (PVC) where the greatest rates of return on international counter pirate investment and policy are to be found. The model includes, (i) cost-benefit analysis at the individual pirate level, based on existing socioeconomic and market data, (ii) the aggregate costs and benefits at the international systems level, and (iii) comprehensive data on the resurgence of piracy by functional classification and sovereign jurisdiction; to include trend, comparator and predictive analysis [77].

A third study, by Fu et al., concentrates on the costs associated with the Far East-Europe trade for container vessels. Calibrated with data between 2003 and 2008, the study models shipping demands and competition in the Far East-Europe container liner shipping service and investigates the economic welfare loss effects due to reduced volumes of trade and shipping, as well as efficiency loss due to geographical re-routing of shipping networks which would be otherwise uneconomical [78].

The analysis by Fu et al. shows that, without government efforts in combating Somali pirates, traffic volumes along the Far East-Europe route would reduce by about 30%, though only about 18% of the traffic would be detoured via the Cape of Good Hope. Their analysis also shows that the overall economic welfare loss is much more substantial, with an expected annual loss of USD 30 billion on the countries and regions served by this shipping route. Fu et al. see the significant loss as supporting the proposition that maritime piracy endangers the sustainability of the current liner shipping's status quo. It also concludes that current naval presence and operations tackling piracy in the western Indian Ocean is justified from the perspective of global economic development as a way to improve economic efficiency and raise aggregate welfare, at least in the short and medium terms. [79]

Beyond the purely financial implications lies an arguably more compelling issue – the human cost of piracy. In the year 2011, the IMB reported that vessels around the world experienced 105 attempted boardings and 176 successful boardings. 113 ships fired upon and 45 were hijacked. 6 persons were assaulted, 802 held hostage, 42 injured, 10 kidnapped, and 8 killed. In 2012, there were 67 attempted boardings and 174 successful boardings. 28 ships were fired upon and 28 were hijacked. 4 persons were assaulted, 585 held hostage, 28 injured, 26 kidnapped, and 6 killed [80].

Seafarers are tortured, physically and mentally abused, shot at, killed, beaten, confined, starved, raped, and used as human shields by pirates. The case of the *MV Renuar*, hijacked on 11 December 2010 and released on 23 April 2011, is a recent example. Somali pirates held the *Renuar*'s Master, Calixto Caniete, and his crew for 133 days under inhuman conditions. Capt. Caniete testified to abuse and deprivation in the hands of the Somali pirate captors. They were confined to only one side of the bridge, allowing for short trips to the toilet. They were held at gunpoint day and night. They were fed rotten rice and given rusty yellowish water to drink. Caniete was personally held responsible, physically abused, and threatened with execution whenever ransom negotiations went sour or when food, water, and fuel ran out. He was forced to give medical attention to their captors and to serve them like their slave [81].

Thousands of seafarers are traumatized by attacks, whether or not the pirates succeed in taking over their vessel. YouTube videos such as that of the hijacked crew of the *MV Leopard* give graphic testimony to this [82]. The prospect of navigating through piracy-affected waters alone is a source of considerable stress that can have a lasting impact on both seafarers and their families. When a seafarer is hijacked, family members are subjected to psychological manipulation by pirates [83] who are frequently inclined to raise the stakes by claiming the hijacked seafarer is either dead or is about to be killed. No matter the financial costs or its effects on commerce, "the potential danger piracy presents to all seafarers, and the fear it induces, which extends to those on large ships and yachts," simply cannot, and must not, be ignored [84].

3.2. Legal Aspects

Article 15 of the 1958 Geneva Convention on the High Seas, and Article 101 of the United Nations Convention on the Law of the Sea (UNCLOS), 1982 provide the world community with what today is generally accepted as the definition of the high seas crime of piracy. By distilling the essence of these articles, it may be said that for an act to be considered piracy under international law, the following conditions or rules must be met:

- the illegal violence rule, i.e., the act must be an illegal act of violence, detention, or depredation;
- the *lucri causa* rule, i.e., the act must be motivated by private gain;
- the two-ship rule, i.e., two ships must be involved in the incident – the victim ship and the pirate ship; and
- the high seas rule, i.e., the act must be committed on the high seas or waters outside the jurisdiction of any state.

When examined in the light of pirate attacks (i.e., outside the present Somali piracy phenomenon), these conditions were always the subject of some controversy and considered as frustrating complications when attempting to identify the crime. The first element on the above list is straightforward. All pirate attacks are illegal acts of violence since these are committed by elements other than naval forces or other public instruments of violence sanctioned by the state.

With regard to the second point, there is controversy whether the reported attacks are motivated by private gain or by public gain. Indeed, some argue that the two are not necessarily mutually exclusive. Logina writes, "Private aims always constitute an important part of public aims, because public aims cannot exist without individuals. If a person truly associates himself/herself with a particular group, the aims of this group are also his/her individual aims [85]."

The third point constitutes the "two-ship rule," which means that for an act to qualify as piracy under UNCLOS, both a pirate ship and a victim ship must be present. In actual fact, the majority of non-Somali piracy attacks do not involve two ships; attacks are usually made while ships are at anchor or tied to the dock or pier. Even in the case of Somali piracy, purists might argue that notwithstanding the use of mother ships to extend the range of pirate boarding teams, most victim ships are boarded by perpetrators using skiffs or rubber boats which are not, strictly speaking, ships.

Finally, the fourth point listed above means that, depending on how Article 58 [86] and "high seas" in Article 101 of UNCLOS are construed, the act would need to have occurred either outside the 12 nautical mile limit (i.e., beyond the territorial sea) or as far out as 200 nautical miles from shore (i.e., beyond the exclusive economic zone). As it happens today, most non-Somali pirate attacks occur landward of the territorial seas of a coastal state. In what might be characterized as a gerrymandering [87] of the oceans, piracy was artificially or virtually eliminated when UNCLOS pushed the high seas to as much as 200 nautical miles from shore.

In its maritime security deliberations, the IMO circumvents the complication posed by the UNCLOS definition of piracy and the imprecise use of the term in certain quarters by resorting to the expanded construction "piracy and armed robbery against ships." IMO defines armed robbery against ships as "any unlawful act of violence or detention or any act of depredation, or threat thereof, *other than an act of piracy*, (italics supplied), directed against a ship or against persons or property on board such a ship, within a State's jurisdiction over such offences [88]."

One crucial implication of identifying an act as piracy under UNCLOS is that it affords any state the option to claim universal jurisdiction by invoking Article 105 [89] Until recently, this remained mainly a hypothetical option because most reported attacks did not meet the UNCLOS criteria. China [90] and India [91] present us with some of the rare examples in contemporary times where piracy cases were prosecuted even in the absence of a nexus with the arresting state. By the mid-2000s the concept of "universal jurisdiction over piracy was largely thought to be a historical artifact with little or no modern relevance [92]." This notion has since been negated by the piracy phenomenon off the coast of Somalia, where most attacks from the mid-2000s onwards have been reported outside what would theoretically be Somalia's exclusive economic zone (EEZ) [93]. Nonetheless, while attacks by Somali pirates easily "fall within the (UNCLOS) definition, which is therefore perfectly adequate to deal with the present situation [94]," states tackling the maritime criminal phenomenon in the Horn of Africa still face numerous challenges.

Kontorovich and Art argue that, "the nominal availability of universal jurisdiction for piracy does not translate in practice into ending impunity for the crime [95]." Because the exercise of universal jurisdiction over piracy cases is only a recent phenomenon, state practice is still in a very early and inefficient stage of development. Nanda observes that, "the needed mechanisms, logistics, and facilities to ensure apprehension and prosecution, detention, extradition, and imprisonment are barely in place [96]." Arresting states invariably transfer suspects to third states. Among these, Kenya has prosecuted more piracy cases where there are no clear Kenyan interests involved [97]. There is an obvious strain on the country's resources, resulting in backlogs that not only delay justice, but also weaken the arrests' deterrent effect. Trials in the courts of arresting states, situated thousands of miles from the actual theatre of operations, are no more efficient, not only because of the manifest delay in transporting suspects but also in assembling witnesses based in different countries around the world [98]. In the worst case, insufficiencies in the domestic legislation of arresting states [99] or unwillingness to commence domestic criminal proceedings [100] leave the naval forces of these countries no choice but to release alleged perpetrators soon after they are captured. The UN Security Council (UNSC) noted "that the lack of capacity, domestic legislation, and clarity about how to dispose of pirates after their capture, has hindered more robust international action against the pirates off the coast of Somalia and in some cases led to pirates being released without facing justice [101]."

Evidence handling and crime-scene preservation are a crucial area that requires improvement. With naval, rather than coast guard or constabulary, forces being deployed to deter and arrest pirates, it is not surprising that evidence collection has been focused on intelligence gathering and maritime target development [102], rather than on building a criminal case against suspected pirates. This lack of skill and knowledge in gathering and handling evidence has affected its admissibility before the courts and allowed many pirates to escape punishment [103].

Failure to observe the human rights of the accused is yet another contributory factor to inefficiency in arrest and prosecution under the current regime of universal jurisdiction over piracy cases. According to Petrig, "It is not rare that criminal prosecutions fail because arrests, investigative steps or handovers are secured in violation of human rights." She also cautions that,

> Even though the legal instruments governing counter-piracy operations do not explicitly mention the applicable human rights norms, enforcement powers cannot be exercised in a legal vacuum and *ad libitum*. Rather, their exercise is restricted by the application of general human rights law. This is insinuated by (UNSC) Resolution 1851 deciding that any measure based on the enforcement powers conferred by that Resolution "shall be undertaken consistent with applicable… human rights law [104]."

Guilfoyle identifies the following four human rights issues as being relevant vis-à-vis counter-piracy operations in the Horn of Africa [105]:

- legal authority to detain suspect pirates at sea and their right to be brought promptly before a judicial authority;
- *non-refoulement* and transferring suspect pirates to regional States for prosecution;
- the application of fair-trial rights in such transfers; and
- in the European Convention on Human Rights (ECHR) context, the right to an effective remedy requiring the ability to challenge one's transfer

A related issue is the question whether arrested piracy suspects are entitled to protections under the law of armed conflict and international law in general [106]. Bahar draws on his experience as the Staff Judge Advocate for the *Nassau* Strike Group during the US Navy's first capture of suspected pirates in recent memory (the *Safina al Bisarat* pirates) and offers the following answer: "Pirates are not combatants or enemy prisoners of war, but they are international maritime criminals entitled to international and constitutional due process protections [107]." Indeed, while the epithet *hostis humani generis* [108] characterises universal abhorrence towards pirates, their torture, maltreatment, and unfair trial will only "call into question the motives and values of states that participate in antipiracy efforts."

To make a complicated situation even more complex, it has been established that a significant number of pirates are actually 15 years old or younger. This drags another area of treaty law into the picture (e.g., International Convention on the Rights of the Child, 1989 Worst Form of Child Labour Convention, 1999) [109]. Nevertheless, because global trade and commerce are dependent on safe and efficient maritime transport, it is only "in every state's best interest that the fight against piracy" is given its best chances for success by ensuring that operations remain "legally and morally beyond reproach [110]."

Numerous other problems related to the legal aspects of counter-piracy programmes have been identified. These include cooperation among law enforcement agencies and institutions; interface between military forces, national police organizations, and Interpol; interface between ship operators and crews and assisting Interpol response; legal capacity building in states affected by piracy; regional judicial and enforcement training; and the possibility for asylum requests by convicted pirates [111].

3.3. Regional Security

Increasingly violent maritime crimes such as piracy can complicate the shaky security climate in any region's maritime domain. After the Horn of Africa, it is probably the Gulf of Guinea (GoG) that suffers from the world's most violent piracy attacks. The GoG region is a highly strategic body of water. The area produces "around 5.2 million barrels per day and is estimated to hold as much as 50.4 billion barrels of oil in proven reserves. By virtue of its vast quantities of natural gas, it is projected to account for one-fifth of global oil production by 2010 and expected to add between two to three million barrels per day to global oil supply [112]."

Unfortunately, the GoG region is also unstable. Equatorial Guinea, the most important new oil-producing nation in the region, also has the most repressive regime; it is a social powder keg set to ignite [113]. The demand for GoG oil could lead to an arms race between world powers and result in the proliferation of weapons in the region [114]. More weapons, more pirates. The secessionist conflict in Nigeria, but a struggle for shares in the oil-rich Niger Delta, "has given way to organized criminal syndicates that deal in oil, arms, and kidnapped foreign workers. An estimated 250,000–300,000 barrels, valued at more than USD 3.8 billion, are stolen each year through "oil bunkering" (the theft of oil from pipelines or storage facilities). Local gangs and political groups are drawn into ethnic violence [115]. The consequences of violence on development, "like its origins, spill across borders, with implications for neighbours, for the region, and globally. Violence in one country can create a 'bad neighbourhood.' For example, the manifestations of conflict in Liberia under President Charles Taylor during the late 1990s hurt Côte d'Ivoire, Guinea, and Sierra Leone." According to the World Bank, the 'bad neighbourhood' affects "economic prospects: estimates suggest that countries lose 0.7 percent of their annual GDP for each neighbour involved in civil war. And a doubling of terrorist incidents in a country is estimated to reduce bilateral trade with each trading partner by some 4 percent [116]."

Back in the Horn of Africa, the 'bad neighbourhood' effect manifests itself in the number of refugees fleeing Somalia. There are around 310,280 Somali refugees in Kenya and 161,468 in Yemen. It has been shown that

> Developing countries that host refugees for protracted periods experience long-term economic, social, political, and environmental impacts. From the moment of arrival, refugees may compete with local citizens for scarce resources such as water, food, housing, and medical services. Their presence increases the demands for education,

health services, infrastructure such as water supply, sanitation, and transportation, and also in some cases, for natural resources such as grazing and firewood [117].

In the case of Somali refugees in the camps in Daadab, Kenya (which hosts one of the largest refugee populations in the world), while it is observed that there are direct and indirect benefits of the camp operation for the local economy, the presence of refugees also results in "depletion of firewood and building materials as well as competition for grazing land in the immediate vicinity of the camps [118]." It is also noted that refugee camps have a tendency to facilitate the cross-border movement of criminal elements and other persons trained in violence [119]. In the Kenyan Shippers Council's assessment, crimes such as piracy have increased "the cost of imports by USD 23.8 million and exports by USD 9.8 million per month." One can naturally expect then that the amount paid to disburse these costs would surely be passed on to consumers [120].

3.4. The UN and IMO Response

United Nations

The United Nation has responded to the problem of piracy off the Horn of Africa with a series of UN Security Council resolutions [121], starting with Resolution 1816, condemning all acts of piracy and armed robbery against ships, urging all states to cooperate with the Transitional Federal Government (TFG) of Somalia in the fight against piracy and armed robbery at sea off the coast of Somalia, and authorizing all states, for a period of six months from the date of the resolution, to:

- enter the territorial waters of Somalia for the purpose of repressing acts of piracy and armed robbery at sea, in a manner consistent with such action permitted on the high seas with respect to piracy under relevant international law; and
- use, within the territorial waters of Somalia, in a manner consistent with action permitted on the high seas with respect to piracy under relevant international law, all necessary means to repress acts of piracy and armed robbery.

The effect of Resolution 1816 has been extended every six months since it was adopted in June 2008. Other UNSC resolutions in the series include exhortations for states to, among others, cooperate in the establishment of anti-piracy courts, respect the human rights of arrested suspects, increase prosecution capacity for suspected pirates, increase development assistance to Somalia, respect the marine resources of Somalia, criminalize piracy under their domestic law, cooperate in transfer arrangements for convicted pirates, etc.

UNSC Resolution 1581 encouraged states "to establish an international cooperation mechanism to act as a common point of contact between and among states, regional and international organizations on all aspects of combating piracy and armed robbery at sea off Somalia's coast." This led to the creation of the Contact Group on Piracy off the Coast of Somalia (CGPCS) on 14 January 2009. The CGPCS has now brought together more than 60 countries and international organizations all working towards the prevention of piracy off the Somali coast. The CGPCS operates through five Working Groups, in which all CGPCS parties may participate, addressing different focus areas [122]:

- Working Group 1 (WG1): responsible for ensuring effective naval operational co-ordination and supporting the building of the judicial, penal and maritime capacity of regional states to ensure they are better equipped to tackle piracy and maritime security challenges;
- Working Group 2 (WG2): provides specific, practical and legally sound guidance to the CGPCS, states and organizations on all legal aspects of counter-piracy. At its tri-annual meetings the participants exchange information on on-going judicial activities, including specific court cases, as well as on relevant capacity building activities in the region. Through this exchange of information, WG2 contributes to a common approach to and understanding of the legal issues. WG2 has developed a number of specific legal tools gathered in a virtual "legal tool box," including on issues such as applicable international law, transfer and ship-riders;
- Working Group 3 (WG3): discusses concerns of the participant states, maritime industry and labour groups regarding actions that should be taken to provide self-defensive actions to protect vessels from hijacking by pirates in the high risk waters off Somalia;
- Working Group 4 (WG4): focuses mainly on the public diplomacy aspect of the problem of combating piracy over the coast of Somalia. It aims at raising awareness of the dangers of piracy and highlighting the best practices to eradicate this criminal phenomenon. Based on the conviction that the most effective way to combat piracy is through working on land, it uses various means of communication and education to inform the public in the area and abroad of the dangers posed by piracy; and
- Working Group 5 (WG5): coordinates international efforts to identify and disrupt the financial networks of pirate leaders and their financiers. The CGPCS has understood from the beginning of its establishment that successful eradication of piracy is impossible without dismantling the illicit funding and financial flows related to piracy taking place on shore.

Aside from the UNSC, a number of UN bodies are heavily involved in counter-piracy activities, such as the United Nations Office on Drugs and Crime (UNODC), United Nations Political Office for Somalia (UNPOS), Operational Satellite Applications Programme (UNOSAT) of the UN Institute for Training and Research (UNITAR), Food and Agricultural Organization (FAO), World Food Programme (WFP), United Nations Development Programme (UNDP), and the International Maritime Organization (IMO).

While not UN bodies, the significant commitment and contributions of the North Atlantic Treaty Organization (NATO), European Union (EU), and International Criminal Police Organization (Interpol) to combating piracy deserve to be mentioned and acknowledged.

International Maritime Organization

The International Maritime Organization, the United Nations specialized agency with responsibility for the safety and security of shipping and the prevention of marine pollution by ships, has been involved in combating piracy since the 1990s [123]. The IMO's anti-piracy programme is a long-term project that began in 1998. Phase one consisted of a number of regional seminars and workshops attended by government representatives from countries in piracy-affected areas of the world; while phase two consisted of a number of evaluation and assessment missions to different regions. Throughout the years, IMO has formulated a body of treaties and recommendations that are useful in the global fight against piracy [124].

Keeping in mind the thousands of seafarers navigating through the world's piracy hotspots on a daily basis, the IMO Council designated "Piracy: orchestrating the response" as the theme for World Maritime Day 2011. IMO also set the following objectives in support of this theme [125]:

- increase pressure at the political level to secure the release of all hostages being held by pirates;
- review and improve the IMO guidelines to maritime administrations and seafarers and promote compliance with industry best management practice and the recommended preventive, evasive, and defensive measures ships should follow;
- promote greater levels of support from, and coordination with, navies;
- promote anti-piracy coordination and cooperation procedures between and among States, regions, organizations, and industry;
- assist states in building capacity in piracy-affected regions of the world, and elsewhere, to deter, interdict, and bring to justice those who commit acts of piracy and armed robbery against ships; and
- provide care, during the post-traumatic period, for those attacked or hijacked by pirates and for their families.

Djibouti Code of Conduct

IMO's aim has been to foster the development of regional agreements on implementation of counter piracy measures. Regional cooperation among States has an important role to play in solving the problem of piracy and armed robbery against ships, as evidenced by the success of the regional counter-piracy operation in the Straits of Malacca and Singapore. The Regional Cooperation Agreement on Combating Piracy and Armed Robbery Against Ships in Asia (ReCAAP), which was concluded in November 2004 by 16 countries in Asia, and includes the ReCAAP Information Sharing Centre (ISC) for facilitating the sharing of piracy-related information, is a good example of successful regional cooperation which IMO seeks to replicate elsewhere. Today, the deteriorating security situation in the seas off war-torn Somalia and the Gulf of Aden (and in the increasingly volatile Gulf of Guinea) are at the heart of the problem.

In January 2009, inspired by the achievements of ReCAAP, an important regional agreement was adopted in Djibouti by States in the region, at a high-level meeting convened by IMO. The Djibouti Code of Conduct (DCoC) concerning the Repression of Piracy and Armed Robbery against Ships in the Western Indian Ocean and the Gulf of Aden recognizes the extent of the problem of piracy and armed robbery against ships in the region and, in it, the signatories declare their intention to cooperate to the fullest possible extent, and in a manner consistent with international law, in the repression of piracy and armed robbery against ships. As of January 2013, 20 of 21 eligible states in the region are signatories to the DCoC [126].

Signatories to the DCoC commit themselves towards sharing and reporting relevant information through a system of national focal points and information centres; interdicting ships suspected of engaging in acts of piracy or armed robbery against ships; ensuring that persons committing or attempting to commit acts of piracy or armed robbery against ships are apprehended and prosecuted; and facilitating proper care, treatment, and repatriation for seafarers, fishermen, other shipboard personnel and passengers subject to acts of piracy or armed robbery against ships, particularly those who have been subjected to violence. Implementation of the DCoC will help to:

- improve communications between States;
- enhance the capabilities of States in the region to deter, arrest and prosecute pirates; improve States' maritime situational awareness; and
- enhance the capabilities of local coast guards.

While the DCoC is heavily influenced by ReCAAP, the one is not the exact duplicate of the other. The DCoC does not explicitly provide for countries outside the region to accede to it. Article 15 of the DCoC provides that it be open for signature by any of the 21 regional states that were participants in the Djibouti Meeting of 26-29 January 2009. In contrast, ReCAAP, having entered into force, is open to accession by states outside the Asian region [127].

Compared to ReCAAP, the wording in the DCoC reveals an instrument that is bolder in its intentions. The DCoC's provisions include, *inter alia*, a more explicit statement on seizure of ships [128], an article relating to embarked officers or "ship riders [129]," and "the sharing of information concerning applicable laws and guidance pertaining to the interdiction, apprehension, investigation, prosecution, and disposition of persons involved in piracy and armed robbery against ships [130]."

In spite of the determined tone of the instrument, nothing in the DCoC "is intended to… create or establish a binding agreement [13]." In other words, the DCoC in its present form is a set of statements of intent rather than a treaty opposable to its parties. In contrast, ReCAAP is an international treaty instrument within the scope of the Vienna Convention on the Law of Treaties [132]. Nonetheless, the DCoC makes a strong appeal for a binding agreement to be concluded within two years of the date at which the Code takes effect [133].

Another significant difference between DCC and ReCAAP is that the former creates not one, but three, ISCs, plus a training center. While ReCAAP has its single ISC in Singapore, DCC designates an ISC each in Kenya (Mombassa), Tanzania (Dar es Salaam), and Yemen. Additionally, Djibouti has offered to establish the regional training center [134].

Commentators refer to ReCAAP as a "model for other regions that are faced with the scourge of piracy and armed robbery [135]" or as a "template for other similar international agreements [136]." Indeed, some very useful lessons can be learned from the ReCAAP experience. The first of these is that a regional agreement is not a silver bullet. Regional agreements are an important element in any comprehensive approach against criminality at sea, but these are effective only when applied together with a multitude of other measures and arrangements. In fact, ReCAAP did not enter into force until after the magnitude and severity of piracy and armed robbery against ships in East Asia had already peaked.

There are many other lessons to be learned from ReCAAP, both in terms of challenges and opportunities. Using ReCAAP as a model reduces the learning curve and hastens the pace for launching the three DCoC-ISCs [137].

CONCLUSION

> We are seeking solutions in three distinct time horizons. In the immediate term, our aim is to contain piracy, thwart pirate attacks and punish those responsible for such attacks; in the mid-term, our strategy is to undermine organized crime gangs that plan and mastermind pirate operations and make it harder for them to engage in, and conduct, such operations; while the long term solution should be for the international community to help the people of Somalia to rebuild their country, including establishing law and order conditions such that crime will no longer be a preferred option for several of them.
>
> - Efthimios Mitropoulos, 2011 [138]

The objective of this chapter was to explore the linkages between political stability, economic development and piracy at sea. In pursuing its objective, this chapter aimed not so much to offer answers or solutions, but more to provide food for thought that might facilitate the formulation of answers and solutions.

The piracy-security-development nexus has been shown to exist in terms of MDGs, state failure and fragility, fishery resources, emergency-relief aid, and development aid. This provides us with a further basis for deeper studies into the nexus that will hopefully contribute to laying the appropriate foundation for recovery and development that will stifle the seeds of criminality.

This part presents three sections in conclusion. First are thoughts on some challenges facing long-term development programmes. Next are thoughts on the way forward vis-à-vis a long-term perspective. Finally, the third section puts forward a few ideas for further research.

Challenges

Rebuilding a failed or collapsed state like Somalia will involve innumerable challenges. In an ideal world, a weak state should have been strengthened before it could fail or collapse [139]. Aside from the enormous amount of time and resources necessary to revive Somalia, there may be a potential contradiction or resistance within the country against a restoration. Section 2.5 of this chapter refers to studies showing how the Somali private sector have had little choice but to adapt to their situation of statelessness and develop the necessary coping mechanisms. In what is probably a testament to the dire conditions under the Barre regime, indicators show how Somalia has been better off under anarchy than under government.

It is almost inconceivable that Somalis in general would not wish for a fully functioning state to promote and orchestrate the population's security and economic wellbeing. However, their only experience of post-independence government has been under a predatory dictatorship. Given the level of corruption within the bureaucracy and the role that security forces historically played in armed violence and criminality against civilians in that country, any apprehension towards programmes to revive a strong central government is only understandable. Development projects "presume that an effective state structure is essential for economic development and human security, but for many Somalis the state is seen as a potential threat and a source of armed conflict [140]." Herein lies the contradiction.

Another challenge is the need to change the perception that "piracy is a global phenomenon but not a global problem [141]." Indeed, in commercial terms, "although an individual ship owner with insufficient insurance cover could be ruined by a single large payment if a ship were to be held for ransom and thereby prevented from working for any length of time, the estimated losses for the shipping industry as a whole remain insignificant [142]." Only a major or significant disruption of maritime trade and commerce can turn piracy into a global problem [143]. While this may be the case, in terms of piracy's impact and costs for international seaborne trade there are other considerations than the purely financial implications. The human cost is a very compelling issue [144]. The vast majority of the hostages held by Somali pirates today are either Filipino or Indian. One cannot help but speculate on the possible scenario if the hundreds of hostages happened to be predominantly nationals of the affluent OECD states instead. One might also imagine the global reaction if an environmental disaster were to result from piracy [145], if oil were to contaminate pristine coasts and cover sea birds and seals, or if the petroleum prices were to double or treble. The level of priority and resources assigned to the problem by western governments and the degree of media attention would conceivably change if this were the case.

The Way Forward

Long-term development programmes targeted at weak or failed states must engage the country's leaders and together "build the legitimate institutions that can provide a sustained level of citizen security, justice, and jobs – offering a stake in society to groups that may otherwise receive more respect and recognition from engaging in armed violence than in lawful activities, and punishing infractions capably and fairly [146]."

The problem in Somalia may not be so much the absence of a state as much as it is the lack or decline of local institutions crucial to stability and development. Some of these local institutions still exist and, though weak, they may very well be important keys to a building-block approach to the Somali problem [147]. The way forward in Somalia would be to adopt a building block or bottom up approach, rather than classic state-building (top down). A government that controls only a few city blocks, and that has no credible public security enforcement apparatus, could be little more than a paper tiger. There is increasing belief that the debacle in "cases such as Afghanistan and Iraq, institutional features of the second phase – constitutions, elections, representative bodies – were implemented before achievement of the first phase, the establishment of a legitimate state monopoly of physical force [148]."

The enforcement and maintenance of law and order are critical to breaking the cycle of insecurity. Without a functioning police force, piracy and other forms of criminality will remain lucrative. These illicit activities will attract young people because of limited employment opportunities. When there is a window of opportunity to revive important sectors such as agriculture or industry, only few young people will be willing and available. Without human resources recovery programmes will fail, jobs will not be generated, and criminality continues to be a viable option; and so the vicious cycle keeps turning.

With traditional fishing grounds replenished, a lucrative fish processing industry in Somalia is a real possibility. Support for the development of fishery resources and the fishing industry should be increased. A profitable fishing industry will not only result in helping create jobs, stimulating the economy, promoting education and training, and technology transfer, it will also symbolically eliminate an excuse Somali communities have used in engaging in piracy.

The global community should consider increased collaboration and support to relatively effective regional governments such as Somaliland and Puntland, provided these regional governments dissociate themselves from any form of pirate activity [149]. Economically and politically stable regions can serve as radiating spokes from which development could spread to the rest of the country.

The development and implementation of any long-term aid programme should closely involve the target states so that there is a feeling of ownership of the solution. The practice of sending a team of experts from western capitals to LDCs to conduct "a 'needs assessment,' and then dictate to the locals" [150] should be avoided at all cost.

Further Research

A number of possible areas of further research could serve the interest of fostering the long-term objective of political and socio-economic stability of piracy-affected areas such as Somalia.

- Piracy and its effects
  - The social, economic and political causes and consequences of piracy on coastal communities
  - The influence of cultural attitudes, practices and structures on piracy
  - Piracy's effects on local economies, particularly employment opportunities, businesses, and trade
  - Local responses to piracy prevention
- Development programmes
  - The role of development aid or partnership programmes in resource-rich and relatively economically affluent countries in areas such as the Gulf of Guinea
  - A comprehensive survey of all bilateral and multilateral aid that flows into Somalia, the status of such programmes, and recommendations for improvement and optimization
  - The development of Somaliland and Puntland to serve as regional centres of excellence from which development can radiate
  - The role of the Somali diaspora
- The development-piracy nexus; build upon the research conducted by Mejia et al. to look into
  - Further differentiation on the effects of piracy on weak as opposed to fragile or failed states
  - The difference between democracy and political stability, keeping in mind that liberal democracy does not automatically flow from political stability, and vice versa
  - Maritime and marine potential
  - Establishment of the Somali EEZ and promotion of marine and ocean resources management, exploration, and exploitation

- Maritime repair and supply – Somalia is ideally situated; the same geographical features that provide it with perfect piracy hunting grounds also make it the perfect stop for ships in need of a wide range of services geared towards the maritime industry
- Maritime labour development – the number of young men that have taken to the sea for whatever reason could speak of the potential for young Somalis to become seafarers
- Fishing industry – determine whether/how much fish stocks have recovered; evaluate current multilateral fisheries projects designed to drive pirates from piracy back to fishing

Article 100 of UNCLOS, obligates all states to "cooperate to the fullest extent in the repression of piracy on the high seas or in any other place outside the jurisdiction of any State." This obligation to cooperate applies not only to short-term counter-piracy operations, but also to long-term development programmes that will enable the country to provide its citizens with the opportunities they deserve. Large-scale criminality will "corrupt government officials, hurt economic development, undermine civil society, and increase ambient levels of violence [151]."

This chapter merely scratches the surface on the linkages between security, development, and piracy. The more lessons the international community can learn from the extreme case of Somalia, the more prepared it will hopefully be in facing – or better yet, preventing – the next piracy powder kegs.

REFERENCES

[1] "For a pirate is not included in the number of lawful enemies, but is the common enemy of all. With him there ought not to be any pledged word nor any oath mutually binding." This quote and translation from Cicero's *De officiis* are borrowed from D. Heller-Roazen, *The enemy of all: piracy and the law of nations*, New York, New York, USA: Zone Books, 2009, p. 16, an exposition of the legal, political, and historical nature of pirates and piracy. It is also discussed in A. P. Rubin, *The law of piracy (2nd ed.)*, Irvington-on-Hudson, New York, USA: Transnational Publishers, 1998, p. 15, n. 49.

[2] A specialised division of the ICC, the IMB is a non-profit making organisation, established in 1981 to act as a focal point in the fight against all types of maritime crime and malpractice. For over 25 years, the IMB has used industry knowledge, experience and access to a large number of well-placed contacts around the world to protect the integrity of international trade by seeking out fraud and malpractice. "ICC Commercial Crime Services," *http://www.icc-ccs.org,* accessed 31 January 2013.

[3] The latest IMB report as of the date of this study is: ICC-IMB, *Piracy and armed robbery against ships report for the period 1 January – 31 December 2012*, Cinnabar Wharf, London, UK: ICC-IMB, 2013. The website "Piracy News & Figures," *http://www.icc-ccs.org/piracy-reporting-centre/piracynewsafigures* complements the data through rolling updates until the annual report is published at year's end.

[4] M. N. Murphy, *Small boats, weak states, dirty money: piracy and maritime terrorism in the modern world*, New York, New York, USA: Columbia University Press, 2009, p. 7.

[5] The World Bank, *World development report 2011: conflict, security, and development*, Washington, DC, USA: The World Bank, 2011, pp. 1-2.

[6] See, for example, discussions in E. A. Anderson, "It's a pirate's life for some: the development of an illegal industry in response to an unjust global power dynamic," *Indiana Journal of Global Legal Studies*, vol. 17, no. 2, 2010, p. 329; K. Czernichowski, "The roots of piracy in Somalia," pp. 135-144, in A. Fireš and I. Varga (eds.), *Crucial problems of international relations through the eyes of young scholars*, Prague, Czech Republic: University of Economics, 2009; X. W. Fu, A. K. Y. Ng, and Y. Y. Lau, "The impacts of maritime piracy on global economic development: the case of Somalia," *Maritime Policy & Management*, vol. 37, no. 7, 2010, p. 677; S. J. Hansen, *Piracy in the greater Gulf of Aden: myths, misconception and remedies*, Oslo, Norway: Norwegian Institute for Urban and Regional Research, 2009, p. 7; S. Percy and A. Shortland, *The business of piracy in Somalia*, Berlin, Germany: DIW Berlin, 2011, p. 4.

[7] See D. Nincic, "Maritime piracy in Africa: the humanitarian dimension," *African Security Review*, vol. 18, no. 3, 2009, pp. 5-6.

[8] R. Baird, "Transnational security issues in the Asian maritime environment: responding to maritime piracy," *Australian Journal of International Affairs*, vol. 66, no. 5, 2012, p. 505.

[9] M. Q. Mejia Jr., P. Cariou, and F.-C. Wolff, "Piracy in shipping," pp. 346-370, in W. K. Talley (ed.), *The Blackwell companion to maritime economics*, Oxford, UK: Blackwell Publishing, 2012.

[10] Freedom House indicators: political rights (scale from 1 "Free" to 7 "Least Free"), civil liberties (scale from 1 "Free" to 7 "Least Free") and freedom status (1 "Free", 2 "Partially Free" and 3 "Not Free").

[11] Mejia, Cariou, Wolff, "Piracy in shipping," p. 363.

[12] *Ibid.*

[13] UN Millennium Project, *Investing in development: a practical plan to achieve the Millennium Development Goals*, London, UK: Earthscan, 2005.

[14] The World Bank, *WDR 2011*, pp. 5-6.

[15] See UNCTAD, "The least developed countries report 2011," *http://unctad.org/en/docs/ldc2011_en.pdf*, accessed 20 December 2012.

[16] According to the report, Somalia is likely to meet Goal 1 by the year 2015. TFG, "2010 Millennium Development Goals progress report Somalia," *http://www.so.undp.org/index.php/Support-towards-reaching-the-MDGs.html*, accessed 20 December 2012.

[17] *Ibid*, p. 33.

[18] Puntland State of Somalia, "Millennium Development Goals progress report 2010 (2nd draft)," pp. 55, 58-59. *http://www.so.undp.org/index.php/Support-towards-reaching-the-MDGs.html*, accessed 20 December 2012.

[19] A. Shortland and M. Vothknecht, "Combating 'maritime terrorism' off the coast of Somalia," *European Journal of Political Economy*, vol. 27, suppl. 1, 2011, p. s135.

[20] See Box 2.6 in The World Bank, *WDR 2011*, p. 80.

[21] S. Gates, H. Hegre, H. Mokleiv-Nygård, and H. Strand, "Consequences of civil conflict," *Background Note to WDR 2011*, Washington, DC, USA: The World Bank, 2010, p. 1.

[22] See Figure 1.5 in The World Bank, *WDR 2011*, p. 60.

[23] The World Bank, *WDR 2011*, pp. 50-51.

[24] A.M. Dirie, "2 Somali pirates killed in rivalry clashes: pirates fight over kidnapped aid workers," *SomaliaReport*, 30 October 2011, *http://www.somaliareport.com/index.php/post/1907*, accessed 20 December 2012.

[25] Shortland, Vothknecht, "Combating 'maritime terrorism,'" pp. s149-s150. The authors show through their statistical analysis that pirates conducted attacks even during the holy month of Ramadan, showing contempt for the Islamic courts.

[26] N. Wadhams, "Somali pirates vs. islamists: a dispute over business," *Time*, 7 May 2010, *http://www.time.com/time/printout/0,8816,1987855,00.html*, accessed 20 December 2012.

[27] A. Lindley, "Leaving Mogadishu: towards a sociology of conflict related mobility," *Journal of Refugee Studies*, vol. 23, no. 1, 2010, pp. 2–22; C. Raleigh "The search for safety: the effects of conflict, poverty and ecological influences on migration in the developing world," *Global Environmental Change*, vol. 21, suppl. 1, 2011, p. s85.

[28] The World Bank, *WDR 2011*, p. 62.

[29] *Ibid.*, p. 60. See also L. L. Dahlberg, "Youth violence in the United States: major trends, risk factors, and prevention approaches," *American Journal of Preventive Medicine*, vol. 14, no.4, 1998.

[30] J. V. Hastings, "Geographies of state failure and sophistication in maritime piracy hijackings," *Political Geography*, vol. 28, no. 4, 2009, pp. 214.

[31] L. Andersen, "Fragile states on the international agenda," pp. 7-9, in L. Engberg-Pedersen, L. Andersen, F. Stepputat, and D. Jung (eds.), *Fragile situations*, Copenhagen, Denmark: Danish Institute for International Studies, 2008.

[32] From R. E. Brooks, "Failed states, or the state as failure?," *The University of Chicago Law Review*, vol. 72, no. 4, 2005, pp. 1159-1196. See also G. Helman and S. Ratner, "Saving failed states," *Foreign Policy*, vol. 89, 1992-1993, pp. 3-20; and J.-G. Gros, "Towards a taxonomy of failed states in the new world order: decaying Somalia, Liberia, Rwanda and Haiti," *Third World Quarterly*, vol. 17, no. 3, 1996, pp. 455-471.

[33] "Fragility and fragile situations: Periods when states or institutions lack the capacity, accountability, or legitimacy to mediate relations between citizen groups and between citizens and the state, making them vulnerable to violence." The World Bank, *WDR 2011*, p. xvi.

[34] UNCTAD, "The least developed countries report 2011," p. iii.

[35] M. N. Murphy, *Somalia: the new Barbary? Piracy and Islam in the Horn of Africa*, New York, New York, USA: Columbia University Press, 2011, pp. 1-2.

[36] Hastings, "Geographies of state failure," pp. 213-223.

[37] R. I. Rotberg, "The new nature of nation-state failure," *The Washington Quarterly*, vol. 25, no. 3, 2002, p. 90.

[38] *Ibid.*, pp. 85–96.

[39] Marine Resources Assessment Group (MRAG), "Review of impacts of illegal, unreported and unregulated fishing on developing countries," Synthesis Report prepared for the *UK Department for International Development* (DFID), July 2005.

[40] L. Ploch, C. M. Blanchard, R. O'Rourke, R. C. Mason, and R. O. King, *Piracy off the Horn of Africa*, Washington, DC, USA: Congressional Research Service, 2011, p. 9.

[41] T. Potgieter and C. Schofield, “Poverty, poaching and pirates: geopolitical instability and maritime insecurity off the Horn of Africa,” *Journal of the Indian Ocean Region*, vol. 6, no. 1, 2010, p. 103.

[42] *Id.*

[43] Hansen, *Piracy in the greater Gulf of Aden.*

[44] A.S. Arky, “Trading nets for guns: the impact of illegal fishing on piracy in Somalia,” *Unpublished Master's Thesis*, Monterey, California, USA: Naval Postgraduate School, 2010, p. 15.

[45] Mwangura, “VLCC *Irene SL* freed by pirates,” 8 April 2011. *http://www.somaliareport.com/index.php/post/477/VLCC_Irene_SL_Freed_By_Pirates,* accessed 20 December 2012.

[46] K. Menkhaus, "Dangerous waters," *Survival*, vol. 51, no. 1, 2009, p. 22.

[47] Hansen, *Piracy in the greater Gulf of Aden*, p. 10.

[48] D. B. Termansen, “Counter piracy off Somalia: a case for applying the comprehensive approach strategy,” *Unpublished Research Paper*, Newport, Rhode Island, USA: Naval War College, 2011, pp. 8-9.

[49] A. Le Sage and N. Majid, “The livelihoods gap: responding to the economic dynamics of vulnerability in Somalia,” *Disasters*, vol. 26, no. 1, 2002, p. 12.

[50] Presumably a popular utterance by Somali pirates; in this case it was one who goes by the name “Red Teeth.” See P. Eichstaedt, *Pirate state: inside Somalia's terrorism at sea*, Chicago, Illinois, USA: Lawrence Hill Books, 2010, p. 165.

[51] Hansen, *Piracy in the greater Gulf of Aden*. See also J. Straziuso, “Upside to Somali piracy: better fishing,” *Toronto Star*, 10 January 2010, *www.thestar.com/news/world/article/748867--upside-to-somali-piracy-better-fishing?bn=1*, accessed 20 December 2012.

[52] Ploch et al., *Piracy off the Horn of Africa*, p. 9.

[53] Arky, “Trading nets for guns,” p. 20. See also G. E. Weir, “Fish, family, and profit: piracy and the Horn of Africa,” *Naval War College Review*, vol. 62, no. 3, 2009, p. 20.

[54] In dollar values, this translates to an increase from USD 6 million in 1950 to USD 32 million in 2002 (based on the value of the dollar in the year 2000). M. Bawumia and U. R. Sumaila, “Fisheries, ecosystems and piracy: a case study of Somalia,” *Working paper # 2010-04*, Vancouver, BC, Canada: Fisheries Centre, University of British Columbia, 2010, p. 17. Available for downloading at *http://www.fisheries.ubc.ca/publications/working/index.php.*

[55] ReliefWeb, “Briefing kit for Somalia.” Downloaded from the UN in Somalia website *http://www.unctsom.org/documents/Key%20Documents%20on%20Somalia.pdf.*, accessed 5 December 2011.

[56] Nincic, “Maritime piracy in Africa,” p. 13.

[57] The scope of the CERF is to pre-position funding for humanitarian action to finance both preparedness and early response to crisis. See CERF, "Analysis of CERF Activities in 2009," p. 2. *http://ochaonline.un.org/cerf/WhatistheCERF /tabid/3534 /language/en-US/Default.aspx*, accessed 5 December 2011.

[58] Nincic, “Maritime piracy in Africa,” p. 11.

[59] R. Middleton, “Piracy in Somalia: threatening global trade, feeding local wars,” *Briefing Paper*, London, UK: Chatham House, 2008.

[60] Integrated Regional Information Networks (IRIN), “Somalia: pirates target food, pushing up prices,” 12 April 2010. *http://www.irinnews.org/ printreport.aspx?reportid=88780*, accessed 20 December 2012.

[61] The World Bank, *WDR 2011*, p. 180.

[62] *Ibid.*, p. 183.

[63] *Ibid.*, p. 195.

[64] *Ibid.*, p. 197.

[65] Andersen, "Fragile states on the international agenda," pp. 7-9.

[66] The World Bank, *WDR 2011*, p. 268.

[67] P. T. Leeson, “Better off stateless-Somalia before and after government collapse,” *Journal of Comparative Economics*, vol. 35, no. 4, 2007.

[68] Powell, R. Ford, and A. Nowrasteh, “Somalia after state collapse: chaos or improvement?,” *Journal of Economic Behavior & Organization*, vol. 67, nos. 3-4, 2008.

[69] J. Coyne, “Reconstructing weak and failed states: foreign intervention and the nirvana fallacy,” *Foreign Policy Analysis*, vol. 2, nr. 4, 2006, pp. 343–360. Coyne further writes, “Attempts to reconstruct weak and failed countries suffer from a nirvana fallacy. Where central governments are absent or dysfunctional, it is assumed that reconstruction efforts by foreign governments generate a preferable outcome. This assumption overlooks (1) the possibility that foreign government interventions can fail, (2) the possibility that reconstruction efforts can do more harm than good, and (3) the possibility that indigenous governance mechanisms may evolve that are more effective than those imposed by military occupiers. It is argued that re-construction efforts focus on resolving the meta-level game of creating self-sustaining liberal democratic institutions while neglecting the nested games embedded within the general meta-game.”

[70] Powell et al., “Somalia after state collapse,” p. 669.

[71] K. Menkhaus, “State collapse in Somalia: second thoughts,” *Review of African Political Economy*, vol. 30, no. 97, 2003, p. 405.

[72] J. A. Mubarak, “The hidden hand behind the resilience of the stateless economy of Somalia,” *World Development*, vol. 25, no. 12, 1997.

[73] Powell et al., “Somalia after state collapse,” p. 669. Also Menkhaus, “State collapse in Somalia,” p. 405.

[74] UN Secretary-General's remarks at the launch of World Maritime Day theme for 2011: “Piracy: Orchestrating the Response,” London, UK, 3 February 2011, *http://www.un.org/apps/sg/sgstats.asp?nid=5073*, accessed 20 December 2012.

[75] A. Bowden, *The economic costs of maritime piracy*, Bloomfield, Colorado, USA: One Earth Future Foundation, 2010.

[76] Geopolicity, “The economics of piracy: pirate ransoms & livelihoods off the coast of Somalia,” 2011, p. 3. *http://geopolicity.com/contact_us.php*, accessed 20 December 2012.

[77] *Ibid.*, p. iv.

[78] Fu et al., “The impacts of maritime piracy,” p. 677.

[79] *Ibid.*, p. 690.

[80] ICC-IMB, *Piracy and armed robbery against ships report for the period 1 January – 31 December 2012*, Cinnabar Wharf, London, UK: ICC-IMB, 2013.

[81] Caniete, "*MV Renuar*: 133 days of fear, hopelessness, and helplessness," in M. Q. Mejia Jr., C. Kojima, M. Sawyer (eds.), *Piracy at sea*, Springer Verlag, *in press*.

[82] "*MV Leopard* crew beg for release from Somali pirates," *http://www.youtube.com/watch?v=ypkgtL6QGy8*, accessed 21 December 2012.

[83] K. Hurlburt, *The human cost of Somali piracy*, Bloomfield, Colorado, USA: One Earth Future Foundation, 2011.

[84] Murphy, *Small boats, weak states, dirty money*, p. 378.

[85] A. Logina, "Definition of piracy: an analysis of its effectiveness in the light of the *Arctic Sea* incident," pp. 267-268, in M. Q. Mejia Jr. (ed.), *Maritime security and crime*, Malmö, Sweden: WMU Publications, 2010.

[86] UNCLOS 1982, Article 58 "Rights and duties of other states in the exclusive economic zone" specifies that, among others, the high seas piracy provisions "and other pertinent rules of international law apply to the exclusive economic zone in so far as they are not incompatible" with Part V of the Convention.

[87] M.Q. Mejia Jr., "Maritime gerrymandering: dilemmas in defining piracy, terrorism, and other acts of maritime violence," *Journal of International Commercial Law*, Vol. 2, No. 2, 2003, pp. 152-75.

[88] International Maritime Organization, "Code of Practice for the Investigation of the Crimes of Piracy and Armed Robbery against Ships," *Resolution A.922(22)*, 22 January 2002, at 2.2 in Annex.

[89] UNCLOS 1982, Article 105 "Seizure of a pirate ship or aircraft" provides that "every State may seize a pirate ship or aircraft, or a ship or aircraft taken by piracy and under the control of pirates, and arrest the persons and seize the property on board. The courts of the State which carried out the seizure may decide upon the penalties to be imposed, and may also determine the action to be taken with regard to the ships, aircraft or property, subject to the rights of third parties acting in good faith."

[90] K. Zou, "New developments in the international law of piracy," *Chinese Journal of International Law*, Vol. 8, No. 2, 2009.

[91] S. Venkiteswaran, "Re: *Alondra Rainbow*," in Mejia, *Maritime security and crime*.

[92] M. Bahar, "Attaining optimal deterrence at sea: a legal and strategic theory for naval anti-piracy operations," *Vanderbilt Journal of Transnational Law*, vol. 40, no. 1, 2006, p. 13.

[93] M. Q. Mejia Jr., "Piracy off the Somali coast," pp. 297-298, in Mejia, *Maritime security and crime*.

[94] Guilfoyle, "Treaty jurisdiction over pirates: a compilation of legal texts with introductory notes," Paper prepared for the *3rd Meeting of Working Group 2 on Legal Issues, The Contact Group on Piracy off the Coast of Somalia*, Copenhagen, Denmark, 26-27 August 2009, p. 4.

[95] Kontorovich and S. Art, "An empirical examination of universal jurisdiction for piracy," *The American Journal of International Law*, vol. 104, no. 3, 2010.

[96] V. P. Nanda, "Maritime piracy: how can international law and policy address this growing global menace?," *Denver Journal of International Law and Policy*, vol. 39, no. 2, 2011, p. 203.

[97] J. T. Gathii, "Kenya's piracy prosecutions," *American Journal of International Law*, vol. 104, no. 3, 2010.

[98] R. P. Kelley, "UNCLOS, but no cigar: overcoming obstacles to the prosecution of maritime piracy," *Minnesota Law Review*, vol. 95, no. 6, 2011.

[99] J. D. Peppetti, "Building the global maritime security network: a multinational legal structure to combat transnational threats," *Naval Law Review*, vol. 55, 2008, pp. 110-112.

[100] R. Geiß and A. Petrig, *Piracy and armed robbery at sea: the legal framework for counter-piracy operations in Somalia and the Gulf of Aden*, Oxford, UK: Oxford University Press, 2011, p. 29.

[101] UN Security Council, *Resolution 1851, S/RES/1851*, 22 December 2008, p. 2.

[102] Bahar, "Attaining optimal deterrence at sea," pp. 58-59.

[103] Fouché, "Sea piracy: the law enforcement approach – overcoming challenges to effective investigation and prosecution of Somali pirates," in M. Q. Mejia Jr., C. Kojima, M. Sawyer (eds.), *Piracy at sea*, Springer Verlag, *in press*.

[104] A. Petrig, "Human rights and counter-piracy operations – no legal vacuum but legal uncertainty," in M. Q. Mejia Jr., C. Kojima, M. Sawyer (eds.), *Piracy at sea*, Springer Verlag, *in press*.

[105] D. Guilfoyle, "Counter-piracy law enforcement and human rights," *International and Comparative Law Quarterly*, vol. 59, no. 1, 2010, p. 159.

[106] M. H. Passman, "Protections afforded to captured pirates under the law of war and international law," *Tulane Maritime Law Journal*, vol. 33, no. 1, 2008.

[107] Bahar, "Attaining optimal deterrence at sea," p. 6.

[108] Latin for "enemy of mankind."

[109] Williamson, "Piracy at sea: the humanitarian impact," presentation at the International conference on piracy at sea *(ICOPAS)*, Malmö, Sweden, 17-19 October 2011.

[110] Passman, "Protections afforded to captured pirates," p. 39-40.

[111] M. Q. Mejia Jr., C. Kojima, M. Sawyer, "The Malmö Declaration: calling for a multi-sectoral response to piracy," in M. Q. Mejia Jr., C. Kojima, M. Sawyer (eds.), *Piracy at sea*, Springer Verlag, *in press*.

[112] G. Onuoha, "Energy and security in the Gulf of Guinea: a Nigerian perspective," *South African Journal of International Affairs*, vol. 16, no. 2, 2009, pp. 245-264.

[113] B. McSherry, "The political economy of oil in Equatorial Guinea," *African Studies Quarterly*, vol. 8, no. 3, 2006, pp. 23-45.

[114] F. Onuoha, "The geo-strategy of oil in the Gulf of Guinea: implications for regional stability, *Journal of Asian and African Studies*, vol. 45, no. 3, 2010, pp. 369-384.

[115] The World Bank, *WDR 2011*, p. 67.

[116] *Ibid.*, p. 65.

[117] M. P. Gomez and A. Christensen, "The impacts of refugees on neighboring countries: a developpment challenge," *Background Note to WDR 2011*, Washington, DC, USA: The World Bank, 2010, p. 6.

[118] *Ibid.*, pp. 7-8.

[119] The World Bank, *WDR 2011*, pp. 77-78.

[120] B. Sanga, "Kenya's Somali incursion cuts piracy costs in Indian Ocean," *Business Daily* (Nairobi), 9 November 2011, *http://allafrica.com/stories/201111091257.html*, accessed 20 December 2012.

[121] UN, "United Nations documents on piracy," *http://www.un.org/depts/los/piracy/piracy_documents.htm*, accessed 20 December 2012.

[122] CGPCS, "Working groups," *http://www.thecgpcs.org/work.do?action=work*, accessed 20 December 2012.

[123] IMO, *http://www.imo.org*, accessed 20 December 2012.

[124] Among them the Convention for the Suppression of Unlawful Acts Against the Safety of Maritime Navigation (SUA), 1988, as amended; the International Ship and Port Facility Security (ISPS) Code; Chapter XI-2 of the International Convention for the Safety of Life at Sea (SOLAS), 1974, as amended; and scores of circulars and recommendations for governments and shipping companies on issues such as the deployment of armed guards on board ships, the prevention and suppression of piracy and armed robbery against ships, as well as the investigation of cases of piracy and armed robbery against ships.

[125] E. E. Mitropoulos, "The Year of the Seafarer and the impacts of piracy," *WMU Journal of Maritime Affairs*, vol. 10, no. 1, 2011, pp. 1-5.

[126] IMO, *http://www.imo.org/ourwork/security/piu/pages/dcoc.aspx*, accessed 30 January 2013.

[127] ReCAAP, Article 18 "Signature and entry into force."

[128] DCoC, Article 4 "Measures to repress piracy."

[129] DCoC, Article 7 "Embarked officers."

[130] DCoC, Article 8.7 "Coordination and information sharing."

[131] DCoC, Article 15(a) "Miscellaneous provisions."

[132] This defines treaty as "an international agreement concluded between States in written form and governed by international law, whether embodied in a single instrument or in two or more related instruments and whatever its particular designation."

[133] DCoC, Article 13 "Consultations."

[134] Resolution 3 adopted at the *IMO Sub-regional meeting on maritime security, piracy and armed robbery against ships for Western Indian Ocean, Gulf of Aden and Red Sea States*, Djibouti, 26-29 January 2009.

[135] Ho, "Combating piracy and armed robbery in Asia: the ReCAAP Information Sharing Centre (ISC)," *Marine Policy*, vol. 33, no. 2, 2008, p. 434.

[136] S. Menefee, "A recap of ReCAAP," p. 198, in Mejia, *Maritime security and crime*.

[137] M. Q. Mejia Jr., "Regional cooperation in combating piracy and armed robbery against ships: learning lessons from ReCAAP," pp. 125-137, in A. Petrig (ed.), *Sea piracy law – Droit de la piraterie maritime*, Berlin, Germany: Dunckler and Humblot, 2010.

[138] E. Mitropoulos, "International Conference on Piracy at Sea: keynote address," in M. Q. Mejia Jr., C. Kojima, M. Sawyer (eds.), *Piracy at sea*, Springer Verlag, *in press*.

[139] Rotberg, "The new nature of nation-state failure," p. 94.

[140] Menkhaus, "Somalia and the Horn of Africa," *Background Case Study to WDR 2011*, Washington, DC, USA: The World Bank, 2011, p. 9.

[141] Murphy, *Small boats, weak states, dirty money*, p. 21.

[142] *Ibid.*, p. 52.

[143] *Ibid.*, p. 378.

[144] See Section 3.1 of this Report. Add to this the humanitarian emergency in the Horn of Africa where half a million Somalis live more or less permanently in refugee camps in

Kenya and Yemen (see Section 3.3 of this Report) – not to mention the hundreds of thousands suffering within Somalia's borders.

[145] Abhyankar, "Maritime crime," in M. Q. Mejia Jr. (ed.), *Contemporary issues in maritime security*, Malmö, Sweden: WMU Publications, 2005.

[146] The World Bank, *WDR 2011*, p. 8.

[147] Hansen, *Piracy in the greater Gulf of Aden*, pp. 62-63.

[148] D. Jung, "State formation and state-building: is there a lesson to learn from sociology?," p. 39, in L. Engberg-Pedersen, L. Andersen, F. Stepputat, and D. Jung (eds.), *Fragile situations*, Copenhagen, Denmark: Danish Institute for International Studies, 2008.

[149] J. P. Pham, "Putting Somali piracy in context," *Journal of Contemporary African Studies*, vol. 28, no. 3, 2010, p. 336.

[150] F. Fukuyama, "'Stateness' first," *Journal of Democracy*, vol. 16, no. 1, 2005, p. 85.

[151] Hastings, "Geographies of state failure," pp. 213-223.

PAPERS AND PUBLICATIONS OF PROFESSOR PROSHANTO K. MUKHERJEE

JOURNAL ARTICLES

P.K. Mukherjee "Mirage at Sea", *The Marine Observer*, Journal of the Meteorological Office, Bracknell, U.K., May 1975.

P.K. Mukherjee, "The Charting and Safe Keeping of Oceans and Waterways: Legal Implications", Vol. 6, No. 3, May 1981 edition of *Dalhousie Law Journal*, Dalhousie Law School, Halifax, Nova Scotia.

P.K. Mukherjee, "The Consent Regime of Oceanic Research in the New Law of the Sea", April 1981 issue of *Marine Policy*, I.P.C. Science and Technology Press Ltd., Guildford, Surrey, U.K.

A.J. Kerr and P.K. Mukherjee, "Who is Qualified to Survey Canada's Off-shore?", *The Canadian Surveyor*, April 1984, Journal of the Canadian Institute of Surveyors, pp. 15 – 25.

Ron McNab, P.K. Mukherjee, Richard Buxton, "Canada's Continental Shelf: An Ocean Mapping Challenge", in *Geos*, Vol. 16 No. 1, 1987, published by Energy, Mines and Resources Canada, p. 18

P.K. Mukherjee, "Overtaking or Crossing: Judicial Interpretation and the Mariner's Dilemma", *Journal of Maritime Law & Commerce*, U.S.A., April 1992, pp. 247-262.

P.K. Mukherjee, "Flagging Options: Legal and Other Considerations"; Proceedings, International Conference on Ports and Shipping in a Changing Economic Environment, *Mariner, Journal of the Master Mariners' Society of Pakistan*, Vol.4, No.1, January/March 1993.

P.K. Mukherjee, "Maritime Cases and Rules of Statutory Construction", published in Vol. 25, No. 2, April 1994 issue of *Journal of Maritime Law and Commerce*, U.S.A.

P.K. Mukherjee, "The Use of Model Legislation in the Development of a Modern Maritime Regime", *WMU Alumni Journal*, 2000.

Proshanto K. Mukherjee, "New Horizons for Flag States", *Maritime Review*, London; Pacific Press Limited, 2000, pp. 110-114.

P.K. Mukherjee, "The Law of Maritime Liens and Conflict of Laws", *Journal of International Maritime Law (JIML)*, Issue 3, December, 2003.

P.K. Mukherjee, "Selected Issues of Law and Ergonomics in Maritime Security", *Journal of International Maritime Law (JIML),*10 [2004] 316.

Proshanto K. Mukherjee, "Transformation of Conventions into National Legislation: Piracy and Suppression of Unlawful Acts" *Journal of International Commercial Law,* University of Wales, Swansea, 2004.

Proshanto K. Mukherjee, "The Anachronism in Maritime Law that is General Average", *WMU Journal of Maritime Affairs*, October 2005, Vol. 4, No. 3 at pp. 195-209.

Maximo Q. Mejia and Proshanto K. Mukherjee, "The SUA Convention 2005: A Critical Evaluation of its Effectiveness in Suppressing Maritime Criminal Acts" in *Journal of International Maritime Law,* (2006) 12 *Journal of International Maritime Law (JIML)*, 170-191.

Proshanto K. Mukherjee, "The New SUA Convention in Perspective" in *Shipping and Transport International,* London: Guthrum House, August 2006, Vol. 6, No. 1, pp.12-15.

Proshanto K. Mukherjee, "Criminalisation and Unfair Treatment: The Seafarer's Perspective" in *Journal of International Maritime Law (JIML)*, September-October 2006, Volume 12, Issue 5, pp.325-336.

Proshanto K. Mukherjee, "Essentials of General Average: A Synoptic Overview of an Ancient Maritime Law" in *WMU Journal of Maritime Affairs,* April 2007, Vol. 6, No. 1, pp. 21-36.

Mejia M.Q. Jr., Mukherjee P.K., Akselsson R., "The ISM Code in the Context of Swedish Port State Control Statistics" in *Ocean Yearbook* 2007, Vol. 21, pp. 405-426.

Proshanto K. Mukherjee, "The ISM Code and ISPS Code – A Critical Legal Analysis of Two SOLAS Regimes" *WMU Journal of Maritime Affairs,* October 2007, Vol. 6, No. 2, pp 147-166.

Proshanto K. Mukherjee and Abhinayan Basu Bal, "A Legal and Economic Analysis of the Volume Contract Concept under the Rotterdam Rules : Selected Issues in Perspective" Vol. 40, No. 4, October 2009 issue of *Journal of Maritime Law and Commerce*, U.S.A., pp. 579 – 607.

Proshanto K. Mukherjee and Abhinayan Basu Bal, "A Legal and Economic Analysis of the Volume Contract Concept under the Rotterdam Rules: Selected Issues in Perspective", Vol. 77 *J. Transp. L. Logist. & Pol'y* [1], 2010, Annapolis MD: Association of Transportation Law Professionals Inc., pp. 27-51.

Proshanto K. Mukherjee & Abhinayan Basu Bal, "To implement or not to implement: Ship source Marine Pollution Law in the Baltic Sea Region", *Baltic Transport Journal*, 3/2010 (35), May/June 2010.

Proshanto K. Mukherjee & Olena Bokareva, "Multimodal Maritime Plus: Some European Perspectives on Law & Policy", (2010), 16 *Journal of International Maritime Law (JIML)*.

Proshanto K. Mukherjee, "Enhancement of Maritime Law Education in the Indian Context", (2010), 3 *NUJS Law Review*, Kolkata, India.

Proshanto K. Mukherjee and Abhinayan Basu Bal, "The Impact of the Volume Contract Concept on the Global Community of Shippers: The Rotterdam Rules in Perspective", (2010), 16 *Journal of International Maritime Law (JIML)*.

PUBLISHED CONFERENCE PROCEEDINGS

P.K. Mukherjee and R.S. Lefebvre, "Fishermen and Oil Pollution Damage: The Regimes of Compensation", *Proceedings: International Research Symposium on Labour Developments in the Fishing Industry*, University of Quebec at Rimouski, P.Q., November 3-4, 1983 pp.73-81, published by Department of Fisheries and Oceans, Canada.

P.K. Mukherjee and Neil M. Anderson, "Copyright, Safety and the Electronic Chart: Towards New Directions in Navigation"; *Proceedings*: *1st Biennial Canadian Hydrographic Conference*, Halifax, Nova Scotia, April 1985, p. 109-115.

Ron MacNab, P.K. Mukherjee and Richard Buxton, "The 1982 U.N. Convention on the Law of the Sea and the Outer Limit of the Continental Shelf: Some Practical Difficulties for Wide Margin States", *Proceedings: "Oceans '87 - The Ocean: An International Workplace"*, Halifax, Nova Scotia, September - October 1987, Vol. 2, p. 698-704.

P.K. Mukherjee and D.H. Gray, "Inter-jurisdictional Boundaries in Tidal and Non-Tidal Rivers" *Proceedings: Oceans '87 - The Ocean: An International Workplace,* Halifax, Nova Scotia, September-October 1987, Vol. 2, p. 688-695.

P.K. Mukherjee, "The Electronic Chart: Legal Issues Old & New". *Proceedings: International Conference on Maritime Law and the Electronic Chart*, Ottawa, November 1990, pp. 18-20.

P.K. Mukherjee, "Copyright Control of Electronic Charts: The Pros and Cons" *Proceedings: International Conference on Maritime Law and the Electronic Chart*, Ottawa, November 1990, pp. 29-38.

P.K. Mukherjee, "Maritime Technology and the Law: The Electronic Chart in Perspective." *Proceedings: Maritime Technology 21st Century, 1992 Conference*, University of Melbourne, Australia.

P.K. Mukherjee, "Issues of Environmental Law and Regulations in the Path towards Port and Maritime Excellence: Opportunities for Research and Development", *Proceedings: Inaugural International Conference on Port and Maritime R&D and Technology*, Singapore, 29-31 October, 2001.

P.K. Mukherjee and Maximo Q. Mejia, "The Legal Framework of Maritime Security in International Law", *Proceedings: Pacem in Maribus 13*, Kiev, Ukraine, 2003.

P.K. Mukherjee, "The Law of Maritime Liens and Conflict of Laws", *Proceedings: International Conference on Maritime Law, China Maritime Law Association,* Shanghai, October 2002, pp. 88-95.

Proshanto K. Mukherjee, "Selected Aspects of the Recognition Regime under the STCW Convention", *Proceedings, International Conference on Port and Maritime R&D and Technology*, Singapore, 10-12 September, 2003, pp. 235-244.

J.U. Schröder, M.Q. Mejia, Jr., P.K. Mukherjee, F.M. Manolis and S. Dreessen, "Potential Consequences of Imprecise Security Assessments" in Detlef Nielsen (Ed.), *Maritime Security and MET: Proceedings of IAMU 6th. Annual General Assembly and Conference*, World Maritime University, Malmö, Sweden, 24-26 October, 2005, Southampton: WIT Press, 2005 at pp. 79-80.

Proshanto K. Mukherjee, "The Role of Higher Education in the Development and Implementation of Maritime Law and Policy", in *Proceedings: Maritime Forum 2008*, Chennai, India, 31 January – 2 February, 2008.

Proshanto K. Mukherjee and Jingjing Xu, "The Legal Framework of Exhaust Emissions from Ships: A Selective Examination from a Law and Economics Perspective", in Neil Bellefontaine and Olof Linden (Eds) *Impacts of Climate Change on the Maritime Industry,* Malmö: *WMU Publications,* 2009, pp. 69 – 101.

Proshanto K. Mukherjee, "Liability and Compensation for Environmental Damage Caused by Ship-Source Pollution: Actionability of Claims" in *Proceedings: International Conference on Marine Pollution Liability and Policy,* Dalian, China, 4-5 June, 2009, pp. 98-117

Proshanto K. Mukherjee & Abhinayan Basu Bal, "A Legal and Economic Analysis of the Volume Contract Concept under the Rotterdam Rules: Selected Issues in Perspective", presented at the Rotterdam Rules 2009 Colloquium, Rotterdam Rules Signing Ceremony, 20 - 23 September 2009, Rotterdam.

Proshanto K. Mukherjee & Abhinayan Basu Bal, "The Impact of the Volume Contract Concept on the Global Community of Shippers: The Rotterdam Rules in Perspective", presented at the Sixth European Colloquium on Maritime Law (ECMLR) on The Legal, Economic, Environmental, Insurance and Commercial Implications of the Rotterdam Rules, 27 - 28 May 2010, Swansea University.

Proshanto K. Mukherjee & Olena Bokareva, "Multimodal Maritime Plus: Some European Perspectives on Law & Policy", presented at the Sixth European Colloquium on Maritime Law (ECMLR) on The Legal, Economic, Environmental, Insurance and Commercial Implications of the Rotterdam Rules, 27 - 28 May 2010, Swansea University.

Books and Monographs

Proshanto K. Mukherjee, *Maritime Legislation,* Malmö: WMU Publications, 2002.

Proshanto K. Mukherjee, Maximo Q. Mejia Jr., Gotthard M. Gauci, (Eds) *Maritime Violence and Other Security Issues at Sea*, Malmö: WMU Publications, 2002.

Proshanto K. Mukherjee and Mark Brownrigg, *Farthing on International Shipping*, 4th Edition, Malmö, WMU Publications. (to be published in 2011)

Proshanto K. Mukherjee, Maximo Q. Mejia Jr., Jingjing Xu, *Ergonomics, Economics, and the Law : The International Regime of Maritime Security,* WMU Research Report Series, No. 1, June 2009

Chapters in Books

P.K. Mukherjee, "Maritime Law" in *A Guide to the Management and Operation of Marine Research and Survey Vessels* published by International Centre for Ocean Development, Halifax, Nova Scotia, 1989, Chapter 1, pp. 1-130.

Ron McNab and P.K. Mukherjee, "The 1982 U.N. Convention on the Law of the Sea and the Outer Limit of the Continental Shelf: Some Practical Difficulties for Wide Margin States", in Donat Pharand and Umberto Leanza (Eds.) *The Continental Shelf and the Exclusive Economic Zone: Delimitation and Legal Regime*, Dordrecht/Boston/London: Martinus Nijhoff, 1993.

Proshanto K. Mukherjee, "Transformation of Conventions into National Legislation: Piracy and Suppression of Unlawful Acts", in Proshanto K. Mukherjee, Maximo Q. Mejia Jr., Gotthard M. Gauci, (Eds.) *Maritime Violence and Other Security Issues at Sea*, Malmö, WMU Publications, 2002, pp. 55-99.

Proshanto K. Mukherjee and Azfar Mohamad Mustafar, "The International Ship and Port Facility Security (ISPS) Code and Human Element Issues", in Maximo Q. Mejia Jr. (Ed) *Contemporary Issues in Maritime Security*, Malmö, WMU Publications, 2005, pp. 277-285.

Proshanto K. Mukherjee & Maximo Q. Mejia, "The ISPS Code: Legal and Ergonomic Considerations" in Maximo Q. Mejia (Ed.) *Contemporary Issues in Maritime Security,* Malmö: WMU Publications, 2005, pp. 33-51.

Proshanto K. Mukherjee, "An Introduction to Maritime Law and Admiralty Jurisdiction" in *The Admiral,* Accra: Ghana Shippers' Council, Buck Press Ltd., 2005, pp. 1-56.

Proshanto K. Mukherjee, "Refuge and Salvage", Chapter 10 in Aldo Chircop and Olof Linden (Eds.), *Places of Refuge for Ships,* Leiden, Boston: Martinus Nijhoff, 2006, pp. 271-297.

Mikis Manolis and Proshanto K. Mukherjee, "Unlawful Acts and the Carriage of Goods by Sea: Liabilities, Defences and Legal Implications", in Maximo Q. Mejia Jr., Jingjing Xu (Ed.) *Coastal Zone Piracy and Other Unlawful Acts at Sea*, Malmö: WMU Publications, 2007, pp. 291 – 311.

Proshanto K. Mukherjee, "A Legal Commentary on the Alondra Rainbow Judgment", in Maximo Q. Mejia Jr., Jingjing Xu (Ed.) *Coastal Zone Piracy and Other Unlawful Acts at Sea*, Malmö: WMU Publications, 2007, pp. 267 – 278.

Proshanto K. Mukherjee, "The Penal Law of Ship-Source Marine Pollution: Selected Issues in Perspective" in *Liber Amicorum Judge Thomas A. Mensah: Law of the Sea, Environmental Law and Settlement of Disputes",* Max Planck Institute for Comparative Public Law and International Law, Leiden Boston: Martinus Nijhoff September 2007, pp. 463 - 496

Proshanto K. Mukherjee, "Liabilities of Ports in Respect of Marine Pollution and Related Matters" in D.R. Thomas (Ed.) *Liability Regimes in Contemporary Maritime Law*, London: Informa, 2007, pp. 53 – 98.

Proshanto K. Mukherjee, "Liability and Compensation for Environmental Damage Caused by Ship-Source Pollution: Actionability of Claims" in Michael G. Faure, Han Lixin and Shan Hongjun (Eds.) *Marine Pollution Liability and Policy: China, Europe and the U.S.*, The Netherlands: Wolters Kluwer, 2010, pp. 75-95

Proshanto K. Mukherjee, "Essentials of the Regimes of Limitation of Liability in Maritime Law", *The Admiral*, Vol. IV, Accra: Ghana Shippers' Council, Unik Image, 2009, pp. 39-57.

Proshanto K. Mukherjee, "Maritime Offences under International Law and the Arctic Sea Incident" in Maximo Q. Mejia (Ed.) *Maritime Security and Crime,* Malmö: WMU Publications, 2010, pp. 255-262

Book Reviews

P.K. Mukherjee, Book Review of Edgar Gold, *Gard Handbook on P&I Insurance*, 5th. Edition, Arendal, Norway, in *Journal of Maritime Law and Commerce,* Vol. 34, No. 3, July 2003.

Proshanto K. Mukherjee, Book Review of Edgar Gold, Aldo Chircop, Hugh Kindred, *Maritime Law (Essentials of Canadian Law)* in *WMU Journal of Maritime Affairs,* (Oct. 2004), Vol. 3, No.2. pp. 211-213.

Proshanto.K. Mukherjee, Book Review of Ajoy Chatterjee, *Auditing the ISM – A Guide for ISM Auditors*, in *WMU Journal of Maritime Affairs,* (Oct. 2005), Vol. 4, No.3. pp. 229-230.

Proshanto K. Mukherjee, Review of Edgar Gold, *Gard Handbook on Protection of the Marine Environment*, 3rd. edition. Arendal, Norway, *Journal of Maritime Law and Commerce*, Baltimore: Jefferson Law Book Co., January 2007, Vol 38, No. 1, pp. 125-126.

Proshanto K. Mukherjee, Review of Dr. Z Oya Özcayir, *Port State Control*, 2nd edition, LLP, 2004, *Journal of International Maritime Law*, July-August 2006, Volume 12, Issue 4, pp.290-291.

Proshanto K. Mukherjee, Review of Wayne K. Talley, *Maritime Safety, Security and Piracy*, London: Informa, 2008, published in the *Journal of International Maritime Law,* 2010.

Proshanto K. Mukherjee, Review of Michael W. D. White, *Australian Marine Pollution Laws*, 2nd edition, The Federation Press, published in the *WMU Journal of Maritime Affairs*, 2011.

Foreword and Editorials

P.K. Mukherjee, "Piracy, Unlawful Acts and Maritime Violence", Editorial in *Journal of International Maritime Law* 10 [2004] 4 pp. 301-302

Proshanto K. Mukherjee, *Foreword* in Maximo Q. Mejia Jr. (Ed.) *Contemporary Issues in Maritime Security*, Malmö: WMU Publications, 2005.

Proshanto K. Mukherjee, *Foreword* in Maximo Q. Mejia Jr., Jingjing Xu (Ed.) *Coastal Zone Piracy and Other Unlawful Acts at Sea*, Malmö: WMU Publications, 2007.

Proshanto K. Mukherjee, "Chandrika Prasad Srivastava: A Tribute to the Founding Chancellor and Chancellor Emeritus of World Maritime University" in Proshanto K. Mukherjee, Maximo Q. Mejia Jr., Jingjing Xu, *Ergonomics, Economics, and the Law : The International Regime of Maritime Security,* WMU Research Report Series, No. 1, June 2009.

Proshanto K. Mukherjee, *Foreword* in Abhinayan Basu Bal, *An Evaluation of the United Nations Convention on Contracts for the International Carriage of Goods Wholly or Partly by Sea (The Rotterdam Rules) Through Critical Analysis,* WMU Research Report Series No. 2, June 2009.

Proshanto K. Mukherjee, *Foreword* in Maximo Q. Mejia Jr. (Ed.) *Maritime Security and Crime*, Malmö: WMU Publications, 2010.

Proshanto K. Mukherjee, "Chandrika Prasad Srivastava : A Tribute to the Founding Chancellor and Chancellor Emeritus of World Maritime University", Editorial in *WMU Journal of Maritime Affairs*, Vol. 9 (2010), No. 2, pp. 135-136.

SPECIAL PUBLICATIONS

P.K. Mukherjee, *Offshore Management* - A Study Guide for the Canada Lands Surveyors Examination; 1989; published by the Canadian Hydrographic Service, Department of Fisheries and Oceans, Ottawa.

P.K. Mukherjee, Co-Author of *Manual on "Technical Aspects of Law of the Sea"* Special Publication of the International Hydrographic Organization, Monaco, July 1993.

P.K. Mukherjee, Co-Author, *Guidelines for Maritime Legislation,* Third Edition, Bangkok: ESCAP, 1991.

Proshanto K. Mukherjee, *Understanding Maritime Transportation Laws*, Seoul: Chung Ang University, Dept. of Shipping and Logistics Management, September 2009.

SEMINAR AND WORKSHOP PAPERS, UNPUBLISHED CONFERENCE PROCEEDINGS AND PUBLIC LECTURES

N.J. Campbell, G.L. Holland, J.D. Bradford and P.K. Mukherjee, "International Aid in Fisheries and Ocean Science and Technology: A Canadian View". Presented at international workshop on *Future of International cooperation in Marine Technology, Science and Fisheries*, sponsored by National Academy of Sciences, National Research Council, Washington, D.C., held at Scripps Institution of Oceanography, La Jolla, California, January, 18-22, 1981.

P.K. Mukherjee and J.F. Abgrall "Compensation for Victims of Oil Spills: Canadian Experience with Fishermen's Claims." Presented at Seminar on *Economic Consequences of Oil Spills*, sponsored by the Environment Committee of the Organization for Economic Cooperation and Development (O.E.C.D.); Paris, France, June 1981.

P.K. Mukherjee, "Liability and the Electronic Chart" in David Underwood (Ed.) *Proceedings: Joint Workshop on the Electronic Chart* sponsored by the Canadian Hydrographers Association and the Hydrographic Society (U.S. Branch), Dartmouth, Nova Scotia, April 1985, p. 19.

P.K. Mukherjee, "International Perspectives in Maritime Law and the Shipping Legislation of Trinidad & Tobago", *Proceedings: The Shipping Bill, 1987*, Seminar sponsored jointly by the Caribbean Fisheries Training and Development Institute and the Nautical Institute; Port-of-Spain, Trinidad, October 1987.

P.K. Mukherjee, "The Legal Implications of the Placement and Maintenance of Navigational Aids", *Canadian Coast Guard Training Seminar*, Cornwall, Ontario, February 1988.

P.K. Mukherjee, "Legal Implications of the Electronic Chart" Peter B. Mushkat (Ed) *Proceedings,- Charting a Course for Electronic Navigation Display in Canada,* St. John's, Newfoundland, June 1988.

P.K. Mukherjee, "The Surveyor's Potential Exposure to Liability", *Hydrographic Seminar sponsored by International Centre for Ocean Development,* University of Toronto, School of Survey Science, June 1988.

P.K. Mukherjee, "The Electronic Chart: Legal Aspects", *Proceedings: Workshop on Electronic Chart, U.S. Hydrographic Conference '88, "The World of Hydrography"*, Baltimore, Md., April 1988.

P.K. Mukherjee, "Roles and Functions of Private Entities in a Marine Pollution Emergency", Lecture delivered at Seminar on *Financial Questions, Liabilities & Compensation for Pollution*, sponsored by the Regional Marine Pollution Emergency Response Centre (REMPEC), of the Mediterranean Action Plan of the Barcelona Convention, held in Malta, October 1990.

P.K. Mukherjee "The International Law of Maritime Liens: A General Overview"; *Proceedings: International Seminar on Maritime Law*, IMLI, Malta, 19th May, 1993.

P.K. Mukherjee, "Fiscal Success Versus Flag State Responsibility". Paper presented at *Association of Malta Shipowners Workshop*, Malta, 26 May, 1994.

P.K. Mukherjee, "The Implementation of IMO Conventions through National Legislation". Paper presented at *IMO Regional Seminar on Legislation for the Adoption and Implementation of IMO Conventions*; Port of Spain, Trinidad and Tobago, September 1998.

P.K. Mukherjee, "The Jamaica International Ship Registry: A One Stop Shop", Paper presented at Maritime Seminar jointly sponsored by the University of the West Indies Norman Manley Law School and the Maritime Authority of Jamaica, Kingston, Jamaica, September 2000.

P.K. Mukherjee, "The Changing Face of the Flag State: Experience with Alternative Registries", *Proceedings, Seminar on Strategies for Canadian Shipping: Forging a New Paradigm,* Toronto, Ontario, October, 2000.

P.K. Mukherjee, "Maritime Safety and the Human Element in the Wake of the Prestige Disaster", *Presentation to Parliament of the European Union,* Brussels, February 2004

Maximo Q. Mejia Jr., Proshanto K Mukherjee, "The International Maritime Law on Piracy at Sea", presented at the *Workshop on Piracy and Non-traditional Threats to Maritime Security in Asia*, organized by the Centre for East and Southeast Asian Studies, Lund University and the Nordic Institute of Asian Studies, 7-8 May 2004, Grand Hotel, Molle, Sweden.

P.K. Mukherjee, "Criminalization of Seafarers: The Modern Maritime Malady", in *Proceedings: Symposium on Seafarers' Rights: Reform*, Greenwich Maritime Institute, University of Greenwich, 11 November, 2005.

Proshanto K. Mukherjee, "Enhancement of Maritime Law Education in the Indian Context", presented at *Shipping and Marine World Expo*, Mumbai 14 February 2008.

Unpublished Papers

P.K. Mukherjee, "The 200-Mile Limit: Its Implications in Fisheries and Marine Scientific Research Policy", 1975.

P.K. Mukherjee, "A Comparative Analysis of Three U.N. Conferences on the Law of the Sea", 1975.

P.K. Mukherjee, "International Organizations and Ocean-related Interests: A Survey of the Functions of ECOSOC, FAO, UNCTAD, and UNEP", 1976.

P.K. Mukherjee, "Maritime Transportation: A Subject of National Interest", 1976.

P.K. Mukherjee, "Setting of Ship Standards in the Law of Vessel Source Pollution: Canadian and International Perspectives", 1978.

P.K. Mukherjee, "Canada and the Liner Conference System: A Critical Survey", 1978.

P.K. Mukherjee, "Towards a Global Regime for the Prevention and Control of Marine Pollution: Canadian Perspectives" 1979.

P. K. Mukherjee, "The Development of Maritime Legislation: An Enquiry into its History, Principles, Uniformity and Preparation" (Ph.D. thesis), 1996

Editorial Activities

Currently Member of the Editorial Boards of the Journal of International Maritime Law and WMU Journal of Maritime Affairs; formerly Member of the Editorial Board of Journal of Maritime Law and Commerce and Editorial Assistant of Dalhousie Law Journal.

About the Authors

Abhinayan BASU BAL

Dr. Abhinayan Basu Bal is presently an Assistant Professor and a post-doctoral researcher at University of Gothenburg, Sweden. He received his PhD from the World Maritime University (WMU), Malmö, Sweden, after pursuing research in the law of carriage of goods by sea. Prior to joining the WMU doctoral programme, Abhinayan attended University College London in the United Kingdom where he earned the degree of Master of Laws specializing in Maritime Law. He also obtained a Master of Business Law from the National Law School of India University, Bangalore, India, a Bachelor of Laws from the University of Burdwan, India and a Bachelor of Science in Economics from the University of Calcutta, India.

Gotthard Mark GAUCI

Dr. Gotthard Mark Gauci is Lecturer in Maritime Regulation and Policy, Plymouth Business School, Plymouth University, having held previous appointments at Plymouth Law School, Swansea University, as well as Cardiff University. After studying law at the Universities of Malta and Southampton, he carried out research leading to his PhD degree from the University of Wales in 1994. He has written various articles and papers on a number of aspects of shipping law. He has been a member of the core faculty of Lloyd's Maritime Training Programme for a number of years. Before joining academia, he practised as an advocate for a number of years in Malta, lecturing part-time at the IMO International Maritime Law Institute. His main research interests are shipping law and environmental law and he has written extensively in these fields. He is a contributor to *Benedict on Admiralty*, and the author of *Oil Pollution at Sea - Civil Liability and Compensation for Damage* (John Wiley & Sons, 1997).

Måns JACOBSSON

Måns Jacobsson was from 1985 to 2006 Director and Chief Executive Officer of the International Oil Pollution Compensation Funds (IOPC Funds) in London. Since his retirement from the IOPC Funds at the end of 2006 he is working as academic lecturer and as a consultant in maritime and environmental matters.

After studies at Princeton University in the United States, Måns Jacobsson studied law at Lund University in Sweden, graduating in 1964.

Måns Jacobsson served in the Swedish judiciary at district court and appellate court level 1964-1970. He worked as legal advisor in the Department for International Civil Law of the Swedish Ministry of Justice 1970-1981 and was Head of that Department 1982-1984, representing Sweden in a number of inter-governmental organisations. He held the post of President of Division of the Stockholm Court of Appeal 1985-2006. He has also served as an arbitrator in Sweden.

Måns Jacobson is member of the Board of Governors of the World Maritime University (WMU) in Malmö (Sweden). He is Visiting Professor at WMU and at the Maritime Universities in Dalian and Shanghai (People's Republic of China) and Honorary Professor at the University of Nottingham (United Kingdom). He is a Visiting Fellow at the IMO International Maritime Law Institute (IMLI) in Malta and member of the Institute of International Shipping and Trade Law at the University of Swansea (United Kingdom). He is also corresponding member of the Academia Nacional de Derecho y Ciencias Sociales in Buenos Aires (Argentina). He is member of the Council of London Shipping Law Centre - Maritime Business Forum and of the Advisory Board of Portius International and EU Port Law Centre in Antwerp.

He is member of the Executive Council of Comité Maritime International (CMI). He is also associate member of Quadrant Chambers, a set of leading barristers in London specialising in commercial law

Måns Jacobsson has published (together with two co-authors) a book on patent law. He has also published numerous articles in various fields of law, such as maritime law, torts, patent law, nuclear law and treaty law.

The University of Southampton (United Kingdom) has conferred upon him the Degree of Doctor of Laws *honoris causa.*

Chie KOJIMA

Dr. Chie Kojima is Associate Professor of International Law at Musashino University, Tokyo, Japan. Aside from holding bachelor's and master's degrees in law, Dr. Kojima earned a Doctor of Laws from Chuo University and a Doctor of the Science of Law from Yale Law School. Previously, she served as Assistant Professor of Maritime Law and Policy at the World Maritime University in Malmö, Senior Research Fellow at Max Planck Institute for Comparative Public Law and International Law in Heidelberg, and law clerk for Judge Hisashi Owada and Judge Vladlen S. Vereshchetin at the International Court of Justice in The Hague. She has been teaching Advanced Treaty Law, the Law of the Sea (Maritime Zones), Law and Policy related to the Marine Environment, and Maritime Security Issues in International Law. She is the co-editor of *Solidarity: A Structural Principle of International Law* (together with Rüdiger Wolfrum, Springer, 2010), an editor of *Max Planck Encyclopedia of Public International Law* (Rüdiger Wolfrum ed., Oxford University Press, online ed., 2008) and the assistant editor of *Law of the Sea, Environmental Law and Settlement of Dispute: Liber Amicorum Judge Thomas A. Mensah* (Tafsir Malick Ndiaye & Rüdiger Wolfrum eds., Martinus Nijhoff Publishers, 2007).

F. Mikis MANOLIS

Dr. Mikis Manolis earned his PhD from the University of Wales in Swansea in conjunction with the World Maritime University. He currently practices with the law firm of Hungerford Tomyn Lawrenson and Nichols in Vancouver, Canada in the area of civil litigation with a focus on maritime, commercial, shareholder, and insurance matters. In addition to his PhD and his broad litigation experience, Dr. Manolis holds a Bachelor of Arts in Political Science from the University of British Columbia, a Master of Arts in Political Science from Dalhousie University, and a Bachelor of Laws from Dalhousie University. He is also a member of the British Columbia Bar, the author/editor of numerous articles and books, and a member of the Canadian Maritime Law Association.

Kofi MBIAH

Dr. Kofi Mbiah has been the Chief Executive Officer of the Ghana Shippers Authority since 1999. He is also the Chairman of the Legal Committee of the International Maritime Organization (IMO). He graduated from the University of Ghana, Legon, in 1980 with a Bachelor of Laws degree and in 1982 he became a Barrister and Solicitor of the Supreme Court of Ghana after graduating as a Barrister at Law,(BL) from the Ghana Law School. He holds a Masters in Marine Management from Dalhousie University, Canada, a Master of Laws from the IMO International Maritime Law Institute, Malta, an MBA from the Ghana Institute of Management and Public Administration, and a PhD in Maritime Administration from the World Maritime University.

Maximo Q. MEJIA Jr.

Dr. Maximo Q. Mejia Jr. is Professor and Head of Maritime Law and Policy at the World Maritime University (WMU), where he has been a member of the resident faculty since 1998. Before joining WMU, Dr. Mejia saw duty on board various naval and coast guard vessels as well as in shore-based maritime administration activities in the Philippines. His assignments included, *inter alia*, Commanding Officer of Port State Control Office Manila, Commander of Coast Guard Station Iligan, Deputy Executive Director of the Presidential Task Force on Maritime Development, and Assistant Chief of Staff for Navigational Safety. He earned his *Bachelor of Science* at the United States Naval Academy (Annapolis, Maryland, USA), *Master of Arts in Law and Diplomacy* at the Fletcher School (Tufts University, Massachusetts, USA), *Master of Science in Maritime Safety Administration* from the World Maritime University (Malmö, Sweden), and *Doctor of Philosophy* from Lund University (Lund, Sweden). Aside from teaching maritime policy, law, human factors, and security-related courses, Prof. Mejia is Secretary of Doctoral Programmes at WMU, Associate Editor of the *WMU Journal of Maritime Affairs*, and co-Editor of the book series *WMU Studies in Maritime Affairs*. He is the editor/co-editor of a number of books on maritime security and the author/co-author of numerous articles published in international academic journals.

Samuel Pyeatt MENEFEE

Dr. Samuel Pyeatt Menefee is a graduate of Yale University (BA, 1972), Oxford (Dip Soc Anth and BLitt, 1973 and 1975), Harvard (JD, 1981), Virginia (LLM and SJD, 1982 and 1993), and Cambridge (MPhil, 1995). Dr. Menefee is Maury Fellow at the Center for Oceans Law & Policy and Senior Associate at the Center for National Security Law, University of Virginia School of Law. He also serves as an Adjunct Professor at World Maritime University, and a Fellow of the ICC-International Maritime Bureau and the Regional Piracy Centre. Menefee was formerly *Rapporteur* of the Joint International Working Group for Uniformity of the Law of Piracy; Chairman of the Working Party on Piracy of the Maritime Law Association of the United States; and Chairman of the Committee on Marine Security of the Marine Technology Society. He has authored numerous articles and monographs about piracy and maritime violence.

Thomas MENSAH

Dr. Thomas A. Mensah was a Judge of the International Tribunal for the Law of the Sea, from 1996 to 2005. He was the first President of the Tribunal from 1996 to 1999. Prior to his election to the Tribunal, Judge Mensah had been a Lecturer of Law University of Ghana and Dean of the Faculty of Law, Associate Legal Officer at the International Atomic Energy Agency, Vienna and Assistant Secretary-General and Director of Legal Affairs and External Relations at the International Maritime Organization (IMO). Judge Mensah has been Cleveringa Professor of Law at Leiden University and Professor of Law and Director, Law of the Sea Institute at the University of Hawaii. From 1995 to 1996 Judge Mensah was the High Commissioner (Ambassador) of Ghana to the Republic of South Africa and he served as the Chairman of the F4 (Environmental Claims) Panel, United Nations Compensation Commission (UNCC), Geneva from 2000 to 2005. Judge Mensah is a Member Institut de droit International (since 1989), Titular Member of the Comité Maritime International (CMI) and a Member of the Advisory Council of the British Institute of International and Comparative Law. He earned his BA from the University of Ghana, LLB from the University of London, and LLM and JSD Yale University Law School. He is the author of numerous articles, monographs and papers in the field of public international law, law of the sea, maritime law and international environmental law.

Chandrika Prasad SRIVASTAVA

Dr. C. P. Srivastava, KCMG, IAS (Retd.), was the longest serving Secretary General of the International Maritime Organization (IMO); he remains Secretary General Emeritus of IMO, and the Founding Chancellor and Chancellor Emeritus of the World Maritime University (WMU). Prior to his entry into the global sphere of maritime affairs in 1974, Dr. Srivastava was Chairman and Managing Director of the Shipping Corporation of India. Previous to that he was Director General of Shipping in the Government of India and on the wider front of public administration, Secretary and Personal Aide to the Late Prime Minister of India, Shri Lal Bahadur Shastri. He had the distinction of being awarded the Padma Bhushan in 1972 and was conferred a knighthood (KCMG) by the Queen of England for his outstanding achievements. Several such national honours were bestowed upon him by the Kings of Sweden, Norway and Spain, and by the Presidents of Germany, Poland, Portugal, Brazil, Argentina and Egypt, among others. He was a member of the prestigious Indian Administrative Service (IAS) and the first chief executive of the Shipping Corporation of India. As such, brought a wealth of experience to bear on his role as Secretary General of IMO (1974-1989) and subsequently as Founding Chancellor of WMU. In recognition of his invaluable and extraordinary service and contribution to his country and the maritime world at large, the President of India bestowed on him the second highest national honour of India, the Padma Vibhushan on Republic Day, 26 January 2009. Dr. Srivastava was educated in Lucknow, India (BA, MA, LLB).

D. Rhidian THOMAS

Professor Thomas is a graduate of the Universities of Wales and Sheffield, and was appointed Professor of Maritime Law and Director of the Institute of Shipping and Trade Law at the School of Law, Swansea in 2000. He served as the Director of the Institute until September 2010. He now retains the title of the Founding Director of the Institute of International Shipping and Trade Law. Previously he was Professor of Law at the University of East Anglia and has taught at the National University of Singapore, University of Windsor, Canada, the University of Gothenberg, Sweden, and at the IMO International Maritime Law Institute in Malta. From 1989 to 1999 he was adjunct Professor of Law on the University of Detroit Mercy London Law Programme and Director of the Lloyd's List Shipping Law Seminars.

He was a member of the Departmental Advisory Committee on Arbitration Law which produced and drafted the Arbitration Act 1996; and is a member of an Advisory Committee which advises the DETR on the implementation of international conventions on shipping. He is a member of the British Maritime Law Association and Chairman of the Sub-committee on Mortgages and Ship Arrest. He is also a member of the Chartered Institute of Arbitrators. He is author of Maritime Liens (vol.14 British Shipping Laws) (1980); *Law* and Practice of Appeals from Arbitration Awards (1994); Default Powers of Arbitrators (1996). He is editor and contributor to Modern Law of Marine Insurance, Volume 1 (1996), and Volume 2 (2002), Marine Insurance: The Law in Transition (2006) and Liability Regimes in Contemporary Maritime Law (2007). He is also a contributor to Marine Insurance at the turn of the Millennium, ed. Professor M. Huybrechts (1999). His journal publications are extensive and reflect his interests in international commercial and maritime law and in arbitration law. He is Editor-in-Chief of the Journal of International Maritime Law and an editor of *Arbitration* International.

Jingjing XU

Dr. Jingjing Xu is Professor of Maritime Law and Economics at the Business School of Plymouth University. She is also the Deputy Director of the Centre for Maritime Logistics, Economics and Finance (CEMLEF). She holds the degree of PhD in Law, the degree of MSc in Shipping Management and the degree of BEcon in Transport Economics. Her teaching and research interests are interdisciplinary in scope touching upon both law and economics in the marine and maritime domain. She has particular interests in the law and policy issues pertaining to marine pollution, maritime safety and security, and marine renewable energy development. She has a significant number of publications and has acted as reviewer for some leading journals. She is Director of Studies or Supervisor to a number of PhD students and have been taking a leading role in many research projects in relation to marine and maritime affairs. In addition to her role at Plymouth University, Dr. Xu is a Visiting Professor at three other Universities including World Maritime University, Lund University in Sweden and Shanghai Maritime University in China. Dr. Xu is an Associate Fellow of the Royal Institute of Navigation, a Fellow of the Higher Education Academy, and a member of various law associations including the British Maritime Law Association and the Society of Legal Scholars.

INDEX

#

A

B

C

F

G

H

I

J

K

L

Q

R

S

U

V

W

Y